Of Risks and Normative Responses

Christina Anikó Simmig

Of Risks and Normative Responses

Unleashing the Potential of Disaster Risk Reduction in Relation to Natural Hazards

Springer

Christina Anikó Simmig
Hamburg, Germany

ISBN 978-3-031-41103-8 ISBN 978-3-031-41104-5 (eBook)
https://doi.org/10.1007/978-3-031-41104-5

This Springer imprint is published by the registered company Springer Nature Switzerland AG
The registered company address is: Gewerbestrasse 11, 6330 Cham, Switzerland

Paper in this product is recyclable.

Acknowledgements

This book is based on a dissertation written as part of a Joint PhD Programme between Macquarie University and the University of Hamburg. Its oral defence took place on 25 January 2023. This study is current as of 9 April 2023.

I am deeply indebted to my supervisors Dr. Francesca Dominello, Prof. Dr. Markus Kotzur, and Prof. Dr. Carlos Bernal Pulido for their support. In addition, my deep gratitude goes to Dr. Kirsten Davies, who encouraged and supported me in applying for the Joint PhD Programme and who has been my supervisor at Macquarie University for over 2 years. Their invaluable and prompt feedback on my drafts have instrumentally shaped my work in terms of both content and writing style. I am grateful for their continuous encouragement and their patience in challenging me to deliver my best work. I would also like to thank my examiners Prof. Dr. Anne van Aaken, Prof. Dr. Anika Klafki, Prof. Dr. Karsten Nowrot, and Prof. Dr. Kirsten Schmalenbach for their prompt evaluation and the fruitful discussion during the oral defence.

I am very grateful to Macquarie University for awarding me a Commonwealth-Funded scholarship to fund my Joint PhD candidature and an additional stipend to finance my one-year research stay at Macquarie University. The research stay gave me the opportunity to gain insights into new research methods and to discuss relevant points for my research. I thank everyone who gifted their precious time.

I would like to sincerely thank my dear colleagues and friends at Macquarie University and the University of Hamburg who made my doctoral studies—despite some lows that are always inherent in such projects—a wonderful and enriching time. Anouk Andres, Dinah Cassebaum, Vivian Elvers, Dr. Alessandra Guida, Verena Kahl, Dr. Khaled Khwaileh, Dr. Manuela Niehaus—your input for my work and your profound encouragement during the various stages of my doctoral studies have helped me through many storms. I also thank Andrea Hearst for proofreading the whole manuscript.

Special thanks to my parents, who supported me in my decisions and always believed in me, and to my grandmother for being a role model to me with her unwavering positive attitude. My final wholehearted thanks belong to my husband for his unfailing love and support in all situations. The completion of this project would not have been possible without his loving support.

Contents

Abbreviations

A1-P1	Art 1 of the Protocol No 1 of the Convention for the Protection of Human Rights and Fundamental Freedoms
ASR	Draft Articles on State Responsibility (International Law Commission)
BVerfG	German Federal Constitutional Court (*Bundesverfassungsgericht*)
BVerwG	German Federal Administrative Court (*Bundesverwaltungsgericht*)
CBA	Cost-Benefit Assessment
Court	European Court of Human Rights
CoE	Council of Europe
COVID-19	Coronavirus Disease 2019
DA	Draft Articles on the Protection of Persons in the Event of Disasters (International Law Commission)
DRR	Disaster Risk Reduction
ECHR	Convention for the Protection of Human Rights and Fundamental Freedoms
EComHR	European Commission of Human Rights
ECtHR	European Court of Human Rights
EFAS	European Flood Awareness System
EU	European Union
HFA	Hyogo Framework for Action 2005-2015
IACtHR	Inter-American Court of Human Rights
ICJ	International Court of Justice
IDL	International Disaster Law
IDNDR	International Decade for Natural Disaster Reduction
ILC	International Law Commission
IPCC	Intergovernmental Panel on Climate Change
IRU	International Relief Union

ISDR	International Strategy for Disaster Reduction
Member states	Member States of the Council of Europe
OIEWG	Open-ended Intergovernmental Expert Working Group on Indicators and Terminology relating to Disaster Risk Reduction
SFDRR	Sendai Framework for Disaster Risk Reduction 2015-2030
UNGA	United Nations General Assembly
UNDP	United Nations Development Programme
UNDRR (formerly UNISDR)	United Nations Office for Disaster Risk Reduction (formerly United Nations International Strategy for Disaster Reduction)
UNDRO	United Nations Disaster Relief Organization
VCLT	Vienna Convention on the Law of Treaties
WTO AB	Appellate Body of the World Trade Organisation

List of Figures

List of Tables

Chapter 1
Introduction

Why, despite advances in the natural and social science of hazards and disasters, do losses continue to increase?
(International Council for Science 2008)

Natural hazards pose a worldwide challenge to the survival and livelihood of people in spite of a growing understanding of disaster risks and disaster risk reducing measures,[1] including within the member states of the Council of Europe ('member states').[2] Experts regularly advise on the risks of natural hazards as well as available and effective risk reduction strategies that individuals and societies could adopt to protect lives and assets. Nevertheless, the current level of implementation of such measures is insufficient to curb the steady increase of disaster losses in Europe,[3] causing significant economic, social, health, cultural and environmental damage.[4] Bearing this in mind, the focus of this book is on means to counteract one obstacle in the way of increasing disaster risk reduction ('DRR') in the context of natural hazards, namely, the influence of the distorted risk perception of laypersons. Psychology has extensively studied how mental processes often lead people to neglect risks from natural hazards, especially the longer it has been since the last disaster manifested.[5] The effects of distorted risk perception are not limited to the personal sphere but can also be one reason why a democratic society's risk management collectively underestimates risks from natural hazards. Building on research indicating that more people would privately and collectively opt for more

---

[1] World Conference on Disaster Reduction (2005), para 3.

[2] See for the member states of the Council of Europe United Nations Inter-Agency Secretariat of the International Strategy for Disaster Reduction and Council of Europe (2011); see in relation to the member states that are also part of the European Union European Spatial Planning Observation Network (2013) and European Commission (2021).

[3] On the steady increase of disaster losses, see EM-DAT, CRED/UCLouvain, Brussels, Belgium.

[4] United Nations Office for Disaster Risk Reduction (2015), para 4.

[5] Sunstein (2002a), p. 70.

C. A. Simmig, *Of Risks and Normative Responses*,
https://doi.org/10.1007/978-3-031-41104-5_1

DRR related to natural hazards if they understood the facts properly,[6] this book argues that the state should strive to mitigate the consequences of distorted risk perception in individual and collective decision-making concerning such hazards. The aim of this book is to explore means to mitigate the consequences of distorted risk perception through the law and adjustments to political decision-making and to inform to what extent the values of autonomy and democracy limit these options for member states.

To mitigate the influence of distorted risk perception related to natural hazards on democratic decision-making, this book argues for implementing deliberative fora in the political decision-making process. Ample empirical evidence suggests that deliberative processes can mitigate the distorting effects of common heuristics and biases in risk perception in the public decision-making process. In addition to the practical merit of deliberation, this book further substantiates the case for deliberative democracy based on normative political theory.

To further inform how the states should complement their risk management to protect individuals and the collective from the consequences of distorted risk perceptions related to common natural hazards, this book sets out a range of measures that member states may lawfully implement. As a starting point, the member states should aim to mitigate distorted risk perceptions through the use of disaster risk communication that takes into account the knowledge about risk perception, through nudging techniques, and financial incentives. To the extent that the collective assesses the consequences of individuals' risk decisions related to natural hazards as an unacceptable risk to the community, the state could further enforce DRR through spatial planning and regulations to control urban development as effective measures to reduce disaster risks.

To highlight the conceptual merits of initiating disaster loss reduction in Europe from the bottom-up by reducing distorted risk perceptions, this book opposes competing proposals from academia and public discourse. These competing proposals are rooted in the fact that, to many scholars, the current lack of collective and individual initiative in DRR seems irrational, considering that science has clearly laid out the severe and likely impacts as well as ways to avert such consequences.[7] Building on this assessment, competing proposals derive a right or even a duty of the state to protect people for their 'own good', if necessary, even without mobilising democratic support. Conversely, this book demonstrates how fundamental rights and democratic values stand in the way of such competing proposals that aim to increase DRR from the top-down. Even when people's risk perceptions are distorted, the values of autonomy and democracy must be the touchstone when navigating the challenges of enhancing DRR.

With this in mind, this book contributes arguments and concrete measures to reduce disaster losses from the bottom up, while respecting democratic requirements for the decision-making process, as well as human rights standards to protect

[6] Spence and So (2021), pp. 2–3; Ivčević et al. (2021).

[7] Crosweller and Wilmshurst (2013), p. 564; Albris et al. (2020), pp. 8–9.

individual autonomy. In this respect, the book addresses the issue of DRR in a novel way by exposing how political barriers to disaster loss reduction can be overcome by giving higher priority to mitigating distorted risk perceptions.

To embark on the exploration of the outlined socio-legal issue, this chapter sets out the context and analytical framework for this book. The following section begins by elaborating on the problem that prompted this book, that is, the unexploited potential for DRR in Europe and the link to mental and cultural biases in risk perception that often lead individuals and collectives to neglect risks from natural hazards. The chapter then sets out the aims of this book and provides information on the methodology and terminology used in this book, and on its structure. Finally, this chapter discusses how competing schools of thought respond to the findings on distorted risk perception concerning natural hazards, as well as the conflicting interests involved.

1.1 Exploring the Problem

To further introduce the overarching issue of this book, this section elaborates on what makes Europeans vulnerable to natural hazards, the lack of legal measures to counter them and the link to biases and heuristics on the individual and democratic decision-making process. Biases and heuristics describe mental processes that reduce the complexity of information by consciously or unconsciously ignoring some information.[8] While these processes are efficient, they can 'lead to severe and systematic errors' in risk perception.[9] This section shows how such distortions in risk perception contribute to a lack of initiative among individuals in Europe in reducing disaster risks, giving rise to the need for public regulations to address this issue. At the same time, the section explores the challenges in mobilising public support for increasing DRR efforts, highlighting how these distortions in risk perception exacerbate the issue. Last, this section introduces the key values pertinent to risk management and the design of collective decision-making processes. These fundamental values form the normative basis of the book's promotion of a bottom-up approach in addressing the repercussions of distorted risk perception at both the individual and collective level.

[8] Tversky and Kahneman (1974), p. 1124.

[9] Ibid; see Glöckner (2016), pp. 16, 21; see further Le Grand and New (2015), pp. 81, 84.

1.1.1 *The Potential for Disaster Risk Reduction in Europe*

In the context of natural hazards, one of the dominant disaster risks in the member states relates to the vulnerable housing situations of people. Despite the increasing understanding of disaster risks and of ways to reduce them, the number of people living in areas prone to natural hazards has increased in Europe and beyond.[10] Additionally, in many European countries, a large proportion of real estate is vulnerable to regional natural hazards.[11] This vulnerability is due to both location and structurally unsuitable construction design.[12] For the most part, these buildings belong to 'historic' settlement areas that existed before the protection regulations under spatial planning or building law came into force.[13] For example, two-thirds of residential buildings in Italy were already built before the law for earthquake-resistant structures, Law 64/1974, came into force in 1974.[14] Even if land use provisions and building codes were in place, '[m]any governments deliberately turned a blind eye' to the practice of illegal constructions, 'on the grounds that it helped fighting poverty and allowed more people to build their own residence at budget prices'.[15]

As Chap. 2 examines in detail, the growing knowledge on the disaster risk factors and means to reduce them in science have provided people with options to deliberately decrease their vulnerability. With respect to the particular example of seismic vulnerability, seismic engineering has identified construction techniques and material capable of reducing the seismic vulnerability of buildings. In relation to the affordability of such measures, a difference between citizens of the member states and many other parts of the world should be noted. The member states score high or even very high on the human development index,[16] which is predicated on criteria such as life expectancy and quality, level of education, and per capital income.[17] It follows that citizens are more likely to have the choice to reduce disaster risks in the context of natural hazards once they have knowledge of the risk. Thus, comparably many Europeans have the means available to reduce disaster risks relating to their situation.[18] For instance, they have a choice to reduce their vulnerability by reinforcing their homes, their risk of exposure by choosing to inhabit low risk areas, or by increasing their capacity to respond to natural hazards by educating and preparing themselves. Although costs may be a deterrent, the main factors that remain are the

[10] Crosweller and Wilmshurst (2013), p. 548.

[11] Artino et al. (2020), p. 10273.

[12] Ibid.

[13] For examples, see on Austria Giese (2011), p. 204; on Italy, see Artino et al. (2020), p. 10273; on Spain, see Carreño et al. (2014), p. 22.

[14] Artino et al. (2020), p. 10273; see further Formisano et al. (2019).

[15] Valensise et al. (2017), p. 297.

[16] Conceição (2020), pp. 343–346.

[17] United Nations Development Programme (2022).

[18] See Zack (2012), p. 819.

lack of awareness of the potentially affected parties,[19] and sometimes the technical complexity and duration of adaptations.[20] The consequent reluctance on the part of individuals, combined with the fact that in many European countries a large proportion of real estate inadequately protects against natural hazards, poses the risk of catastrophic consequences for individuals and society as a whole.

Nevertheless, many member states still often allow people to live with disaster risk, despite knowledge about the possibility of potentially fatal threats. This is exemplified by the inhabitation of the island Santorini in Greece. Particularly detailed research has identified Santorini as one of the most dangerous volcanoes in Europe.[21] Risk assessments further characterise the residents and visitors as highly vulnerable in case of an eruption.[22] Despite the knowledge of this risk, people are allowed to live within the potentially affected zone, and Greece only recently activated a Civil Protection Plan in case there is an eruption.[23] Similarly, people are allowed to inhabit the flanks of Mount Etna in Italy, despite the increased probability of flank eruptions and ensuing lava flows surrounding Mount Etna.[24] Moreover, it has been found that interventions are urgently needed to improve seismic safety in Italy as approximately 50% of residential buildings are exposed to seismic risks.[25] Since the total government programme for earthquake protection is less than 1% of the amount that would be needed to bring all buildings to a seismic safe level, the vulnerability remains very high.[26] Further examples can be found in Austria and Germany, where houses in flood-prone areas pose a similar challenge.[27] For the example, around 270,000 residential buildings in Germany are located in high-risk flood zones.[28] Since 2000, the share of new residential buildings in flood-prone zones has even slightly increased.[29] Also, in the aftermath of the 2021 volcanic eruptions on La Palma, one of the Canary Islands belonging to Spain, legal and scientific experts criticised how urbanisation was permitted in the affected area, despite the fact that other eruptions had already previously occurred.[30]

The contrast between scientific progress made in reducing disaster risks and the increasing disaster losses demonstrates the claim made by Georg Kent that '[d]

---

[19] Ivčević et al. (2021).

[20] Artino et al. (2020), p. 10275.

[21] Dominey-Howes and Minos-Minopoulos (2004), pp. 286–287.

[22] Ibid, p. 291.

[23] Ibid, pp. 291–292, 304, 305; General Secretariat for Civil Protection (2020).

[24] Dibben (2008).

[25] Artino et al. (2020), p. 10274.

[26] Spence and So (2021), p. 216.

[27] Giese (2011); Bundesanstalt für Gewässerkunde (Federal Institute of Hydrology) (2019); Faßbender (2015); Köck (2017); Jablonski (2014), pp. 31–55.

[28] Gesamtverband der Versicherer (2023).

[29] Ibid.

[30] Álvarez and Brunet (2021).

isaster protection is not only about science'.[31] If there is a lack of individual initiative in implementing measures to reduce disaster risks, ensuring the protection of life and property requires the establishment of legal standards of protection, as well as their review by respective institutions to be effective.[32] However, while all member states have national legislation on natural hazard risk management, their approach and effectiveness vary. In the last decades, a large number of countries reportedly adopted DRR policies and legal frameworks, and yet, the efforts of many countries still underachieve the goal of effective protection.[33] In fact, the international community has identified the lack of national implementation and strengthening of organisational, legal and policy frameworks for DRR at the domestic level as the primary challenge in reducing losses caused by natural hazards.[34] This is due to a lack of reallocation of organisational and financial resources needed for the actual operationalisation of the adopted frameworks and principles.[35]

1.1.2 The Implications of Distorted Risk Perception for Risk Management

Insights into the mental and cultural biases in risk perception can help uncover one obstacle impeding the allocation of greater resources towards public DRR initiatives in the context of natural hazards. The 'errors' behind mental processes are not limited to the personal sphere but also affect collective safety.[36] Due to the same heuristics, a society can collectively over- or underestimate risks.[37] Thus, the public demand for, or resistance to, DRR is subject to people's risk perception that may contrast with experts' evaluation of scientifically determined facts. As such, in democratically organised states biased risk perceptions over objective risk are likely to be reflected in laws, policies, and regulations.[38] This could be an issue among the member states, all of which have avowed themselves to democracy, as clarified in

[31] Kent (2001), p. 137.

[32] Ibid.

[33] Childs (2013), p. 11; DasGupta and Shaw (2017), p. 16; Aronsson-Storrier and da Costa (2017), p. 503; Fisher (2010), p. 566; see International Federation of Red Cross (2013), p. 12; International Federation of Red Cross and Red Crescent Societies (IFRC) and United Nations Development Programme (2014), p. 78; Gesamtverband der Deutschen Versicherungswirtschaft e. V. (2021).

[34] World Conference on Disaster Reduction (2004), para 102.

[35] Childs (2013), p. 11.

[36] Spence and So (2021), pp. 2–3.

[37] Viscusi (1992), p. 10.

[38] Alemanno (2016), p. 201.

the Preamble of the European Convention on Human Rights[39] ('ECHR') and in the Preamble and art 3 of the Statute of the Council of Europe.[40]

Particularly, the difference between foresight and hindsight is known to influence the public demand for risk regulation.[41] On the one hand, the phenomenon of the 'probability neglect', which Chap. 2 presents in detail,[42] explains the catalytic function of the occurrence of disasters for the development of DRR frameworks.[43] The occurrence of a disaster may temporarily increase the 'dread factor' related to a risk, and thus the desire for protection. This phenomenon is known as 'crisis effect'.[44] At the individual level, the phenomenon explains the recorded rise in insurance purchases after disasters triggered by natural hazards struck.[45] For example, in the German Federal State of Rhineland-Palatinate, only 37% of houses were insured against natural hazards before the disaster in Ahrtal in 2021.[46] After the disaster, the insurance rate has risen to 42%.[47] However, this phenomenon is not limited to the individual sphere but also affects the design of law.[48] A highly salient detrimental outcome, which triggers strong emotions among people, can give rise to public demand for law, although the probability of harm has not changed.[49] For instance, experts have predicted that the 2021 volcanic eruptions on La Palma will lead to much more rigorous legislation and urban planning.[50] The eruption is expected to serve as a wake-up call, highlighting the importance of robust regulations and improved urban planning practices to enhance safety and resilience in the affected area. Although the probability and seriousness of harm has not changed, the phenomenon of the 'probability neglect' can lead people to believe future events are more likely than can be scientifically proven. In this regard, Germany's decision to phase out nuclear power after the 2011 Fukushima Daiichi nuclear disaster, which galvanised numerous anti-nuclear protests, is another textbook example of induced changes in law due to the crisis effect. Remarkably, the decision to suspend the extension of operating times for nuclear power plants, which had only been decided in October 2010, was made a mere three days after the disaster. In Germany, the

[39] Convention for the Protection of Human Rights and Fundamental Freedoms, opened for signature 4 November 1950, 213 UNTS 221 (entered into force 3 September 1953).

[40] Statute of the Council of Europe, opened for signature 5 May 1949, 87 UNTS 103 (entered into force 3 August 1949).

[41] Sunstein (2002a), p. 69.

[42] See Sect. 2.1.1.

[43] See Sommario and Venier (2018), p. 33, who assert this correlation between the Indian Ocean tsunami and the adoption of the HFA; Briceño (2015), p. 4.

[44] Stefanovic (2003), p. 242; Baan and Klijn (2004), p. 118.

[45] Slovic (2000), p. 14.

[46] Gesamtverband der Deutschen Versicherungswirtschaft e. V. (2019), p. 53.

[47] Gesamtverband der Deutschen Versicherungswirtschaft e. V. (2022).

[48] Sunstein (2002a), pp. 63, 67.

[49] Ibid, p. 69.

[50] Álvarez and Brunet (2021).

term 'Fukushima effect' has since come to refer to the political impact of a sudden change in reporting and public opinion on an issue.[51]

Additionally, this bias may give rise to public demands for specific DRR measures that would have prevented harm in the past but which, from a scientific perspective, do not effectively reduce future damage. An example from the hometown of the author of this book, the Hanseatic City of Hamburg, concerns the tightening of dog breeding laws in 2001. After two dogs, deliberately trained to fight by their convicted owner, attacked and killed a child, public and political attention turned to their breed, which belonged to a list of breeds classified as so-called attack dogs.[52] As a result, shortly after the incident, Hamburg enacted the strictest keeping and breeding regulations and bans of all German federal states with regard to certain breeds.[53] Veterinarians and animal welfare organisations have argued that the political focus on the breed is misguided, as the problem is usually not so much the dog but the owner.[54] As such, bite attacks are often committed by dogs whose breed is not on any attack dog list, for example, German Shepherds and Labradors.[55] Moreover, there are still neither statistical surveys nor studies that justify the blanket treatment of attack dogs.[56] Against this background, the origin of the law to regulate so-called 'dangerous dogs' is seen by experts as being directly related to the high emotions surrounding the cruel death of the child.[57]

On the other hand, the phenomenon of the 'hindsight bias' can lead people to condemn a previous policy simply because the risk manifested itself. This can lead to people accusing the state of not having taken preventive measures, even though they had no active interest in spending on risk reduction before the disaster.[58] As such, Chap. 2 presents studies that confirm the consequences for people's *ex post* judgment of liability.[59] The perception of negligence through the hindsight lens is based on the fact that people tend to construct a narrative of avoidability after the fact.[60] This applies even if the event was not foreseeable.[61] This perception of the state's negligence in not preventing a disaster can affect people's trust in the effectiveness of public risk management and the government as a whole. Yet, people's trust in government is an important factor for the stability and performance of democratic systems.[62] The existence of trust in institutions is the prerequisite for the

---

[51] Heinrich et al. (2018), p. 9; see Blome (2021).

[52] Stein (2019); Wenig (2020).

[53] Stein (2019); Tsokos (2019), pp. 63–64.

[54] Stein (2019) and Wenig (2020).

[55] Stein (2019).

[56] Ibid.

[57] Ibid.

[58] Kamin and Rachlinski (1995), p. 90.

[59] See Sect. 2.1.2.

[60] Pedersen (2013), pp. 60–61.

[61] On so-called 'black swan' events, see Sect. 2.1.2.

[62] See Pharr et al. (2000).

'coordination of actions over large domains of space and time, which in turn permits the benefits of more complex, differentiated, and diverse societies'.[63]

On the flip side, the presented mechanisms behind public risk perception may constitute an obstacle for a government to regulate a risk in foresight. A state may find it harder to publicly justify expenses to avoid damage that is not feared, and consequently not perceived as a threat by the public.[64] People's focus on a desired outcome can even make them perceive opposing risk assessment as 'obstructionism'.[65] As a result, a widespread lack of fear can decrease the investment in public risk management in democracies. In fact, studies have suggested that political systems that are subject to legislative periods, tend to mostly prioritise people's short-term demands.[66] Irrespective of empirical and statistical knowledge about a risk's probability, the more time has passed since its last manifestation, the more likely it is that people will neglect the probability of a risk.[67] Such ignorance creates vulnerabilities, as Nassim N Taleb's example of a turkey illustrates:

> Consider a turkey that is fed every day. Every single feeding will firm up the bird's belief that it is the general rule of life to be fed every day … On the afternoon of the Wednesday before Thanksgiving, something unexpected will happen to the turkey. It will incur a revision of belief.[68]

Similarly, the fact that severe damage from natural hazards is rare makes people vulnerable to their feeling that they will be spared. It may be for this reason that the benefits of long-term risk reducing measures in the context of natural hazards are likely to be neglected in democratic processes.

1.1.3 The Need for a Bottom-Up Approach to Increase Disaster Risk Reduction

With regard to the status quo of private and public DRR measures despite increasing disaster losses, experts vehemently call for domestic and international policies to reduce the vulnerability of individuals and societies to natural hazards.[69] With the goal of facilitating the implementation of more risk reducing measures in mind, this book promotes measures aimed at mitigating the consequences of distorted risk

63 Warren (1999), p. 3, citing Luhmann (1979); Giddens (1990).

64 Hugenbusch and Neumann (2016), p. 6; Viscusi (1992), pp. 10–11.

65 Baan and Klijn (2004), p. 116; for an example, see Sect. 4.1.2.1.

66 Hugenbusch and Neumann (2016), p. 6.

67 Sunstein (2002a); see further Loewenstein et al. (2001), p. 276; Gross (2016), p. 314; Viscusi (1992), pp. 9–10.

68 Taleb (2010), p. 40.

69 Wisner et al. (2004); International Law Commission (2016), Commentary on Draft Article 9 para 12; Raju and da Costa (2018), p. 280; International Federation of Red Cross and Red Crescent Societies (IFRC) and United Nations Development Programme (2014).

perception, all while upholding the autonomy and equality of citizens. In doing so, this book promotes a bottom-up approach to generate the necessary private, public and political will to increase DRR measures. As such, this approach acknowledges that public DRR must be democratically legitimised and covered by a rationale that justifies public risk management.

In contrast to the bottom-up approach for increasing DRR advanced in this book, the findings on biases and heuristics that distort individual and collective decision-making have also given rise to several competing proposals. Based on the perceived 'irrationality' of people's risk perception, these schools of thought seek to legitimise risk reducing measures without the individuals or even collective consent. Such proposals can be seen as embodying a top-down approach to increase DRR. The political philosophy of 'paternalism' embodies the underlying idea.[70] Gerald Dworkin has defined paternalism as 'the interference with a person's liberty of action justified by reasons referring exclusively to the welfare, good, happiness, needs, interests or values of the person being coerced'.[71] Similar to the concept of beneficence, *paternalism* promotes the benefit of another individual.[72] However, paternalism deviates from beneficence, as it is not constricted by the expressed will of the beneficiary.[73] As such, governmental paternalism seeks 'to address a failure of judgment or reasoning of an individual, at least as perceived by the government'.[74] The arguments for paternalistic regulation gained first momentum in the 1970s with the emergence of empirical findings on people's perceptions of risk in psychology.[75] Building on these findings, some commentators argue for the state's moral or even legal obligation to protect the individual from 'risk to self'.[76] The term 'risk to self' refers to persons exposing themselves to risks, for instance, the risks of natural hazards. One rationale for intervention focusses on the protection of individual interests, such as health and life, while the other aims to realise the 'authentic self' of individuals by intervening with their behaviours that do not correspond to their goals and desires. Similarly, the observed influence of heuristics and biases on the democratic decision-making process have given new impetus to an old question in normative political theory. In light of the distortions in people's risk evaluations, the question is as to whether democracy is the most convincing political system for politically legitimate decision-making. Competing schools of thought assign a leading role to experts in public decision-making processes with the claim to realise the objectively or subjectively best solution for the 'incompetent' citizen. However, this book's examination of fundamental values reveals ethical, legal, and normative political shortcomings within these competing rationales. These findings further

[70] See Alemanno (2016), p. 199.

[71] Dworkin (1972), p. 65; Flanigan (2017).

[72] Maclean (2009), p. 51.

[73] Ibid.

[74] Le Grand and New (2015), p. 15.

[75] For a short overview of the historical development, see ibid, pp. 80–82.

[76] See Alemanno (2016), p. 198.

reinforce the necessity of pursuing the objective of improved DRR through a bottom-up approach.

To begin with, the consideration of the value of autonomy in the state's response to distorted risk perception is pivotal in rejecting such top-down approaches. Private autonomy grants the individual freedom to make decisions based on adequate knowledge, competence, and in a voluntary capacity.[77] In this context, 'voluntary capacity' refers to the absence of compulsion or fear. 'Competence' refers to the capacity of autonomy and may exclude very young or insane persons.[78] This capacity is sometimes also referred to as 'responsibility'.[79] Based on this conceptualisation of the 'freedom to make decisions', the value of autonomy attaches to the manner in which a decision is made and carried out, and not to the outcome of a specific decision. Thus, this conceptualisation of autonomy respects the existence of different notions of what constitutes a satisfying life, as embodied in the principle of pluralism.[80] As such, autonomy not only constitutes an independent value besides happiness itself but is a condition for the pursuit of happiness.[81] It thus has intrinsic, as well as instrumental value for the pursuit of happiness.[82] These values substantiate the ethical obligation of actors to refrain from intervening in other's autonomous risk-taking. As long as an individual *autonomously* takes a risk in the context of natural hazards, that is, informed, voluntarily and responsibly, the individual generally enjoys the negative right to not be interfered with. In this regard, it is important to recognise that decisions to take risks in the context of natural hazards are not necessarily involuntarily borne. For instance, some people choose to live close to flood prone rivers, earthquake faults, or volcanoes, because they prioritise fertile farmland and reliable freshwater sources over the avoidance of potential harm.[83] In case of such voluntary decisions, interferences require an overriding justification to not offend the illustrated value of autonomy, even if an interference is supposed to serve the individual's 'own good'.[84] As such, DRR measures that do not infringe upon autonomy typically include those that prioritise informing and empowering individuals rather than imposing strict mandates. Beyond such autonomy promoting measures, interferences may be justified when they protect society from the consequences of individual risk-taking. The findings on distortions in risk perception, however, cannot justify interferences aimed at effectively reducing disaster risks associated with natural hazards. As a result, the value of autonomy places

[77] Haworth (1984), p. 8; Schneewind (2010), p. 249.

[78] Van de Poel and Fahlquist (2012), p. 884.

[79] Ibid.

[80] Alemanno (2016), p. 199.

[81] Schneewind (2010), p. 248; Haworth (1984), p. 5; Flanigan (2017), p. 294.

[82] Maclean (2009), pp. 23–29.

[83] Kelman and Mather (2008), pp. 190–191; Dibben (2008), p. 289; Wachinger et al. (2013), p. 1054.

[84] Alemanno (2016), p. 199; see further Le Grand and New (2015), pp. 111–135; for a detailed analysis, see Sect. 4.2.

constraints on paternalistic approaches to justify the implementation of effective DRR to curb the steady increase of disaster losses related to natural hazards.

Similarly, attempts to paternalistically reshape the political system suffer from normative flaws that underscore the need for bottom-up approaches. In accordance with this book, most contemporary political philosophy considers democracy, in the sense of equal opportunity for self-governance for all, a necessary requirement of political legitimacy.[85] The concept of political legitimacy concerns the rationales for the legitimate use of political power.[86] In other words, the concept of political legitimacy describes 'why a government has the right to coercively impose and enforce law'.[87] Political theory usually assesses political legitimacy in terms of two sources of legitimacy.[88] First, political legitimacy can derive from procedural or *input*-oriented legitimacy, which requires the authority's actions to be responsive to the '*authentic preferences* of citizens' in order to respect their right to self-governance.[89] The right of self-governance derives from the right to liberty.[90] An equal voice in the collective decision-making process allows the individual to exercise control over issues that affect his or her domain.[91] As such, democracy's basic idea of the 'rule by the people'[92] derives political legitimacy from the fact that decisions are responsive to the people's preferences.

Competing schools of thought rely on the second source of legitimate decision-making to justify paternalistic governmental systems aiming to restructure risk management. The second source is instrumental or *outcome*-oriented legitimacy, which relates to the production of 'good outcomes'.[93] The production of 'good outcomes' by empowering experts in political decision-making is often advocated by these competing schools of thought as a means to establish political legitimacy in non-democratic state political systems.[94] They use the empirical findings in psychology as an argument against democratic structures and advocate for alternative state political systems, such as the rule by experts who are considered to be 'people who know best'.[95] However, the analysis reveals normative and practical flaws in such purely, or at least primarily, outcome-oriented justifications that rely on a notion of objective rationality. These flaws render undemocratically constituted

[85] Peter (2017), para 4.

[86] Ripstein (2004).

[87] Paletta (2011), pp. 870–871.

[88] See Brettschneider (2005), pp. 423–424; see further Min and Wong (2018), p. 2 with further references.

[89] Scharpf (1997), p. 19; Christiano and Bajaj (2022), para 2.2.1.

[90] Christiano and Bajaj (2022), para 2.2.1; Fung (2007).

[91] Christiano and Bajaj (2022), para 2.2.1.

[92] Waldron (2012), p. 187.

[93] Brettschneider (2005), p. 424; Holst (2012), p. 50.

[94] Runciman (2018), p. 180; see Holst (2012), p. 41.

[95] Runciman (2018), p. 180; see Holst (2012), p. 41.

political decision-making unacceptable from a normative standpoint.[96] Therefore, adjustments in the political decision-making process to mitigate the influence of distorted risk perception must be achieved through enhancement within the democratic system.[97]

In sum, when addressing distorted risk perception, it is important to respect values of autonomy and democratic principles. A bottom-up approach can empower individuals, promote inclusivity, and ensure that decisions are made in a transparent, participatory, and accountable manner. Ultimately, this leads to more robust and legitimate risk management outcomes. At the same time, as advocated in this book, a bottom-up approach can facilitate an increase in DRR. Building on the outlined issue, the following sections of this chapter set out the objective of this book, and provide information on the methodology, structure, terminology, scope, academic context and significance of this book.

1.2 Research Focus and Aims of the Book

The overarching focus of this book is to examine how member states should complement their risk management related to common natural hazards in light of distorted risk perception, with the aim to facilitate the reduction of disaster losses. This issue is explored through the discussion of three sub-questions. First, why do disaster losses related to natural hazards increase when knowledge and means of risk reduction are available? Second, what substantive measures could member states implement to mitigate the consequences of distorted risk perception relating to natural hazards without unjustifiably interfering with individuals' rights? Third, with regard to the necessary democratic support for such measures, how should member states adjust their collective decision-making processes to mitigate the influence of distorted risk perception while respecting citizens as autonomous and equal?

In answering the first research sub-question, the book argues that the member states' administrative and legal framework is currently not taking account of people's distorted risk perceptions regarding natural hazards. People are inclined to underestimate the risk posed by natural hazards and neglect DRR due to misconceptions relating to the effectiveness of risk reduction or the effectiveness of existing measures. By discussing the existence and extent of these misperceptions, this book aims to explain the neglect of DRR at both the private and political level in the member states. Moreover, the law only provides limited protection against the consequences of distorted risk perception. There is a lack of specialised risk prevention or mitigation law binding on all member states. The scientific findings on the effectiveness of DRR and people's distorted perception of risk is also not sufficient to give rise to positive human rights obligations to take long-term risk reduction

[96] Holst (2012), p. 52; see further Fischer (1990), pp. 21–26.

[97] Green (1981), p. 11.

measures. By discussing the interpretation of relevant human rights under the ECHR, the book aims to demonstrate that, for the foreseeable future, the ECHR is likely to require state action only in the case of imminent and clearly identifiable natural hazards. The interpretation of fundamental law thus amounts to a disaster response-oriented approach, which excludes prevention of property damage in most cases. Closing the gaps in legal protection against the consequences of distorted risk perception related to common natural hazards therefore depends on member states taking the initiative.

However, while there is a case to be made that more people likely would recognise the benefits of DRR for themselves and society once they have properly understood the risk and DRR benefits, the question remains of how the state may respond to this information without unjustifiably interfering with individual autonomy. Thus, in relation to the second sub-question, the book assesses a selection of recommended DRR measures in terms of their effectiveness in protecting life and property and the conditions for their compatibility with the legally guaranteed protection of private autonomy. In this regard, the book takes up the concern that state measures to reduce risks can undermine individual autonomy, even in cases where individuals' risk perception is distorted. As a result, the analysis identifies a number of measures that aim to adjust people's behaviour towards natural hazards, while remaining below the threshold of interference with autonomy. With respect to effective yet intrusive DRR measures, the analysis contours the scope of justified interferences to protect the collective from the consequences of individual risk decisions in relation to natural hazards. Conversely, the book also discusses competing arguments, prompted by the findings on distortions in people's risk perception, that advocate for state interventions to protect individuals for their 'own good'.

The range of permissible DRR measures presented differs in terms of effectiveness in protecting life and property. The more effective, the higher the cost and level of intrusion associated with it. Accordingly, the introduction of such DRR measures depends on democratic support. For this reason, in addressing the third sub-question, the book argues for the implementation of deliberative processes to mitigate the influence of distorted risk perception regarding natural hazards in political decision-making, all while respecting democratic values. By discussing concepts of political science, the book aims to advance the research that has established that discursive methods of deliberation are effective and legitimate tools when the perception of facts is distorted.

1.3 Research Methodology

The book is a socio-*legal* appraisal of discussed responses to increase DRR related to natural hazards in light of the consequences of distorted risk perception for the individual and the collective. Since the research methodology must align with the different aspects of the research question,[98] the approach in the book is to draw on a combination of research methodologies.

To answer the first sub-question on the reasons for the increase in disaster losses despite possible remedial measures, the book examines the extent to which the law applies to DRR and reasons for the lack of individual and collective initiative. This examination firstly involves a desk-based synthesis of critical legal analyses found in the literature, specifically focusing on the exploration of the current legal framework within domestic and specialised international law. The review concentrates on the analysis of the law applicable to member states in relation to natural hazards, with a particular emphasis on floods and earthquakes. Furthermore, considering the competing arguments supporting a broader interpretation of the state's positive obligations under the ECHR, the book also reviews the interpretation of the ECHR as applicable general law. This aspect invites a doctrinal research methodology to identify and interpret specialised and general law. Doctrinal research is designed to analyse what the law is in a specific context.[99] It 'aims to systematise, rectify and clarify the law on any particular topic by a distinctive mode of analysis of authoritative texts that consist of primary and secondary sources'.[100] The process of doctrinal research consists of 'selecting and weighing material taking into account hierarchy and authority, as well as understanding social context and interpretation'.[101] In the context of human rights research, the doctrinal methodology specifically involves a 'process of identifying the applicable human rights norms, their legal nature and scope of application, and their correct interpretation'.[102] In European human rights law, the response to this question flows from the interpretation of the ECHR under the established interpretation methodology, as well as a review of prior case law. The identification and interpretation of the law serves to conclude that the member states' law is currently predominantly disaster response-oriented, which falls short in effectively preventing property damage.

To further address a reason for the lack of political will to implement long-term cost-efficient DRR, the book explores deviations in prevailing risk perception and facts about natural hazards and the ability to reduce risk. To that end, the research relies on a desk-based synthesis of academic literature from a variety of fields, namely psychology, disaster studies, risk studies, and epistemology. In carrying this out, a link emerges between people's distorted risk perception and the untapped DRR potential at the private level. To establish how distortions in risk perception further affect the design and (non-) development of policies, the study draws on theoretical and epistemic insights from political science.

Where the second sub-question addresses how a state *may* protect people from the consequences of their distorted perception concerning the risks from natural

[98] See Siems (2009), p. 12; Schrama (2011), pp. 148–149, 151, 161.

[99] Chynoweth (2008), p. 30.

[100] McConville and Chui (2017), p. 3.

[101] Dobinson and Johns (2017), p. 24.

[102] Scheinin (2017), p. 20.

hazards, the answer requires a desk-based synthesis of discussed DRR measures and an examination of the limits set by positive law, that is, the ECHR. This interpretation of the law in relation to these DRR measures again draws on doctrinal research methodology to conclude a set of lawful measures to reduce the consequences of distorted risk perception.

When the third sub-question asks how the design of public decision-making should take into account the findings on risk perception research it goes beyond research into *de lege lata*. Instead, this issue is of a *normative jurisprudential* nature. Normative jurisprudence evaluates how law *ought* to be or *ought* to become.[103] To answer the question of how public decision-making should accommodate the findings of risk perception research, the research requires a theoretical research methodology. Theoretical research focusses on 'the ideas and assumptions which make up the theories upon which rules are based'[104] and thereby 'fosters a more complete understanding of the conceptual bases of legal principles'.[105] The understanding of the underlying theoretical considerations of collective decision-making processes within the member states provides the foundation for the book's proposal for adjusting the political decision-making process in response to findings from behavioural studies. To attain this understanding, the theoretical analysis delves into both moral and political theories. Moral theory addresses how a person ought to be, and ought to act, as part of a community,[106] while political theory focusses on how a state should be organised.[107] Both theories hold significance in normative jurisprudence.[108]

1.4 Structure of the Book

This book is divided into six chapters. This chapter defines the book's research focus and aims, its structure and scope, and its significance and contribution to society and literature. This book is concerned with the normative response to the influence of distorted risk perception on individual and public negligence of DRR. So far, this chapter has examined the strategic neglect of natural hazard risks in land use and construction procedures within Europe and how distorted risk perception plays a role in this public neglect. Building upon these identified problems, the chapter has outlined the case for a normative response from the bottom-up, rooted in the introduced values of autonomy and democratic values. To contextualise the

[103] For an overview of different views on normative jurisprudence, see Bayón (2013), pp. 5–7.

[104] Hutchinson (2018), p. 68.

[105] Pearce et al. (1987), p. 17.

[106] Gomez (2017), p. 174.

[107] See Kaldis (2002).

[108] Bayón (2013), p. 7; Finnis (2014), p. 135; see further West (2011), p. 6; Leiter (2013), p. 162, citing Kelsen (2005), p. 1.

examination in this book, the chapter further sets out the competing approaches aimed at enhancing public DRR measures. What emerges from the examination is the challenge to balance the value of the individual's autonomy with the value of other interests threatened by their risk-taking and with the collective interest to not be affected by individual decision-making.

Chapter 2 explores in detail one reason for the neglect of DRR by discussing existing research on people's distorted perception of risks in the context of natural hazards. To that end, the chapter analyses the factual ability to reduce the impact of natural hazards, specifically floods and earthquakes, and how laypersons perceive such capacities. The analysis demonstrates a discrepancy between the people's perception of risks and the reduction of risks from natural hazards, and the scientific facts about the extent to which humankind can protect life and property from natural hazards. To explain this discrepancy, the analysis additionally presents how the culturally conditioned relationship between natural hazards and psychological phenomena distorts the perception of risks associated with natural hazards. In doing so, the chapter provides knowledge about risk distortions that are relevant for designing measures to mitigate the risks.

To further complement this chapter's discussion of the need for legal measures to increase DRR, Chap. 3 examines how international law does not respond to the ever-increasing disaster losses resulting from natural hazards. On the one hand, it highlights the lack of specialised international law concerning DRR, and on the other hand, how the ECHR is also not designed to engage in comprehensive DRR. In discussing competing arguments, the chapter demonstrates that the ECHR rarely necessitates long-term preventive measures to reduce vulnerable living situations against natural hazards. Building on an examination of the Court's case law and the object and purpose of human rights, the chapter shows that neither the long-term cost-effective potential of DRR in safeguarding life and property, nor the findings on distortions in risk perception lead to significantly stricter due diligence on the part of the state. Consequently, the current regulatory regime on the international level, combined with the lack of domestic law discussed in the present chapter, leaves a gap in legal protection against the consequences of distorted risk perception related to natural hazards. This gap substantiates the need for further exploration of measures to mitigate these consequences in both individual and collective decision-making in Chaps. 4 and 5.

Chapter 4 legally examines a number of recommended DRR measures by experts with regard to their compatibility with the rights of individuals under the ECHR. While some decision-support measures do not interfere with fundamental rights, the chapter also discusses more effective risk reduction measures that require justification. It emerges from the discussion that land-planning and enforcement of buildings codes in high-risk areas are very effective long-term DRR measures. However, in certain cases, it becomes necessary to compensate individuals to strike a fair balance between the individual right to property and community interests. Conversely, with competing arguments in mind, the analysis maintains that the objective of interfering with individuals' rights for their 'own good' is insufficient to provide justification, primarily due to the imperative of respecting the value of autonomy.

The identified lawful means to promote or enforce DRR, that states could implement if democratic support was given, leads Chap. 5 to examine deliberative democracy as an avenue to mobilise democratic demand for DRR. To that end, Chap. 5 examines how deliberative processes can mitigate the influence of distorted risk perception on public risk evaluation and explores the advantages of deliberative democracy under normative political theory. The chapter further strengthens the case for deliberative processes by discussing competing schools of thought that propose empowering experts to make rational risk decisions for the public to mitigate the influence of distorted risk perception. The discussion highlights the flaws of such proposals with respect to their practical implementation and their compatibility with normative political theory, particularly the concept of political legitimacy.

The final chapter concludes the book by articulating the potential of strengthening bottom-up DRR through deliberative processes in collective decision-making and by promoting disaster risk communication that takes into account distortions in risk perceptions. The chapter also identifies the weaknesses of arguments to increase DRR based on paternalistic reasoning if necessary, even without first mobilising the necessary political support.

1.5 Terminology

The analysis of this book is carried out in the context of natural hazards and concerns the legitimacy and political facilitation of DRR measures in light of evidence on people's distorted risk perceptions. However, it is important to acknowledge that the relevant sociological concepts of natural hazards, disaster risks, and DRR have undergone an evolution that has led to a conceptual blurring. In fact, the concepts resemble a 'definitional minefield' in disaster studies as well as legal studies.[109] As such, it is necessary to clarify the terminology that is used in the field and to define the terms used in the process of determining which risks to respond to and how to respond to them.

1.5.1 The Term of 'Natural Hazards'

The term 'hazards' refers to phenomena, processes or human activity that can negatively impact human life or health, economic assets, and the environment.[110] Hazards are usually categorised as either natural hazards or human made hazards. *Natural hazards* are generally associated with predominantly natural processes and

[109] Alexander (2005), pp. 26–28; see further Kotzur (2012), p. 271; Bartolini (2018), p. 11; Focarelli (2020), para 6.

[110] See UN General Assembly (2016), p. 18.

phenomena.[111] In contrast, *human made hazards*, also called anthropogenic hazards, refer to human accidental, negligible, or deliberate activities and choices that entirely or predominantly induce the hazard.[112]

These definitions make it clear that the character of hazards is no longer determined by their appearance, as was the case in the past. Examples have shown that prima facie appearances can obscure the real reason for the emergence of a hazard. It is hardly surprising to find disasters in history, whose prima facie natural appearance led to a premature classification as a disaster being triggered by a natural hazard. The case of the 1963 landslide of the Vajont Dam in northern Italy constitutes one of the best-known examples.[113] During the filling of the reservoir, a massive landslide caused a flood that was fatal for almost 2000 people.[114] The landslide first appeared to be a natural hazard but later turned out to have been induced by the reservoir's varying water level.[115] Thus, despite its prima facie natural appearance, the landslide constituted a human made hazard. Consequently, even though examples of natural hazards often refer to storms, floods, tsunamis, volcanic eruptions, heat waves, cold spells, droughts, earthquakes, avalanches, or landslides, the naturalness of a hazard depends on there being a lack of proof of predominantly human induction.[116]

1.5.2 The Disaster (Risk) Conceptualisation in Modern Disaster Studies

Today's disaster studies build on the distinction between hazards and disasters, which this book observes. Only in combination with *vulnerability*, *exposure*, and lack of *capacity* to cope, do hazards become *disasters*,[117] and their extent also depends on these social risk factors.[118] In relation to natural hazards whose occurrence itself cannot be avoided, the impact on people can only be reduced by decreasing social risk factors.

---

[111] Ibid; United Nations Inter-Agency Secretariat of the International Strategy for Disaster Reduction (2004), p. 5.

[112] UN General Assembly (2016), p. 18; International Law Commission (2016), Commentary to Draft Article 3 para 10; Focarelli (2020), para 6. It should be noted, however, that this definition excludes armed conflicts and other situations of social instability in the context of disaster. Armed conflicts do not present a disaster per se but are subject to international humanitarian law.

[113] Ghirotti (2012), p. 359; Sossai (2018), p. 119.

[114] EM-DAT, CRED/UCLouvain, Brussels, Belgium.

[115] Ghirotti (2012), pp. 366, 370.

[116] Focarelli (2020), para 6.

[117] Field et al. (2012), p. 69.

[118] Fisher (2010), pp. 551–552; United Nations Inter-Agency Secretariat of the International Strategy for Disaster Reduction (2004), pp. 36–37; Lauta (2018), p. 46.

The concept of *vulnerability* refers to the specific conditions that increase the susceptibility to the impacts of hazards.[119] These conditions are determined by physical, social, economic, and environmental factors or processes. The concept of *exposure* focusses on the spatial element of individuals being located in hazard-prone areas.[120] Reversely, the concept of *capacity* describes positive conditions that enable a society 'to manage and reduce disaster risks and strengthen resilience'.[121] Accordingly, disaster risk is defined as the 'potential loss of life, injury, or destroyed or damaged assets which could occur to a system, society or a community in a specific period of time, determined probabilistically as a function of *hazard, exposure, vulnerability and capacity*'.[122] Thus, the common disaster definition in disaster studies emphasises the social and sociological dimension beside the physical dimension.[123] This relationship can be described by the following formula:[124]

$$\textit{Risk of a Disaster} = \frac{\text{Hazard} \times \text{Vulnerability} \times \text{Exposure}}{\text{Coping Capacity}}$$

Building on this conceptualisation, the following axioms for disasters can be derived. Most disasters involve a human made component.[125] Beside the possible human influence on the rise and gravity of hazards, the social factors of vulnerability, exposure, and lack of capacity are all ascribed to the human made component.

Against this background, the former UN Secretary-General Kofi Annan noted that '[t]he term "natural disasters" has become an increasingly anachronistic misnomer. In reality, it is human behaviour that transforms natural hazards into what should be called unnatural disasters'.[126] In fact, the often-used term 'natural disaster' can only refer to exceptional disasters that are triggered by purely natural processes and are objectively irresistible. Beyond this narrow scope of application for the term 'natural disaster', disaster studies avoid this term, as it seems inextricably intertwined with its former connotation of being unavoidable.[127] To express this current disaster conceptualisation, this book uses the proposed term 'disaster triggered by natural hazards'.[128]

---

[119] See UN General Assembly (2016), p. 24.

[120] See ibid, p. 18.

[121] See ibid, p. 12.

[122] Ibid, p. 14 (emphasis added).

[123] Bartolini (2018), p. 12.

[124] Field et al. (2012), p. 69.

[125] Kloepfer (2017), p. 144; Jaeckel (2001), p. 155.

[126] Annan (1999), para 11.

[127] Briceño (2015), p. 1; Wachinger et al. (2013), p. 1062; Raju and da Costa (2018), p. 285.

[128] Briceño (2015), p. 1.

1.5.3 The Current Disaster Risk Reduction Terminology

Policies aimed 'at preventing new and reducing existing disaster risk and managing residual risk' have become recognised under the terms of DRR.[129] Although the term 'risk' is subject to some ambiguity depending on the discipline and context,[130] risk in a broad sense is commonly described as the product of the probability of a given harm materialising, times the gravity of said harm.[131] Trouwborst sums it up simply as: [132]

$$risk = probability\, of\; harm \times gravity$$

The DRR concept comprises different categories of measures that target different levels of effectiveness. As such, DRR is commonly categorised into prevention, mitigation, and preparation. Historically, international instruments and the literature have defined these subcategories inconsistently. This is partly due to the wide array of actors involved in the development of DRR. For this reason, the Open-Ended Intergovernmental Expert Working Group ('OIEWG') was tasked to recommend an updated terminology relating to DRR.[133]

According to the OIEWG, today's concept of DRR is understood as measures that aim not only at *reducing* existing disaster risk and managing residual risk but also at *preventing* new disaster risk.[134] The recommendation of the OIEWG on terminology relating to DRR defines *prevention* as activities and measures that avoid existing as well as new disaster risks.[135] The concept includes the elimination of those risk factors that exclude the risk of a disaster.[136] Such preventive measures include dams or embankments to avoid certain flood risks, the prohibition of settlement in high risk zones through land use control, and seismic engineering designs to preclude the collapse of buildings.[137] Notably, the concept does not suggest that all disaster risks can be entirely avoided.[138]

If the risk cannot be avoided itself, *mitigation* aims to lessen or minimise the negative impacts of a hazardous event.[139] As such, the meaning of 'mitigation' in DRR differs from environmental law, where the term refers to the reduction of

---

129 UN General Assembly (2016), p. 16.

130 Pettersen (2016), p. 40.

131 Jaeckel (2017), p. 37; Trouwborst (2006), p. 27; German Advisory Council on Global Change (2000), pp. 52–53.

132 Trouwborst (2006), p. 27.

133 General Assembly (2015).

134 UN General Assembly (2016), p. 16; Kelman et al. (2017), pp. 3–4.

135 UN General Assembly (2016), p. 21.

136 Ibid, pp. 14, 21.

137 Ibid, p. 21.

138 Ibid, pp. 14, 21.

139 Ibid, p. 20; International Law Commission (2013), para 141.

greenhouse gas emissions that are considered to be the cause of climate change.[140] In relation to DRR, the OIEWG lists examples of mitigation such as engineering techniques, hazard resistant construction, environmental and social policies, and public awareness as measures to lessen the scale or intensity of natural hazards.[141]

The third concept, *preparation*, refers to the 'knowledge and capacities … to effectively anticipate, respond to and recover from the impacts of likely, imminent or current disasters'.[142] This category includes an array of measures, including for instance early warning systems, emergency management systems, evacuation plans, and stockpiling of equipment, food and medicine.[143] The response includes the evacuation of already or soon to be exposed people and their subsequent protection. To that effect, these measures do not aim at reducing the risk by building up defence or by pre-emptively avoiding exposure but to escape the risk once it materialises. This last category under DRR thus incorporates the traditional idea of disaster management.[144]

1.5.4 Risk Governance and Risk Evaluation

With respect to the challenge of collectively deciding whether and how to regulate a risk, such as in the context of natural hazards, the concept of 'risk governance' is relevant. The term '[r]isk governance refers to a complex of coordinating, steering and regulatory processes conducted for collective decision making involving *uncertainty*'.[145] The emphasis on 'uncertainty' makes it clear that the concept of risk governance relates to situations that philosophers call *contingency*.[146] Contingency refers to an event, or an action, that could possibly happen or not.[147] Thus, risk governance includes collective decision making relating to situations in which science is unable to predict with reasonable certainty the time and place of a potential threat, the options to respond to it, and the consequences of this response.[148] The process by which a society assesses risks is referred to as 'risk evaluation'.[149]

---

140 UN General Assembly (2016), p. 20.

141 Ibid.

142 Ibid, p. 21.

143 For an overview of the definitions and models of preparedness, see Buckle (2012), pp. 484–485; UN General Assembly (2016), p. 21.

144 International Law Commission (2013), para 38.

145 Renn and Klinke (2016), p. 204 (emphasis added); for an overview of the development and ambiguity of this recently coined term, see Hermans et al. (2012), pp. 1095–1104.

146 Renn (2008), p. 1.

147 Silver (2018) and Øhrstrøm and Hasle (2020).

148 Renn (2008), pp. 2–3.

149 Ibid, p. 149.

The current conceptualisation of the risk evaluation process differentiates acceptable, tolerable, and intolerable risks.[150] Acceptable risks are commonly defined as risks that are accepted in a certain context on the basis of societal values.[151] In case of acceptable risks, no further risk management is expected.[152] In contrast, tolerable risks require further measures, to render them acceptable.[153] Tolerable risks relate to risks, whose associated benefit is considered worth securing if reasonable risk reduction measures are taken.[154] The benefits of intolerable risks, on the other hand, are judged insufficient to run the risk.[155] Consequently, risk management is called upon to prohibit or phase out the risky activity.[156] These categories are applicable to risky activities that create or aggravate risk agents, such as prima facie natural hazards. Yet, the three categories may further apply to the design of risk-absorbing systems that protect against natural risk agents, such as buildings.[157] As such, the risk-absorbing system's level of vulnerability to hazards is open to risk evaluation.[158] In practice, the delineation between acceptable, tolerable, and intolerable risks is the most difficult and most controversial task of risk management.[159]

1.6 Scope of the Book

With regard to the scope of this book, some limitations must be noted. First, the overarching issue of this book is of a legal sociological nature. The book sets out legal and policy measures to reduce the consequences of distorted risk perception and argues for their necessity. The main purpose is thus not a systematic and neutral exploration of the current law in the CoE member states but an investigation of the extent to which the law (does not) respond to increasing disaster losses, to what extent it sets barriers for solutions and how political support for solutions can be gained. Reference points for arguing the need for legal and political measures in response to distorted risk perception are scientific findings on risks of natural hazards, benefits and costs of DRR and the perception of these. In this respect, the book relies on a desk-based synthesis of the existing body of research and does not itself collect epistemic data.

---

[150] Ibid; Renn and Klinke (2016), p. 210; Rausand and Haugen (2020), pp. 102–104; Murphy and Gardoni (2012), p. 989.

[151] Rausand and Haugen (2020), pp. 99–102; see also Renn (2008), p. 149.

[152] Renn and Klinke (2016), p. 210; Rausand and Haugen (2020), pp. 102–104; Kemp (2016), p. 167.

[153] Renn and Klinke (2016), p. 210.

[154] Ibid; Rausand and Haugen (2020), pp. 102–104; Renn (2008), p. 149; Kemp (2016), p. 167.

[155] Renn and Klinke (2016), p. 210; Rausand and Haugen (2020), pp. 102–104; Renn (2008), p. 149; Kemp (2016), p. 167.

[156] Renn and Klinke (2016), p. 210.

[157] Renn (2008), p. 149.

[158] Ibid.

[159] Renn and Klinke (2016), p. 208; Renn (2008), p. 149.

Second, the examination of legal measures to reduce the consequences of distorted risk perception in the context of natural hazards focusses on human rights under the ECHR. As such, this book does not purport to provide a complete analysis of the lawfulness of DRR measures for each member state's constitutional framework. Instead, this book examines the permissibility of different DRR measures on the basis of Europe's shared fundamental rights as enshrined in the ECHR.[160] The ECHR constitutes Europe's most important human rights instrument.[161] After the exclusion of Russia from the CoE in March 2022,[162] the ECHR comprises 46 member states and approximately 676 million Europeans. In the words of the European Court of Human Rights ('the Court'), the ECHR establishes the 'public order of Europe'.[163] The judgments of the Court are legally binding,[164] and since their enforcement is monitored by the Committee of Ministers,[165] the Court has a 'remarkably good' record of execution of judgments.[166] The member states are required to execute judgments whenever a violation has been found by taking all necessary measures.[167]

Third, this book's analysis is carried out in the context of natural hazards. As indicated by its definition above,[168] this term encompasses a broad field of natural risks to humans and their assets. However, for the purpose of this book, it is not necessary to present a complete account of natural hazard risks and unexploited DRR potential in member states. In fact, an account that does justice to the comprehensive nature of the natural hazard concept would require a separate research project. Instead, this book adopts the understanding of the natural hazard as discussed above to examine a few salient examples of seemingly 'irrational' individual and societal behaviours towards known risks of natural hazards in Europe. For this reason, this book particularly focusses on hydrometeorological and geophysical hazards, when contextuality is important for the analysis. These types of natural hazards are among the most common natural hazards in Europe.[169] In particular, flooding

---

[160] However, it should be noted that national constitutions sometimes provide stricter individual protection than the ECHR. The ECHR only establishes minimum standards, see generally Petzold (1993), pp. 60–61.

[161] Pedersen (2008), p. 84; Stahl (2012), p. 78; Frowein (2009), para 17; Polakiewicz (2019), paras 28, 71.

[162] Following the Russian Federation's invasion of Ukraine on 24 February 2022, the Committee of Ministers adopted Resolution CM/Res(2022)2 on the cessation of the Russian Federation's membership of the Council of Europe on 16 March.

[163] EComHR, *Austria v Italy,* Decision, 11 January 1961, p. 20.

[164] See Article 46 (1) of the ECHR.

[165] See Article 46 (2) of the ECHR.

[166] Leuprecht (1993), p. 800; Polakiewicz (2019), para 17.

[167] Leuprecht (1993), p. 800.

[168] See Sect. 1.5.1.

[169] EM-DAT, CRED/UCLouvain, Brussels, Belgium.

already represents Europe's most frequent disaster triggered by natural hazards.[170] Hydrometeorological and geophysical hazards also cause the greatest economic damage in Europe.[171]

Fourth, scientists confirm that the expected increase in the number and intensity of extreme weather events, such as heavy rainfall, is linked to human induced climate change.[172] In this context, the analysis in this book is confined to the challenges related to legally attributing individual disasters to anthropogenic climate change rather than natural causes. Beyond that, the separate question might arise as to whether there is a legal obligation to 'prevent' or 'mitigate' the increase in risk by reducing greenhouse gas emissions. This complex question, which is the subject of much current research[173] and a growing case law,[174] is beyond the scope of the research question and aim of this book.

Last, the analysis of proposals for adapting the member state's political system in response to distorted risk perception zeros in on moral and state philosophical theories that are relevant to the member states. Although each of the 46 member states has its own historical and cultural background, they share certain economic, ethical, and political concepts.[175] The CoE was the first European political organisation founded with the aim of achieving closer unity between its members.[176] The member states themselves have affirmed in the preambles of their most important treaties 'their devotion to the spiritual and moral values which are the common heritage of their peoples and the true source of individual freedom, political liberty and the rule of law, principles which form the basis of all genuine democracy'.[177] These values form the benchmark for assessing proposals for adapting the member state's political system.

---

[170] Field et al. (2012), p. 258; EM-DAT, CRED/UCLouvain, Brussels, Belgium, EM-DAT recorded 664 floods in member states of the CoE between 1900 and 2023. The next most frequent disasters triggered by natural hazards are storms with 570 counts and earthquakes with 283 counts (as per 10 April 2023). However, it should be noted that EM-DAT considers situations or events as disasters, which overwhelms local capacity, necessitating a request to national or international level for external assistance as disaster.

[171] Over the last 20 years, EM-DAT records US $109.7 billion in flood-related damages and US $145.9 billion in earthquake-related damages in the member states, see EM-DAT, CRED/UCLouvain, Brussels, Belgium.

[172] Clarke et al. (2022).

[173] Boyle (2012), Lewis (2018) and Kahl (2022).

[174] See, e.g., IACtHR, *State Obligations in Relation to the Environment in the Context of the Protection and Guarantee of the Rights to Life and to Personal Integrity - Interpretation and Scope of Articles 4(1) and 5(1) of the American Convention on Human Rights,* Advisory Opinion, 15 November 2017; BVerfG, *Klimaschutz,* Order, 24 March 2021, BVerfGE 157, 30.

[175] Baade (2017), p. 308.

[176] Preamble and art 1 (a) of the Statute of the Council of Europe, opened for signature 5 May 1949, 87 UNTS 103 (entered into force 3 August 1949).

[177] Statute of the Council of Europe, opened for signature 5 May 1949, 87 UNTS 103 (entered into force 3 August 1949); see further Convention for the Protection of Human Rights and Fundamental Freedoms, opened for signature 4 November 1950, 213 UNTS 221 (entered into force 3 September 1953).

1.7 Contextualising the Problem in Terms of Competing Schools of Thought

So far, this chapter has elaborated on the problem that inspired this book, that is, the asymmetry between the potential to save lives and property from natural hazards and the lack of legal frameworks to help realise this potential in member states. This book identifies the knowledge of mental and cultural biases in risk perception as a viable starting point to reduce this asymmetry. To provide a contextual backdrop for exploring approaches to mitigate the consequences of distorted risk perception, this subsection sets out the contrasting schools of thought found in the existing literature and the stance taken by this book in opposition to them.

1.7.1 Common Rationales for Public Risk Regulation

First, in relation to risk management, this chapter has already argued that, despite increasing disaster losses, the status quo of private and public DRR measures warrants public measures to reduce them.[178] While Chap. 4 assesses the lawfulness of proposed measures by commentators in the literature in relation to fundamental rights, this section aims to provide an overview of the normative discussion in the literature and highlight critical points that the following chapters of this book discuss.

To begin with, proposals for measures to mitigate the consequences of distorted risk perception must respect fundamental rights to protect the individual sphere of freedom. At the international level, the member states have set such limits to their risk management by adopting the ECHR, which obliges the member states to abstain from interfering with the individuals' rights and freedoms under the ECHR.[179] In this respect, it must be noted that the intended protection of the individual can at the same time encroach on his or her freedom.[180] In other words, the principle of personal autonomy, as an underlying principle in the interpretation of these rights and freedoms,[181] constitutes the main ethical and legal argument against a paternalistic approach to enforce protection against risks.[182] As a result, state measures against the consequences of distorted risk perception in relation to natural hazards must not interfere or must be covered by a rationale that justifies the proposed interference.

The arguments in the literature for state regulation usually feature three main rationales, which also apply to the field of DRR. Two of these rationales aim to

---

[178] See Sect. 1.1.

[179] Shelton and Gould (2013), pp. 562–563.

[180] Flanigan (2017), p. 294; Le Grand and New (2015), p. 105.

[181] ECtHR, 5th Sec., *Prilutskiy v Ukraine*, Judgment, 26 February 2015, para 32.

[182] Flanigan (2017), p. 294; Le Grand and New (2015), p. 105.

protect the individual from 'risk to self'.[183] The term 'risk to self' refers to persons exposing themselves to risks, for instance, the risks of natural hazards. One rationale for intervention focusses on the protection of individual interests, such as health and life, while the other aims to realise the 'authentic self' of individuals by intervening with their behaviours that do not correspond to their goals and desires. As such, the rationale that aims to protect the health or life of the individual from natural hazards and the rationale that seeks to realise the individual's 'authentic self' share a *beneficent* or *paternalistic* character. If the measure is covered by the explicit will of the beneficiary, it is of a *beneficent* character that does not interfere with the value of autonomy.[184] Only measures against the will of the individual, that is, *paternalistically* motivated goals, are problematic in terms of justification. The third rationale seeks to prevent 'risk to others'.[185] This rationale protects communal interests from individuals' risk-taking, thereby embodying a *non-paternalistic* in rationale. The analysis reveals that only this last rationale would be suitable to justify an increase in the necessary safety levels for reducing rising disaster losses.

1.7.1.1 The Rationale of Protecting the Individuals' Interests

The first usually advanced rationale for intervening in people's decisions in the context of natural hazard risks is the protection of individual's interests, such as life, health, and property. Over the past centuries, the understanding of the purpose of the state has changed to include the protection of individuals' interests from private risks in some areas.[186] In sociology, risks are commonly categorised as *public* and *private risks*, with the natural hazards discussed in this book typically falling into the *private risk* category.[187] The sociological categorisation is associated with differences in the evaluation of risks in terms of their meaning to society.[188] It is based on relevant differences in ethical and political philosophical perspectives on the justification for societal risk regulation. As such, the decision of whether to ignore or

---

[183] Alemanno (2016), p. 198.

[184] See Maclean (2009), p. 51.

[185] Alemanno (2016), p. 198.

[186] Doron (2016), p. 20; Heun (2011), pp. 18–19.

[187] Commonly, the academic literature defines *private* risks as that are discretely generated, localised, within personal control, or of natural origin. Examples of *human made private* risks would constitute cars or wood stoves, while *natural private* risks refer to natural toxins, for instance. In contrast, *public* risks pose threats to human safety or health, are centrally or mass-produced, widely distributed, and largely beyond the direct understanding and control of individual risk bearers. According to this definition, textbook examples of *public* risks are nuclear power plants, chemical additives in food, or vaccinations. Yet, risks may not neatly fall into one of these categories. On the contrary, a risk may be located somewhere between the poles of the private-public continuum. For instance, risks posed by mass transportation have a public risk character, while the individual still maintains a choice in bearing the risk, see Huber (1985), pp. 277–278; Gillette and Krier (1990), p. 1029; Ambrus (2017), p. 103.

[188] Ambrus (2017), p. 103; Gillette and Krier (1990), pp. 1028–1029; Huber (1985).

regulate a risk depends on questions, such as whether the risk is human made or natural, and whether the risk is voluntary chosen or involuntarily imposed.[189] Until the eighteenth century, the prevailing understanding of the state's purpose dictated that the assessment of *private risk* fell within the individual's realm, along with the corresponding responsibility for the outcomes of their decisions.[190] However, over the centuries, the notion of an individual's exclusive responsibility for *private risks* has been challenged.[191]

Today, it is a central and fundamental goal in the modern state, as well as the state's primary source of legitimacy, to provide protection to its citizens against risks to their legal interests.[192] At the international level, the member states have codified this goal by adopting the ECHR, which obliges the member states to ensure the protection of individual's rights, including those pertaining to life and property. In this regard, judiciary and quasi-judiciary bodies on human rights all over the world have repeatedly found that human rights can give rise to positive obligations in addition to their primarily negative obligation.[193] Based on an effective interpretation of the object and purpose of the ECHR in conjunction with the individual rights, the Court infers the existence of positive obligations, even if the relevant Articles do not explicitly mention them, such as to the right to property.[194] The case law even recognises that natural circumstances can threaten the protected interests just as much as state acts.[195] Regarding such positive obligations, certain commentators advocate for a broader interpretation of the state's positive obligations to safeguard individuals from natural hazards under the ECHR. This broader interpretation could potentially facilitate the advancement of DRR in the member states.[196] However, as Chap. 3 examines in detail, it is the combination of the rank of the right to property with the inherent characteristics of natural hazards that precludes a

[189] See Möller (2012), p. 60; Hansson (2004); Dworkin (2015); Cranor (1993), p. 128; van de Poel and Fahlquist (2012), pp. 890–895; Ross and Athanassoulis (2012), p. 839; see Shrader-Frechette (2005), p. 96; Renn (2008), p. 3.

[190] Doron (2016), p. 20; see further Ambrus et al. (2017), p. 4.

[191] Doron (2016), p. 20; Heun (2011), pp. 18–19.

[192] For more details, see Isensee (1983); Arends (2008), p. 263; Dyzenhaus (2001), p. 462; Stahl (2012), pp. 88–89; Stoll (2003), pp. 6–8; Heun (2011), pp. 15–16.

[193] For the International Covenant on Civil and Political Rights, see General Comment No. 6. It considers that the 'expression "inherent right to life" cannot properly be understood in a restrictive manner, and the protection of this right requires that States adopt positive measures', see UN Human Rights Committee (1982), para 5; for the American Convention on Human Rights the Inter-American Court of Human Rights also found that a 'State has a legal duty to take reasonable steps to prevent human rights violations', see IACtHR, *Velasquez Rodriguez Case,* Judgment, 29 July 1988, p. 174; for the European Convention on Human Rights, see ECtHR, *Marckx v Belgium,* Judgment, 13 June 1979, Eur Court HR (ser A) 31, para 31; ECtHR, *Airey v Ireland,* Judgment, 9 October 1979, Eur Court HR (ser A) 32, para 32.

[194] Krieger (2014), p. 189; Starmer (1999), pp. 194–195.

[195] Starmer (1999), p. 194.

[196] Lauta and Rytter (2016).

comprehensive DRR obligation under the ECHR.[197] Instead, the positive obligations of member states in relation to natural hazards particularly revolves around response-oriented measures. A duty to raise the general level of safety for protection against natural hazards cannot be derived from the ECHR.

In addition to the voices that argue for a more extensive obligation of the state based on the rationale to protect individuals' interests, other commentators argue that this rationale at least permits state interventions. As such, some scholars argue that the value of autonomy behind people's unfettered decisions is inferior vis-à-vis the value of life and health.[198] For instance, Frank B Cross argues that considering subjective values in collective decision-making processes would seem innocuous but would result in the non-trivial cost of failing to maximise lifesaving.[199] Others also remind those who reject state interferences in private risk decisions that the many advances in public health

> would not have happened unless the state acknowledged its responsibility for the health of the population. Nanny state name-calling may be a flippant and reflexive response to policies one does not like. Ultimately, however, it is a call for the state to be agnostic about the health of citizens.[200]

Conversely, and in accordance with this book, other scholars argue that such argumentation unduly neglects the value of autonomy. In particular with respect to the protection of health, this line of argument would effectively make the legitimacy of people's ends dependent on how the state judges these goals.[201] Even if a decision may seem 'unhealthy' to a third party, autonomy would protect the individual from paternalistic state interference due to the pluralistic understanding of happiness.[202] As such, the concept of autonomy accepts that happiness is a state of mind that one cannot conceptualise in abstract ends or means. Thus, while health and welfare may be ends in themselves to some, to others they may merely constitute the means to self-fulfilment.[203] To the latter, health has merely instrumental value that 'allows us to follow our life plans and achieve our goals'.[204] A different assessment may only be justified if the risk concerns the future ability to make autonomous decisions. In this respect, it should be noted that the value of autonomy would also protect its continuation.[205] This continuation of autonomy would be terminated by, for example, death. Thus, building on this argumentation, interventions in autonomous

[197] See Sect. 3.2.4.

[198] Cross (1998), p. 35; Conly (2013, 2014).

[199] Cross (1998), p. 35.

[200] Magnusson (2015), p. 1080.

[201] Le Grand and New (2015), p. 102.

[202] See Maclean (2009), pp. 36–38; Dröge (2003), pp. 329–330.

[203] Maclean (2009), p. 28.

[204] Ibid.

[205] Flanigan (2017), p. 301; see Smith (2002), p. 238; Le Grand and New (2015), p. 127; Maclean (2009), pp. 36–38.

decisions involving such risks may be justified to *protect* the value of autonomy.[206] Yet, in detail, the question remains of how *certain* a danger to life and health must be in order to justify an intervention in autonomy. The delineation carried out in Chap. 4 demonstrates that this rationale cannot justify further precautionary measures that would raise the safety standard through increased DRR.

1.7.1.2 The Rationale of Realising the Individual's Authentic Self

The second rationale discussed for justifying state interferences in autonomy with DRR measures concerns the ambition to realise people's 'authentic values' to promote the value of autonomy.[207] Scholars point out that the empirical findings on people's perceptions of risk in psychology, which Chap. 2 explores in detail,[208] give reason to suspect a 'disjunction' between the ends people presumably want and the way in which they reach them. The empirical findings suggest that people tend to make 'irrational, weak-willed, uninformed, and inconsistent' risk decisions.[209] The influence of cognitive and cultural mechanisms would 'interfere with our appreciation of even quite simple facts, and lead us to choose ineffective means to our ends'.[210] Against this background, some scholars argue that the realisation of people's authentic values was justified as promotion of the value of autonomy.[211] This line of argument relies on the concept of so-called 'reasoning failures', which describe a 'disjunction between the ends we want and how to get them'.[212] Such disjunctions would allow the state to ensure that the individual is acting autonomously enough when pursuing self-harming conduct, since reasoning failures would constitute a mild form of 'autonomy failure',[213] which are a well-established justification for interfering in private risk-taking.[214] Le Grand and New define an autonomy failure as 'a prior diminution of the individual's capacity for autonomous decision making'.[215] Typical examples for such autonomy failures constitute conditions of mental disability, mental illness, or the immaturity of children.[216] Virtually all legal systems apply the concept of autonomy failures to protect certain individuals

---

206 Le Grand and New (2015), pp. 111, 120–121; Feinberg (1989), p. 126; see further Maclean (2009), p. 28; Renn (2008), p. 96.

207 Sunstein (2002b), p. 53; Sunstein (2005), p. 126; see further Evans (2006), p. 222; Slovic (2000), p. 285; Breyer (1993), p. 55; Kahan et al. (2006), pp. 1075–1076.

208 See Sect. 2.1.

209 Flanigan (2017), p. 306.

210 Conly (2014), p. 349.

211 Ibid.

212 Le Grand and New (2015), p. 103.

213 Feinberg (1989), pp. 117–127; Le Grand and New (2015), pp. 119–132.

214 Le Grand and New (2015), p. 106; see further Conly (2014); Flanigan (2017), p. 306.

215 Le Grand and New (2015), p. 106.

216 Ibid, pp. 116–117; Goodin (1993), pp. 232–234.

in the context of private risks. Restrictions concerning the drinking or smoking age are examples for such laws.[217] In fact, as Chap. 3 shows, cases of autonomy failures in decision-making increase the state's due diligence to protect affected individuals against natural hazards.[218] However, a relevant, albeit controversial, question for the focus of this book is when the justification for interventions based on 'autonomy failures' applies to situations of reasoning failures.

The justification for state interventions in private risk-taking based on 'reasoning failures' has been put forward in many contexts, such as the field of international trade,[219] the field of medical ethics,[220] in particular with respect to vaccinations,[221] or with respect to the risks from climate change.[222] Another much discussed example constitutes the smoking of cigarettes.[223] The fact that nicotine is addictive, and that most smokers state their wish to quit smoking, brings the voluntariness of a smokers' decision to continue smoking into question.[224] In response to such disjunctions, some scholars argue that a corrective intervention is 'necessary, even if it is sometimes unwelcome, to allow people to live the lives they truly want to live'.[225] This rationale also applies in the context of natural hazards, where a distorted perception of risk can prevent people from achieving their goals.

On the flip side, the empirical evidence on risk perception simultaneously suggests that full voluntariness 'is an extremely rare, if not unattainable ideal'.[226] To that effect, a broad interpretation of 'reasoning failures' and their justifying power would annul the intended protection of autonomy by given rights through the backdoor.[227] Thus, the rationale bears the risk of serving as a smokescreen for paternalism unless a differentiated approach, as set out in Chap. 4,[228] is employed. To distinguish permissible from impermissible state intervention in cases of reasoning failures, Chap. 4 draws upon moral and political philosophy, which is reflected in ECHR jurisprudence. As a result, the analysis shows that the differentiated approach allows only a narrow scope of permissible interventions.

---

217 See generally Le Grand and New (2015), pp. 50–51.

218 See Sect. 3.2.3.2.

219 See for example Howse (2000).

220 See for instance Varelius (2006).

221 See Zolkefli (2017) and Flanigan (2014).

222 Wang and Kim (2018).

223 Viscusi (1992), pp. 23–25; Conly (2016); Doucet (2017); Grill and Voigt (2016).

224 Dworkin (1972), p. 82; Goodin (1989), pp. 579–587.

225 Conly (2014).

226 Le Grand and New (2015), pp. 119–120, who refer to Feinberg (1989).

227 See generally Dröge (2003), p. 330.

228 See Sect. 4.2.2.

1.7.1.3 The Rationale of Protecting the Collective Against Harm

The third rationale for intervening in individual autonomous decision-making aims to protect the collective against harm emanating from individual risk-taking. As such, this rationale builds on the harm principle, which states that 'every individual should be free to act as he or she perceives to be in self-interest, subject only to limits established to protect the interests of others'.[229] From the perspective of political philosophy, protecting individual third parties, or society as a whole, from the harmful consequences of individual risk-taking is one of the natural obligations of the state.[230] In fact, the harm principle's rationale for balancing individuals' autonomy in a pluralistic society shapes most of today's risk regulation. For instance, smoking bans in public places seek to protect other individuals from passive smoking.[231] As such, the question arises to what extent the harm principle permits a restriction of personal autonomy in the context of natural hazards. One consideration is the financial burden of individual risk-taking on the public.

In this regard, disasters regularly prompt governments to undertake costly rescue operations and financial support for survivors.[232] For example, between 1991 and 2010, the international community spent almost 70% of their international aid allocated to disasters on disaster response and 23.3% on reconstruction and rehabilitation.[233] Considering these costs, Robert W McGee asks whether it is fair to force the general public to pay for the consequences of voluntary decisions to take known private risks.[234] For instance, taxpayers 'who have enough sense not to live in a flood zone should not be forced' to pay for the post-disaster relief system.[235]

The evaluation of such proposals in this book requires some contextualisation of societal needs. Building on the goal of a functioning society, it is reasonable to question the desirability of strictly applying the harm principle, that is, to forbid or sanction every private risk-taking behaviour that creates a risk for the community. A strict extension of the harm principle to the context of risk would sanction actions that implicate a nonzero risk of resulting in interferences with other people's rights.[236] For instance, it would prohibit activities, such as driving a car or mowing a lawn for the nonzero risk of causing an accident or ricocheting rocks, which can kill a third party.[237] Thus, a desire for maximising the protection of community interests from the consequences of individual risk-taking would need to accept

[229] Green (1981), p. 11.

[230] See Heun (2011), pp. 25–26.

[231] BVerfG, Judgment, 30 July 2008, BVerfGE 121, 317.

[232] See Heun (2011), p. 23; Linnerooth-Bayer (2012), p. 652.

[233] Kellett and Caravani (2013), p. 5.

[234] McGee (2008), p. 548.

[235] Ibid.

[236] Hansson (2012), p. 46; Hansson (2003), p. 298; Hansson (2023), paras 5.3–5.4; Schroeder (1986), pp. 509–510.

[237] Hansson (2012), p. 46; Schroeder (1986), p. 501.

Isaiah Berlin's famous conclusion that values are regularly incommensurate.[238] The achievement of one end will often entail losses at the other end, that is, individual freedom.[239] Worse, a strict interpretation of the harm principle would effectively frustrate the functioning of human society.[240] Notably, no one is exempted from the possibility of contributing conditions to future harm unless no one ever did anything.[241] Even cooking meals or heating homes creates environmental pollution that increases health risks to others.[242] Thus, with respect to the goal of a functioning society, 'a truly absolute right against harm is impossible to defend'.[243] Instead, this goal requires to reasonably balance the protection of individuals' rights to non-interference on the one hand, and the interests of the community on the other.[244] Chapter 4's assessment of certain measures provides examples of how this rationale would justify an increase in the safety standard if there were a public demand for it.

1.7.2 Competing Proposals on the Design of Political Decision-Making Processes

It follows from the difficulties of balancing the different interests in risk management that the epistemic knowledge about risks and DRR options is in itself not action-guiding but risk management constitutes a complex balancing act.[245] This delineation of private and public responsibility and the allocation of collective resources to risk reduction measures is a matter of the national decision-making process.[246] With the goal of mitigating the influence of distorted risk perception in political decision-making in mind, a special focus in this book is on the advantages of appropriately structured deliberative processes in public decision-making. As Chap. 5 presents in detail, public participation in policy-making through deliberative processes can help mitigate the effects of distorted risk perception in collective decision-making processes while respecting citizens as autonomous and equal.[247] To achieve this objective, the structure of deliberative processes incorporates key elements such as procedural norms, moderation, and the active involvement of relevant stakeholders, including experts. These components work together to create a framework that fosters effective communication, encourages critical analysis, and

[238] Berlin (1958).

[239] Stoll (2003), p. 269.

[240] Hansson (2012), p. 46; Byskov (2020), p. 260; Hansson (2003), p. 298.

[241] See MacLean (2012), pp. 794–795.

[242] See the example provided by ibid.

[243] Schroeder (1986), p. 526; see Stoll (2003), p. 269.

[244] Viscusi (1992), p. 10; Byskov (2020), pp. 260–261.

[245] Möller (2012), p. 71.

[246] Baade (2017), p. 330.

[247] See Sect. 5.1.2.

ensures the inclusion of diverse perspectives, ultimately enabling informed decision-making. Deliberate processes give participants the opportunity to overcome their distorted perception of risk and bring their 'reasoned' assessment of risk into the collective decision-making process. Such 'reasoned' assessments refer to epistemically robust arguments that all affected people could agree upon or can at least be expected to agree upon by the force of the 'better argument'.[248] In other words, the deliberative process respects risk evaluation as a complex socio-economic-political process that is based on the collective *subjective evaluation* of the *objective facts* about risks.[249] By supporting participants in assessing risks based on a proper understanding of the facts during the deliberative process, this book argues that implementing deliberate processes can even strengthen democratic values. The conceptualisation of autonomy and liberty suggests that a state's risk regulation should respond to the '*authentic preferences* of citizens' in order to respect their right to self-governance.[250] Yet, the evidence suggests that people would judge the acceptability of risks differently, if they could unbiasedly apply scientific facts in its judgment.[251] Thus, mitigating the influence of distorted risk perception through deliberative processes promotes democratic values.

Conversely, in light of the challenge that distorting risk perception poses to collective decision-making processes, a competing school of thought uses the empirical findings in psychology as an argument against democratic structures. The complex considerations behind risk management, in addition to the identified fallacies of people's intuitive disaster risk perception, could cast doubt on the extent to which lay people's preferences should inform public risk regulation. If '[t]he reduction of collective risks is the natural obligation of government',[252] then the state's reliance on expertise in risk management would be preferable to promote the 'common good', which serves as one source of political legitimacy. In this respect, this competing school of thought relies on a conceptualisation of the 'common good' that assumes the existence of contextually 'correct outcomes' and conditions the political legitimacy of the decision-making procedure on its capacity to arrive at these outcomes.[253] Accordingly, if non-democratic processes contribute to better approximate these correct outcomes, political legitimacy would not depend on the inclusion of democratic values in the decision-making process.[254] For instance, alternative state political systems, such as epistocracy, derive political legitimacy from the production of 'good outcomes' by 'people who know best'.[255]

[248] Habermas (2015), p. 37; see generally Holst (2012), p. 51; cf. Schumpeter (2010), p. 226.

[249] Renn (2008), p. 151.

[250] Scharpf (1997), p. 19; Christiano and Bajaj (2022), para 2.2.1.

[251] See Viscusi (1992), p. 25; Christiansen and Hallsson (2017), pp. 62–63; Ivčević et al. (2021).

[252] Heun (2011), p. 26.

[253] See Peter (2017), para 4.1.

[254] See ibid.

[255] Runciman (2018), p. 180; see Holst (2012), p. 41.

While this book agrees that the polity could undoubtedly benefit from improved means of determining people's 'authentic' risk acceptance, it argues that such improvements need to be achieved by enhancing the political process within the democratic system. In this regard, this book defends the democratic system against such state political systems as the theoretically more reasonable approach to improve the 'authenticity' of public risk management. It argues that the proposed promotion of the collective good based on experts' decisions irrespective of people's preferences or consent ignores human-rights based free choices, belittles the democratic sovereign, and amounts to paternalism.[256] Moreover, the argument for prioritising expertise may further suffer from ill-founded trust in the experts' abilities to not only deliver scientific insights but also to realise the collective good. As such, the result of the discussion of competing schools of thought in Chap. 5 reinforces the argument put forth in this book, advocating for the inclusion of deliberative fora in the collective decision-making process to mitigate the influence of bias and heuristics.

1.8 Significance of the Book

By combining insights from the scientific, social science and legal disciplines in this book's analysis, the book makes an original contribution to legal and political studies. Behaviour studies have long explored behaviour patterns. In fact, it has been argued that '[m]any conferences are being held, research projects carried out and books written asking the very same question in relation to the many other ways in which we, as a species, make strange and seemingly irrational choices in relation to our personal and collective safety'.[257] Yet, the legitimacy of targeted responses to these patterns of behaviour has received little overall attention in the literature to date.[258] In this regard, this book builds a bridge between science and sociological studies and studies of law and normative political theory.[259]

The analysis in this book further contributes to enhancing public understanding of the influence and consequences of risk perception patterns relating to natural hazards. As a result, this research contributes to society's greater appreciation of the importance of DRR measures, on the one hand, and bias correction measures, on the other. Moreover, this book's research offers political entities a substantiated approach to facilitate legislative changes to reduce neglected risks of natural hazards.

256 Goodin (1993) and Smiley (1989).

257 Crosweller and Wilmshurst (2013), p. 564.

258 Van Aaken (2017), p. 84; Schweizer (2016), p. 94.

259 For the need of interdisciplinary research, see generally Schrama (2011), p. 161; see further De Boer et al. (2006).

The importance of this book also lies in its timing. Currently, there is a window of opportunity to increase private and public risk reduction measures before the frequency and intensity of natural hazards is projected to increase. For the future, scientists project more frequent occurrence of extreme events—such as floods—in all regions of the world due to environmental degradation and climate change.[260] Heavy precipitation days and extremes in heavy precipitation intensity, as well as precipitation contribution, will also likely increase.[261] As a consequence, the probability of flash floods increases,[262] which entail the highest fatality risk among natural hazards.[263] Recent records already demonstrate the risk of dam failures because of increased precipitation.[264] The results of this book will assist member states and individuals to adopt a proactive approach. In this way, this book contributes to member states playing their part in achieving the global targets as agreed in the Sendai Framework for Disaster Risk Reduction (2015–2030).[265] These include the goals to substantially reduce global disaster mortality by 2030, and to reduce direct economic loss, damage to critical infrastructure and disruption of basic services due to disasters.[266]

1.9 Conclusion

This book is an examination of how the state should legally and politically respond to people's distorted risk perception in the field of natural hazards to decrease disaster losses, all while respecting citizens as autonomous and equal individuals. On the one hand, the book contours what measures the state must and may take to protect both individuals and the collective from the consequences of distorted risk perception. On the other hand, the book suggests ways to politically facilitate an increase in the standard of protection in the face of the influence of risk perception without undermining democratic values, such as the values of liberty and political equality.

This chapter has provided an overview of the book by outlining the research questions and identifying how the book makes an original and significant contribution to the literature on disaster risk reduction. It has summarised how each chapter will address the research question and fulfil the aims of the book. In doing so, this

---

260 Farber (2014), p. 12; Cohen and Bradley (2010), p. 95; International Federation of Red Cross and Red Crescent Societies (2012), p. 21; Cubie and Hesselman (2015), p. 40, who refer to Human Rights Council (2009), paras 8, 23; Crosweller and Wilmshurst (2013), pp. 561–562; Edwards (2013).

261 Field et al. (2012), p. 198, Table 3-3; Freer et al. (2013), p. 195.

262 European Environment Agency (2008), p. 13.

263 European Environment Agency (2004), pp. 9, 75; Field et al. (2012), p. 258; European Commission (2021), pp. 17–18.

264 Field et al. (2012), p. 258.

265 United Nations Office for Disaster Risk Reduction (2015).

266 Ibid, para 18.

chapter has identified a key issue in this field—balancing the need for DRR with the need to preserve individual autonomy and mobilise democratic support. With respect to preserving individual autonomy, this chapter has examined three rationales for justifying public interferences with individual's autonomy. One rationale is the protection of legal interests from the consequences of natural hazards. Another rationale builds on the claim that people would assess risks differently if they were not influenced by prejudices and heuristics. In this respect, the state should help people realise their 'authentic self'. The third rationale relates to the protection of common capacities and resources from the consequences of individual choices. With respect to the need to mobilising democratic support, the discussion revealed that decisions regarding disaster risk management involve complex and controversial ethical, political, and scientific questions.[267] Even if science gives societies options for action, the infinite number of risks on the one hand and the goal of a functioning society on the other hand compel societies to have to choose which risks should be ignored and which should be reduced. The subjectivity and complexity of disaster risk management, raises the question of who should decide on public risk management and how, especially considering the influence of people's distorted risk perceptions.

The scope and origin of people's distorted risk perceptions is the major focus of the following chapter. To that end, Chap. 2 establishes the factual knowledge about the potential to protect life and property from natural hazards and examines the extent to which doubts are justified as to whether individual risk decisions are based on scientifically correct perceptions of the facts.

References

Albris K, Lauta KC, Raju E (2020) Disaster knowledge gaps: exploring the interface between science and policy for disaster risk reduction in Europe. Int J Disaster Risk Sci 11(1):1–12. https://doi.org/10.1007/s13753-020-00250-5

Alemanno A (2016) Risk and regulation. In: Burgess A, Alemanno A, Zinn JO (eds) Routledge handbook of risk studies. Routledge, Abingdon, pp 191–203

Alexander D (2005) An interpretation of disaster in terms of changes in culture, society and international relations. In: Perry RW, Quarantelli EL (eds) What is a disaster? New answers to old questions. Xlibris, Philadelphia, pp 25–38

Álvarez C, Brunet JM (2021) ¿De quién es la tierra creada por el volcán de La Palma? El País, 23 September 2021. https://elpais.com/sociedad/2021-09-23/de-quien-es-la-tierra-creada-por-el-volcan.html. Accessed 19 June 2023

Ambrus M (2017) The European Court of Human Rights as governor of risk. In: Ambrus M, Rayfuse RG, Werner W (eds) Risk and the regulation of uncertainty in international law, 1st edn. Oxford University Press, Oxford, pp 99–115

Ambrus M, Rayfuse RG, Werner W (2017) Risk and international law. In: Ambrus M, Rayfuse RG, Werner W (eds) Risk and the regulation of uncertainty in international law, 1st edn. Oxford University Press, Oxford, pp 3–9

[267] Lauta (2018), p. 50.

Annan K (1999) Report of the Secretary-General on the work of the organization. UN Doc A/54/1

Arends JFM (2008) From Homer to Hobbes and beyond — aspects of 'security' in the European tradition. In: Brauch HG, Behera NC, Chourou B, Dunay P, Grin J, Kameri-Mbote P, Liotta PH, Mesjasz C, Spring ÚO (eds) Globalization and environmental challenges: reconceptualizing security in the 21st century, vol 3. Springer, Heidelberg, pp 263–277

Aronsson-Storrier M, da Costa K (2017) Regulating disasters? The role of international law in disaster prevention and management. Disaster Prev Manag 26(5):502–513. https://doi.org/10.1108/DPM-09-2017-0218

Artino A, Caponetto R, Evola G, Margani G, Marino EM, Murgano E (2020) Decision support system for the sustainable seismic and energy renovation of buildings: methodological layout. Sustainability 12(10273):1–21. https://doi.org/10.3390/su122410273

Baade B (2017) Der Europäische Gerichtshof für Menschenrechte als Diskurswächter, vol 263. Springer, Heidelberg

Baan PJ, Klijn F (2004) Flood risk perception and implications for flood risk management in the Netherlands. Int J River Basin Manag 2(2):113–122. https://doi.org/10.1080/15715124.2004.9635226

Bartolini G (2018) A taxonomy of disasters in international law. In: Zorzi Giustiniani F, Sommario E, Casolari F, Bartolini G (eds) Routledge handbook of human rights and disasters. Routledge, Abingdon, pp 10–26

Bayón JC (2013) The province of jurisprudence underdetermined. In: Ferrer Beltrán J, Moreso JJ, Papayannis DM (eds) Neutrality and theory of law, vol 106. Springer, Dordrecht, pp 1–16

Berlin I (1958) Two concepts of liberty. An inaugural lecture delivered before the University of Oxford on 31 October 1958. Clarendon Press, Oxford

Blome N (2021) Jahrhundert-Regen: Bitte nicht noch einen "Fukushima-Moment": Eine Kolumne von Nikolaus Blome. DER SPIEGEL (online), 19 July 2021. https://www.spiegel.de/politik/deutschland/hochwasser-katastrophe-bitte-nicht-noch-einen-fukushima-moment-kolumne-a-73af5773-7c17-4441-ac8c-702bf495a1ae. Accessed 19 June 2023

Boyle A (2012) Human rights and the environment: where next? EJILAW 23(3):613–642. https://doi.org/10.1093/ejil/chs054

Brettschneider C (2005) Balancing procedures and outcomes within democratic theory: core values and judicial review. Polit Stud 53(2):423–441. https://doi.org/10.1111/j.1467-9248.2005.00536.x

Breyer S (1993) Breaking the vicious circle: toward effective risk regulation. The Oliver Wendell Holmes Lectures, vol 1992. Harvard University Press, Cambridge

Briceño S (2015) Looking back and beyond Sendai: 25 years of international policy experience on disaster risk reduction. Int J Disaster Risk Sci 6(1):1–7. https://doi.org/10.1007/s13753-015-0040-y

Buckle P (2012) Preparedness, warning and evacuation. In: Wisner B, Gaillard JC, Kelman I (eds) The Routledge handbook of hazards and disaster risk reduction. Routledge, London, pp 493–504

Bundesanstalt für Gewässerkunde (Federal Institute of Hydrology) (2019) Hochwassergefahren- und Hochwasserrisikokarten in Deutschland (Status 2019). https://geoportal.bafg.de/karten/HWRM/#. Accessed 19 June 2023

Byskov MF (2020) Utilitarianism and risk. J Risk Res 23(2):259–270

Carreño ML, Barbat AH, Cardona OD, Marulanda MC (2014) Holistic evaluation of seismic risk in Barcelona. In: Alexander D, Birkmann J, Kienberger S (eds) Assessment of vulnerability to natural hazards: a European perspective. Elsevier, Amsterdam, pp 21–52

Childs D (2013) Implementation of the Hyogo Framework for action: summary of reports 2007–2013. United Nations Office for Disaster Risk Reduction. https://www.undrr.org/quick/11319. Accessed 19 June 2023

Christiano T, Bajaj S (2022) Democracy. In: Zalta EN (ed) The Stanford Encyclopedia of Philosophy. https://plato.stanford.edu/entries/democracy/. Accessed 19 June 2023

Christiansen A, Hallsson BG (2017) Democratic decision making and the psychology of risk. Les ateliers de l'éthique/The Ethics Forum 12(1):51–83. https://doi.org/10.7202/1042278ar

Chynoweth P (2008) Legal research. In: Knight A, Ruddock L (eds) Advanced research methods in the built environment. Wiley-Blackwell, Chichester, pp 28–38

Clarke B, Otto F, Stuart-Smith R, Harrington L (2022) Extreme weather impacts of climate change: an attribution perspective. Environ Res Clim 1(12001):1–25. https://doi.org/10.1088/2752-5295/ac6e7d

Cohen R, Bradley M (2010) Disasters and displacement: gaps in protection. J Int Hum Leg Stud 1(1):95–142. https://doi.org/10.1163/187815210X12766020139884

Conceição P (2020) The next frontier: human development and the Anthropocene. Human Development Report, New York

Conly S (2013) Against autonomy: justifying coercive paternalism. Cambridge University Press, Cambridge

Conly S (2014) Against autonomy: justifying coercive paternalism. J Med Ethics 40(5):349. https://doi.org/10.1136/medethics-2013-101444

Conly S (2016) The case for banning cigarettes. J Med Ethics 42(5):302–303. https://doi.org/10.1136/medethics-2016-103520

Cranor CF (1993) Regulating toxic substances: a philosophy of science and the law, Environmental ethics and science policy series. Oxford University Press, New York

Cross FB (1998) Facts and values in risk assessment. Reliab Eng Syst Saf 59(1):27–40. https://doi.org/10.1016/S0951-8320(97)00116-6

Crosweller HS, Wilmshurst J (2013) Natural hazards and risk: the human perspective. In: Rougier J, Hill LJ, Sparks RSJ (eds) Risk and uncertainty assessment for natural hazards. Cambridge University Press, Cambridge, pp 548–569

Cubie D, Hesselman M (2015) Accountability for the human rights implications of natural disasters: a proposal for systemic international oversight. NQHR 33(1):9–41

DasGupta R, Shaw R (2017) Disaster risk reduction: a critical approach. In: Kelman I, Mercer J, Gaillard JC (eds) The Routledge handbook of disaster risk reduction including climate change adaptation. Taylor & Francis, Milton, pp 12–23

De Boer Y, de Gier A, Verschuur M, de Wit B (2006) Building bridges: researchers on their experiences with interdisciplinary research in the Netherlands. RMNO, KNAW, NWO and COS, Den Haag

Dibben CJ (2008) Leaving the city for the suburbs—the dominance of 'ordinary' decision making over volcanic risk perception in the production of volcanic risk on Mt Etna, Sicily. J Volcanol Geotherm Res 172(3–4):288–299. https://doi.org/10.1016/j.jvolgeores.2007.12.014

Dobinson I, Johns F (2017) Legal research as qualitative research. In: McConville M, Chui WH (eds) Research methods for law, 2nd edn. Edinburgh University Press, Edinburgh

Dominey-Howes D, Minos-Minopoulos D (2004) Perceptions of hazard and risk on Santorini. J Volcanol Geotherm Res 137(4):285–310. https://doi.org/10.1016/j.jvolgeores.2004.06.002

Doron C-O (2016) The experience of 'risk': genealogy and transformations. In: Burgess A, Alemanno A, Zinn JO (eds) Routledge handbook of risk studies. Routledge, Abingdon, pp 17–26

Doucet M (2017) The costs and benefits of a cigarette ban. J Med Ethics 43(6):411–412. https://doi.org/10.1136/medethics-2017-104172

Dröge C (2003) Positive Verpflichtungen der Staaten in der Europäischen Menschenrechtskonvention. Beiträge zum ausländischen öffentlichen Recht und Völkerrecht, Bd. 159. Springer, Heidelberg

Dworkin G (1972) Paternalism. Monist 56(1):64–84. https://doi.org/10.5840/monist197256119

Dworkin G (2015) The nature of autonomy. Nordic J Stud Educ Policy 1(28479):1–8. https://doi.org/10.3402/nstep.v1.28479

Dyzenhaus D (2001) Hobbes and the legitimacy of law. Law Philos 20(5):461. https://doi.org/10.2307/3505220

Edwards TL (2013) Hydrometeorological hazards under future climate change. In: Rougier J, Hill LJ, Sparks RSJ (eds) Risk and uncertainty assessment for natural hazards. Cambridge University Press, Cambridge, pp 151–189

EM-DAT, CRED/UCLouvain, Brussels, Belgium. www.emdat.be. Accessed 19 June 2023

European Commission (2021) Commission staff working document: overview of natural and man-made disaster risks the European Union may face. SWD(2020) 330 final/2

European Environment Agency (2004) Impacts of Europe's changing climate: an indicator-based assessment. EEA Report, Copenhagen

European Environment Agency (2008) Impacts of Europe's Changing Climate: 2008 indicator-based assessment. EEA Report, vol 2008, 4. Office for Official Publications of the European Communities, Luxembourg

European Spatial Planning Observation Network (2013) Territorial dynamics in Europe - natural hazards and climate change in European regions. Territorial observation, vol 7. ESPON, Luxembourg

Evans JH (2006) Between technocracy and democratic legitimation: a proposed compromise position for common morality public bioethics. J Med Philos 31(3):213–234. https://doi.org/10.1080/03605310600732834

Farber DA (2014) International law and the disaster cycle. In: Caron DD, Kelly MJ, Telesetsky A (eds) The international law of disaster relief. Cambridge University Press, Cambridge, pp 7–20

Faßbender K (2015) Die Bewältigung von Extremhochwasser durch Wasser- und Bauplanungsrecht – unter besonderer Berücksichtigung von Starkregenereignissen. ZUR 26(10):525–531

Feinberg J (1989) Harm to self. The moral limits of the criminal law, vol 3. Oxford University Press, New York

Field CB, Barros V, Stocker TF, Dahe Q (2012) Managing the risks of extreme events and disasters to advance climate change adaptation: special report of the Intergovernmental Panel on Climate Change. Cambridge University Press, New York

Finnis J (2014) What is the philosophy of law? Am J Jurisprud 59(2):133–142. https://doi.org/10.1093/ajj/auu012

Fischer F (1990) Technocracy and the politics of expertise. SAGE Publishing, Newbury Park

Fisher D (2010) Legal implementation of human rights obligations to prevent displacement due to natural disasters. In: Kälin W, Williams R, Koser K, Solomon A (eds) Incorporating the guiding principles on international displacement into domestic law: issues and challenges. American Society of International Law, Washington, D.C., pp 551–591

Flanigan J (2014) A defense of compulsory vaccination. HEC Forum 26(1):5–25. https://doi.org/10.1007/s10730-013-9221-5

Flanigan J (2017) Seat belt mandates and paternalism. J Moral Philos 14(3):291–314. https://doi.org/10.1163/17455243-46810050

Focarelli C (2020) Duty to protect in cases of natural disasters. In: Wolfrum R, Peters A (eds) Max Planck Encyclopedia of Public International Law. https://opil.ouplaw.com/display/10.1093/law:epil/9780199231690/law-9780199231690-e781. Accessed 19 June 2023

Formisano A, Vaiano G, Fabbrocino F (2019) Seismic and energetic interventions on a typical South Italy residential building: cost analysis and tax detraction. Front Built Environ 5(12):1–15. https://doi.org/10.3389/fbuil.2019.00012

Freer J, Beven KJ, Neal J, Schumann G, Hall J, Bates P (2013) Flood risk and uncertainty. In: Rougier J, Hill LJ, Sparks RSJ (eds) Risk and uncertainty assessment for natural hazards. Cambridge University Press, Cambridge, pp 190–233

Frowein JA (2009) European Convention for the protection of human rights and fundamental freedoms (1950). In: Wolfrum R, Peters A (eds) Max Planck Encyclopedia of Public International Law. https://opil.ouplaw.com/display/10.1093/law:epil/9780199231690/law-9780199231690-e790. Accessed 19 June 2023

Fung A (2007) Democratic theory and political science: a pragmatic method of constructive engagement. Am Polit Sci Rev 101(3):443–458. https://doi.org/10.1017/S000305540707030X

General Assembly (2015) Establishment of an Open-Ended Intergovernmental Expert Working Group on indicators and terminology relating to disaster risk reduction: GA Res 69/284

General Secretariat for Civil Protection (2020) Γενικό Σχέδιο Αντιμετώπισης Εκτάκτων Αναγκών και Άμεσης/Βραχείας Διαχείρισης των Συνεπειών από την Εκδήλωση Ηφαιστειακής Δραστηριότητας στο Ηφαιστειακό Σύμπλεγμα Σαντορίνης με την κωδική ονομασία "ΤΑΛΩΣ" [trans: General plan for dealing with extraordinary needs and immediate/short-term management of consequences from the volcanic activity event at the Santorini volcanic complex with the code name "TALOS"]. https://civilprotection.gov.gr/sites/default/files/ap_941_06-02-2020_egkrisi_kai_apostoli_1is_ekdosis_genikoy_shedioy_ifaisteioy_santorinis_ada_ovit46mtlv-thvi_0.pdf. Accessed 19 June 2023

German Advisory Council on Global Change (2000) World in transition: strategies for managing global environmental risks. Springer, Berlin

Gesamtverband der Deutschen Versicherungswirtschaft e. V. (2019) Naturgefahrenreport 2019: Die Schaden-Chronik der deutschen Versicherer. https://www.gdv.de/resource/blob/51710/%20e5eaa53a9ec21fb9241120c1d1850483/naturgefahrenreport-%202019%2D%2D-schaden-chronik-data.pdf. Accessed 19 June 2023

Gesamtverband der Deutschen Versicherungswirtschaft e. V. (2021) Positionspapier des Gesamtverbandes der Deutschen Versicherungswirtschaft für ein zeitgemäßes und nachhaltiges Bauordnungs- und Bauplanungsrecht, das den Herausforderungen durch Klimawandel und Extremwetterereignissen zuverlässig begegnen kann. https://www.gdv.de/resource/blob/66384/3b4b78bbd97fe50268d7bdb1d42a9d58/positionspapier-bauen-data.pdf. Accessed 19 June 2023

Gesamtverband der Deutschen Versicherungswirtschaft e. V. (2022) Nur die Hälfte der Gebäude in Deutschland sind richtig gegen Naturgefahren versichert. https://www.gdv.de/gdv/themen/schaden-unfall/nur-die-haelfte-der-gebaeude-in-deutschland-sind-richtig-gegen-naturgefahren-versichert-12176. Accessed 19 June 2023

Gesamtverband der Versicherer (2023) Neue GDV-Berechnungen: Zu viele Neubauten in Überschwemmungsgebieten. https://www.gdv.de/gdv/medien/medieninformationen/neue-gdv-berechnungen-zu-viele-neubauten-in-ueberschwemmungsgebieten%2D%2D129294. Accessed 19 June 2023

Ghirotti M (2012) The 1963 Vaiont Landslide, Italy. In: Stead D, Clague JJ (eds) Landslides: types, mechanisms and modeling. Cambridge University Press, Cambridge, pp 359–372

Giddens A (1990) The consequences of modernity. Stanford University Press, Stanford

Giese K (2011) Baurechtliche Maßnahmen zum Schutz des Baubestandes vor Hochwassergefahren. Baurechtliche Blätter 14(5):203–231. https://doi.org/10.1007/s00738-011-0026-0

Gillette CP, Krier JE (1990) Risk, courts, and agencies. Univ Pa Law Rev 138(4):1027–1109. https://doi.org/10.2307/3312245

Glöckner A (2016) Psychology and disaster: why we do not see looming disasters and how our way of thinking causes them. Glob Policy 7:16–24. https://doi.org/10.1111/1758-5899.12289

Gomez C (2017) Ethics and disaster risk reduction including climate change adaptation. In: Kelman I, Mercer J, Gaillard JC (eds) The Routledge handbook of disaster risk reduction including climate change adaptation. Taylor & Francis, Milton, pp 174–186

Goodin RE (1989) The ethics of smoking. Ethics 99(3):574–624. https://doi.org/10.1086/293100

Goodin RE (1993) Democracy, preferences and paternalism. Policy Sci 26(3):229–247. https://doi.org/10.1007/BF00999718

Green HP (1981) The role of law in determining acceptability of risk. Ann N Y Acad Sci 363(1):1–12. https://doi.org/10.1111/j.1749-6632.1981.tb20712.x

Grill K, Voigt K (2016) The case for banning cigarettes. J Med Ethics 42(5):293–301. https://doi.org/10.1136/medethics-2015-102682

Gross M (2016) Risk and ignorance. In: Burgess A, Alemanno A, Zinn JO (eds) Routledge handbook of risk studies. Routledge, Abingdon, pp 310–317

Habermas J (2015) Inclusion of the other: studies in political theory. Polity Press, Cambridge

Hansson SO (2003) Ethical criteria of risk acceptance. Erkenntnis 59(3):291–309. https://doi.org/10.1023/A:1026005915919

Hansson SO (2004) Weighing risks and benefits. Topoi 23(2):145–152. https://doi.org/10.1007/s11245-004-5371-z

Hansson SO (2012) A panorama of the philosophy of risk. In: Roeser S, Hillerbrand R, Sandin P, Peterson M (eds) Handbook of risk theory: epistemology, decision theory, ethics, and social implications of risk. Springer, Dordrecht, pp 27–54

Hansson SO (2023) Risk. In: Zalta EN (ed) The Stanford Encyclopedia of Philosophy. https://plato.stanford.edu/entries/risk/. Accessed 19 June 2023

Haworth L (1984) Autonomy and utility. Ethics 95(1):5–19. https://doi.org/10.1086/292594

Heinrich P, Adrian C, Kalashnikova O, Schäfer F, Evert S (2018) A transnational analysis of news and tweets about nuclear phase-out in the aftermath of the Fukushima incident. In: Witt A, Diesner J, Rehm G (eds) Proceedings of the LREC 2018 "Workshop on Computational Impact Detection from Text Data". ELRA, Paris, pp 8–16

Hermans MA, Fox T, van Asselt MB (2012) Risk governance. In: Roeser S, Hillerbrand R, Sandin P, Peterson M (eds) Handbook of risk theory: epistemology, decision theory, ethics, and social implications of risk. Springer, Dordrecht, pp 1094–1117

Heun W (2011) Risk management by the government and the constitution. In: Duttge G, Lee SW (eds) The law in the information and risk society. Universitätsverlag Göttingen, Göttingen, pp 15–29

Holst C (2012) What is epistocracy? In: Øyen SA, Lund-Olsen T, Vaage NS (eds) Sacred science? On science and its interrelations with religious worldviews. Wageningen Academic Publishers, Wageningen, pp 41–54

Howse R (2000) Democracy, science, and free trade: risk regulation on trial at the World Trade Organization. Mich Law Rev 98(7):2329–2357. https://doi.org/10.2307/1290307

Huber P (1985) Safety and the second best: the hazards of public risk management in the courts. Colum Law Rev 85(2):277–337. https://doi.org/10.2307/1122439

Hugenbusch D, Neumann T (2016) Cost-benefit analysis of disaster risk reduction: a synthesis for informed decision making. Aktion Deutschland Hilft e.V. https://www.aktion-deutschland-hilft.de/fileadmin/fmdam/pdf/publikationen/ADH_Studie_EN_rev3.pdf. Accessed 19 June 2023

Human Rights Council (2009) Report of the Office of the United Nations High Commissioner for Human Rights on the Relationship between Climate Change and Human Rights. UN Doc A/HRC/10/61

Hutchinson T (2018) Researching and writing in law, 4th edn. Thomson Reuters, Sydney

International Council for Science (2008) A science plan for integrated research on disaster risk: addressing the challenge of natural and human-induced environmental hazards. International Council for Science, Paris

International Federation of Red Cross (2013) Better laws, safer communities?: Emerging themes on how legislation can support disaster risk reduction. https://www.preventionweb.net/files/globalplatform/entry_bg_paper~ifrcdlpbetterlawssafercommunities2013.pdf. Accessed 19 June 2023

International Federation of Red Cross and Red Crescent Societies (2012) World Disasters Report: focus on forced migration and displacement. https://www.ifrc.org/sites/default/files/2012_WDR_Full_Report.pdf. Accessed 19 June 2023

International Federation of Red Cross and Red Crescent Societies (IFRC) and United Nations Development Programme (2014) Effective law and regulations for disaster risk reduction: a multi-country report, New York. https://disasterlaw.ifrc.org/sites/default/files/media/disaster_law/2020-09/DRR%20Report%20%28full%20version%29%20final_page_LR.pdf. Accessed 19 June 2023

International Law Commission (2013) Sixth report on the protection of persons in the event of disasters. UN Doc A/CN.4/662

International Law Commission (2016) Draft articles on the protection of persons in the event of disasters, with commentaries. Yearbook of the International Law Commission, 2016, vol II, Part Two, pp 26–58

Isensee J (1983) Das Grundrecht auf Sicherheit: Zu den Schutzpflichten des freiheitlichen Verfassungsstaates. Vortrag gehalten vor der Berliner Juristischen Gesellschaft am 24. November 1982 - erweiterte Fassung. Schriftenreihe der Juristischen Gesellschaft zu Berlin, vol 79. De Gruyter, Berlin

Ivčević A, Mazurek H, Siame L, Bertoldo R, Statzu V, Agharroud K, Estrela Rego I, Mukherjee N, Bellier O (2021) Lessons learned about the importance of raising risk awareness in the

Mediterranean region (North Morocco and West Sardinia, Italy). Nat Haz Earth Syst Sci 21(12):3749–3765. https://doi.org/10.5194/nhess-21-3749-2021

Jablonski S (2014) Hochwasserschutzrecht: Herausforderungen - Rechtsgrundlagen - Ansatzpunkte und Instrumente. Leipziger Schriften zum Umwelt- und Planungsrecht, vol 26. Nomos, Baden-Baden

Jaeckel L (2001) Schutzpflichten im deutschen und europäischen Recht: Eine Untersuchung der deutschen Grundrechte, der Menschenrechte und Grundfreiheiten der EMRK sowie der Grundrechte und Grundfreiheiten der Europäischen Gemeinschaft. Leipziger Schriften zum Völkerrecht, Europarecht und ausländischen öffentlichen Recht, vol 4. Nomos, Baden-Baden

Jaeckel AL (2017) The international seabed authority and the precautionary principle: balancing deep seabed mineral mining and marine environmental protection, Publications on ocean development series, vol 83. Brill, Leiden

Kahan DM, Slovic P, Braman D, Gastil J (2006) Fear of democracy: a cultural evaluation of Sunstein on risk. Harv Law Rev 119(4):1071–1109

Kahl V (2022) A human right to climate protection – necessary protection or human rights proliferation? NQHR 40(2):158–179. https://doi.org/10.1177/09240519221092595

Kaldis B (2002) Moral conflict and the idea of order: on the relationship between ethics and political philosophy. Archiv für Rechts- und Sozialphilosophie 88(3):419–442

Kamin KA, Rachlinski JJ (1995) Ex post ≠ ex ante: determining liability in hindsight. Law Hum Behav 19(1):89–104. https://doi.org/10.1007/BF01499075

Kellett J, Caravani A (2013) Financing disaster risk reduction: a 20 year story of international aid. Global Facility for Disaster Reduction and Recovery at the World Bank and the Overseas Development Institute. https://cdn.odi.org/media/documents/8574.pdf. Accessed 19 June 2023

Kelman I, Mather TA (2008) Living with volcanoes: the sustainable livelihoods approach for volcano-related opportunities. J Volcanol Geotherm Res 172(3–4):189–198. https://doi.org/10.1016/j.jvolgeores.2007.12.007

Kelman I, Mercer J, Gaillard JC (2017) Editorial introduction to this handbook: why act on disaster risk reduction including climate change adaptation? In: Kelman I, Mercer J, Gaillard JC (eds) The Routledge handbook of disaster risk reduction including climate change adaptation. Taylor & Francis, Milton, pp 3–8

Kelsen H (2005) Pure theory of law, 2nd edn. Lawbook Exchange, Clark

Kemp R (2016) Quantitative risk management and its limits: a UK engineering perspective. In: Burgess A, Alemanno A, Zinn JO (eds) Routledge handbook of risk studies. Routledge, Abingdon, pp 164–178

Kent G (2001) The human right to disaster mitigation and relief. Environ Haz 3(3):137–138. https://doi.org/10.3763/ehaz.2001.0315

Kloepfer M (2017) Zur Vermeidung von Naturkatastrophen durch Recht. Deutsches Verwaltungsblatt:141–149

Köck W (2017) Rechtliche Anforderungen an das Bauen in Überschwemmungs- und Risikogebieten. In: Faßbender K, Köck W (eds) Aktuelle Fragen und Entwicklungen im Hochwasserschutzrecht: Dokumentation des 21. Leipziger Umweltrechtlichen Symposions des Instituts für Umwelt- und Planungsrecht der Universität Leipzig und des Helmholtz-Zentrums für Umweltforschung - UFZ am 07. und 08. April 2016, 1st edn. Nomos, Baden-Baden, pp 147–172

Kotzur M (2012) EU law on disaster preparedness and response. German Yearb Int Law 55:253–278

Krieger H (2014) Positive Verpflichtungen unter der EMRK: Unentbehrliches Element einer gemein-europäischen Grundrechtsdogmatik, leeres Versprechen oder Grenze der Justiziabilität? ZaöRV 74(2):187–213

Lauta KC (2018) Disasters and responsibility. Normative issues for law following disasters. In: O'Mathúna DP, Dranseika V, Gordijn B (eds) Disasters: core concepts and ethical theories. Springer, Cham, pp 43–53

Lauta KC, Rytter JE (2016) A landslide on a mudslide? Natural hazards and the right to life under the European Convention on Human Rights. J Hum Rights Environ 7(1):111–131. https://doi.org/10.4337/jhre.2016.01.05

Le Grand J, New B (2015) Government paternalism: nanny state or helpful friend? Princeton University Press, Princeton

Leiter B (2013) The demarcation problem in jurisprudence: a new case for skepticism. In: Ferrer Beltrán J, Moreso JJ, Papayannis DM (eds) Neutrality and theory of law, vol 106. Springer, Dordrecht, pp 161–174

Leuprecht P (1993) The execution of judgments and decisions. In: Macdonald RS, Matscher F, Petzold H (eds) The European system for the protection of human rights. Nijhoff, Dordrecht, pp 791–800

Lewis B (2018) Environmental human rights and climate change: current status and future prospects. Springer, Singapore

Linnerooth-Bayer J (2012) Financial mechanisms for disaster risk. In: Wisner B, Gaillard JC, Kelman I (eds) The Routledge handbook of hazards and disaster risk reduction. Routledge, London, pp 652–663

Loewenstein GF, Weber EU, Hsee CK, Welch N (2001) Risk as feelings. Psychol Bull 127(2):267–286. https://doi.org/10.1037/0033-2909.127.2.267

Luhmann N (1979) Trust and power. Polity, Cambridge

Maclean AR (2009) Autonomy, informed consent and medical law: a relational challenge, Cambridge law, medicine, and ethics, vol 8. Cambridge University Press, Cambridge

MacLean D (2012) Ethics and risk. In: Roeser S, Hillerbrand R, Sandin P, Peterson M (eds) Handbook of risk theory: epistemology, decision theory, ethics, and social implications of risk. Springer, Dordrecht, pp 791–804

Magnusson RS (2015) Case studies in nanny state name-calling: what can we learn? Public Health 129(8):1074–1082. https://doi.org/10.1016/j.puhe.2015.04.023

McConville M, Chui WH (2017) Introduction and overview. In: McConville M, Chui WH (eds) Research methods for law, 2nd edn. Edinburgh University Press, Edinburgh, pp 1–17

McGee RW (2008) An economic and ethical analysis of the Katrina disaster. Int J Soc Econ 35(7):546–557. https://doi.org/10.1108/03068290810886948

Min JB, Wong JK (2018) Epistemic approaches to deliberative democracy. Philos Compass 13(6):e12497. https://doi.org/10.1111/phc3.12497

Möller N (2012) The concepts of risk and safety. In: Roeser S, Hillerbrand R, Sandin P, Peterson M (eds) Handbook of risk theory: epistemology, decision theory, ethics, and social implications of risk. Springer, Dordrecht, pp 55–85

Murphy C, Gardoni P (2012) The capability approach in risk analysis. In: Roeser S, Hillerbrand R, Sandin P, Peterson M (eds) Handbook of risk theory: epistemology, decision theory, ethics, and social implications of risk. Springer, Dordrecht, pp 980–997

Øhrstrøm P, Hasle P (2020) Future contingents. In: Zalta EN (ed) The Stanford Encyclopedia of Philosophy. https://plato.stanford.edu/entries/future-contingents/. Accessed 19 June 2023

Paletta D (2011) Political legitimacy. In: Chatterjee DK (ed) Encyclopedia of global justice. Springer, Dordrecht, pp 870–872

Pearce DC, Campbell EM, Harding D (1987) Australian law schools: a discipline assessment for the Commonwealth Tertiary Education Commission, vol 5. Australian Government Publishing Service, Canberra

Pedersen OW (2008) European environmental human rights and environmental rights: a long time coming? Georgetown Int Environ Law Rev 21(1):73–111

Pedersen OW (2013) Environmental risks, rights and Black Swans. Environ Law Rev 15(1):55–62. https://doi.org/10.1350/enlr.2013.15.1.176

Peter F (2017) Political legitimacy. In: Zalta EN (ed) The Stanford Encyclopedia of Philosophy. https://plato.stanford.edu/entries/legitimacy/. Accessed 19 June 2023

Pettersen K (2016) Understanding uncertainty: thinking through in relation to high-risk technologies. In: Burgess A, Alemanno A, Zinn JO (eds) Routledge handbook of risk studies. Routledge, Abingdon, pp 39–48

Petzold H (1993) The convention and the principle of subsidiarity. In: Macdonald RS, Matscher F, Petzold H (eds) The European system for the protection of human rights. Nijhoff, Dordrecht, pp 41–62

Pharr SJ, Putnam RD, Dalton RJ (2000) A quarter-century of declining confidence. J Democ 11(2):5–25. https://doi.org/10.1353/jod.2000.0043

Polakiewicz J (2019) Council of Europe (COE). In: Wolfrum R, Peters A (eds) Max Planck Encyclopedia of Public International Law. https://opil.ouplaw.com/display/10.1093/law:epil/9780199231690/law-9780199231690-e607. Accessed 19 June 2023

Raju E, da Costa K (2018) Governance in the Sendai: a way ahead? Disaster Prev Manag 27(3):278–291. https://doi.org/10.1108/DPM-08-2017-0190

Rausand M, Haugen S (2020) Risk assessment: theory, methods, and applications, Wiley series in statistics in practice, 2nd edn. Wiley, Hoboken

Renn O (2008) Risk governance: coping with uncertainty in a complex world, Earthscan risk in society series. Routledge, London

Renn O, Klinke A (2016) Risk governance: concept and application to technological risk. In: Burgess A, Alemanno A, Zinn JO (eds) Routledge handbook of risk studies. Routledge, Abingdon, pp 204–215

Ripstein A (2004) Authority and coercion. Philos Public Aff 32(1):2–35. https://doi.org/10.1111/j.1467-6486.2004.00003.x

Ross A, Athanassoulis N (2012) Risk and virtue ethics. In: Roeser S, Hillerbrand R, Sandin P, Peterson M (eds) Handbook of risk theory: epistemology, decision theory, ethics, and social implications of risk. Springer, Dordrecht, pp 833–856

Runciman D (2018) How democracy ends. Profile Books, London

Scharpf FW (1997) Economic integration, democracy and the welfare state. J Eur Public Policy 4(1):18–36. https://doi.org/10.1080/135017697344217

Scheinin M (2017) The art and science of interpretation in human rights law. In: Andreassen BA, Sano H-O, McInerney-Lankford S (eds) Research methods in human rights: a handbook. Edward Elgar, Cheltenham, pp 17–37

Schneewind JB (2010) Autonomy, obligation, and virtue: an overview of Kant's moral philosophy. In: Schneewind JB (ed) Essays on the history of moral philosophy. Oxford University Press, Oxford, pp 248–276

Schrama W (2011) How to carry out interdisciplinary legal research - some experiences with an interdisciplinary research method. ULR 7(1):147–162. https://doi.org/10.18352/ulr.152

Schroeder CH (1986) Rights against risks. Colum Law Rev 86(3):495. https://doi.org/10.2307/1122636

Schumpeter JA (2010) Capitalism, socialism and democracy. Routledge, London

Schweizer M (2016) Nudging and the principle of proportionality: obliged to nudge? In: Mathis K, Tor A (eds) Nudging - possibilities, limitations and applications in European law and economics. Springer, Cham, pp 93–119

Shelton D, Gould A (2013) Positive and negative obligations. In: Shelton D (ed) The Oxford handbook of international human rights Law (online edn.). https://doi.org/10.1093/law/9780199640133.003.0025

Shrader-Frechette K (2005) Flawed attacks on contemporary human rights: Laudan, Sunstein, and the cost-benefit state. Hum Rights Rev 7(1):92–110. https://doi.org/10.1007/s12142-005-1004-1

Siems MM (2009) The taxonomy of interdisciplinary legal research: finding the way out of the desert. J Commonwealth Law Leg Educ 7(1):5–17. https://doi.org/10.1080/14760400903195090

Silver S (2018) Contingency in philosophy and history, 1650–1800. Textual Pract 32(3):419–436. https://doi.org/10.1080/0950236X.2018.1442391

Slovic P (2000) The perception of risk. Earthscan risk in society. Taylor & Francis, London

Smiley M (1989) Paternalism and democracy. J Value Inq 23(4):299–318. https://doi.org/10.1007/BF00136925

Smith P (2002) Drugs, morality and the law. J Appl Philos 19(3):233–244. https://doi.org/10.1111/1468-5930.00218

Sommario E, Venier S (2018) Human rights law and disaster risk reduction. QIL Zoom-in 49:29–47

Sossai M (2018) States' failure to take preventive action and to reduce exposure to disasters as a human rights issue. In: Zorzi Giustiniani F, Sommario E, Casolari F, Bartolini G (eds) Routledge handbook of human rights and disasters. Routledge, Abingdon, pp 119–131

Spence R, So E (2021) Why do buildings collapse in earthquakes? Building for safety in seismic areas. Wiley-Blackwell, Hoboken

Stahl S (2012) Schutzpflichten im Völkerrecht - Ansatz einer Dogmatik: Ein Beitrag zu Grund, Inhalt und Grenzen der völkerrechtlichen Schutzpflichtendogmatik im Bereich konventionell geschützter Menschenrechte. Beiträge zum ausländischen öffentlichen Recht und Völkerrecht, Bd. 232. Springer, Heidelberg

Starmer K (1999) European human rights law: The Human Rights Act 1998 and the European Convention on Human Rights. Legal Action Group, London

Stefanovic IL (2003) The contribution of philosophy to hazards assessment and decision making. Nat Haz 28(2–3):229–247. https://doi.org/10.1023/A:1022965604958

Stein A (2019) Sind Kampfhunde wirklich gefährlicher als andere Hunde? Hamburger Abendblatt, 8 October 2019. https://www.abendblatt.de/ratgeber/article227313827/Sind-Kampfhunde-wirklich-gefaehrlicher-als-andere-Hunde.html. Accessed 19 June 2023

Stoll P-T (2003) Sicherheit als Aufgabe von Staat und Gesellschaft: Verfassungsordnung, Umwelt- und Technikrecht im Umgang mit Unsicherheit und Risiko. Jus Publicum, vol 101. Mohr Siebeck, Tübingen

Sunstein CR (2002a) Probability neglect: emotions, worst cases, and law. Yale Law J 112(1):61–107. https://doi.org/10.2307/1562234

Sunstein CR (2002b) Risk and reason: safety, law, and the environment. Cambridge University Press, Cambridge

Sunstein CR (2005) Laws of fear: beyond the precautionary principle. The Seeley lectures, vol 6. Cambridge University Press, Cambridge

Taleb NN (2010) The Black Swan: the impact of the highly improbable, 2nd edn. Random House Trade Paperbacks, New York

Trouwborst A (2006) Precautionary rights and duties of states. Nova et vetera iuris gentium. Martinus Nijhoff, Boston

Tsokos M (2019) Die Zeichen des Todes: Neue Fälle von Deutschlands bekanntestem Rechtsmediziner, 4th edn. Droemer, München

Tversky A, Kahneman D (1974) Judgment under uncertainty: heuristics and biases. Science 185(4157):1124–1131. https://doi.org/10.1126/science.185.4157.1124

UN General Assembly (2016) Report of the Open-Ended Intergovernmental Expert Working Group on indicators and terminology relating to disaster risk reduction. UN Doc A/71/644

UN Human Rights Committee (1982) General comment no. 6: Article 6 (right to life). UN Doc CCPR/C/GC/36

United Nations Development Programme (2022) Technical notes: Human Development Report 2021/22. https://hdr.undp.org/sites/default/files/2021-22_HDR/hdr2021-22_technical_notes.pdf. Accessed 19 June 2023

United Nations Inter-Agency Secretariat of the International Strategy for Disaster Reduction (2004) Living with risk: a global review of disaster reduction initiatives, Volume II - Annexes. United Nations, Geneva

United Nations Inter-Agency Secretariat of the International Strategy for Disaster Reduction, Council of Europe (2011) Climate change adaptation and disaster risk reduction in Europe: a review of risk governance. https://www.undrr.org/quick/11207. Accessed 19 June 2023

United Nations Office for Disaster Risk Reduction (2015) Sendai Framework for disaster risk reduction 2015–2030. UN Doc A/CONF.224/L.2

Valensise G, Tarabusi G, Guidoboni E, Ferrari G (2017) The forgotten vulnerability: a geology- and history-based approach for ranking the seismic risk of earthquake-prone communities of the Italian Apennines. Int J Disaster Risk Reduct 25:289–300. https://doi.org/10.1016/j.ijdrr.2017.09.014

van Aaken A (2017) Judge the nudge: in search of the legal limits of paternalistic nudging in the EU. In: Alemanno A, Sibony A-L (eds) Nudge and the law: a European perspective. Hart, Oxford

van de Poel I, Fahlquist JN (2012) Risk and responsibility. In: Roeser S, Hillerbrand R, Sandin P, Peterson M (eds) Handbook of risk theory: epistemology, decision theory, ethics, and social implications of risk. Springer, Dordrecht, pp 877–907

Varelius J (2006) The value of autonomy in medical ethics. Med Health Care Philos 9(3):377–388. https://doi.org/10.1007/s11019-006-9000-z

Viscusi WK (1992) Fatal tradeoffs: public and private responsibilities for risk. Oxford University Press, New York

Wachinger G, Renn O, Begg C, Kuhlicke C (2013) The risk perception paradox-implications for governance and communication of natural hazards. Risk Anal 33(6):1049–1065. https://doi.org/10.1111/j.1539-6924.2012.01942.x

Waldron J (2012) Democracy. In: Estlund DM (ed) The Oxford handbook of political philosophy. Oxford University Press, New York, pp 187–203

Wang J, Kim S (2018) Analysis of the impact of values and perception on climate change skepticism and its implication for public policy. Climate 6(4):99. https://doi.org/10.3390/cli6040099

Warren ME (1999) Introduction. In: Warren ME (ed) Democracy and trust. Cambridge University Press, Cambridge, pp 1–21

Wenig P (2020) Der Tag in Hamburg, als der kleine Volkan starb. Hamburger Abendblatt, 11 July 2020. https://www.abendblatt.de/hamburg/article229489848/kampfhunde-pitbull-hamburg-kind-tod-volkan-zerfleischen-prozess-senat-gesetz-trauer-sechsjaehriger-kleinkind-polizei-justiz-hunde-tiere-zeus-gipsy-american-staffordshire-wilhelmsburg-tierschutz.html. Accessed 19 June 2023

West R (2011) Normative jurisprudence: an introduction. Cambridge introductions to philosophy and law. Cambridge University Press, Cambridge

Wisner B, Blaikie P, Cannon T, Davis I (2004) At risk: natural hazards, people's vulnerability, and disasters, 2nd edn. Routledge, London

World Conference on Disaster Reduction (2004) Review of the Yokohama strategy and plan of action for a safer world. UN Doc A/CONF.206/L.1

World Conference on Disaster Reduction (2005) Hyogo Framework for Action 2005–2015: building the resilience of nations and communities to disasters. UN Doc A/CONF.206/6

Zack N (2012) Disaster relief. In: Chadwick RF, Callahan D, Singer P (eds) The encyclopedia of applied ethics, vol 1, 2nd edn. Academic Press, Cambridge, pp 817–825

Zolkefli Y (2017) Evaluating the concept of choice in healthcare. Malays J Med Sci 24(6):92–96. https://doi.org/10.21315/mjms2017.24.6.11

Chapter 2
The Ability to Reduce a Natural Hazard's Impact and Its Perception

> *Their perceptions may be so far from reality that you and I know that they're absurd, but that's how they feel about it and that's the way they perceive things. So, in discussing the subject, we really have to distinguish between the reality of what may or may not occur, the analysis of it, and the perception of it. (Starr 1980, p. 4)*

The previous chapter provided an overview of the book and the issues it seeks to address. The first issue of the research question considers why disaster losses related to natural hazards increase in the member states of the Council of Europe ('member states') when knowledge and means of risk reduction are available. The book identifies one reason for the rise of disaster losses as people's neglect of the risks of natural hazards, which the administrative and legal frameworks of the member states fail to mitigate. To substantiate this claim, this chapter begins by exploring the distorted risk perceptions held by individuals and the factual ability to reduce the impact of natural hazards, particularly hydrometeorological and geophysical hazards. The existence of distorted perceptions raises doubts about the 'authenticity' of individual decision making when it comes to responding to the risks in the context of natural hazards. In this regard, studies suggest that more people would privately and collectively opt for more DRR related to natural hazards if they understood the facts properly.[1] Building on the discussion of people's distorted risk perceptions in this chapter, the following chapter shows that without the creation of additional administrative and legal measures, people are partly unprotected from the consequences of their distorted risk perception. Although the state must intervene in exceptional cases, fundamental individual rights do not oblige the state to support individuals in challenging their distorted risk perceptions in order to make authentic decisions. However, as the discussion in this book develops it is clear that there are various

[1] Spence and So (2021), pp. 2–3; Ivčević et al. (2021).

C. A. Simmig, *Of Risks and Normative Responses*,
https://doi.org/10.1007/978-3-031-41104-5_2

approaches in how states could respond to distorted risk perceptions, to promote and enforce more disaster risk reduction ('DRR') at the private and collective level. The book provides an in-depth analysis of these arguments on the normative response to distorted risk perceptions, and at the same time provides insights into how individual autonomy and democratic values set limits to these arguments.

To establish the link between lack of DRR and individual perceptions of risk and DRR, this chapter contrasts findings on people's perceptions and facts. What emerges from the discussion in this chapter is that lay people often underestimate or overestimate the factual capacity of disaster risk management. First, the understanding of 'natural disasters' as being inevitable and therefore unavoidable, still resonates in people's perception, even though this conceptualisation has long been discredited. Second, even when people recognise that there are ways to reduce risks associated with natural hazards, they often attribute the wrong characteristics to them, which weakens risk reduction efforts. Third, the development of DRR has also given rise to unrealistic, yet regularly observed, expectations in societies towards the effectiveness of DRR. Such obsolete and unrealistic expectations have a negative impact on the protection of life and property, as an incorrect sense of helplessness or confidence may decrease the alertness to risks.

The examination in this chapter begins by presenting a taxonomy of mechanisms influencing people's risk perception. To contextualise the cultural origin of these common risk perception patterns, this chapter secondly traces the historical evolution of the disaster narrative in disaster studies, culture, and politics. Thirdly, to put these risk perception biases to the reality test, this chapter contours the factual capacity to reduce disaster losses. In doing so, this chapter addresses insights from epistemology and risk studies. Additionally, it explores the capacity to reduce disaster losses from hydrometeorological and geophysical hazards in more detail.

2.1 Taxonomy of People's Risk Perception

The role of mental processes in people's decision-making, such as biases and heuristics, has been studied extensively in psychology. The term heuristic refers to 'mental shortcuts' or 'rules of thumb'.[2] These mental processes reduce the complexity of information by, consciously or unconsciously, ignoring some information.[3] In fact, scholars often find a discrepancy between people's perception of risk and scientific knowledge about risks.[4] As such, the effects of these mental processes are not limited to the field of DRR. At the individual level, people choose to eat unhealthy

[2] Crosweller and Wilmshurst (2013), p. 550.

[3] Tversky and Kahneman (1974), p. 1124.

[4] Christiansen and Hallsson (2017), pp. 53–58; see Kahan et al. (2006), pp. 1071–1072; Crosweller and Wilmshurst (2013), p. 564; Laudan (1997), pp. 6–11, 17–19; Laudan (1994), pp. 14–16, 23.

food, smoke, do too little exercise or not use sunscreen.[5] At the collective level, societies continue with activities that change the world's climate and destroy the biodiversity that they depend on.[6] Such observations have long prompted psychologists to study these 'very deeply embedded, but hopefully not inaccessible, aspects of the human condition'.[7] This section elaborates on the cognitive patterns behind apparently contradictory and occasionally dangerous decisions, such as the neglect of certain disaster risks.[8]

2.1.1 The Probability Neglect

Firstly, the perception of scientifically asserted risk is often influenced by a well-researched phenomenon known as 'probability neglect'.[9] Cass R Sunstein described this phenomenon, and its roots as follows

> When it comes to risk, a key question is whether people can imagine or visualize the worst-case outcome. When the worst case produces intense fear, surprisingly little role is played by the stated probability that that outcome will occur. An important function of strong emotions is thus to drive out quantitative judgments, including judgments about probability, by making the best case or the worst case seem highly salient.[10]

With respect to the saliency of outcomes, time plays an important role.[11] The more recent the manifestation of a risk, thus the more vivid the memories, the more a situation is perceived as unsafe. On the other hand, if the individual does not consider risk reducing measures appropriate or feasible, people tend to not acknowledge a probable hazard.[12] As such, a probable hazard particularly runs the risk of denial, if even its discussion could negatively affect the vulnerable people's livelihoods.[13] For instance, according to a 2004 study of Dominey-Howes and Minos-Minopoulos, the greatest fear of residents on Santorini was the negative impact of an eruption on the key role of tourism industry, and not the fear for their lives.[14] Against this backdrop, only 23% of residents believed that the loss of life would have the greatest impact on their community, despite the lack of civil protection planning guidelines for

[5] See generally Crosweller and Wilmshurst (2013), p. 564.

[6] Masson-Delmotte et al. (2021) and Ceballos et al. (2017).

[7] Crosweller and Wilmshurst (2013), p. 564.

[8] Ibid; Spence and So (2021), pp. 2–3.

[9] Sunstein (2002); see further Loewenstein et al. (2001), p. 276; Gross (2016), p. 314; Viscusi (1992), pp. 9–10.

[10] Sunstein (2002), p. 70.

[11] Ibid, p. 64.

[12] Crosweller and Wilmshurst (2013), p. 554; Spence and So (2021), pp. 2–3.

[13] Crosweller and Wilmshurst (2013), p. 554.

[14] Dominey-Howes and Minos-Minopoulos (2004).

Santorini at the time of the study.[15] In other words, only few residents were aware of the fact that even a medium-sized eruption could kill relatives and friends and cause severe damage to the land and properties.[16] The risk perception of the vast majority neglected this risk.

2.1.2 The Hindsight Bias

The perception of a past event's probability is moreover affected by the mere fact of its manifestation. The fact that harm occurred, foregrounds how unlikely its occurrence was beforehand.[17] A study by Kamin and Rachlinki illustrates the hindsight biases' consequences for people's *ex post* judgment of liability.[18] In their experiment, one group was presented with facts about the possibility of a fictitious flood and the measures to prevent it. In contrast to this foresight condition, another group was confronted with the fact that the town decided against taking measures, and that a preventable flood occurred.[19] Over three quarters of participants in the foresight condition found a flood not sufficiently probable to allocate monetary resources of the fictitious town.[20] However, the same facts with the additional knowledge about the outcome, led the majority of participants to judge the authority's conduct as negligent.[21]

This is even the case when the event was unforeseeable, such as in cases of 'black swan events'.[22] According to a definition by Nassim N Taleb, Black Swan events are beyond 'regular expectations, because nothing in the past can convincingly point to its possibility',[23] and consequently they exclude a reliable prediction of their appearance.[24] However, 'human nature makes us concoct explanations for its occurrence after the fact, making it explainable and predictable'.[25]

---

[15] Ibid, pp. 291–292, 304, 305.

[16] Ibid, p. 305.

[17] Sunstein (2002), p. 69.

[18] Kamin and Rachlinski (1995).

[19] Ibid, p. 93.

[20] Ibid, p. 98.

[21] Ibid, p. 99.

[22] While the black swan theory refers to the broader problem of induction in epistemology, Taleb's 'black swan' events comprise a narrower scope. They only refer to unexpected events of a certain magnitude, which are rationalised in hindsight, see Taleb (2010), p. xxii.

[23] Ibid.

[24] Pettersen (2016), p. 42.

[25] Taleb (2010), p. xxii.

2.1.3 *The 'Dread' Factor in Risk Perception of Natural Hazards*

In addition to the time of last manifestation and their feelings towards risk-reducing measures, the context of risk also influences people's emotional perception. Thus, how strongly people feel about an expected outcome generally depends on the risk's characteristics, besides the asserted probability or seriousness of potential harm.[26] These characteristics are often referred to as 'dread factors'.

The dread factor depends on the extent to which people feel they could control or manage a possibly harmful event and whether the risk includes an element of choice.[27] If someone feels that he or she could personally evade the consequences of the harmful event, the risk may be perceived as less serious.[28] Notably, the perception of personal abilities is often misplaced, as past studies have well documented.[29] For example, surveys show that almost 90% of drivers considered their driving skills above the median driver.[30]

Then again, if the risk is taken involuntarily, such as preservatives in food, it may be perceived as more serious.[31] Previous studies suggested that people are roughly one thousand times more likely to accept even higher risks from voluntary activities, such as skiing, than from involuntary activities.[32] Psychometric studies further show that there is a strong correlation between taking a risk voluntarily and the personal perception of being able to control that risk.[33]

The psychometric paradigm indicates that people tend to take a risk voluntarily, and are prone to perceive it as controllable, if the risk is a familiar one.[34] If the risk is familiar, people also tend to assume that the risk is understood by themselves, and by science.[35] In contrast, individuals tend to perceive new risks as unknown to themselves, as well as not understood by science.[36] Simultaneously, they perceive the new risk as uncontrollable.[37] To this effect, nature is often considered familiar, while industrial processes are dreaded more due to their newness.[38]

---

[26] Slovic (2000), p. 285.

[27] Ambrus (2017), p. 103; Renn (2008), p. 94; Baan and Klijn (2004), p. 116; Cross (1998), pp. 30–32.

[28] Renn (2008), p. 94; see Lindell and Perry (2012), pp. 619–620.

[29] Cross (1998), p. 35; Svenson (1981).

[30] Svenson (1981), p. 146; Camerer and Kunreuther (1989), p. 569.

[31] Baan and Klijn (2004), pp. 117–118.

[32] Starr (1969), p. 1237; Fischhoff et al. (1978), pp. 128, 143; Cross (1998), p. 32.

[33] Fischhoff et al. (1978), p. 144, see Table 5; Slovic (2000), p. 283; Cross (1998), p. 35.

[34] Fischhoff et al. (1978), pp. 133, 144.

[35] Ibid.

[36] Ibid.

[37] Ibid.

[38] Renn (2008), p. 107.

2.1.4 Semantic Risk Patterns

What characteristics people assign to different risk types is often determined by socially and culturally internalised '*semantic risk patterns*'.[39] Semantic risk patterns allow the efficient judgment of risks based on few salient characteristics, thereby reducing the complexity.[40] In this respect, natural hazards and human made hazards actually share similar determinants.[41] Their occurrence is of a rare and stochastic nature that regularly allows little warning time.[42] Nevertheless, they belong to two different semantic risk patterns.[43] Human made hazards are perceived as random events that could happen anytime. This increases the dread factor, since most people 'feel more threatened by unexpected danger or by being unprepared than by danger that arises either on a regular basis or where there is enough time for risk control measure to be taken'.[44] Additionally, people perceive risks from human made hazards as the consequence of non-personally made decisions and actions. This perception as involuntary, yet avoidable risk, further increases the dread factor.

The perception of natural hazards, on the other hand, often suffers from two misconceptions that both reduce the dread factor. The first misconception concerns a tendency to believe in a temporal regularity behind the occurrence of natural hazards.[45] The comforting belief in a deterministic behaviour of natural hazards thus decreases the feeling of being randomly exposed. It rather suggests the potential to duly prepare in time, or the unnecessity to prepare oneself at all. As such, survivors of the '100-year flood' in Germany in 2013 believed that they would not have to endure another comparable hazard during their lifetime.[46] The missing feeling of immediacy then reduces the likelihood of people actively seeking information or taking other preparatory measures.[47]

Secondly, natural hazards are often perceived as a predetermined stroke of fate, and not the consequence of choices and missing actions.[48] To this end, Ortwin Renn finds that the 'possibility for controlling natural disaster and lessening their impacts have not yet anchored themselves sufficiently in people's awareness of allowing the risks from natural disasters to be assessed in the same way as those from

[39] Ibid, pp. 93–94, 145; see Kahan et al. (2006), pp. 1084–1088; see further regarding 'cultural cognition theory' Christiansen and Hallsson (2017), pp. 56–58.

[40] Renn (2008), pp. 94, 110–111.

[41] Ibid, pp. 111–113.

[42] Ibid.

[43] Ibid.

[44] Ibid, p. 111.

[45] Ibid, p. 113; Crosweller and Wilmshurst (2013), p. 554.

[46] Crosweller and Wilmshurst (2013), p. 554; Wachinger et al. (2013), p. 1059; see Renn (2008), p. 113.

[47] Lindell and Perry (2012), pp. 623–624.

[48] Renn (2008), p. 113.

technological accidents'.[49] The inability to avoid the occurrence of natural hazards itself causes feelings of helplessness.[50] People often react to this feeling by either accepting the hazard as fate, or by denying its existence as a result of the probability neglect.[51]

2.1.5 *The Faith in the Effectiveness of Risk Determination and Reduction*

Although it has been claimed that the 'assumption of inevitability is deeply engrained and has been difficult to shake'[52] in the context of disasters triggered by natural hazards, the modernisation has also given rise to a diametrically opposed but equally inaccurate understanding of the state's DRR capacity. In the second half of the twentieth century, society became 'increasingly preoccupied with the future (and also with safety)'.[53] Beck describes modern society as 'a risk society … [that is] increasingly occupied with debating, preventing and managing risks that it itself has produced'.[54] Steve Rayner seconds Beck by characterising the current era as the 'age of assessment'[55] that is underpinned by a growing 'obsession with risk'.[56] The idea of identifying unwanted future events for the purpose of avoiding them became what has been described as a 'defining characteristic of the late modernity'.[57] In extreme forms, societies' aspiration to gain control over the future can even amount to the belief in science's ability to completely predict harms and their causality.[58] This 'Total Predetermination Fallacy' flows from a safety paradigm that emerged in the 1950s.[59] Pariès compares this safety paradigm with the 'search of the modern Grail: a world where nothing goes wrong, a perfect world'.[60] The ideal of eliminating risks altogether with the help of risk determination is referred to as the 'zero-risk society'.[61] A contemporary example of a cultural belief in 'zero risk' is Japan with its *anzen shinwa*, the safety myth, which relates to its state of technology.[62] The

---

[49] Ibid.

[50] Wachinger et al. (2013), p. 1062.

[51] Crosweller and Wilmshurst (2013), p. 554; Wachinger et al. (2013), p. 1062.

[52] Sun (2016), p. 32.

[53] Giddens and Pierson (1998), p. 209.

[54] Beck (2006), p. 332.

[55] Rayner (2003), p. 163.

[56] See Rayner (2007), p. 165.

[57] Ibid.

[58] Giddens and Pierson (1998), p. 209.

[59] Pariès (2017), pp. 42–44.

[60] Ibid, p. 43.

[61] Slovic (1987), p. 280.

[62] Nöggerath et al. (2011), p. 37.

result, as Corinne Bieder has put it, has been 'the illusion of control' through the creation of 'a pathological relation to risk', which may not be commensurate to the risks as they are experienced in reality.[63]

2.1.6 The Factor of Herd Mentality

One factor that can reinforce both tendencies to underestimate risk and to overestimate safety is the 'herd mentality'. An example of these effects is the reportingly increasing inhabitation of the flanks of Mount Etna. The probability of flank eruptions and of ensuing lava flows surrounding Mount Etna does not seem to impact on the individuals' decision to continually move up Etna's flanks.[64] The influence of 'herd mentality' on people's risk perception may evoke a false sense of security among the respective inhabitants. In fact, the tendency of people to adopt a behaviour accelerates the more individuals have already adopted it.[65] Social psychology and political science refer to this tendency as the 'bandwagon effect'.[66] The more people neglect a risk, or take a risk seriously, the more people will adopt the same behaviour.[67] Even if people understand a risk, and the necessary measures to reduce it, their trust in the risk decision of another individual or group may still drive their behaviour.[68] A recent example constitutes the globally observed mass stockpiling of toilet paper in response to the pandemic of Coronavirus Disease 2019 in March 2020.[69] With this 'herd mentality' in mind, the example of other people already living in the proximity of Mount Etna is considered to be a factor in people's decision to move up its flanks.[70]

---

63 Bieder (2017), p. 112.

64 Dibben (2008).

65 Matsumoto (2009), 'Bandwaggon Effect', p. 75; Colman (2015), 'Bandwaggon Effect', p. 77; Crosweller and Wilmshurst (2013), p. 550.

66 Matsumoto (2009), 'Bandwaggon Effect', p. 75; Colman (2015), 'Bandwaggon Effect', p. 77.

67 See Crosweller and Wilmshurst (2013), p. 550.

68 See Wachinger et al. (2013), p. 1054.

69 Although the respiratory pathogen would not increase the personal consumption, and continued production was reportedly secured, people dreaded shortages due to the collective behaviour, see Corkery and Maheshwari (2020) and Frankel (2020).

70 Crosweller and Wilmshurst (2013), p. 550.

2.2 Historical Overview of the Shifts in the Disaster Narrative

As the previous section pointed out, some mental mechanisms are culturally and socially conditioned. To contextualise their origin, it is useful to juxtapose the cultural shifts in the conceptualisation of disasters. Over the centuries, the conceptualisation of disasters, particularly those triggered by natural hazards, has significantly changed. With the changing understanding of their causes, foreseeability, and of the potential resistance against them, the assignment of blame for the consequences of natural hazards has also shifted.[71]

2.2.1 *Individual Blame Under the Sin-Centred Narrative*

The oldest understanding of disasters is based on the idea that human sin can elicit disasters. As such, disasters feature in many cultural or religious traditions.[72] Often, they are portrayed as an instrument of a higher power reacting to human activities, for example, in form of 'angry gods sending disasters as punishment'.[73] Widely known examples from the Old Testament are Noah's Flood or the destruction of Sodom and Gomorrah by 'fire and brimstone'. Other examples build on historical disasters. Such as, Herodotus, who claimed the tsunami which struck the Greek Potidaea in 479 BC, was Poseidon punishing the Persians for laying siege to Potidaea.[74] More recently, adherents of different religions have linked the 2004 Indian Tsunami and the 2010 Haiti earthquake to various committed sins.[75] In reverse, surviving such calamities is often understood as reward for pursuing a devoted life.[76] In this sin-centred narrative, humans have an active part in the inducement of disasters, and are therefore to blame.

2.2.2 *The Dominant Hazard Disaster Paradigm*

These recent examples show that the sin centred-narrative of 'natural disasters' still exists even today. However, the common perception of disasters has significantly changed due to the increased understanding of natural laws.[77] Over time, scientific

[71] Lauta (2014), p. 138.

[72] For a detailed overview and analysis, see Chester et al. (2012).

[73] O'Mathúna (2018), pp. 28–29, 31; Sun (2016), pp. 29–30.

[74] O'Mathúna (2018), p. 28, citing Molesky (2016), p. 150.

[75] O'Mathúna (2018), pp. 28–29, citing among others Lutzer and Graham (2011).

[76] O'Mathúna (2018), p. 29, citing Lutzer and Graham (2011) and Molesky (2016).

[77] Sun (2016), p. 29.

findings have been able to explain natural hazards as the result of physical processes in nature, instead of sinful human behaviour.[78] However, even though by the twentieth century natural hazards were no longer attributed to wrongful human behaviour, their manifestation were still deemed exceptional and their negative consequences *a priori* outside the human, or legal, ambit.[79] In fact, for most of the last century risk studies viewed natural processes as the most significant in determining the '*cause*' of a disaster triggered by natural hazards.[80] This so-called dominant hazard disaster paradigm places the rare, improbable, and extreme character of disasters at its centre.[81] As such, disasters have traditionally been dismissed as unavoidable events 'against which little can be done except hope for the best and prepare for the worst'.[82] Just as disaster management was consequently restricted to disaster response preparation and execution, any allegations of state failures merely centred on the post-disaster phase.[83]

2.2.3 The Emergence of System Blame

The disaster narrative has kept on shifting with the development of scientific understanding, which has demonstrated how people may influence the rise, course, and outcome of disasters. As such, scientific research has led to a reconceptualisation of natural events as an amplifier of pre-existing social and political conditions.[84] At its core, this notion is not exactly new.[85] In 1756, Jean-Jacques Rousseau already challenged the myopic conceptualisation of 'natural disasters'. Referring to the Great Lisbon Earthquake in 1755, he remarked how 'it was hardly nature who assembled there twenty thousand houses of six or seven stories. If the residents of this large city had been more evenly dispersed and less densely housed, the losses would have been few or perhaps none at all'.[86] However, it has only been since the late 1970s that social circumstances have been accepted in the scholarship as inextricably intertwined in disaster causation.[87] Prominent scholars have sought 'some radical rethinking on the nature of "natural" disasters'[88] and argued it was necessary to take

[78] Ibid, pp. 29–30.

[79] Lauta (2016), pp. 96, 109; Sun (2016), p. 30; Lauta and Rytter (2016), p. 120.

[80] Wisner et al. (2004), pp. 7, 10; Lauta and Faure (2016), p. 180.

[81] Gaillard and Texier (2010), p. 81; Lauta and Faure (2016), p. 180.

[82] Fisher (2010), p. 551; Popovski (2014), pp. 98–99.

[83] Sun (2016), pp. 31–32.

[84] Wisner et al. (2004); Sommario and Venier (2018), pp. 29–30.

[85] Sun (2016), p. 31.

[86] Rousseau in a letter to François-Marie Arouet de Voltaire from 18 August 1756, cited in Molesky (2016), p. 331.

[87] DasGupta and Shaw (2017), p. 13; Gaillard and Texier (2010), p. 82.

[88] O'Keefe et al. (1976).

the 'naturalness out of the natural disasters'.[89] The last few decades have further yielded a broad body of research that seeks to amend the scientifically obsolete, yet publicly still widespread narrative, that hazards unavoidably cause disasters.[90]

2.2.3.1 The Relevance of Social Risk Factors for a Hazard's Impact

As discussed in the previous chapter,[91] hazards only become disasters in combination with social disaster risk factors, namely, vulnerability, exposure and lack of capacity to cope, according to modern disaster research. Recent disasters demonstrate how these three social disaster risk factors impact on the effects of a natural hazard on human life. On 12 January 2010, an earthquake reaching a magnitude of 7.0 on the Richter scale struck Haiti and killed 222,570 people.[92] In contrast, the earthquake that hit Chile almost 1 month later, which had a magnitude of 8.8, and as such released 500-times more energy,[93] killed only 526 people.[94] No two earthquakes are comparable, but the significant difference in the death toll was the result of the pre-existing conditions in the two affected countries.[95] While Chile has invested in mitigating known seismic risks,[96] Haiti has not, and consequently suffered from its pre-existing vulnerability and a lack of earthquake experience.[97]

While these examples demonstrate the different outcomes that can result depending on the extent to which social risk factors are reduced, other examples show how human conduct can actively increase vulnerability. The 2004 Hurricane Jeanne in Haiti and the Dominican Republic is an example that demonstrates the fatal, albeit inadvertent, impacts that increased vulnerability created by human activities can cause. Although sharing the same island and having roughly the same population, the hurricane killed 2754 people in Haiti and 11 people in the Dominican Republic.[98] Research has identified a 89% correlation between the amount of deforestation and incidence of victims per exposed number of people.[99] In the literature, Haiti's particular physical vulnerability due to deforestation is seen as one of the main reasons for the disproportionate death toll compared to the Dominican Republic.[100] Today's

[89] Ibid.

[90] Bartolini (2018), p. 11; Lauta (2016).

[91] See Sect. 1.5.2.

[92] EM-DAT, CRED/UCLouvain, Brussels, Belgium; Lomnitz and Wisner (2012), pp. 319–320.

[93] Lauta (2016), p. 93; Lomnitz and Wisner (2012), pp. 320–321.

[94] EM-DAT, CRED/UCLouvain, Brussels, Belgium.

[95] Lauta and Faure (2016), p. 181.

[96] Wyndham (2014), p. 8.

[97] Between 1900 and 2018, Chile experienced 31 earthquakes, while Haiti was struck by two earthquakes, see EM-DAT, CRED/UCLouvain, Brussels, Belgium; Lomnitz and Wisner (2012), pp. 319–321.

[98] EM-DAT, CRED/UCLouvain, Brussels, Belgium.

[99] Peduzzi (2005).

[100] Felima (2009), pp. 19–20; Peduzzi (2005), p. 3.

disaster conceptualisation in disaster studies pays tribute to this human influence on the disaster outcome.

2.2.3.2 From 'Disaster Management' to 'Risk Management' in Political Discourse

The changed disaster conception, and its consequences for DRR, have also found their way into international political discourse, albeit not in binding international law. For centuries, the answer to disasters has been dominated by a reactive policy on relief action.[101] Disaster management focussed on the response to disasters, rather than on their mitigation. The earliest international attempt to reduce losses in the context of disaster was the International Relief Union ('IRU') which was established in 1927 but was quickly disbanded.[102] As indicated by the name, the IRU's focus was to provide humanitarian relief to victims of natural hazards. The organisation's purpose was 'to furnish to the suffering population first aid and to assemble for this purpose funds, resources and assistance of all kinds' in accordance with Article 2 (1) of the IRU Convention.[103] This mostly included the provision of food, shelter, clothes and medical services during and after a 'disaster'. This focus echoes the traditional narrative of disasters being beyond human control, and that the only room for human action lies in responding to this calamity as effectively as possible.[104] In fact, the characterisation of natural hazards being an 'Act of God' was still strong even in the early sixties.[105]

It was not until four decades ago, that the international community, through the Office of the United Nations Disaster Relief ('UNDRO'), established in 1971, voiced its concerns over 'the actual and potential consequences of natural hazards' on a global scale and called for much greater emphasis on 'pre-disaster planning and prevention'.[106] Indeed, it was by the end of the 1960s, that the narrative had begun to veer away from merely accepting extreme events towards efforts to 'tame the forces of nature', for example through sea walls and dams.[107] The shift from mere disaster response to the active management of risk became more visible in the priorities that were set for UNDRO. One of UNDRO's tasks was to 'mobilize, direct and coordinate the relief activities of the various organizations of the UN system'.[108] In addition, the UNDRO's mandate also included to 'promote the study, prevention,

[101] Office of the United Nations Disaster Relief Co-ordinator (1980), p. 3; International Law Commission (2012), para 114; Sun (2016), pp. 31–32.

[102] Zorzi Giustiniani (2018), pp. 7–8; Farber (2014), pp. 13–14; Cubie (2017), pp. 248–249.

[103] Convention Establishing an International Relief Union (IRU), signed 12 July 1927, 135 LNTS 247 (entered into force 27 December 1932).

[104] Sun (2016), pp. 31–32.

[105] DasGupta and Shaw (2017), p. 13.

[106] Office of the United Nations Disaster Relief Co-ordinator (1980), p. 3.

[107] DasGupta and Shaw (2017), p. 13.

[108] General Assembly (1971), p. 86.

control and prediction of natural disasters, including the collection and dissemination of information concerning technological developments'.[109] These developments marked the emergence of the DRR concept. However, the vagueness of UNDRO's objectives, its limited funding and lack of specialised staff, proved to be an obstacle to meaningful progress in DRR. Nevertheless, the emerging recognition of disasters as the product of complex risk factors besides natural hazards in the late 1970s and 1980s helped advance the DRR approach.[110] This was further enhanced by United Nation's designation of the 1990s as the 'International Decade for Natural Disaster Reduction' ('IDNDR').[111] During this time, the international community took important first steps towards the institutionalisation of DRR at the UN level. The 1994 Yokohama Strategy for a safer World and its Plan of Action,[112] provided the first global guidelines on 'natural disaster' prevention, preparedness, and mitigation.[113] In addition, the IDNDR concluded with the establishment of the 'International Strategy for Disaster Reduction' and a permanent UN inter-agency secretariat.[114]

The last decades have seen the rise of the disaster risk concept in the numerous international soft-law instruments. The 'Review of the Yokohama Strategy and Plan of Action for a Safer World' has already emphasised the growing national trend to focus on disaster risk management indiscriminately on all types of risk.[115] The following Hyogo Framework for Action 2005–2015[116] ('HFA') picked up on the conceptual developments in disaster studies by referring to disasters as the product of hazards and other risk factors.[117] As such, it seeks to reflect 'a holistic and multi-hazard approach to disaster risk management'.[118] The HFA also represents a terminological cesura by completely replacing the term 'natural disaster'.[119] Instead the HFA refers to 'disasters caused by hazards of natural origin and related environmental and technological hazards and risks'.[120] The framework thus acknowledges the terminological fallacy that the term 'natural disaster' inherits.

Its successor, the Sendai Framework for Disaster Risk Reduction (2015–2030)[121] ('SFDRR') manifests the shift from disaster management towards disaster risk

[109] Ibid.

[110] DasGupta and Shaw (2017), p. 13; Lauta and Faure (2016), p. 180; Wisner et al. (2004), p. 10.

[111] General Assembly (1987).

[112] World Conference on Natural Disaster Reduction (1994); endorsed by the General Assembly in 1994, see General Assembly (1994), pp. 3–5.

[113] Zorzi Giustiniani (2018), p. 10; Sommario and Venier (2018), p. 33.

[114] Zorzi Giustiniani (2018), p. 10.

[115] World Conference on Disaster Reduction (2004), para 49.

[116] World Conference on Disaster Reduction (2005).

[117] World Conference on Natural Disaster Reduction (1994), p. 1 para 3.

[118] World Conference on Disaster Reduction (2005), p. 1 Fn 3.

[119] Briceño (2015), pp. 1–2.

[120] World Conference on Disaster Reduction (2005), p. 1 Fn 3.

[121] United Nations Office for Disaster Risk Reduction (2015).

management,[122] as it particularly embraces a 'whole-risk-approach'.[123] The strengths of SFDRR relate to its focus on risk management, the enhancement of resilience, and the prevention of new risks.[124] It understands disaster risk 'in all its dimensions of vulnerability, capacity, exposure of persons and assets, hazard characteristics and the environment',[125] which mirrors the disaster risk conceptualisation in disaster studies.[126] Similarly, the International Law Commission's ('ILC') Draft Articles on the Protection of People in the Event of a Disasters ('DA')[127] align with the conceptualisation of disasters in contemporary disaster studies.[128] The understanding of disasters as a risk that can be reduced is reflected in DA 9(1), which includes the duty to 'reduce the risk of disasters by taking appropriate measures, including through legislation and regulations, to prevent, mitigate, and prepare for disasters'.[129] As such, the emphasis on disaster risks in DA 9, irrespective of the type of hazard, similarly aligns with the disaster conception in today's disaster studies. This shows how the concept of disaster risk has gained acceptance in international discourse, even though it has not found its way into binding law.

2.3 The Factual Ability and Challenges to Reduce Risk

The historical overview above demonstrates how scientific and technological progress has changed the understanding of how people can deal with natural hazards. At the political and scientific level, a modern conceptualisation of disasters as the cumulation of risk factors has expanded the understanding of available action from purely reactive to preventive measures. However, along the historical development, people's risk perceptions and risk reduction measures have evolved considerably differently. On the one hand, the taxonomy of risk perceptions demonstrates that the 'sin-centred disaster narrative' as well as the 'dominant hazard disaster paradigm' persist in lay people's perceptions. On the other hand, the development of risk studies has also given rise to societal expectations 'that "science" can deliver a complete, objective, and definitive truth to orient public decisions about risks'.[130] While

[122] Raju and da Costa (2018), p. 280.

[123] Nicoletti (2012), pp. 183, 196; Bartolini (2018), p. 18; DasGupta and Shaw (2017), pp. 13–17; Bartolini et al. (2015), p. 41.

[124] Zorzi Giustiniani (2018), p. 17.

[125] United Nations Office for Disaster Risk Reduction (2015), para 23.

[126] Ibid, Foreword.

[127] In its 68th session, the International Law Commission adopted a draft preamble and 18 draft articles, together with commentaries thereto, UN Doc A/CN.4/L.871 (2 May–10 June and 4 July–12 August 2016).

[128] Bartolini et al. (2015), p. 41.

[129] Notably, this duty is weaker than a previous version of the Draft Article, which included the duty to take 'necessary' measures. See General Assembly (2014).

[130] Doron (2016), p. 25.

this expectation on the accuracy of science is rarely expressed explicitly in regulation making processes, it often implicitly shapes them.[131] As the following discussion demonstrates, both poles on the risk perception scale represent an inaccurate idea of the factual capacity and challenges of disaster risk reduction. To that end, the discussion contours the factual ability to determine disaster risks in the context of natural hazards, to foresee their manifestation, and the ability to reduce them.

2.3.1 The Conditions of Risk Determination

The determination of risks to lives and property involves an examination of the *risk agent*, for instance a natural hazard, as well as the *risk-absorbing system*, for instance the human organism or a building inhabiting people.[132] The examination of the *risk agent* seeks to determine the probability that a risk-agent of a certain gravity arises. The examination of the *risk-absorbing system* seeks to ascertain the possibility and likelihood of negative effects of the risk-agent on the risk-absorbing system. The central role of probability in risk management entails that 'a basic understanding of probability is increasingly turning into a necessity' to comprehend the capacity of risk management.[133]

2.3.1.1 The Sources of Knowledge for Probability Calculation

Knowledge about the probability of an event, and its probable damage to a risk absorbing system, has its source in epistemic knowledge and historical data. First, models based on epistemic knowledge about the physical world can yield a theoretical probability. The textbook example of a fair die illustrates this relationship. The epistemic knowledge that the imagined die has six identical faces enables the exact calculation of the theoretical probability based on the basic axioms of probability theory.[134] However, real life situations comprise of extraordinarily complex systems of known and unknown factors. As a consequence, the exact theoretical probability cannot be determined.[135] However, more research can decrease *epistemic uncertainty*.[136] Secondly, by observing the *frequency of events*, statistical theory further allows the estimation of 'random variations and chance outcomes in the physical world'.[137]

[131] Christoforou (2003), p. 209; Camerer and Kunreuther (1989), p. 575; Stoll (2003), p. 267.

[132] See Renn (2008), p. 178.

[133] Van Coile (2016), p. 38.

[134] Ibid, pp. 28–29.

[135] Ibid, pp. 29–30.

[136] Kastenberg (2015), p. 177; Pariès (2017), p. 44.

[137] Kastenberg (2015), p. 177; see van Coile (2016), pp. 29–32; Pariès (2017), p. 44.

While this 'aleatory uncertainty can only be estimated better' by observing more events, no epistemic research can reduce it.[138]

2.3.1.2 The Unequal Challenges in Risk Analyses

In practice, the level of difficulty in determining the probability of the occurrence and gravity of a possible threat to a risk-absorbing system varies. Some possible threats have a 'simple' or 'linear' nature.[139] They are characterised by a comparably low level of difficulty in identifying and quantifying the risk agent and its causal factors, and the risk-absorbing system and its vulnerability.[140] In this regard, there exists a high level of epistemic knowledge of the relevant factors, as well as sufficient and reliable data.[141] The remaining uncertainty about the spectrum of possible damages, and their respective probability, is consequently low.[142] Examples of such linear risks refer to regularly recurring natural hazards, such as seasonal floods, or certain human-made hazards, such as car accidents.[143]

Yet, other possible threats pose challenges 'beyond the usual agent-consequence analysis'.[144] A possible threat may causally depend on a multitude of interdependent factors, which makes the identification and quantification of the causal links difficult.[145] Such 'complex risks' may require sophisticated models of probabilistic inferences to determine the probability of harm.[146] However, the limitedness or lack of epistemic knowledge or data may also entail 'the inability to provide accurate and precise quantitative assessments between a causing agent and an effect'.[147]

2.3.1.3 The Consequences for the Risk Concept

Different degrees of knowledge or non-knowledge shape the conceptualisation of the risk concept. In technical terms, the risk concept divides into four sub-categories. Depending on the degree of knowledge about the probability and gravity, the harm is qualified as *certainty*, risk *stricto sensu*, *uncertainty*, or *ignorance*.[148] *Certainty* is when 'the outcome is known and it is certain that the event will take place'.[149] The

---

138 Kastenberg (2015), p. 177.

139 Renn (2008), p. 178; Renn et al. (2011), p. 234.

140 Renn (2008), pp. 178, 186, 189; Renn et al. (2011), p. 234.

141 Renn (2008), pp. 178, 186, 189; Renn et al. (2011), p. 234.

142 Renn (2008), pp. 178, 189.

143 Ibid, p. 178; Renn et al. (2011), p. 234.

144 Renn et al. (2011), p. 234.

145 Renn and Klinke (2016), p. 210; Renn et al. (2011), p. 234; Renn (2008), p. 186.

146 Renn et al. (2011), p. 234.

147 Renn and Klinke (2016), p. 210.

148 Ambrus (2017), p. 102.

149 Ibid.

concepts of risk *stricto sensu* and *uncertainty* both describe the existence of knowledge about the outcome. However, *uncertainty* implies there is a lack of knowledge about the probability of the harm's occurrence, while '*risk stricto sensu*' infers some available knowledge about its probability.[150] Lastly, situations exist where there is neither knowledge about the outcome nor about the probability and these are referred to as *ignorance*.[151] This category deserves a closer look since it stands in direct conflict with the examined social perception of science's omnipotence to determine risks.

2.3.1.4 The Limitations of Knowledge

On the one hand, the concept of ignorance refers to known limits of knowledge.[152] In this case, 'we know we do not know'.[153] As previously explained, this known lack of knowledge impedes the accuracy of quantitative assessment of an identified causing agent and an identified effect. Yet, risk assessments can indicate the known lack of knowledge. On the other hand, the concept of ignorance also refers to unknown knowledge gaps.[154] If neither epistemic knowledge, nor a precedence, point to a threat, risk assessments have a blind spot. The famous statement of Donald H Rumsfeld, made while he was former United States Secretary of Defence, captures these differences in the knowledge spectrum:

> [A]s we know, there are known knowns; there are things we know we know. We also know there are known unknowns. That is to say we know there are some things we do not know. But there are also unknown unknowns - the ones we don't know we don't know.[155]

Such knowledge spectrum represents a core epistemological insight of the inability to guarantee the correctness, and completeness, of our knowledge.

2.3.1.4.1 The Epistemological Limitations of Knowledge

The philosophical branch of epistemology concerns the question of whether and how knowledge perceived from observations and experiments can claim validity.[156] It is sometimes called the theory of knowledge.[157] The famous black swan reference illustrates the epistemological insight of the uncertainty of knowledge: Before Europeans landed in Australia all swans were presumed to be white based on the

150 Ibid.

151 Ibid; Gross (2016), p. 311.

152 Gross (2016), p. 311.

153 Pettersen (2016), p. 41.

154 Gross (2016), p. 311.

155 US Department of Defence (2002).

156 Krob (2009); see further Aven (2016), p. 66.

157 Krob (2009).

empirical evidence, which lacked any contradicting sightings.[158] The sighting of the first black swan in Western Australia invalidated the derived 'knowledge'. In the words of the German philosopher of science, Karl Popper, '[n]o number of sightings of white swans can prove the theory that all swans are white, but the sighting of just one black swan may disprove it'.[159] From an epistemological perspective, past performances cannot certainly ensure future performance.

2.3.1.4.2 Types of Black Swan Events

Due to this epistemological blind spot, two types of unknown events may surprise societies. The first type of unknown-unknown events are such events beyond our range of experience.[160] Such events are unknown to science, and consequently unanticipated.[161] An example of an unknown-unknown event are new types of viruses.[162] Another type of unknown event that Rumsfeld's statement overlooks are 'unknown knowns'.[163] This type refers to events that are unknown in some contexts, while they are known in other contexts or to others.[164] As a consequence, the event may not be anticipated by the risk determination. The 1986 Lake Nyos disaster in Cameroon constitutes a historical example of such an event. Over one night, 1700 people mysteriously died within 25 km. Only in hindsight were scientists able to explain that a massive cloud of carbon dioxide gas had bubbled up from a magma chamber beneath the Lake.[165] While the possibility of such so-called limnic eruption at Lake Nyos was unknown in foresight, the general possibility of such eruptions was not unknown to the scientific community. In fact, just 2 years earlier, a limnic eruption occurred in Cameroon at Lake Monoun.

2.3.2 *The Certainty of Predicting Natural Hazards*

Building on this theoretical knowledge about the capacity of risk determination, it is now possible to contextualise the foreseeability of natural hazards. The level of certainty of predicting natural hazards varies depending on the type of hazard and the individual case. Generally, the more often a hazard recurs, the lower are

---

158 Runde (2009), p. 493.

159 Popper (1985), p. 101.

160 Gilbert et al. (2016), pp. 383–384; Aven (2017), pp. 28–30; Aven (2016), pp. 68–69; Pettersen (2016), p. 42.

161 Gilbert et al. (2016), pp. 383–384; Aven (2017), pp. 28–30; Aven (2016), pp. 68–69.

162 Aven (2016), p. 68.

163 Pettersen (2016), p. 41.

164 Aven (2017), pp. 28–29; Aven (2016), p. 68.

165 Wisner et al. (2004), p. 9.

remaining uncertainties.[166] Accordingly, the previous analysis identified regularly recurring natural hazards as an example of linear or routine risk problems.[167] Yet, apart from the regularly recurring natural hazards, '[u]ncertainty is ubiquitous in natural hazards'.[168] On the one hand, hazard risk analyses generally suffer from a lack of historical data on the hazard.[169] On the other hand, it is 'hard to think of any natural hazard process where the physics is adequately understood'.[170] To illustrate these challenges in more detail, the analysis turns to hydrometeorological and geophysical hazards as two examples.

2.3.2.1 Hydrometeorological Hazards

In terms of hydrometeorological hazards, the historical records comprise a length of about 150 years for some variables.[171] While this is long in comparison to other hazards,[172] it is too short to reliably estimate the return periods of rare hydrometeorological hazards,[173] particularly since the collection of more reliable and complete data sets only began a few decades ago.[174] Even today, many states still fail to 'systematically collect disaster-related facts, data, and information'.[175]

Moreover, the certainty of hydrometeorological hazard risk analyses further suffers from incomplete epistemic understanding. The internal variability of the earth system due to natural and anthropogenic influence, as well as chaos and oscillations, constitute ultimately unresolvable challenges.[176] The imperfect knowledge and chaos factor significantly decrease the certainty of predicting beyond a few days.[177] The predictability limit of hydrometeorological hazards has been estimated to be 2 weeks.[178]

Similarly, the prediction of flood hazards faces a variety of non-stationary uncertainties.[179] For example, rainfall variability and the uncertainties in the development of cascading effects affect the accuracy of flood hazard mapping.[180] Since 2002, the

---

166 Renn (2008), p. 178.

167 Ibid.

168 Hill et al. (2013), p. 4.

169 See Gilbert et al. (2016), p. 384; Smolka (2006), p. 2160.

170 Hill et al. (2013), p. 8.

171 Edwards and Challenor (2013), p. 112; Freer et al. (2013), p. 192.

172 Edwards and Challenor (2013), p. 117.

173 Ibid, p. 112.

174 Ibid.

175 Weichselgartner and Pigeon (2015), p. 110.

176 Edwards and Challenor (2013), p. 112.

177 Ibid, pp. 112–113.

178 Ibid, p. 112.

179 Freer et al. (2013), pp. 220–221.

180 Ibid, p. 220.

European Flood Awareness System ('EFAS'), has been providing probabilistic flood early warning information up to 10 days in advance.[181] For instance, the EFAS had already detected the first signs of the 2021 European Floods 3 days earlier.[182] In the following days, scientists were able to concretise the extent and areas of the predicted flood almost precisely.[183] Between 10 and 14 July 2021, they had issued more than 25 continuously updated warnings for specific regions.[184]

2.3.2.2 Geophysical Hazards

In contrast to hydrometeorological hazards, the risk determination of earthquakes can often rely on historical records, which often trace back more than 2000 years.[185] While this provides a starting point for statistical probability calculations, a crucial obstacle to more certainty remains the lack of direct knowledge of the Earth's interior.[186] This lack of direct access means that scientists can merely derive indirect knowledge of the Earth's interior from seismic waves.[187] Moreover, since the launch of the global positioning system in the late 1970s, further knowledge can be derived by observing the motions of tectonic plates.[188]

Nevertheless, the forecasting of earthquakes is 'still in a primitive stage'.[189] Earthquake early warning systems may only provide a short term warning by recording the seismic waves at the epicentre and transmit the information to their expected arrival location.[190] Since the electronic signal travels faster than the waves' energy through rock and soil, the delay time yields a short warning.[191] For instance, Mexico City's early warning system usually provides a 50-second warning.[192]

---

181 European Commission (2021), p. 18.

182 Moody (2021); The Copernicus Emergency Management Service (2021).

183 Moody (2021).

184 The Copernicus Emergency Management Service (2021).

185 Lomnitz and Wisner (2012), p. 316.

186 Ibid, pp. 311–312.

187 Ibid.

188 Ibid, p. 313.

189 Ibid, pp. 315–316, citing National Research Council (U.S.) (2003), p. 149.

190 Lomnitz and Wisner (2012), p. 318.

191 Ibid.

192 Ibid.

2.3.2.3 Potential for Improving the Certainty of Predictions

While more physical research generally decreases epistemic uncertainty,[193] science still expects limited improvement in the predictability of hazards.[194] In light of the known complexity of modelling natural hazards, some scholars scale down the expectations of more certain hazard predictability.[195] More research and modelling would often even result in more overall uncertainty, as it may reveal more uncertain model parameters.[196]

Although scientists have only limited expectations to improve the predictability of natural hazards, they still have identified some potential to improve the certainty of hazard risk analyses. The certainty of the risk agent's analysis could benefit from increasing the systematic data collection. As such, non-governmental organisations, such as the International Council for Science, campaign for a global agreement on pre-determined methodologies for consistent data management.[197] It is against this backdrop, that the SFDRR highlights the importance of promoting 'the collection, analysis, management and use of relevant data and practical information and ensure its dissemination'.[198]

2.3.3 The Ability to Protect Individuals and Assets Against Natural Hazards

After having contoured the current capacity and obstacles to risk determination and prediction in the context of natural hazards, the analysis now turns to examine the capacity to protect people's lives and property against such hazards. The implementation of DRR can avoid or significantly reduce the negative effects of hazards on a community or a society. A successful example constitutes the extensive disaster control policies in China. While floods killed 140,000 people in 1931 and 33,000 people in 1954, China was able to reduce the death toll in similar floods to 3000 in 1998.[199] In member states, the reported number of deaths per disaster triggered by natural hazards demonstrates a decreasing trend throughout the last 100 years (Fig. 2.1), despite an increasing number of disasters (Fig. 2.2).

---

[193] Kastenberg (2015), p. 177.

[194] Edwards and Challenor (2013), pp. 112–128.

[195] Hill et al. (2013), p. 9.

[196] Ibid.

[197] International Council for Science (2008), pp. 16, 31–33.

[198] United Nations Office for Disaster Risk Reduction (2015), para 24 a.

[199] Annan (1999).

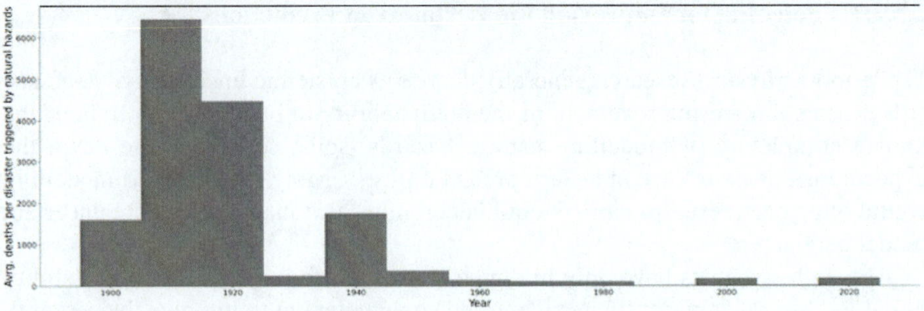

Fig. 2.1 Histogram of the average number of deaths per disaster triggered by natural hazards in the member states of the Council of Europe between 1900 and 2023. (Data sourced from 'EM-DAT, CRED/UCLouvain, Brussels, Belgium – www.emdat.be', accessed 10 April 2023)

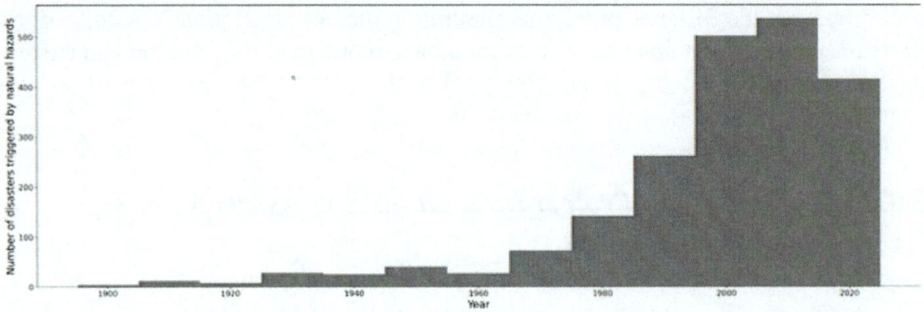

Fig. 2.2 Histogram of total number of disasters triggered by natural hazards in the member states of the Council of Europe between 1900 and 2023. (Data sourced from "EM-DAT, CRED/UCLouvain, Brussels, Belgium – www.emdat.be", accessed 10 April 2023)

On the one hand, this success is due to increased living standards.[200] With a higher standard of living, people's *vulnerability* and *exposure* to disasters, on average, has decreased, while their *response capacity* has increased. On the other hand, China's success may also be attributable to the rise of DRR in the second half of the twenty-first century. To contextualise the capacity of DRR in more detail, this book again turns to hydrometeorological and geophysical hazards. In relation to these two natural hazards, disaster risk management has been able to identify concrete measures to increase protection against hazards that were formerly considered irresistible.

[200] See Govind (2014), p. 248, who identifies the lack of development as a key indicator of where a disaster might occur.

2.3.3.1 Protection Against Earthquakes

Earthquakes remain one of the most often used example of an irresistible event in legal literature.[201] Yet, comparisons of the death toll after earthquakes among countries such as Japan or Chile on the one hand, and Haiti on the other hand, demonstrate that earthquakes are not necessarily irresistible.[202] In fact, seismic engineering has identified construction techniques and material capable of reducing the seismic vulnerability of buildings. Lomnitz and Wisner even claim that '[i]n principle, all structures could be made earthquake-resistant'.[203] Some techniques may even retrospectively decrease buildings' seismic vulnerability, such as seismic upgrading or the more effective retrofitting technique.[204] An earthquake in Italy in August 2016 epitomized the effectiveness of such techniques. The earthquake hit, among others, two Italian towns, Amatrice and Norcia, with roughly equal force.[205] Norcia had enforced seismic protection standards after an earthquake in 1979. Some scholars identify this as the reason why the 2016 earthquake left Norcia practically unscathed, in contrast to Amatrice where almost 300 people were killed and $5 billion in damages was caused.[206]

In addition to the implementation and enforcement of respective building codes, earthquake early warning systems may also effectively reduce the fatality risk. It has been claimed that even a short time frame may allow 'drivers to pull over, fire fighters and ambulance teams can drive their vehicles outside depots that might collapse, [and] gas and other inflammable pipelines can be shut off by automatic valves'.[207]

Last, preparing the community may further reduce the fatality risk. Such preparation may involve education on the recommended conduct in the event of an earthquake. Preparedness may further involve raising awareness of objects and furniture in the home that can cause injury in case of an earthquake, and how they can be secured in advance.[208] As such, Tokyo's low earthquake fatality rate is not only low due to one of the strictest anti-quake construction codes in the world, but its regular provision of training to prepare individuals.[209]

---

[201] International Law Commission (1980), p. 66 para 4; Paddeu (2012), pp. 382–283, 401; Hentrei and Soley (2011), para 12.

[202] See Sect. 2.2.3.1.

[203] Lomnitz and Wisner (2012), p. 315.

[204] Formisano et al. (2019), pp. 5–8.

[205] Valensise et al. (2017), pp. 289–291.

[206] Ibid, pp. 290–292; for the data see EM-DAT, CRED/UCLouvain, Brussels, Belgium.

[207] Lomnitz and Wisner (2012), p. 318.

[208] Ibid, p. 319.

[209] Popovski (2014), p. 108; see further Lomnitz and Wisner (2012), pp. 316, 319.

2.3.3.2 Protection Against Floods

Similarly, with respect to floods, disaster studies have developed methods to reduce the social risk factors.[210] The most prominent techniques are dams, dikes, and levees.[211] However, disaster studies advise caution with respect to some of these river training structures as they may simultaneously and inadvertently increase flood risks. On the one hand, some river training structures may successfully decrease the flood exposure in one place, while aggravating it on another place.[212] For this reason, since the late nineteenth century, many countries have supplemented earlier dams and channel modifications with upstream storage reservoirs to reduce the risk of flooding.[213] On the other hand, river training structures may steadily increase people's vulnerability in the long term.[214] River training structures may reduce people's awareness towards flood risks due to an inflated sense of safety.[215] Additionally, the effectiveness of such structures usually depends on regular and costly maintenance which may become neglected with decreasing awareness of the risks.[216]

In addition to structural river training, flood protection measures involve zoning regulation and land-use planning.[217] For instance, attempts are being made to increase natural retention again through financial incentives for unsealing measures and the promotion of natural watercourse development, for example, through river restoration and dyke relocation.[218] Another factor relates to resilient building designs.[219] For instance, single-storey buildings offer less protection in a flood.[220] As such, disaster risk management recommends multi-storey buildings with first floors, assigned other functions other living space, such as parking.[221] Zoning regulation and land-use planning may further take account of the needs of different vulnerable groups. For instance, urban planning may avoid building care homes for the elderly in flood plains due to the increased challenges in evacuating.[222]

---

[210] Schmuck (2012), p. 253.

[211] Ibid, p. 255.

[212] Ibid.

[213] Tarlock and Albrecht (2018), p. 48.

[214] Etkin (1999), pp. 70–73.

[215] Schmuck (2012), p. 255; see further Slovic (1987).

[216] Schmuck (2012), p. 255.

[217] Ibid; European Commission (2017), p. 17; Tarlock and Albrecht (2018), p. 48.

[218] See generally Tarlock and Albrecht (2018), pp. 48–49.

[219] Schmuck (2012), p. 255; European Commission (2017), p. 17; Tarlock and Albrecht (2018), p. 48.

[220] Schmuck (2012), p. 255.

[221] Ibid.

[222] Ibid.

2.4 Conclusion

This chapter has explored some common deviations between people's perception of risks and the factual ability to reduce disaster risks. The growing knowledge on the disaster risk factors and DRR have provided people with options to deliberately change the future. While this 'may seem obvious to modern readers', the conception that human activities shape the future is in fact the result 'of fairly recent developments in our own culture, and contrasts sharply with more fatalistic views of nature and society'.[223] This finding echoes in the presented taxonomy of people's risk perception, which points towards three misperceptions in particular.

First, in some cases, people do not recognise the potential of partially or fully reducing disaster risks from natural hazards through individual or collective measures. However, disasters triggered by natural hazards are in fact no longer categorically inevitable.[224] Except for certain hazards from space that humanity in present times cannot resist nor escape,[225] science and technology have developed measures that can prevent or mitigate the fatal consequences of almost all natural hazards. This technological progress gives societies the choice to build up the 'defence' of the risk-absorbing system with the aim of reaching a level of robustness that may withstand the hazard.[226] Secondly, a society may choose to 'escape' before a hazard manifests.[227] Thirdly, a society may decide to avoid the possible exposure to certain hazards. Examples of this option are zoning regulations or banning activities to prevent hazards from occurring or to minimise their effects.

Conversely, even if people perceive disasters triggered by natural hazards as susceptible to mitigation, risk perception research shows that people tend to have a greater willingness to accept certain risks of natural origin rather than human made risks. In this regard, the severity of consequences is only one of the risk characteristics important to people's judgment of risks' acceptability.[228] With respect to these other risk characteristics, scholars have noted that people are prone to effectuate 'double standards for acceptable risk'.[229] In fact, people may tolerate greater risks if they are familiar, and if the potential consequences have an immediate effect in

---

[223] Renn (2008), p. 1.

[224] Sun (2016), p. 29.

[225] Despite all technical advancements, some hazards are currently irresistible. As such, science has identified hazards from space, which the international community could absolutely and objectively not resist. For instance, humanity's current technology would offer no effective measure to respond to asteroids of a certain size. An asteroid with a diameter below 10 km would potentially eradicate the human species. Even the impact of an asteroid below 3 km in diameter would kill most people in the aftermath, see McGuire (2012), p. 401; Chapman (2007), p. 152.

[226] Such physical protection against natural hazards are for instance dams or seismic reinforced buildings. See Lauta and Rytter (2016), pp. 127–129; Renn (2008), p. 179.

[227] Evacuation plans are examples of this strategy.

[228] Fischhoff et al. (1978), pp. 133, 148–149.

[229] Ibid, p. 149, see also pp. 143–144.

contrast to delayed consequences.[230] In other words, the familiarity and immediacy of a risk are more important to people's acceptability judgment, than the scientifically determined probability of a harmful event. In this regard, natural processes are often considered familiar, while industrial processes are dreaded more due to their newness.[231] The widespread misperception of natural hazards as occurring deterministically also leads to them not being perceived as an immediate risk. Thus, although natural hazards often share similar risk determinants as human made hazards, cognitive mechanisms and culturally predetermined so-called 'semantic risk patterns' play a major role in facilitating people's biased perception of natural hazards. Presumably, people's 'authentic self' would judge risks differently if it could unbiasedly apply scientific facts on the risk of natural hazards in its judgment.[232]

On the flip side, the review of the conditions of risk determination also frustrates the expectation of a 'zero risk' society. Even if society sought to maximise the reduction of risks, the complete avoidance of risk is impossible.[233] First of all, the capacity to wilfully prevent a threat from resulting in harm is predicated on the existence of knowledge of the threat, even if it is uncertain. As such, 'avoidability exists only in the presence of a "general capacity on the part of an agent to foresee an outcome and to take steps to avoid its occurrence."'[234] In this vein, the examination of the capacity to anticipate hazards has found the unavoidable possibility of black-swan events that can 'only be understood *post hoc*'.[235] With respect to such unknown threats, a state can only invest in the resilience and antifragility of the capabilities necessary to handle the unexpected.[236] For instance, such measures may aim at reducing the overall vulnerability, or at designing a flexible and robust emergency management.[237] While such measures decrease social risk factors, their efficiency suffers from the lack of knowledge about the threat. Beyond such cases, the efficiency of risk reduction measures increases with the certainty and precision of risk analysis which depends on the quantity of epistemic knowledge and historical data. In this regard, it must be noted that the capacity to predict the manifestation of specific natural hazards in an area is often short-term, and the capacity has only comparably little potential of improving the certainty or warning time.

Moreover, in contrast to the 'zero risk' expectation, the analysis showed how some risk reducing measures may also create new risks in the future. Thus, despite the abstract existence of effective DRR measures, uncertainties challenge the effective implementation of DRR. In this regard, it must be emphasised that science will never be able to guarantee absolute safety, since so-called 'theoretical uncertainty'

---

[230] Ibid, pp. 143–144, 149; Renn (2008), p. 107.

[231] Renn (2008), p. 107.

[232] See Viscusi (1992), p. 25; Christiansen and Hallsson (2017), pp. 62–64; Glöckner (2016), p. 21.

[233] Viscusi (1992), pp. 3–6.

[234] Cardi (2005), p. 943, who cites Perry (2001), p. 73.

[235] Krieger (2016), p. 339; Pettersen (2016), p. 42.

[236] Aven (2017), p. 33; Pariès (2017), p. 43; Renn (2008), p. 179.

[237] Renn (2008), p. 179.

always remains.[238] Risk analyses cannot reach absolute *epistemic certainty*, but have and always will have a blind spot, even though knowledge continuously expands.[239] Thus, science must be understood as only being able to procure the most reliable 'statements that can be made, at the time being, on a subject matter'.[240] In the words of the German Constitutional Court, science can only present the newest state of unrefuted possible fallacy.[241] However, this finding does not refute the value of scientific risk analyses in public decision making *per se*.

Building on this understanding of the extent to which biases and heuristics interfere with people's decision-making, the following chapters examine the extent to which the law does and could protect people from the consequences of distorted risk perception. While Chap. 4 makes proposals for DRR measures that are compatible with the current legal framework, Chap. 3 begins by showing how current international law does not respond to ever-increasing disaster losses due to natural hazards. In addition to a lack of specialised international law, a detailed examination demonstrates that the interpretation of generally applicable international obligation to protect life and property is response-oriented in most cases. Given the examined uncertainty of most natural hazards in terms of a long-term specification of a place or time of manifestation, the chapter argues that fair balance of individual and collective interests only rarely requires long-term DRR, such as adjustments to planning or building laws. As a consequence, the ECHR is not designed to engage in comprehensive DRR, which would decrease disaster losses overall. Combined with the lack of specific obligations in national law outlined in Chap. 1, Chap. 3 supports the need for complementing the risk management approach.

References

Ambrus M (2017) The European Court of Human Rights as governor of risk. In: Ambrus M, Rayfuse RG, Werner W (eds) Risk and the regulation of uncertainty in international law, 1st edn. Oxford University Press, Oxford, pp 99–115

Annan K (1999) An increasing vulnerability to natural disasters. International Herald Tribune, 10 September 1999. https://www.nytimes.com/1999/09/10/opinion/IHT-an-increasing-vulnerability-to-natural-disasters.html. Accessed 19 June 2023

Aven T (2016) The reconceptualization of risk. In: Burgess A, Alemanno A, Zinn JO (eds) Routledge handbook of risk studies. Routledge, Abingdon, pp 58–72

Aven T (2017) A conceptual foundation for assessing and managing risk, surprises and Black Swans. In: Motet G, Bieder C (eds) The illusion of risk control: what does it take to live with uncertainty? Springer, Cham, pp 23–39

[238] See on the term 'theoretical uncertainty' WTO AB Report, *EC Measures Concerning Meat and Meat Products (Hormones),* 16 January 1998, para 186.

[239] Gross (2016), p. 311; Stoll (2003), p. 268.

[240] Hansson (2013), p. 70.

[241] BVerfG, *Kalkar I,* Judgment, 8 August 1978, BVerfGE 49, 89–147, at para 143.

Baan PJ, Klijn F (2004) Flood risk perception and implications for flood risk management in the Netherlands. Int J River Basin Manag 2(2):113–122. https://doi.org/10.1080/15715124.2004.9635226

Bartolini G (2018) A taxonomy of disasters in international law. In: Zorzi Giustiniani F, Sommario E, Casolari F, Bartolini G (eds) Routledge handbook of human rights and disasters. Routledge, Abingdon, pp 10–26

Bartolini G, Natoli T, Riccardi A (2015) Report of the expert meeting on the ILC's draft articles on the protection of persons in the event of disasters: international law and disasters working papers series 03. Roma Tre University Department of Law

Beck U (2006) Living in the world risk society. Econ Soc 35(3):329–345. https://doi.org/10.1080/03085140600844902

Bieder C (2017) Conclusion. In: Motet G, Bieder C (eds) The illusion of risk control: what does it take to live with uncertainty? Springer, Cham, pp 107–112

Briceño S (2015) Looking back and beyond Sendai: 25 years of international policy experience on disaster risk reduction. Int J Disaster Risk Sci 6(1):1–7. https://doi.org/10.1007/s13753-015-0040-y

Camerer CF, Kunreuther H (1989) Decision processes for low probability events: policy implications. J Policy Anal Manag 8(4):565. https://doi.org/10.2307/3325045

Cardi WJ (2005) Reconstructing foreseeability. Boston Coll Law Rev 46(5):921–988

Ceballos G, Ehrlich PR, Dirzo R (2017) Biological annihilation via the ongoing sixth mass extinction signaled by vertebrate population losses and declines. Proc Natl Acad Sci U S A 114(30):E6089–E6096. https://doi.org/10.1073/pnas.1704949114

Chapman CR (2007) The asteroid impact hazard and interdisciplinary issues. In: Bobrowsky PT, Rickman H (eds) Comet/asteroid impacts and human society: an interdisciplinary approach. Springer, Berlin, pp 145–162

Chester D, Duncan AM, Sangster H (2012) Religious interpretations of disaster. In: Wisner B, Gaillard JC, Kelman I (eds) The Routledge handbook of hazards and disaster risk reduction. Routledge, London, pp 109–120

Christiansen A, Hallsson BG (2017) Democratic decision making and the psychology of risk. Les ateliers de l'éthique/The Ethics Forum 12(1):51–83. https://doi.org/10.7202/1042278ar

Christoforou T (2003) The precautionary principle and democratizing expertise: a European legal perspective. Sci Public Policy 30(3):205–212. https://doi.org/10.3152/147154303781780443

Colman AM (2015) A dictionary of psychology, 4th edn Oxford paperback reference. Oxford University Press, Oxford

Corkery M, Maheshwari S (2020) Is there really a toilet paper shortage? The New York Times, 13 March 2020. https://www.nytimes.com/2020/03/13/business/toilet-paper-shortage.html. Accessed 19 June 2023

Cross FB (1998) Facts and values in risk assessment. Reliab Eng Syst Saf 59(1):27–40. https://doi.org/10.1016/S0951-8320(97)00116-6

Crosweller HS, Wilmshurst J (2013) Natural hazards and risk: the human perspective. In: Rougier J, Hill LJ, Sparks RSJ (eds) Risk and uncertainty assessment for natural hazards. Cambridge University Press, Cambridge, pp 548–569

Cubie D (2017) The international legal protection of persons in humanitarian crises: exploring the acquis humanitaire. Hart, Oxford

DasGupta R, Shaw R (2017) Disaster risk reduction: a critical approach. In: Kelman I, Mercer J, Gaillard JC (eds) The Routledge handbook of disaster risk reduction including climate change adaptation. Taylor & Francis, Milton, pp 12–23

Dibben CJ (2008) Leaving the city for the suburbs—the dominance of 'ordinary' decision making over volcanic risk perception in the production of volcanic risk on Mt Etna, Sicily. J Volcanol Geotherm Res 172(3–4):288–299. https://doi.org/10.1016/j.jvolgeores.2007.12.014

Dominey-Howes D, Minos-Minopoulos D (2004) Perceptions of hazard and risk on Santorini. J Volcanol Geotherm Res 137(4):285–310. https://doi.org/10.1016/j.jvolgeores.2004.06.002

Doron C-O (2016) The experience of 'risk': genealogy and transformations. In: Burgess A, Alemanno A, Zinn JO (eds) Routledge handbook of risk studies. Routledge, Abingdon, pp 17–26

Edwards TL, Challenor PG (2013) Risk and uncertainty in hydrometeorological hazards. In: Rougier J, Hill LJ, Sparks RSJ (eds) Risk and uncertainty assessment for natural hazards. Cambridge University Press, Cambridge, pp 100–150

EM-DAT, CRED/UCLouvain, Brussels, Belgium. www.emdat.be. Accessed 19 June 2023

Etkin D (1999) Risk transference and related trends: driving forces towards more mega-disasters. Glob Environ Change B Environ Haz 1(2):69–75. https://doi.org/10.1016/S1464-2867(00)00002-4

European Commission (2017) Commission staff working document: overview of natural and man-made disaster risks the European Union may face. SWD(2017) 176 final

European Commission (2021) Commission staff working document: overview of natural and man-made disaster risks the European Union may face. SWD(2020) 330 final/2

Farber DA (2014) International law and the disaster cycle. In: Caron DD, Kelly MJ, Telesetsky A (eds) The international law of disaster relief. Cambridge University Press, Cambridge, pp 7–20

Felima CA (2009) Haiti's disproportionate casualties after environmental disasters: analyzing human vulnerabilities and the impacts of natural hazards. J Haitian Stud 15(1–2):6–28

Fischhoff B, Slovic P, Lichtenstein S, Read S, Combs B (1978) How safe is safe enough? A psychometric study of attitudes towards technological risks and benefits. Policy Sci 9(2):127–152. https://doi.org/10.1007/BF00143739

Fisher D (2010) Legal implementation of human rights obligations to prevent displacement due to natural disasters. In: Kälin W, Williams R, Koser K, Solomon A (eds) Incorporating the guiding principles on international displacement into domestic law: issues and challenges. American Society of International Law, Washington, D.C., pp 551–591

Formisano A, Vaiano G, Fabbrocino F (2019) Seismic and energetic interventions on a typical South Italy residential building: cost analysis and tax detraction. Front Built Environ 5(12):1–15. https://doi.org/10.3389/fbuil.2019.00012

Frankel TC (2020) The toilet paper shortage is real. But it should be brief. The Washington Post, 13 March 2020. https://www.washingtonpost.com/business/2020/03/13/toilet-paper-shortage/. Accessed 19 June 2023

Freer J, Beven KJ, Neal J, Schumann G, Hall J, Bates P (2013) Flood risk and uncertainty. In: Rougier J, Hill LJ, Sparks RSJ (eds) Risk and uncertainty assessment for natural hazards. Cambridge University Press, Cambridge, pp 190–233

Gaillard JC, Texier P (2010) Religions, natural hazards, and disasters: an introduction. Religion 40(2):81–84. https://doi.org/10.1016/j.religion.2009.12.001

General Assembly (1971) Resolutions adopted by the General Assembly during its twenty-sixth session: GA Res 8429. UN Doc A/8429

General Assembly (1987) International decade for natural disaster reduction: GA Res 42/169. UN Doc A/RES/42/169

General Assembly (1994) International decade for natural disaster reduction: GA Res 49/22. UN Doc A/RES/49/22

General Assembly (2014) Report of the International Law Commission: sixty-sixth session. UN Doc A/69/10

Giddens A, Pierson C (1998) Conversations with Anthony Giddens: making sense of modernity. Stanford University Press, Stanford

Gilbert RB, Habibi M, Nadim F (2016) Accounting for unknown unknowns in managing multi-hazard risks. In: Gardoni P, LaFave JM (eds) Multi-hazard approaches to civil infrastructure engineering, vol 35. Springer, Cham, pp 383–412

Glöckner A (2016) Psychology and disaster: why we do not see looming disasters and how our way of thinking causes them. Glob Policy 7:16–24. https://doi.org/10.1111/1758-5899.12289

Govind P (2014) Utilizing international climate change adaptation funding to reduce risks of natural disasters in the developing world. In: Caron DD, Kelly MJ, Telesetsky A (eds) The international law of disaster relief. Cambridge University Press, Cambridge, pp 245–269

Gross M (2016) Risk and ignorance. In: Burgess A, Alemanno A, Zinn JO (eds) Routledge handbook of risk studies. Routledge, Abingdon, pp 310–317

Hansson SO (2013) Defining pseudoscience and science. In: Boudry M, Pigliucci M (eds) Philosophy of pseudoscience: reconsidering the demarcation problem. University of Chicago Press, Chicago, pp 61–77

Hentrei S, Soley X (2011) Force Majeure. In: Wolfrum R, Peters A (eds) Max Planck Encyclopedia of Public International Law. https://opil.ouplaw.com/display/10.1093/law:epil/9780199231690/law-9780199231690-e1042. Accessed 19 June 2023

Hill LJ, Sparks RSJ, Rougier J (2013) Risk assessment and uncertainty in natural hazards. In: Rougier J, Hill LJ, Sparks RSJ (eds) Risk and uncertainty assessment for natural hazards. Cambridge University Press, Cambridge, pp 1–18

International Council for Science (2008) A science plan for integrated research on disaster risk: addressing the challenge of natural and human-induced environmental hazards. International Council for Science, Paris

International Law Commission (1980) Yearbook of the International Law Commission 1978: documents of the thirtieth session (excluding the report of the Commission to the General Assembly). UN Doc A/CN.4/SER.A 1978/Add.l (Part 1)

International Law Commission (2012) Fifth report on the protection of persons in the event of disasters. UN Doc A/CN.4/652

Ivčević A, Mazurek H, Siame L, Bertoldo R, Statzu V, Agharroud K, Estrela Rego I, Mukherjee N, Bellier O (2021) Lessons learned about the importance of raising risk awareness in the Mediterranean region (North Morocco and West Sardinia, Italy). Nat Haz Earth Syst Sci 21(12):3749–3765. https://doi.org/10.5194/nhess-21-3749-2021

Kahan DM, Slovic P, Braman D, Gastil J (2006) Fear of democracy: a cultural evaluation of Sunstein on risk. Harv Law Rev 119(4):1071–1109

Kamin KA, Rachlinski JJ (1995) Ex post ≠ ex ante: determining liability in hindsight. Law Hum Behav 19(1):89–104. https://doi.org/10.1007/BF01499075

Kastenberg WE (2015) Ethics, risk and safety culture: reflections on Fukushima and beyond. In: Tanaka S, Carson C, Ahn J, Juraku K, Jensen M, Nagasaki S (eds) Reflections on the Fukushima Daiichi nuclear accident: toward social-scientific literacy and engineering resilience. Springer, Cham, pp 165–187

Krieger K (2016) Resilience and risk studies. In: Burgess A, Alemanno A, Zinn JO (eds) Routledge handbook of risk studies. Routledge, Abingdon, pp 335–343

Krob J (2009) Epistemology. In: Birx HJ (ed) Encyclopedia of time: science, philosophy, theology & culture. SAGE, Los Angeles

Laudan L (1994) The book of risks: fascinating facts about the chances we take every day. Wiley, New York

Laudan L (1997) Danger ahead: the risks you really face on life's highway. Wiley, New York

Lauta KC (2014) New fault lines? On responsibility and disasters. Eur J Risk Regul 5(2):137–145. https://doi.org/10.1017/S1867299X0000355X

Lauta KC (2016) Human rights and *natural* disasters. In: Breau SC, Samuel K (eds) Research handbook on disasters and international law. Edward Elgar, Cheltenham, pp 91–110

Lauta KC, Faure MG (2016) Disaster risk management. In: Burgess A, Alemanno A, Zinn JO (eds) Routledge handbook of risk studies. Routledge, Abingdon, pp 179–188

Lauta KC, Rytter JE (2016) A landslide on a mudslide? Natural hazards and the right to life under the European Convention on Human Rights. J Hum Rights Environ 7(1):111–131. https://doi.org/10.4337/jhre.2016.01.05

Lindell MK, Perry RW (2012) The protective action decision model: theoretical modifications and additional evidence. Risk Anal 32(4):616–632. https://doi.org/10.1111/j.1539-6924.2011.01647.x

Loewenstein GF, Weber EU, Hsee CK, Welch N (2001) Risk as feelings. Psychol Bull 127(2):267–286. https://doi.org/10.1037/0033-2909.127.2.267
Lomnitz C, Wisner B (2012) Earthquake. In: Wisner B, Gaillard JC, Kelman I (eds) The Routledge handbook of hazards and disaster risk reduction. Routledge, London, pp 310–321
Lutzer E, Graham F (2011) Act of god?: Answers to tough questions about god's role in natural disasters. Tyndale House Publishers, Illinois
Masson-Delmotte V, Zhai P, Pirani A, Connors SL, Péan C, Berger S, Caud N, Chen Y, Goldfarb L, Gomis MI, Huang M, Leitzell K, Lonnoy E, Matthews JB, Maycock TK, Waterfield T, Yelekçi O, Yu R, Zhou B, IPCC (2021) Climate change 2021: the physical science basis. Contribution of Working Group I to the Sixth Assessment Report of the Intergovernmental Panel on Climate Change. Intergovernmental Panel on Climate Change (IPCC). https://report.ipcc.ch/ar6/wg1/IPCC_AR6_WGI_FullReport.pdf. Accessed 19 June 2023
Matsumoto DR (2009) The Cambridge dictionary of psychology. Cambridge University Press, Cambridge
McGuire B (2012) Hazards from space. In: Wisner B, Gaillard JC, Kelman I (eds) The Routledge handbook of hazards and disaster risk reduction. Routledge, London, pp 399–410
Molesky M (2016) This Gulf of Fire: The Great Lisbon Earthquake, or Apocalypse in the Age of Science and Reason. Vintage Books, New York
Moody O (2021) Germany knew the floods were coming, but the warnings didn't work. The Sunday Times, 18 July 2021. https://www.thetimes.co.uk/article/germany-knew-the-floods-were-coming-but-the-warnings-didnt-work-cn99wjxzs. Accessed 19 June 2023
National Research Council (U.S.) (2003) Living on an active earth: perspectives on earthquake science. National Academies Press, Washington, D.C. https://doi.org/10.17226/10493
Nicoletti B (2012) The prevention of natural and man-made disasters: what duties for states? In: de Guttry A, Gestri M, Venturini G (eds) International disaster response law. T. M. C. Asser Press, The Hague, pp 177–198
Nöggerath J, Geller RJ, Gusiakov VK (2011) Fukushima: the myth of safety, the reality of geoscience. Bull At Sci 67(5):37–46. https://doi.org/10.1177/0096340211421607
O'Mathúna DP (2018) Christian theology and disasters: where is god in all this? In: O'Mathúna DP, Dranseika V, Gordijn B (eds) Disasters: core concepts and ethical theories, vol 11. Springer, Cham, pp 27–42
Office of the United Nations Disaster Relief Co-ordinator (1980) Natural disaster and vulnerability analysis: report of expert group meeting, 9-12 July 1979. United Nations, Geneva
O'Keefe P, Westgate K, Wisner B (1976) Taking the naturalness out of natural disasters. Nature 260(5552):566–567. https://doi.org/10.1038/260566a0
Paddeu FI (2012) A genealogy of force majeure in international law. Br Yearb Int Law 82(1):381–494
Pariès J (2017) Recognizing complexity in risk management: the challenge of the improbable. In: Motet G, Bieder C (eds) The illusion of risk control: what does it take to live with uncertainty? Springer, Cham, pp 41–55
Peduzzi P (2005) Tropical cyclones: paying a high price for environmental destruction. Environment and Poverty Times:3
Perry SR (2001) Responsibility for outcomes, risk, and the law of torts. In: Postema GJ (ed) Philosophy and the law of torts. Cambridge University Press, New York, pp 72–130
Pettersen K (2016) Understanding uncertainty: thinking through in relation to high-risk technologies. In: Burgess A, Alemanno A, Zinn JO (eds) Routledge handbook of risk studies. Routledge, Abingdon, pp 39–48
Popovski V (2014) State negligence before and after natural disasters as human rights violations. In: Hobson C, Bacon P, Cameron R (eds) Human security and natural disasters. Routledge, London, pp 94–110
Popper KR (1985) The problem of induction. In: Popper KR, Miller DW (eds) Popper selections. Princeton University Press, Princeton, pp 101–117
Raju E, da Costa K (2018) Governance in the Sendai: a way ahead? Disaster Prev Manag 27(3):278–291. https://doi.org/10.1108/DPM-08-2017-0190

Rayner S (2003) Democracy in the age of assessment: reflections on the roles of expertise and democracy in public-sector decision making. Sci Public Policy 30(3):163–170. https://doi.org/10.3152/147154303781780533

Rayner S (2007) The rise of risk and the decline of politics. Environ Haz 7(2):165–172. https://doi.org/10.1016/j.envhaz.2007.05.003

Renn O (2008) Risk governance: coping with uncertainty in a complex world, Earthscan risk in society series. Routledge, London

Renn O, Klinke A (2016) Risk governance: concept and application to technological risk. In: Burgess A, Alemanno A, Zinn JO (eds) Routledge handbook of risk studies. Routledge, Abingdon, pp 204–215

Renn O, Klinke A, van Asselt M (2011) Coping with complexity, uncertainty and ambiguity in risk governance: a synthesis. Ambio 40(2):231–246. https://doi.org/10.1007/s13280-010-0134-0

US Department of Defence (2002) US Department of Defence news briefing - Secretary Rumsfeld and Gen. Myers. http://archive.defense.gov/Transcripts/Transcript.aspx?TranscriptID=2636. Accessed 19 June 2023

Runde J (2009) Dissecting the Black Swan. Crit Rev 21(4):491–505. https://doi.org/10.1080/08913810903441427

Schmuck H (2012) Flood. In: Wisner B, Gaillard JC, Kelman I (eds) The Routledge handbook of hazards and disaster risk reduction. Routledge, London, pp 244–256

Slovic P (1987) Perception of risk. Science 236(4799):280–285. https://doi.org/10.1126/science.3563507

Slovic P (2000) The perception of risk. Earthscan risk in society. Taylor & Francis, London

Smolka A (2006) Natural disasters and the challenge of extreme events: risk management from an insurance perspective. Philos Trans A Math Phys Eng Sci 364(1845):2147–2165. https://doi.org/10.1098/rsta.2006.1818

Sommario E, Venier S (2018) Human rights law and disaster risk reduction. QIL Zoom-in 49:29–47

Spence R, So E (2021) Why do buildings collapse in earthquakes? Building for safety in seismic areas. Wiley-Blackwell, Hoboken

Starr C (1969) Social benefit versus technological risk. Science 165(3899):1232–1238. https://doi.org/10.1126/science.165.3899.1232

Starr C (1980) Introductory remarks. In: Schwing RC, Albers WA (eds) Societal risk assessment: how safe is safe enough? Springer, Boston, pp 1–4

Stoll P-T (2003) Sicherheit als Aufgabe von Staat und Gesellschaft: Verfassungsordnung, Umwelt- und Technikrecht im Umgang mit Unsicherheit und Risiko. Jus Publicum, vol 101. Mohr Siebeck, Tübingen

Sun LG (2016) Climate change and the narrative of disaster. In: Peel J, Fisher D (eds) The role of international environmental law in disaster risk reduction. Brill, Leiden, pp 27–48

Sunstein CR (2002) Probability neglect: emotions, worst cases, and law. Yale Law J 112(1):61–107. https://doi.org/10.2307/1562234

Svenson O (1981) Are we all less risky and more skillful than our fellow drivers? Acta Psychol 47(2):143–148. https://doi.org/10.1016/0001-6918(81)90005-6

Taleb NN (2010) The Black Swan: the impact of the highly improbable, 2nd edn. Random House Trade Paperbacks, New York

Tarlock D, Albrecht J (2018) Potential constitutional constraints on the regulation of flood plain development: three case studies. J Flood Risk Manag 11(1):48–55. https://doi.org/10.1111/jfr3.12274

The Copernicus Emergency Management Service (2021) The Copernicus Emergency Management Service forecasts, warns, and monitors devastating floods in Germany, Netherlands, Belgium and Switzerland. EMS Information Bulletin Nr 144. https://emergency.copernicus.eu/mapping/node/144264. Accessed 19 June 2023

Tversky A, Kahneman D (1974) Judgment under uncertainty: heuristics and biases. Science 185(4157):1124–1131. https://doi.org/10.1126/science.185.4157.1124

United Nations Office for Disaster Risk Reduction (2015) Sendai Framework for Disaster Risk Reduction 2015–2030. UN Doc A/CONF.224/L.2

Valensise G, Tarabusi G, Guidoboni E, Ferrari G (2017) The forgotten vulnerability: a geology- and history-based approach for ranking the seismic risk of earthquake-prone communities of the Italian Apennines. Int J Disaster Risk Reduct 25:289–300. https://doi.org/10.1016/j.ijdrr.2017.09.014

van Coile R (2016) Probability. In: Burgess A, Alemanno A, Zinn JO (eds) Routledge handbook of risk studies. Routledge, Abingdon, pp 27–38

Viscusi WK (1992) Fatal tradeoffs: public and private responsibilities for risk. Oxford University Press, New York

Wachinger G, Renn O, Begg C, Kuhlicke C (2013) The risk perception paradox-implications for governance and communication of natural hazards. Risk Anal 33(6):1049–1065. https://doi.org/10.1111/j.1539-6924.2012.01942.x

Weichselgartner J, Pigeon P (2015) The role of knowledge in disaster risk reduction. Int J Disaster Risk Sci 6(2):107–116. https://doi.org/10.1007/s13753-015-0052-7

Wisner B, Blaikie P, Cannon T, Davis I (2004) At risk: natural hazards, people's vulnerability, and disasters, 2nd edn. Routledge, London

World Conference on Disaster Reduction (2004) Review of the Yokohama Strategy and Plan of Action for a Safer World. UN Doc A/CONF.206/L.1

World Conference on Disaster Reduction (2005) Hyogo Framework for Action 2005–2015: building the resilience of nations and communities to disasters. UN Doc A/CONF.206/6

World Conference on Natural Disaster Reduction (1994) Yokohama Strategy and Plan of Action for a Safer World: guidelines for natural disaster prevention, preparedness and mitigation. http://www.unisdr.org/files/8241_doc6841contenido1.pdf. Accessed 19 June 2023

Wyndham JM (2014) Science and technology: strengthening the human rights response to natural disasters. Hum Rights Defender 23(1):8–10

Zorzi Giustiniani F (2018) Something old, something new: disaster risk reduction in international law. QIL Zoom-in 49:7–27

Chapter 3
The International Obligations in the Context of Natural Hazards

> *[W]hile the State's obligations to respond [to a disaster] ... are comprehensive and undisputed, the scope of the State's obligation to deter disaster risk is less far-reaching, and less clear-cut. (Lauta and Rytter 2016, p. 113)*

The core question of this book is how member states of the Council of Europe ('member states'), given the consequences of distorted risk perception, should complement their risk management to facilitate the reduction of disaster losses related to common natural hazards. The previous chapter has identified people's distorted risk perceptions as a relevant factor in the increase of disaster losses related to natural hazards despite available knowledge and means of risk reduction. In this regard, Chap. 2 has presented and evaluated common risk perception patterns by juxtaposing them to the factual ability to protect life and property from often occurring natural hazards in the member states. On the one hand, the chapter concluded that while the certainty of risk analysis varies, and although its findings may neither be definitively correct, nor complete, science still gives society options to respond to risks from natural hazards with disaster risk reduction ('DRR') measures. However, due to biases and heuristics, important aspects of this scientific knowledge are commonly misperceived or not perceived at all by laypersons. On the other hand, Chap. 2 also exposed the widespread false belief that risks could be reduced to zero. In both cases, the distorted perception of facts reduces the likelihood that individuals take private measures to reduce the risk to their lives, physical integrity, and property, or publicly demand more collective DRR measures.

Given the harmful consequences of such distorted perception of facts, the aim of this chapter is to further substantiate the need for complementing the risk management approach in view of current regulatory regimes. As already outlined in Chap. 1, there is a lack of national legislation to prevent or mitigate the increasing disaster

C. A. Simmig, *Of Risks and Normative Responses*,
https://doi.org/10.1007/978-3-031-41104-5_3

losses related to natural hazards.[1] This chapter complements this finding by showing how international law does not respond to the ever-increasing disaster losses due to natural hazards. On the one hand, it presents a respective lack of specialised international law. On the other hand, it shows that the generally applicable obligations under the European Convention on Human Rights ('ECHR')[2] are also not designed to facilitate in comprehensive DRR. In this regard, this chapter demonstrates that the ECHR very rarely requires long-term preventive measures such as land-planning policies or retrofitting of buildings. The recommendation of experts that these long-term measures can protect life and property in a cost-effective way has no meaningful impact on the scope of positive obligations. Nor do psychological findings on the misperception of common natural hazards by humans lead to a relevant extension of the positive obligation with respect to the risk prevention and mitigation. As a result, the design of generally applicable positive obligations, combined with the lack of specialised international and domestic law, leaves a gap in the legal protection of property against most natural hazards. This gap invites Chaps. 4 and 5 to explore legal and political measures to complement disaster risk management.

To draw these conclusions, this chapter first outlines the current lack of specialised international legislation to prevent or mitigate disaster losses related to natural hazards. To this end, the chapter draws on a synthesis of critical analytical findings of other commentators on existing specialised international law. The analysis then turns to determining the contextual scope of obligations under the ECHR. The existence of positive obligations under the ECHR is hardly questioned, whereas an uncertainty remains as to when, and to what extent, the Convention imposes them.[3] In fact, despite the increasing general recognition of links between human rights and disasters,[4] the interplay between human rights law and DRR remains underexplored in the literature.[5] In fact, most of the commentary in the literature focusses on human rights issues during and after a disaster struck,[6] with only little attention being paid to the pre-disaster phase. For this reason, to demonstrate the limited scope of positive obligations relating to preventive DRR measures, this chapter must also explore the general case law under the ECHR in combination with a literature-review. As a starting point, this chapter presents the findings of the European Court of Human Rights ('the Court') on the right to life and property in the relevant case law relating to natural hazards. However, these established findings are not sufficient to determine the contextual scope of obligations beyond the

[1] See Sects. 1.1.1 and 1.1.2.

[2] Convention for the Protection of Human Rights and Fundamental Freedoms, opened for signature 4 November 1950, 213 UNTS 221 (entered into force 3 September 1953).

[3] Russell (2010), p. 285, citing Starmer (1999), p. 140; Krieger (2014), p. 189.

[4] Lauta (2016), pp. 108–109.

[5] Hilson (2009), p. 354; Kälin (2012), p. 147; Hesselman (2015), p. 224; Ambrus (2017), p. 99; Creta (2018), p. 145. This assessment is shared by Sommario and Venier (2018), p. 31.

[6] For contributions on the duty to provide food, water, clothing, shelter and health services to the affected population, see Davies (2012), Jansen-Wilhelm (2015), Philip (2015), Sykes (2014) and Spieker (2015).

cases assessed. The reason is that the Court's main task is to establish whether a state violated the ECHR in the individual case.[7] In doing so, the Court does not abstractly elaborate the doctrine that underpins its decision. As a result, an individual case only sheds light on which criteria are relevant for the interpretation of the positive obligation in the context of the individual case.[8] These criteria, however, may not be relevant or complete beyond the context for which they were originally conceived. Given the fact that the Court has rarely had the opportunity to assess the state's obligations in relation to natural hazards, uncertainties remain in determining the contextual scope of obligation beyond the cases assessed.[9] To demonstrate how the ECHR is not designed to engage in comprehensive DRR, particularly to mitigate the consequences of distorted risk perception, the analysis deduces the relevant factors for the rise and scope of positive obligations. To that aim, an analysis of the general case law with a view to comparable constellations of interests is necessary. Building on the understanding of the relevant factors, the analysis then demonstrates that the factual preconditions for the rise of positive obligations in the context of natural hazards are usually only given in the short term before their manifestation. This allows the state to take measures to save lives, for instance, through warnings and evacuation. However, bearing in mind that buildings cannot be moved out of the danger zone, the short time-window excludes options to protect property. As a result, positive obligations may serve to protect life, but not property, from the consequences of neglected long-term DRR in the context of natural hazards.

3.1 Overview of the International Law Landscape Relating to Natural Hazards

International law currently lacks binding targets to reduce disaster risks in relation to floods and earthquakes, despite international avowals in support of DRR.[10] Against this background, the subsisting gap between practical need and actual national measures has given rise to regular calls for a stronger international framework in the international discourse.[11] As such, an internationally binding DRR instrument has been sought as it is believed it could serve as a 'helpful tool … to make the case for greater attention to this critical activity'.[12] Nonetheless, international disaster law has so far consisted only of numerous soft-law instruments for

[7] Gerards (2019), p. 10; Greer and Wildhaber (2012), especially pp. 663–666.

[8] See Ebert and Sijniensky (2015), p. 343.

[9] Xenos (2007), p. 232.

[10] Bartolini et al. (2015), pp. 42–43.

[11] Ibid.

[12] Comment by the International Federation of Red Cross and Red Crescent Societies, see International Law Commission (2016b), p. 38.

DRR that focus on identifying and remedying individual's vulnerabilities to natural hazards,[13] and obliging commitments seem unlikely at present. As such, an examination of the international law landscape reveals a discrepancy between the recognition of the benefits of DRR and action taken.

3.1.1 International Law

The first major international framework was the Hyogo Framework for Action 2005–2015[14] ('HFA'), which was set up in response to devastation of the 2004 Indian Ocean Tsunami, one of the deadliest disasters in recorded history.[15] This framework was the first to explain, describe and detail the efforts necessary from the various actors to substantially reduce disaster losses.[16] The HFA further led to the first important successes in the implementation of DRR strategies as evidenced by the self-reporting mechanism of the HFA.[17] Nevertheless, the HFA did not manage to decrease the disaster losses to a level that DRR was expected to achieve.[18] Although countries adopted relevant laws, their implementation was weak,[19] and most disaster financing was still dedicated to post-disaster phases.[20]

The subsequent Sendai Framework for Disaster Risk Reduction (2015–2030)[21] ('SFDRR') broadened the scope of application.[22] While the HFA covered 'disasters caused by hazards of natural origin and related environmental and technological hazards and risks',[23] the SFDRR has extended the scope to any 'risk of small-scale and large-scale, frequent and infrequent, sudden and slow-onset disasters caused by natural or man-made hazards, as well as related environmental, technological and

[13] See proclamation by the UN General Assembly of the International Decade for Natural Disaster Reduction calling for the international community to dedicate the 1990s to the promotion of international co-operation in the field of natural disaster reduction in General Assembly (1987); World Conference on Disaster Reduction (2005) (endorsed by the General Assembly in UNGA Resolution 60/195 of 22 December 2005); United Nations Office for Disaster Risk Reduction (2015) (endorsed by the General Assembly in UNGA Resolution 69/283 of 23 June 2015).

[14] World Conference on Disaster Reduction (2005).

[15] Farber (2014), pp. 14–15.

[16] Zorzi Giustiniani (2018), p. 10; Sommario and Venier (2018), p. 33.

[17] Sommario and Venier (2018), p. 33; Childs (2013).

[18] Sommario and Venier (2018), p. 34; Zorzi Giustiniani (2018), p. 11; see Raju and da Costa (2018), p. 285, who finds that the implementation of post-HFA laws and policies 'has been weak or non-existent'.

[19] Raju and da Costa (2018), p. 285.

[20] Zorzi Giustiniani (2018), p. 11, citing Kellett and Caravani (2013); DasGupta and Shaw (2017), p. 16.

[21] United Nations Office for Disaster Risk Reduction (2015).

[22] Zorzi Giustiniani (2018), p. 17.

[23] World Conference on Disaster Reduction (2005), p. 1 Fn 3.

biological hazards and risks'.[24] In contrast to previous instruments, the SFDRR has focussed on strengthening monitoring mechanisms, standards and reporting duties.[25] Nevertheless, scholars still criticise the lack of specific baselines and quantitative targets.[26] The SFDRR also includes seven, initially vague, global targets that have been specified by an Open-Ended Intergovernmental Expert Working Group ('OIEWG') in 2016.[27] As such, the OIEWG has recommended, and the United Nations General Assembly ('UNGA') has adopted,[28] 38 global indicators in an attempt to provide globally comparable and objective benchmarks.[29] This is the first time that the international community has defined a global target for the progression of DRR.[30] However, the non-binding nature of these instruments exemplifies the states' hesitance to practically commit to DRR.[31]

The latest addition to the international DRR framework is the Draft Articles on the Protection of People in the Event of a Disaster ('DA') by the International Law Commission ('ILC').[32] The 2016 completed Draft Articles include in DA 9(1) the duty to reduce disaster risks 'by taking appropriate measures, including through legislation and regulations, to prevent, mitigate, and prepare for disasters'.[33] Although the ILC has recommended the elaboration of a convention on the basis of the DA in 2016,[34] deliberations in the UNGA have not yet been completed.[35] While the UNGA considered this recommendation at its 76th session in 2021, the issue was ultimately decided for a deferral to a working group of the Committee.[36] The working group will meet for four full consecutive days at the 78th and 79th sessions of the Assembly in 2023 and 2024, respectively.[37] Yet, even if the DA are eventually transformed into a binding treaty, as things stand, a wide range of situations would remain unregulated at the international level. This is because a 'disaster' in the sense of DA 3(a) inter alia presupposes a serious disruption of the functioning of society.

[24] United Nations Office for Disaster Risk Reduction (2015), para 15.

[25] Zorzi Giustiniani (2018), p. 19; Bartolini et al. (2015), p. 42.

[26] Chatterjee et al. (2015), pp. 180–183; Raju and da Costa (2018), pp. 280–281.

[27] UN General Assembly (2016). The intergovernmental expert working group was established by the General Assembly in its resolution 69/284 of 25 June 2015.

[28] General Assembly (2017).

[29] Zorzi Giustiniani (2018), p. 19; UN General Assembly (2016), pp. 5–9.

[30] United Nations Office for Disaster Risk Reduction (2015), p. 5.

[31] Sossai (2018), pp. 120–121; Saunders (2014), p. 29; Thorp (2013), p. 432; Zorzi Giustiniani (2018), p. 18; Raju and da Costa (2018), pp. 285–286.

[32] In its 68th session, the International Law Commission adopted a draft preamble and 18 draft articles, together with commentaries thereto, UN Doc A/CN.4/L.871 (2 May–10 June and 4 July–12 August 2016).

[33] Notably, this duty is weaker than a previous version of the Draft Article that included the duty to take 'necessary' measures, see General Assembly (2014).

[34] General Assembly (2016).

[35] Bartolini (2017).

[36] General Assembly (2021).

[37] Ibid.

Consequently, the duty to reduce disaster risks in DA 9(1) requires a higher threshold of gravity to apply than the SFDRR.[38] Flavia Zorzi Giustiniani qualifies this high threshold as epitomising a 'reactive approach', which she explains resulted from DA 9's late insertion in the project.[39] In fact, the ILC's project originally, and still mainly, addresses legal questions in relation to the disaster response.[40] Thus, even with the adoption of a convention, the field of DRR would remain largely unregulated internationally.

Two findings stand out from the overview of the state of international law. The decades-long development of soft law instruments shows that the long-term strategic importance of DRR has been recognised at the international level. However, this process has not yet produced binding targets.

3.1.2 *The Council of Europe*

Apart from minimum standards for the protection of human rights, which are discussed in detail in the second and third sections of this chapter, there are currently no Council of Europe ('CoE') agreements requiring the reduction of risks relating to natural hazards. By now, the member states have concluded more than 200 international treaties under the umbrella of the CoE.[41] Some of these make explicit provisions to protect against specific human made hazards, such as 'dangerous activities'.[42] For instance, the CoE has adopted the Convention on Civil Liability for Damage Resulting from Activities Dangerous to the Environment.[43] This Convention aims at ensuring adequate compensation for damages, including loss of life, personal injury and damage to property,[44] that are attributable to the performance of dangerous activities.[45] Notably, there are no similarly specialised conventions for cases where the occurrence of damage caused by natural hazards constitutes a breach of due diligence obligations of the state that could give rise to claims for compensation. The only agreement with reference to disasters triggered by natural hazards represents the 'Co-operation Group for the Prevention of, Protection

[38] Zorzi Giustiniani (2018), p. 23.

[39] Ibid.

[40] International Law Commission (2009), para 29.

[41] Statute of the Council of Europe, opened for signature 5 May 1949, 87 UNTS 103 (entered into force 3 August 1949).

[42] For relevant European standards, see ECtHR, *Öneryildiz v Turkey,* Judgment, 30 November 2004, Eur Court HR XII 79, pp. 107–108 paras 59–60; Xenos (2007), p. 237.

[43] Convention on Civil Liability for Damage Resulting from Activities Dangerous to the Environment, opened for signature 21 June 1993 ETS No 150.

[44] Wilkinson (1993), p. 133; Article 2(7) of the Convention on Civil Liability for Damage Resulting from Activities Dangerous to the Environment.

[45] Article 1 of the Convention on Civil Liability for Damage Resulting from Activities Dangerous to the Environment.

Against, and Organisation of Relief in Major Natural and Technological Disasters (EUR-OPA)',[46] which has 22 members to date. However, this partial agreement mainly aims at strengthening cooperation and does not regulate which measures must at least be taken to reduce risks.

Notably, as the CoE has no legislative competence, binding conventions and agreements depend on the consent of the member states wanting to accede to the respective multilateral international treaty.[47] Even if the treaty was elaborated and adopted by the CoE, the member states are not obliged to sign or ratify them.[48]

3.1.3 The European Union

Of the 46 member states, 27 states are additionally members of the European Union ('EU'). Although EU law offers some prime examples for supranational obligations to reduce certain disaster risks, member states largely define the acceptable level of safety for themselves. In this respect, EU law also does not provide an effective means to mitigate the consequences of distorted risk perception in the context of natural hazards.

Art 196 (1) of the Treaty on the Functioning of the European Union[49] ('TFEU') obliges the EU to 'encourage cooperation between Member States in order to improve the effectiveness of systems for preventing and protecting against natural or man-made disasters'. Although this provision touches on the context of disasters triggered by natural hazards, it does not aim to determine where the balance lies between autonomy and other important interests such as life and property with respect to DRR. On the contrary, it reserves this decision to the member states.[50] According to Article 196 of the TFEU, the EU is only competent to implement measures to support, coordinate or supplement the measures of the member states of the EU, as already follows from Article 6 of the TFEU.[51] It must therefore limit itself to accompanying measures that do not displace the EU's member states from their primarily responsible role.[52] Moreover, the disaster notion in Article 196 of the TFEU must be understood more narrowly than in sociological disciplines, such as

---

[46] Established by the Committee of Ministers of the Council of Europe in Setting Up a Co-Operation Group for the Prevention of, Protection against, and Organisation of Relief in Major Natural and Technological Disasters, 20 March 1987.

[47] Polakiewicz (2019), para 11.

[48] Ibid.

[49] Treaty on the Functioning of the European Union, opened for signature 13 December 2007, 2016/C 202/47 (entered into force 1 December 2009).

[50] Kotzur (2015), TFEU Article 196 para 7.

[51] Nettesheim (2021), AEUV Article 196 para 25.

[52] Ibid.

the disaster definition in modern disaster studies described above.[53] Generally, the disaster notion remains unstandardised within international disaster law.[54] Nevertheless, a common criterion of a disaster is a serious disruption of the functioning of society.[55] This constitutes a high applicability threshold that epitomises a reactive approach in contrast to other frameworks, such as the SFDRR.[56] Furthermore, 'systems for preventing and protecting' against disaster do not refer to mitigating the possibility of disasters occurring, but to measures taken to respond adequately to a disaster in an emergency.[57] In other words, the 'linguistically unsound' provision actually refers to traditionally preparatory measures.[58] Thus, even if the general objective of raising the standard of protection through cooperative efforts can be inferred from the provision, its material scope is narrow and the legal consequences an expression of restrained support.[59]

However, as a supranational organisation with legislative powers, the European Union has enacted regulations for some types of natural hazards. For instance, Directive 2007/60/EC deals with the assessment and management of flood risks.[60] This Directive not only includes the obligation to assess and map flood risks, but also to take adequate risk reduction measures.[61] However, commentators have criticised the fact that the Directive does not require specific results or safety standards.[62] Nor does the directive give guidance on the prioritisation of measures in this respect.[63]

Another example includes the European standards under EN 1998 Eurocode 8[64] that aim at reducing the vulnerability of structures in the event of an earthquake.[65] These standards establish common guidelines for the design of buildings and other construction works in seismic zones. However, the implementation of these

---

[53] Kotzur (2012), p. 271; Nettesheim (2021), AEUV Article 196 paras 12–19; Classen (2015), AEUV Article 196 para 4; (2015), TFEU Article 196 para 2.

[54] Bartolini (2018), p. 10; International Law Commission (2009), para 31.

[55] See Bartolini (2018), pp. 16–19; International Law Commission (2016a), Draft Article 3(a); UN General Assembly (2016), p. 13; Nettesheim (2021), AEUV Article 196 paras 12–19; Classen (2015), AEUV Article 196 paras 4–5.

[56] Zorzi Giustiniani (2018), p. 23.

[57] Nettesheim (2021), AEUV Article 196 paras 22–23; Classen (2015), AEUV Article 196 paras 6–7.

[58] Nettesheim (2021), AEUV Article 196 paras 21–24; Classen (2015), AEUV Article 196 paras 6–7.

[59] See Nettesheim (2021), AEUV Article 196 para 22.

[60] Directive 2007/60/EC of the European Parliament and of the Council of 23 October 2007 on the Assessment and Management of Flood Risks, 2007/L 288/27.

[61] European Commission (2021), p. 18.

[62] Priest et al. (2016).

[63] Ibid.

[64] Ref. No. EN 1998-1:2004: E, https://eurocodes.jrc.ec.europa.eu/showpage.php, accessed 19 June 2023.

[65] European Commission (2021), p. 30.

standards in national legislation is not obligatory.[66] The voluntary adoption of standards is a fundamental principle of the European standardisation system.[67] Even when the Eurocode 8 standards have been integrated into national building codes, as in Italy, the vulnerability remains in relation to already existing buildings.[68] For example, in Italy only 5% of homes have been built in the last two decades. Bearing in mind that approximately 50% of residential buildings are exposed to seismic risks,[69] 'the legacy of unsafe buildings remains very large' according to Robin Spence and Emily So.[70]

Last, it is also worth mentioning Article 5(5)(b) of the Regulation 1301/2013/EU on the European Regional Development Fund,[71] which states that the objective of the Fund is to support investments to address specific risks, ensure disaster resilience and develop disaster management systems. While the financial support can promote DRR, the risk reduction ultimately depends on the initiative of and successful implementation in the EU member states. In doing so, the Regulation also does not provide an effective means to mitigate the consequences of distorted risk perception in the context of natural hazards.

3.2 The Positive Obligations Under the ECHR in the Context of Natural Hazards

The overview of specialised international law in the previous section exposed the current lack of provisions to mitigate the increase in disaster losses related to natural hazards. In addition, this chapter argues that generally applicable obligations under the ECHR are also not designed to engage in comprehensive DRR. Although human rights under the ECHR do not systematically address the rights and needs of people affected by a disaster, the general articles find application in the context of disasters. In fact, in the last two decades, the Court has assessed the rise and scope of positive obligations under the right to life and property against threats emanating from natural hazards in internationally ground-breaking cases.[72] From the perspective of international human rights law, the Court's finding of a positive obligation to protect from natural hazards was 'revolutionary'.[73] The judgments of the Court in the

[66] Sousa et al. (2015), p. 25.

[67] Ibid.

[68] Spence and So (2021), p. 216.

[69] See Sect. 1.1.1.

[70] Spence and So (2021), p. 216.

[71] Regulation (EU) No 1301/2013 of the European Parliament and of the Council of 17 December 2013, OJ L 347 289.

[72] International Law Commission (2013), para 51; Sommario and Venier (2018), pp. 41–46; Lauta and Rytter (2016), p. 112.

[73] Popovski (2014), p. 99.

context of disasters are a beacon in the current discourse on DRR obligations of states and have undeniable value in promoting the importance of DRR.[74]

However, the following analysis shows that positive obligations particularly revolve around response-oriented measures and as such very rarely require long-term preventive measures such as land-planning policies or retrofitting of buildings. This response-orientation stems from the need to safeguard personal autonomy and protect the community from 'impossible or disproportionate burdens'. These aims require the application of the *principle of prevention* to interpreting positive obligations relating to risks.[75] The principle of prevention is one of two general principles for governing risks that has crystallised in law alongside the precautionary principle. The precautionary principle requires the adoption of necessary protective measures against serious or irreversible damages, despite scientific uncertainties.[76] In contrast, the principle of prevention only requires protective measures in the face of *certainty* of harm.[77] Since this is only the case in the short term for the most common natural hazards, there is a chance of saving lives through effective preparation and implementation of disaster response measures, but not in terms of property.

3.2.1 The General Principles on the Failure to Implement DRR Under the ECHR

This chapter's analysis of the positive obligations under the ECHR begins by presenting and assessing the Court's findings in cases relating to natural hazards to contour the scope of the positive obligations owed by member states. As explained at the beginning of this chapter, the Court generally does not couch its considerations in individual cases on a theoretical basis. Yet, in the last decade, the Court system has adopted elements of a 'constitutional justice approach'.[78] Inter alia, the Court introduced the concept of so-called 'general principles' that provide more general directions in cases involving questions of fundamental importance for the interpretation of the ECHR.[79] The reason is the Court's recognition that a 'case-law that is developed on a strict case-by-case basis necessarily leads to uncertainty as to both the exact purport of each judgment and the precise contents of the Court's doctrine'.[80] In regards to the context of disasters, the Court has developed such 'general principles' for the interpretation of obligations under the ECHR.

---

[74] Raju and da Costa (2018), p. 282.

[75] Ambrus (2017), p. 104; Seminara (2016), p. 737; Pedersen (2013), p. 61.

[76] Trouwborst (2006), pp. 91–96; Ambrus (2017), p. 103; Sands et al. (2018), pp. 230–232.

[77] Ambrus (2017); Trouwborst (2009), p. 105.

[78] Jahn (2014), pp. 838–841.

[79] Ibid, pp. 822, 836–839.

[80] ECtHR, *Fischer v Austria,* Judgment, 26 April 1995, Eur Court HR (ser A) 312, para 16 (Judge Martens).

3.2.1.1 The 'Disaster'-Term in the General Principles and Case Law

The presentation of these general principles relating to the disaster-context must begin with a contextual account of the disaster term. When the Court's general principles refer to the term 'disaster', it does not have a limiting effect on the rise and scope of the positive obligations as is the case with international disaster law ('IDL') instruments. Notably, the Court's case law often refers to '*disaster*' or 'natural *disasters* [sic]'.[81] For instance, in *Özel v Turkey,* the Court referred to an 'obligation to prevent *disasters*' on the part of the state.[82] Usually, the 'disaster' term plays a pivotal role in IDL to 'identify the situations in which protection may or shall be invoked'.[83] Yet, by juxtaposing the applicability of IDL and the ECHR, it can be shown that the disaster term does not play a comparable role in the Court's interpretation.

As for IDL, it is inherent in the system that a 'disaster' and other terms are not uniformly defined, but 'have been tailored to their specific scope of application'.[84] In order to express the corresponding political will, legal instruments define the concept of disaster with varying degrees of narrowness.[85] However, a common criterion of a disaster in IDL is nevertheless a serious disruption of the functioning of society, even if the latest disaster definitions in important IDL instruments differ in detail.[86] For instance, the International Law Commission ('ILC') in their Draft Articles on the Protection of People in the Event of a Disasters ('DA') aimed at a high threshold by requiring even more criteria in addition to a serious disruption of the functioning of society.[87] In contrast, the disaster definition by the Open-Ended Intergovernmental Expert Working Group on Indicators and Terminology relating to Disaster Risk Reduction ('OIEWG') sought a disaster definition following the broad conceptualisation of disaster risks in the Sendai Framework for Disaster Risk Reduction (2015–2030).[88] To that end, the definition of disasters considers the 'serious disruption of the functioning of a *community* or a society *at any scale*'.[89]

---

[81] ECtHR, *Öneryildiz v Turkey,* Judgment, 30 November 2004, Eur Court HR XII 79, p. 93 para 20; ECtHR, *Budayeva and others v Russia,* Judgment, 20 March 2008, Eur Court HR II 267, for instance at p. 279 para 29, p. 283 para 105, p. 284 para 111, p. 291 para 141; ECtHR, 1st Sec., *Kolyadenko and Others v Russia,* Judgment, 28 February 2012, for instance, paras 112–142, 206; ECtHR, 2nd Sec., *Özel and Others v Turkey,* Judgment, 17 November 2015, paras 170–174, 180.

[82] ECtHR, 2nd Sec., *Özel and Others v Turkey,* Judgment, 17 November 2015, para 172 (emphasis added).

[83] International Law Commission (2009), para 31.

[84] Bartolini (2018), p. 13.

[85] Ibid, p. 10; International Law Commission (2009), para 31.

[86] International Law Commission (2016a), Draft Article 3(a); UN General Assembly (2016), p. 13; see Bartolini (2018), pp. 16–19.

[87] International Law Commission (2016a), Commentary on Draft Article 3 paras 5–10.

[88] United Nations Office for Disaster Risk Reduction (2015), para 15.

[89] UN General Assembly (2016), p. 13 (emphasis added).

In juxtaposition, the Court used the 'disaster' term in cases that would not have met the ILC's and OIEWG's thresholds for a 'disaster'.[90] The facts of most assessed cases neither tested nor exceeded the state's capacity to cope with the event by its own means. For instance, the facts of *Budayeva v Russia* referred to a series of mudslides that swept through the town of Tyrnauz, and resulted in eight casualties.[91] Only the facts of *Özel v Turkey*[92] would satisfy the disaster definitions in DA 3(a) and the OIEWG's recommendation. *Özel v Turkey* related to an earthquake with a magnitude of 7.4 on the Richter scale that struck the İzmit region in August 1999.[93] It killed nearly 18,000 people and gave rise to international assistance in the disaster response.[94] These facts would qualify as a 'disaster' according to both instruments in IDL. However, the other cases demonstrate a disconnection of the Court's used terminology from developments in disaster studies and IDL.[95] Thus, when the Court uses the term 'disaster', it does not imply the requirement of 'a serious disruption of the functioning of society' for the rise of positive obligations.

Instead, the case law demonstrates that the rise of positive obligations depends on the effects on the individual. As such, risks need to meet certain criteria to give rise to positive obligations. In other words, not every risk to an interest covered by the ECHR engages positive obligations.[96] Instead, the state's obligation to provide effective protection is only triggered by a *real risk* to the interest at stake.[97] The meaning of the term 'real risk' has been summarised as 'one that is objectively verified'.[98] The required 'reality of the existence of the risk'[99] is given if the conduct

---

90 Cubie (2017), pp. 171–172; Sossai (2018), p. 126, who further refers to Bartolini (2015), p. 159; see further Bartolini (2018), pp. 12, 20; Bartolini et al. (2015), p. 44.

91 ECtHR, *Budayeva and others v Russia,* Judgment, 20 March 2008, Eur Court HR II 267, p. 296 para 161.

92 ECtHR, 2nd Sec., *Özel and Others v Turkey,* Judgment, 17 November 2015.

93 Ibid, para 16.

94 Ibid.

95 Cubie (2017), pp. 171–172; Sossai (2018), p. 126, who further refers to Bartolini (2015), p. 159; see further Bartolini (2018), pp. 12, 20; Bartolini et al. (2015), p. 44.

96 Seminara (2016), p. 734; Xenos (2007), p. 236.

97 Seminara (2016), p. 734; for instance, the ambit of Article 2 (1) 1 ECHR is engaged if a threat to the physical integrity of the individual exists, see ECtHR, *Osman v United Kingdom,* Judgment, 28 October 1998, para 116; ECtHR, *Budayeva and others v Russia,* Judgment, 20 March 2008, Eur Court HR II 267, pp. 292–293 para 146; with respect to Article 3 of the ECHR, the rise of positive obligations depends on a real risk of exposure to torture or to inhuman or degrading treatment or punishment, see ECtHR, *Soering v United Kingdom,* Judgment, 7 July 1989, Eur Court HR (ser A) 161, paras 90–91.

98 High Court of Justice, *W, Re An Application For Judicial Review*, 27 October 2004, NIQB 67, para 17, quoted in House of Lords, *Re Officer L,* 31 July 2007, UKHL 36, para 20, quoted in ECtHR, 4th Sec., *Van Colle v United Kingdom,* Judgment, 13 November 2012, para 61.

99 House of Lords, *Re Officer L,* 31 July 2007, UKHL 36, para 20, quoted in ECtHR, 4th Sec., *Van Colle v United Kingdom,* Judgment, 13 November 2012, para 61.

or situation is capable of harming a protected interest.[100] In such cases, the respective threat must at least be *likely* to cause a legally relevant harm to a protected interest.[101] On the other hand, the respective threat must be *likely* to occur.[102] Even if a hypothetical threat would be certainly harmful in a relevant manner, the issue does not give rise to positive obligation if the threat is unlikely to manifest.[103] Mónika Ambrus has rightly interpreted the required existence of a *real risk* as an application of the preventive principle, as it represents 'an implicit distinction between risk and uncertainty [in the scientific sense]'.[104] If the possible outcomes and their probability are known, then the state's obligation is one of reasonable prevention.[105]

The underlying reasoning for the threshold of a *real risk*, which is decisive for the response-oriented scope of positive obligation in the context of natural hazards, is explored in the following sections.[106] Prior to this discussion, this subsection further contrasts the scope of due diligence that the Court has derived for the protection of life and property in the event of a *real risk* from natural hazards.

3.2.1.2 The Developed General Principles Relating to the Right to Life

The Court has established general principles in relation to the right to life under Article 2 of the ECHR in the context of natural hazards. Article 2(1) of the ECHR prohibits the intentional deprivation of life, but also provides the general obligation that '[e]veryone's right to life shall be protected by law'. The developed general principles address the rise of the state's obligation, the content of the obligation, as well as the obligation's limitations in the context of natural hazards.

The positive obligation under Article 2(1) of the ECHR applies to any context, 'whether public or not, in which the right to life may be at stake'.[107] There is no *a priori* limit to the contexts in which positive obligations can arise.[108] To that effect, positive obligations can arise in the context of natural hazards. However, the Court clarified that not just any risk of a natural hazard constitutes a *real risk* that gives rise

---

[100] McBride (1999b), HR45-6; ECtHR, *Makaratzis v Greece,* Judgment, 20 December 2004, Eur Court HR XI 195, paras 52–55.

[101] ECtHR, *Dawn Bromiley v United Kingdom,* Decision, 23 November 1999, pp. 9–10; McBride (1999b), HR45-6; Seminara (2016), p. 737; Ambrus (2017), p. 104.

[102] ECtHR, *LCB v United Kingdom,* Judgment, 9 June 1998, Eur Court HR III 49, para 52; Ambrus (2017), p. 104.

[103] Seminara (2016), p. 737.

[104] Ambrus (2017), p. 104.

[105] Ibid, p. 103, citing Trouwborst (2009), p. 105.

[106] See Sects. 3.2.2–3.2.4.

[107] ECtHR, *Centre for Legal Resources on Behalf of Valentin Câmpeanu v Romania,* Judgment, 17 July 2014, Eur Court HR V 1, para 130; ECtHR, *Öneryildiz v Turkey,* Judgment, 30 November 2004, Eur Court HR XII 79, p. 110 para 71; ECtHR, 1st Sec., *Kolyadenko and Others v Russia,* Judgment, 28 February 2012, para 158.

[108] Costa (2008), p. 453; also cited in Stoyanova (2018), p. 310.

to a positive obligation. Positive obligations would apply in so far as the case's circumstances 'point to the *imminence of a natural hazard* that had been *clearly identifiable*'.[109] This would particularly apply to cases of 'a *recurring calamity* affecting a *distinct area* developed for human habitation or use'.[110] Thus, the Court limited the applicability of positive obligations to natural hazards by qualifying the required risk.

Once the positive obligation arises, the state must 'take *all appropriate steps to safeguard life* for the purposes of Article 2'.[111] This results, above all, in the primary duty of the state to establish 'a legislative and administrative framework designed to provide effective deterrence against threats to the right to life'.[112] The Court interprets this obligation as entailing a positive obligation to take regulatory measures, and to adequately inform the public about any life-threatening emergency.[113] Yet, as a general rule, the scope of the positive obligation would depend on the 'origin of the threat' and the extent to which the risk is 'susceptible to mitigation'.[114] Beyond these general indicators, the Court has remained vague when contouring the due diligence to implement regulatory measures to protect the right to life from natural hazards. In individual cases, the Court has concluded that preventive measures can include preparing a defence infrastructure, ensuring the functioning of the early warning system ('EWS'),[115] and 'appropriate spatial planning and controlled urban development' if necessary.[116] Moreover, the state may be obliged to adopt 'measures to reinforce the State's capacity to deal with the unexpected and violent nature of such natural phenomena'.[117] This last specification embodies the traditional approach to disaster management in contrast to disaster *risk* management.[118] The

---

[109] ECtHR, *Budayeva and others v Russia,* Judgment, 20 March 2008, Eur Court HR II 267, p. 290 para 137; ECtHR, 2nd Sec., *Özel and Others v Turkey,* Judgment, 17 November 2015, para 171 (emphasis added).

[110] ECtHR, *Budayeva and others v Russia,* Judgment, 20 March 2008, Eur Court HR II 267, p. 290 para 137; ECtHR, 2nd Sec., *Özel and Others v Turkey,* Judgment, 17 November 2015, para 171 (emphasis added).

[111] ECtHR, *Budayeva and others v Russia,* Judgment, 20 March 2008, Eur Court HR II 267, pp. 288–289 para 129 (emphasis added).

[112] Ibid, pp. 288–299 para 129.

[113] Ibid, p. 289 para 131.

[114] Ibid, p. 290 para 137; ECtHR, 1st Sec., *Kolyadenko and Others v Russia,* Judgment, 28 February 2012, para 161; ECtHR, 2nd Sec., *Özel and Others v Turkey,* Judgment, 17 November 2015, para 171.

[115] ECtHR, *Budayeva and others v Russia,* Judgment, 20 March 2008, Eur Court HR II 267, conclusion of the Court, p. 306 para 2.

[116] ECtHR, 2nd Sec., *Özel and Others v Turkey,* Judgment, 17 November 2015, para 174; see ECtHR, *Budayeva and others v Russia,* Judgment, 20 March 2008, Eur Court HR II 267, conclusion of the Court p. 306 para 2.

[117] ECtHR, 2nd Sec., *Özel and Others v Turkey,* Judgment, 17 November 2015, para 173.

[118] See Sect. 2.2.3.2.

required reinforcement of the 'State's capacity to deal' takes after the concept of preparation in DRR.[119]

With respect to the choice of means to fulfil positive obligations, the Court has acknowledged a particularly wide margin of appreciation for protective measures in the context of natural hazards.[120] The doctrine of the margin of appreciation refers to the scope of review of the state's decisions by the Court.[121] It is not the purpose of human rights to precisely determine resource-allocation and policy choices.[122] Not only does the state enjoy a wide margin of appreciation with respect to difficult social and technical spheres, this margin is even wider with regard to the different avenues of protection from natural hazards.[123] The reasoning behind this wide margin of appreciation also affects the standard of proportionality, which is also referred to as the 'fair balance' test.[124] The Court has continuously reiterated that it must not impose an 'impossible or disproportionate burden' on the authorities without consideration being given to the operational choices which they must make in terms of priorities and resources.[125] This consideration is given even more weight in relation to protecting lives from natural hazards.[126]

3.2.1.3 The Developed General Principles Relating to the Right to Property

The Court has also established general principles in relation to the right to property under Article 1 of the Protocol No 1 of the ECHR ('A1-P1') in the context of natural hazards. The general rule of A1-P1 lays down the individual's right 'to the peaceful enjoyment of his possessions'. The concept of 'possession' under A1-P1 particularly encompasses immovable and movable property.[127] While the Court did not further identify the necessary measures of protection, it made clear that the scope of

[119] See Sect. 1.5.3.

[120] ECtHR, *Budayeva and others v Russia,* Judgment, 20 March 2008, Eur Court HR II 267, pp. 289–290 para 134; ECtHR, *Fadeyeva v Russia,* Judgment, 9 June 2005, Eur Court HR IV 255, p. 283 para 96; ECtHR, 1st Sec., *Kolyadenko and Others v Russia,* Judgment, 28 February 2012, para 160.

[121] Cot (2007), para 1.

[122] Da Costa (2014), p. 67; Kothari and Kälin (2005).

[123] ECtHR, *Budayeva and others v Russia,* Judgment, 20 March 2008, Eur Court HR II 267, p. 290 para 135; ECtHR, *Hatton and Others v United Kingdom,* Judgment, 8 July 2003, Eur Court HR VIII 189, paras 100–101.

[124] Crawford (2011), paras 2; Mowbray (2010).

[125] ECtHR, *Öneryildiz v Turkey,* Judgment, 30 November 2004, Eur Court HR XII 79, p. 121 para 107; ECtHR, *Budayeva and others v Russia,* Judgment, 20 March 2008, Eur Court HR II 267, p. 290 para 135; ECtHR, 1st Sec., *Kolyadenko and Others v Russia,* Judgment, 28 February 2012, para 160.

[126] ECtHR, *Budayeva and others v Russia,* Judgment, 20 March 2008, Eur Court HR II 267, p. 290 para 135.

[127] Grabenwarter and Pabel (2021), § 25 para 3.

reasonably required measures is narrower than those involved in the right to life.[128] In particular, A1-P1 does not require the state 'to take preventive measures to protect private possessions in all situations and all areas prone to flooding or other natural disasters [sic]'.[129]

Accordingly, the state also enjoys a wider a margin of appreciation with regard to the protection of property than in the context of the right to life.[130] If the state's negligent conduct has caused or contributed to the material damage, the positive obligation may be fulfilled by the payment of an appropriate compensation.[131] Yet, in the context of natural hazards, the Court has denied the existence of an obligation to compensate the full market value of the damaged property.[132] The appropriate level of compensation depends on how clearly the damage can be attributed to the fault of the state, how serious the fault of the state was and what other measures have been taken by the authorities.[133] The complexity of the situation, the number of owners affected and the economic, social and humanitarian aspects of the disaster relief must also be taken into account.[134]

3.2.1.4 Assessment of the Developed General Principles

An examination of the presented general principles in relation to the right to life and property provides some guidance on the minimum standard of protection required by the state in the context of natural hazards. As such, the legal requirement of an *imminent* and *clearly identifiable* natural hazard suggests that the positive obligation will in practice often exclude long-term and comprehensive risk reducing measures, such as adjustments to planning law or building law. As a result, the presented general principles indicate that the obligation of member states mostly translates into saving lives through effective preparation and implementation of disaster response.

In addition, when comparing the general principles, the stricter due diligence to protect life than to protect property is apparent. In this regard, the rank of the right at stake affects the scope of positive obligation.[135] Although all human rights are generally indivisible, some rights have special weight. As such, Articles 2 and 3 of the ECHR 'express the most fundamental values of human civilisation'[136] and

---

[128] ECtHR, *Budayeva and others v Russia,* Judgment, 20 March 2008, Eur Court HR II 267, p. 299 para 175.

[129] ECtHR, 4th Sec., *Hadzhiyska v Bulgaria,* Decision, 15 May 2012, para 16.

[130] ECtHR, *Budayeva and others v Russia,* Judgment, 20 March 2008, Eur Court HR II 267, p. 299 para 175.

[131] Ibid, paras 180–185.

[132] Ibid, para 182.

[133] Ibid, p. 182.

[134] Ibid.

[135] Balcerzak (2020), pp. 169–170; see generally Starmer (1999), p. 196.

[136] Costa (2008), p. 452.

enshrine two of the 'basic values of the democratic societies making up the Council of Europe'.[137] As for the right to life, its nature makes its violation irreversible.[138] This inherently prevents remedies after the breach from being able to restore the previous *status quo*. Consequently, this right demands special protection.[139] Its position on the top of the catalogue of human rights,[140] as well as the fact that Article 2 of the ECHR is one of the 'non-derogable' rights, underscores its rank in the ECHR.[141] Thus, Article 2 of the ECHR's high rank extends the range of protection that the state has to provide, when compared with other Convention rights. As a consequence, the Court has highlighted in the context of disasters that the fundamental importance of Article 2 of the ECHR entails the positive obligations to do '*everything within the authorities' power* in the sphere of disaster relief' for its protection.[142] In contrast, the obligation to protect the right to the peaceful enjoyment of possessions under A1-P1 did not provide the same level of protection. Since the latter right is not absolute, the scope of measures that are reasonably necessary are narrower and the authorities enjoy a wider margin of appreciation to choose measures for protecting private possessions from natural hazards than in deciding what measures are needed relating to human life.[143]

However, the general principles alone are not sufficient to assess the protection required under the ECHR against the consequences of distorted risk perception in the context of natural hazards. The general principles do not provide any guidance on the extent to which individuals' vulnerability due to distorted risk perception affects the scope of due diligence. The assessment is further complicated by the lack of explanation of the contextual balancing of interests in the general principles. This circumstance has already led to disagreement among commentators on the contextually required level of protection. In fact, some scholars admit an uncertainty about how the presented case law applies to situations that go beyond the facts assessed in the few existing cases.[144] Fostered by the lack of clarity about the content of the general principles, commentators have also criticised the general principles as arbitrary and argued that the ECHR would impose broader obligations in the context of

---

[137] With respect to Article 2 of the ECHR, see ECtHR, *McCann and Others v United Kingdom,* Judgment, 27 September 1995, Eur Court HR (ser A) 324, para 147; with respect to Article 3 of the ECHR, see ECtHR, *Soering v United Kingdom,* Judgment, 7 July 1989, Eur Court HR (ser A) 161, para 88.

[138] Xenos (2007), p. 238.

[139] Starmer (1999), p. 199.

[140] Grabenwarter and Pabel (2021), § 20 para 1.

[141] Ibid; van Dijk and van Hoof (1998), p. 308.

[142] ECtHR, *Budayeva and others v Russia,* Judgment, 20 March 2008, Eur Court HR II 267, p. 299 para 175 (emphasis added); ECtHR, 4th Sec., *Hadzhiyska v Bulgaria,* Decision, 15 May 2012, para 15 (emphasis added).

[143] ECtHR, *Budayeva and others v Russia,* Judgment, 20 March 2008, Eur Court HR II 267, p. 299 para 175; ECtHR, 4th Sec., *Hadzhiyska v Bulgaria,* Decision, 15 May 2012, para 15; ECtHR, *Vladimirov v Bulgaria,* Decision, 25 September 2018, para 35.

[144] Hesselman (2015), p. 224; see also Sossai (2018), p. 126; see further Ambrus (2017), p. 99.

natural hazards.[145] The remainder of this section provides a comprehensive understanding of the factors that influence the scope of due diligence to show that the ECHR is not designed to mitigate the consequences of distorted risk perception in the context of natural events.

3.2.2 *The Goal of Effective Protection Under the ECHR*

The following subsections theoretically deduce the contextual due diligence in response to natural hazards. With respect to the remaining uncertainties in the presented general principles relating to natural hazards, it is necessary to substantiate the general principles of the Court by exploring the underlying rationales of its interpretation of the ECHR. This analysis is carried out through an analysis of the ECHR's object and purpose and the Court's general case law. In doing so, the analysis ultimately concludes that the ECHR justifiably applies the preventive principle, which in the case of natural hazards entails in particular a positive obligation to take response-oriented measures.

To shed light on the reasoning for the Court's interpretation of the ECHR in the context of natural hazards, the examination begins by exploring the interpretive methodology for ascertaining the meaning of ECHR Articles. Typical for human rights law, the ECHR frames the protected rights in general wording that omits a definition of its exact scope.[146] Further, the ECHR does not specify the rights' corresponding obligations, but proclaims these in one comprehensive provision, Article 1 of the ECHR.[147] This Article merely assigns the general duty to 'secure' treaty rights. The reason for this deliberate ambiguity in the wording is the intended universal and comprehensive protection of chosen human interests for an indefinite time frame. Such intended protection requires a wording that stipulates the protected interest for an infinite number of possible scenarios.[148] Although human rights law's ambit thus tends to be broad and open-textured, the rise and scope of state obligations in any given contexts, such as the disaster context, can be determined based on the principle of effective interpretation.

Notably, the principle of effective interpretation is also not mentioned in the ECHR. Instead, the principle belongs to the Court's developed interpretation

---

[145] Lauta and Rytter (2016).

[146] Çalı (2020), p. 508.

[147] Ibid, p. 509, referring to similar provisions in American Convention on Human Rights, signed 22 November 1969, OAS Treaty Series No 36 (entered into force 18 July 1978), International Covenant on Economic, Social and Cultural Rights, opened for signature 16 December 1966, 993 UNTS 3 (entered into force 3 January 1976) and African Charter on Human and Peoples' Rights, opened for signature 27 June 1981, 21 ILM 58 (entered into force 21 October 1986).

[148] Çalı (2020), p. 510.

methodology.[149] Yet, this interpretative method cannot be described as clear-cut.[150] As a consequence, member states and scholars have criticised the Court's current interpretation of the scope of obligation under the ECHR, deeming it to exceed the original design of the ECHR and the expectations of member states.[151] Several European countries have actively challenged the legitimacy of the Court's jurisprudence as so-called 'judicial activism'.[152] The fact that the original consent of member states to the ECHR did not explicitly extend to this interpretative methodology would render the ensuing jurisprudence illegitimate.[153] Some prominent commentators even go as far as describing the developed methodology as a 'banner under which the Strasbourg court has assumed power to legislate what they consider to be required by "European public order"'.[154]

This general controversy also fed into the reception of the case law in the context of disasters. In *Öneryildiz v Turkey*,[155] the Government of Turkey[156] specifically reproached the Court for surpassing previous case law. *Öneryildiz v Turkey* was the first landmark case to address the state's obligation in relation to disasters, even though the case concerned a human made hazard.[157] According to Turkey, the inclusion of situations of unintentional death in the scope of the right to life would give rise 'to an unprecedented extension of the positive obligations inherent in that provision'.[158] In the Turkish government's legal opinion, Article 2 of the ECHR would neither allow a teleological nor broad interpretation.[159] In other words, Turkey raised the ongoing controversy on the Court's methods of interpretation in regard to its developed general principles relating to disasters. Ultimately this expressed criticism disputes the basis of the general principles in the ECHR, and thus their legally

---

[149] Xenos (2012), pp. 3–4.

[150] Mowbray (2005), p. 61; Marochini (2014), pp. 77–82; however, in *Demir and Baykara v Turkey*, the Court dedicated full section to explaining its methodology, see ECtHR, *Demir and Baykara v Turkey,* Judgment, 12 November 2008, Eur Court HR V 395.

[151] Golsong (1993); Baade (2017), p. 5.

[152] Bossuyt (2015); Mahoney (1990); Krieger (2014), pp. 193–199; Baade (2017), pp. 4–9, who lists cases that sparked criticism in several European countries; Costa (2013), p. 265; Xenos (2012), pp. 3–4.

[153] Baade (2017), p. 10; Marochini (2014).

[154] Hoffmann (2009), para 36; for a comment on Lord Hoffmann's speech, see Spano (2014), pp. 492–497.

[155] ECtHR, *Öneryildiz v Turkey,* Judgment, 30 November 2004, Eur Court HR XII 79.

[156] In a *note verbale* of 3 June 2022, the Permanent Representation of Turkey requested international organisations to use of 'Türkiye' instead of 'Turkey' for all affairs. The country name change became effective upon receipt of the letter. Since all cases discussed in this book date from before that date, the book follows the practice of the Court and uses the former country name 'Turkey' in reference to the past.

[157] *Öneryildiz v Turkey* dealt with a methane explosion in a rubbish tip that caused a fatal landslide and killed 39 people, ECtHR, *Öneryildiz v Turkey,* Judgment, 30 November 2004, Eur Court HR XII 79, pp. 92–93 para 18.

[158] Ibid, para 66.

[159] Ibid, para 67.

binding nature. To dispel this concern, it is necessary to address the basis and consequences of this interpretive principle in more detail.

3.2.2.1 The Legal Basis of the Principle of Effectiveness

Although the ECHR does not mention the interpretive principle of effectiveness, it traces back to the general rule in Article 31(1) of the *Vienna Convention on the Law of Treaties*[160] ('VCLT'),[161] which reflects customary international law.[162] With this legal basis in mind, it is, however, striking that the Court's approach to interpretation deviates from this general rule. In contrast to the Court's overall teleological approach, Article 31 of the VCLT assigns equal weight to all mentioned means of interpretation, that is, the wording, context, and the object and purpose.[163] The equal weighting of the interpretative reference-points mentioned in Article 31 of the VCLT is expressed by its heading, which reads 'General Rule of Interpretation'. It is emphasised in the singular to express 'that the application of the means of interpretation in the article would be a single combined operation' in which all elements are considered simultaneously.[164] The justification for this deviation from the '*lex generalis*', that is, the VCLT, derives from the object and purpose of the ECHR, which underpins the Court's overall teleological approach.[165]

The object and purpose of the ECHR, 'as a treaty for the collective enforcement of human rights and fundamental freedoms', consists in the protection of individual

---

[160] Vienna Convention on the Law of Treaties, opened for signature 23 May 1969, 1155 UNTS 331 (entered into force 27 January 1980).

[161] International Law Commission (1966), p. 219 para 6; the ILC also refers to the practice of international courts, see ICJ, *Corfu Channel (United Kingdom v Albania),* Merits, 9 April 1949, ICJ Rep 4, p. 24; Merrills (1993), p. 98; Dörr (2018), p. 578 para 34.

[162] Articles 31–33 of the VCLT have been consistently and adamantly found to constitute customary international law, see ICJ, *Legality of Use of Force (Serbia and Montenegro v Belgium),* Judgment, 15 December 2004, ICJ Rep 720–765, para 98; ICJ, *Kasikili/Sedudu Island (Botswana v Namibia),* Judgment, 13 December 1999, ICJ Rep 1045–1109, para 18 ('neither Botswana nor Namibia are parties to the [Convention], but … both of them consider Article 31 … is applicable inasmuch as it reflects customary international law'); ICJ, *LaGrand (Germany v United States of America),* Judgment, 27 June 2001, ICJ Rep 466–517, para 99 ('customary international law, reflected in Article 31'); Permanent Court of Arbitration, *The Rhine Chlorides Arbitration Concerning the Auditing of Accounts (Netherlands v France),* Award, 12 March 2004, para 59 ('The Tribunal further notes that the International Court of Justice and other tribunals have affirmed on a number of occasions that these provisions are a codification of customary law'); Villiger (2009), p. 440.

[163] O'Connell (1970), p. 255; International Law Commission (1966), p. 220 para 9; Çalı (2020), p. 507; Fitzmaurice (2015), pp. 746–747; Aust (2013), pp. 185–187; Villiger (2009), pp. 435–436 para 29; for arguments that the 'object and purpose' is only a subsidiary element, see Sinclair (1984), pp. 118–119.

[164] International Law Commission (1966), pp. 219–220 para 8; Dörr (2018), p. 580 para 38.

[165] Scheinin (2017), p. 21; Fitzmaurice (2015), p. 755.

human beings.[166] This can be deduced from the preamble that considers the 'maintenance and further realisation of Human Rights and Fundamental Freedoms' a method by which 'greater unity between its Members' can be pursued. Additionally, Article 1 of the ECHR stipulates that 'High Contracting Parties shall secure to everyone within their jurisdiction the rights and freedoms' as defined in the Convention. As such, the parties to the ECHR have agreed on a type of treaty, whose aim differs from the 'ideal type of treaty' incorporated in the VCLT.[167] The VCLT was written for a reciprocal treaty concept that regulates the exchange of rights and obligations between states, and whose interpretation is reserved for the same states.[168] The ECHR, in contrast, aims at the establishment of a long-term framework of legally binding rights for third party beneficiaries, whose legal force does not depend on a corresponding performance.[169] As such, one of the earlier decisions under the ECHR states that

> obligations … in the Convention are essentially of an objective character, being designed rather to protect the fundamental rights of individual human beings from infringement by any of the High Contracting Parties than to create subjective and reciprocal rights for the High Contracting Parties themselves.[170]

Consequently, the ECHR's special character necessitates 'to seek the interpretation that is most appropriate in order to realise the aim and achieve the object of the treaty, not that which would restrict to the greatest possible degree the obligations undertaken by the Parties'.[171] In other words, the Convention is intended to guarantee rights that are practical and effective, not theoretical or illusory.[172] Thus, the Court's overall teleological approach to interpreting the scope of obligations originates in the member states' consent as set out in the ECHR. The object and purpose of the ECHR demands its interpretation and application so as to give the rights fullest weight and effect.[173]

---

[166] ECtHR, *Soering v United Kingdom,* Judgment, 7 July 1989, Eur Court HR (ser A) 161, para 87.

[167] Matscher (1993), p. 66; International Law Commission (1966), p. 219 para 6; Scheinin (2017), pp. 22, 26; International Law Association (2004), para 22; McGrogan (2014), p. 348; see Brölmann (2005), pp. 392–395.

[168] Scheinin (2017), pp. 22, 36; as also demonstrated by Brölmann (2005), p. 383; Craven (2000), pp. 500–504.

[169] ECtHR, *Ireland v United Kingdom,* Judgment, 18 January 1978, Eur Court HR (ser A) 25, p. 82 para 239; Scheinin (2017), p. 22; Herdegen (2020), p. 31; Craven (2000), p. 504; for the opposing view, that the VCLT's bilateral treaty concept can adequately accommodate human rights treaties, see Simma (1994), pp. 364–376.

[170] EComHR, *Austria v Italy,* Decision, 11 January 1961, p. 19.

[171] ECtHR, *Wemhoff v Federal Republic of Germany,* Judgment, 27 June 1968, Eur Court HR (ser A) 7, p. 19 para 8.

[172] ECtHR, *Airey v Ireland,* Judgment, 9 October 1979, Eur Court HR (ser A) 32, para 24; ECtHR, *Christine Goodwin v United Kingdom,* Judgment, 11 July 2002, Eur Court HR VI 1, p. 26 para 74; ECtHR, *Soering v United Kingdom,* Judgment, 7 July 1989, Eur Court HR (ser A) 161, para 87; ECtHR, *Osman v United Kingdom,* Judgment, 28 October 1998, para 116.

[173] Merrills (1993), p. 98.

3.2.2.2 The Inherent Principle of Fair Balance with Communal Interests

Even though the ECHR and its numerous protocols do not explicitly mention the standard of 'proportionality' to balance different interests, the Court and commentators infer the 'search for a fair balance' as a general principle from the Convention as a whole.[174] Already in its earliest jurisprudence, the Court has described the search for a fair balance of 'the general interest of the community and the protection of the individual's fundamental rights' as an inherent principle of the ECHR.[175] As a consequence of this 'fair balance' test, the scope of obligation inevitably varies.[176] In particular, the scope of obligation must have

> regard to the diversity of situations obtaining in Contracting States and the choices which must be made in terms of priorities and resources. Nor must such an obligation be interpreted in such a way as to impose an impossible or disproportionate burden on the authorities.[177]

As such, this conception takes account of policy considerations relevant to a functioning society. In other words, the obligation and its degree of stringency imposed on public authorities must strike an appropriate balance with the general rights of the community.[178] As a consequence, a state is not legally responsible to meet an absolute standard that demands the aversion of the risk, irrespective of any other considerations.[179]

3.2.2.3 The Margin of Appreciation

Since only the goal of human rights is defined, there are often several possibilities for achieving it in the context. As long as the means provide effective protection, the choice of means to meet the positive obligations is left to the states as a matter of their discretion.[180] In this regard, the margin of appreciation doctrine limits the scope of review of the state's decisions by third parties, such as the Court.[181] The breadth of the margin determines the intensity of review, and therefore, the state's

---

[174] See, e.g., ECtHR, *Soering v United Kingdom,* Judgment, 7 July 1989, Eur Court HR (ser A) 161, para 89; Schweizer (2016), pp. 96–97; Arai-Takahashi (2015), p. 451; Eissen (1993); McBride (1999a); Crawford (2011), para 13; van Dijk and van Hoof (1998), p. 81; Mowbray (2010).

[175] See, e.g., ECtHR, *Rees v United Kingdom,* Judgment, 17 October 1986, Eur Court HR (ser A) 106, para 37; Mowbray (2010), p. 290.

[176] ECtHR, *Appleby and Others v United Kingdom,* Judgment, 6 May 2003, Eur Court HR VI 185, p. 199 para 40.

[177] Ibid.

[178] House of Lords, *Re Officer L,* 31 July 2007, UKHL 36, para 21, cited in ECtHR, 4th Sec., *Van Colle v United Kingdom,* Judgment, 13 November 2012, para 61.

[179] House of Lords, *Re Officer L,* 31 July 2007, UKHL 36, para 21; McBride (1999b), HR43, HR52.

[180] Klatt (2011), p. 716.

[181] Cot (2007), para 1.

discretion.[182] In this way, the doctrine grants a degree of flexibility towards the state as the principle actor in shaping social coexistence, that is, the nation state.[183] Accordingly, it is not up to the Court to prioritise its view of the best policy to deal with social, economic and urban problems over the views of the local authorities.[184]

Thus, at the heart of the doctrine lies the recognition that the national authorities have a comparative advantage in assessing the facts, as well as the social requirements in question.[185] This is aligned with concerns of democratic legitimacy, since socio-political questions are not up to unelected international judges to decide upon.[186] Substantively, the margin of appreciation doctrine is a direct result of the consideration of the subsidiarity principle.[187] It has been a 'long-standing and fundamental jurisprudential tool' in the Court's decision-making,[188] even before an explicit reference to the subsidiarity principle was added to the ECHR itself.[189] The principle of subsidiarity expresses the preference for allocating and exercising governmental functions at the lowest level in a system of multi-level governance.[190] In other words, higher levels should only assume responsibilities or functions insofar as the lower level is not able to do so.[191] The principle further acknowledges that lower governance levels are in a better position, 'by reason of their direct and continuous contact with the vital forces',[192] to strike the balance between individual and community interests.[193] As such, the principle of subsidiary takes account of two considerations. On the one hand, it respects individuals and communities as autonomous in deciding the appropriate course of action in accordance with their preferences.[194] On the other hand, it recognises the individual's responsibility for his or

---

[182] Crawford (2011), para 20.

[183] Cot (2007), para 1.

[184] ECtHR, *Öneryildiz v Turkey,* Judgment, 30 November 2004, Eur Court HR XII 79, p. 121 para 107.

[185] Cot (2007), para 19; ECtHR, *Handyside v United Kingdom,* Judgment, 7 December 1976, Eur Court HR (ser A) 24, para 48; ECtHR, *Dudgeon v United Kingdom,* Judgment, 22 October 1981, Eur Court HR (ser A) 45, para 52; Petzold (1993), p. 59.

[186] Cot (2007), para 20; Krieger (2014), pp. 196–197; Legg (2012), Ch 4.

[187] Petzold (1993), p. 59; Feichtner (2007), para 29; see further Protocol No 15 to the Convention for the Protection of Human Rights and Fundamental Freedoms, opened for signature 24 June 2013, No 213 CETS (entered into force 1 August 2021); Mowbray (2015), p. 339.

[188] Mowbray (2015), p. 341.

[189] The respective protocol No. 15 entered into force on 1 August 2021, Protocol No 15 to the Convention for the Protection of Human Rights and Fundamental Freedoms, opened for signature 24 June 2013, No 213 CETS (entered into force 1 August 2021). The restatement of the principle of subsidiarity in the Preamble of the ECHR was required by the Brighton Declaration on the future of the Strasbourg Court of April 2012.

[190] Feichtner (2007), para 1; Petzold (1993), p. 60.

[191] Petzold (1993), p. 41.

[192] ECtHR, *Handyside v United Kingdom,* Judgment, 7 December 1976, Eur Court HR (ser A) 24, para 48.

[193] Feichtner (2007), para 2; Petzold (1993), p. 60.

[194] Feichtner (2007), para 2.

her well-being, as well as the community's responsibility for the well-being of its members.[195]

The breadth of the margin differs in each case, depending on the rank and nature of the right in dispute, as the previous comparison of the developed general principles in the context of natural hazards has illustrated.[196] In addition, the breadth of the margin depends on the intensity of the contested encroachment, the nature of the pursued interest, and the existence or absence of a European standard among the member states.[197] Thus, the margin of appreciation becomes narrower the more fundamental the right at issue, the more intense the encroachment, and the stronger the European consensus in question.[198] By contrast, in the context of social and economic policies, the Court has granted the state a wide margin of appreciation.[199]

3.2.3 The Relevant Factors for Determining the Loss of Autonomy

The explored effective interpretation of the object and purpose of the ECHR revealed how the extent of positive obligations is inter alia determined by the effect of the threat on the individual.[200] In this regard, relevant in determining a threat to a protected interest is the extent to which autonomy is threatened or lost. Because of this conceptualisation of *effective* protection, 'different nuances and gradations of positive obligation exist, according to how much help the individual needs for the ensuring of his or her autonomy'.[201] The Court itself has emphasised 'that the notion of personal autonomy is an important principle underlying the Convention guarantees'.[202] As a result, the protective measures required ultimately depend on what is necessary to preserve or restore the autonomy of the individual in relation to a protected interest as '[t]he demands on the state increase with the diminished free choice of the individual'.[203] In addition, the due diligence must not impose a disproportionate burden on the state. In this regard, critical discussion has focussed in

[195] Ibid.

[196] See Sect. 3.2.1.4.

[197] ECtHR, 4th Sec., *Mosley v United Kingdom,* Judgment, 10 May 2011, paras 108–111; Cot (2007), para 3; Krieger (2014), pp. 204–205; O'Donnell (1982), pp. 479–490; Macdonald (1993).

[198] For a detailed analysis, see Legg (2012), pp. 200–218.

[199] EComHR, *James and Others v United Kingdom,* Judgment, 21 February 1986, Eur Court HR (ser A) 91, para 46; ECtHR, *Öneryildiz v Turkey,* Judgment, 30 November 2004, Eur Court HR XII 79, p. 121 para 107; Peukert (2009), Artikel 1 des 1. ZP, p. 657 para 44.

[200] Dröge (2003), pp. 388–389.

[201] Ibid, p. 388.

[202] ECtHR, 5th Sec., *Prilutskiy v Ukraine,* Judgment, 26 February 2015, para 32; see for the almost identical quotation in relation to Article 8 of the ECHR ECtHR, *Pretty v United Kingdom,* Judgment, 29 April 2002, Eur Court HR III 155, p. 193 para 61.

[203] Dröge (2003), pp. 388–389.

particular on whether the individual or the community bears the responsibility for his or her knowingly carrying out activities that are *risky* for the protected legal interest.[204] Considering the comparatively high level of education in Europe, this question is particularly relevant. There are usually opportunities to learn about the risks of natural hazards and the possibilities of disaster preparedness. However, the question is to what extent the community can be expected to intervene if the individual does not use these opportunities. Given the focus of this book, the question is particular to what extent the examined distorted risk perception in relation to natural hazards affects the scope of positive obligations.[205]

This subsection explores the concept of autonomous decision-making in general case law and the extent to which the ECHR requires its protection. As the following review of general case law shows, 'diminished choice' refers to the fact that the possibility of self-determined redress is impaired to a degree that likely has unintended, yet relevant consequences for the protected interests. The review of general case law also allows this subsection to identify factors that diminish the freedom of choice and thus affect the rise and scope of positive obligations, including in the context of natural hazards. Building on the understanding of the protection of autonomous decision-making, this subsection concludes how the impact of biases and heuristics on people's authentic decision-making, as explored in Chap. 2 in relation to risks from natural hazards,[206] affects the rise and scope of positive obligations. The examination gives examples on how the knowledge of biases and heuristics can affect positive obligations in the context of natural hazards, particularly in relation to the right to life. However, the examination also reveals that as long as people have access to information about the risk and remedies, as well as the means to use these to their benefit, a relevant impairment of autonomous decision-making is only present when there is a degree of *certainty* relating to the risk. Yet, as Chap. 2 explained, in the case of the frequently occurring natural hazards, *certainty* is often only given in the short term.[207] It follows that, in most cases, the lack of certainty prevents the rise of a positive obligation to take preventive and mitigative risk reduction despite the impact of the biases and heuristics on people's decision-making. The reason is that the concept of autonomy also limits the scope of protective obligations, which the following first subsection establishes in more detail.

---

[204] See, for instance, the controversy in the partly Dissenting Opinion of Judge Gölcüklü in ECtHR, *Mahmut Kaya v Turkey*, Judgment, 28 March 2000, Eur Court HR III 149, p. 35; Mowbray (2004), pp. 18–19; McBride (1999b), HR 45, 51.

[205] See Sect. 2.1.

[206] See Sect. 2.1.

[207] See Sect. 2.3.2.

3.2.3.1 The Protection of Autonomy Against Paternalistic Interference

First, freedom vis-à-vis the state must include the right to take some risks and dangers for protected interests.[208] The taking of risks can be an expression of the individual's autonomy that neither requires nor allows state interferences. In this vein, the Court's interpretation of the aim of positive obligations respects that autonomy is a prerequisite for happiness, which itself is a state of mind that one cannot conceptualise in abstract ends or means.[209] As a consequence of this value of autonomy, a person may even have a negative right that forbids interventions by the state, for instance, if people decide to live near rivers to gain a beautiful view, despite knowledge of the increased vulnerability in case of floods.[210] The rights do not aim at protecting the legal interest itself, but at protecting the right to the respective legal interest.[211]

The case of *Prilutskiy v Ukraine*[212] demonstrates how the value of autonomy restrains the rise and scope of positive obligations. This case concerned the death of the applicant's son during a privately organised game that involved driving to various locations to solve riddles. The applicant's son died in a collision of his team's car with a pillar. The cause of the collision was found to be the driving teammate's failure to abide by the speeding limit.[213] Beyond the general traffic safety regulations, which included sanctions for their violations, the applicant claimed that the state should have subjected these games to a licensing requirement to fulfil its obligation under the right to life.[214]

It is important to note that *in casu* the state had no, nor ought to have had knowledge, of the threat to the specific individual.[215] Consequently, the Court's assessment zeroed in on the effectiveness of the abstract protective domestic legislative and administrative framework in deterring threats to the right to life. The Court acknowledged that driving in traffic constitutes a dangerous activity. Such dangerous activities require the state to take appropriate steps to safeguard life. In this regard, the Court noted the existing traffic safety regulations that target the dangers of participating in traffic. *In casu*, the manifested risk did not differ from these inherent dangers. With respect to the question as to whether the state should still have taken more strict measures, the Court cautioned that

> the positive obligations under Article 2 should not be unduly impaired by paternalistic interpretations, bearing in mind that the notion of personal autonomy is an important principle

---

208 ECtHR, 5th Sec., *Prilutskiy v Ukraine,* Judgment, 26 February 2015, para 32; Dietlein (2005), p. 223; Dröge (2003), p. 329; Jablonski (2014), p. 83.

209 See Sect. 1.1.3.

210 See Heun (2011), p. 380.

211 See Opsahl (1993), p. 211, quoting Fawcett (1987), p. 37.

212 ECtHR, 5th Sec., *Prilutskiy v Ukraine,* Judgment, 26 February 2015.

213 Ibid, para 28.

214 Ibid, para 29.

215 Ibid, paras 36–37.

> underlying the Convention guarantees, primarily those pertinent to private life. The Court has observed that the ability to conduct one's life in a manner of one's own choosing may also include the opportunity to pursue activities perceived to be of a physically or morally harmful or dangerous nature for the individual concerned, and improper State interference with this freedom of personal choice may give rise to an issue under the Convention…[216]

In other words, even though the death was tragic, the individual's taking of risk was 'voluntary enough'.[217] The risks pertaining to speeding must have been known by the son who was an adult who 'enjoyed a freedom to act and decided to participate in the game of his own free will, having taken upon himself the responsibility to follow the existing rules'.[218] As a result, a positive obligation to implement stricter regulation of individual failures to abide by the traffic regulations could not be deduced from the right to life.

The outlined limitation that the concept of autonomy imposes on the rise and scope of positive obligations also applies to the context of individuals' voluntary exposure to risks from natural hazards. The ECHR does not oblige the state to protect individuals from harmful consequences of their 'own choosing', regardless of whether the risk is human made or natural. On the contrary, such an interpretation may interfere with the autonomy of the individual guaranteed by the Convention rights. A justified paternalistic intervention in the individual's autonomy requires a high certainty and seriousness of the threat, as Chap. 4 discusses in detail.[219] However, if risks are not taken of one's own choosing, a positive obligation of the state to protect individuals from the consequences of their actions may arise. The evaluation of the extent to which the examined influence of biases and heuristics on individual decisions triggers positive obligations requires an examination of which factors impair freedom of choice. Based on a review of general case law, the following section presents the relevant factors in relation to the threat in addition to the victim and provides examples of their relevance in the context of natural hazards.

3.2.3.2 Factors Decreasing Autonomous Decision-Making

Due to the value of autonomy, positive obligations only arise when the autonomy of the individual is impaired or significantly endangered. This depends, inter alia, on factors associated with the threat, such as the *seriousness and immediacy of the threat* to a protected legal interest.[220] Depending on these factors, a review of the Court's case law and the literature reveals three different forms that positive obligations under the ECHR can take to ensure effective protection of rights:

---

[216] Ibid, para 32.

[217] Feinberg (1989), pp. 117–127.

[218] ECtHR, 5th Sec., *Prilutskiy v Ukraine,* Judgment, 26 February 2015, para 36.

[219] See Sects. 4.1.4 and 4.2.2.

[220] Starmer (1999), p. 196.

1. States are primarily obliged to create a domestic *legislative and administrative framework* that provides effective deterrence against *real risks* to legally protected interests.[221] This constitutes the so-called 'basic' obligation.[222] This obligation is also reflected in the general principles related to natural hazards, both in respect of the right to life and A1-P1.[223] For instance, situations can oblige the state to enact appropriate spatial planning and to control urban development.[224] To fulfil the positive obligation, these provisions have to be effective, meaning they need to be backed up by law enforcement.[225]

   With respect to situations where individuals knowingly engage in behaviour that is risky to the protected legal interest, the rise of the basic obligation also depends on how widespread the risky behaviour is. The more widespread the risky behaviour, the more stringent the due diligence to adapt the national legal and administrative framework to reduce said behaviour. A case review in the context of the right to life demonstrates this correlation with respect to the primary duty of putting in place a *protective domestic legislative and administrative framework*. In principle, the conceptualisation of positive obligations as a balance between individual and collective interests draws the line of due diligence requirements relating to the *legislative and administrative framework* at individual recklessness.[226] For instance, the Court decided in *Bône v France* that the attempt to alight from a train on the side of the tracks, despite warnings about the serious risks, constitutes reckless conduct.[227] *In casu*, this reckless conduct created an autonomous causal sequence that led to the victim being fatally hit by another train.[228] Another example of reckless behaviour is swaying on the top bar of a movable goal, which is knowingly not fixed to ground, despite the foreseeable risk of causing the goal to turn over and hurt the individual.[229] All of these examples demonstrate that the individual ought to have foreseen that their conduct could *likely* set off a *real* and *immediate* threat to respective interests. So long as the state does not unjustifiably interfere with the individual's autonomy, the state may protect individuals against the consequences of reckless behaviour,

[221] See, e.g., ECtHR, *Young, James and Webster v United Kingdom,* Judgment, 13 August 1981, Eur Court HR (ser A) 44, p. 49; ECtHR, *Osman v United Kingdom,* Judgment, 28 October 1998, para 115; ECtHR, *Öneryildiz v Turkey,* Judgment, 30 November 2004, Eur Court HR XII 79, p. 115 para 89; ECtHR, *Budayeva and others v Russia,* Judgment, 20 March 2008, Eur Court HR II 267, pp. 288–289 para 129.

[222] Starmer (1999), p. 196; Mowbray (2004), p. 16.

[223] See Sects. 3.2.1.2–3.2.1.3.

[224] ECtHR, 2nd Sec., *Özel and Others v Turkey,* Judgment, 17 November 2015, para 174; ECtHR, *Budayeva and others v Russia,* Judgment, 20 March 2008, Eur Court HR II 267, p. 289 para 133.

[225] ECtHR, *Osman v United Kingdom,* Judgment, 28 October 1998, para 115.

[226] See, e.g., ECtHR, 3rd Sec., *Molie v Romania,* Decision, 1 September 2009, para 44.

[227] ECtHR, 2nd Sec., *Bône v France,* Decision, 1 March 2005.

[228] Ibid.

[229] ECtHR, 3rd Sec., *Molie v Romania,* Decision, 1 September 2009, para 46.

which a fortiori constitutes reasoning failures. However, the state is not internationally responsible to protect individuals against their own reckless behaviour.[230]

Then again, an exception constitutes a case of numerous and serious gaps in the protective framework. In such cases, the state cannot hide behind the victim's recklessness.[231] Moreover, if the state learns about individuals' systemic neglect of due diligence or even breaches of the law, the state may not remain passive.[232] As such, the growth of seriously risky behaviour into a widespread social phenomenon may oblige authorities to put additional measures into place for the public's protection from reasoning failures.[233] With respect to natural hazards, for instance, the state's knowledge of a widespread ignorance of early warnings would require additional state action to meet its due diligence. If less intrusive measures do not effectively protect life, forced evacuations may become necessary.[234]

2. Positive obligations can further entail the obligation to *adequately inform the public* about *real risks* that threaten a right.[235] Only when individuals have information are they enabled to make choices based on their own assessment of risks.[236] This dimension has been first addressed in *Guerra and Others v Italy*,[237] which involved the state's failure to inform the applicants about the risks of living near a chemical plant and the procedures to be followed in the event of an accident. In the context of Article 2 of the ECHR, the Court has placed particular emphasis on the public's right to information as one preventive measure to ensure the effective protection of rights.[238] In *Öneryildiz v Turkey*, the Court emphasised the role of information as a prerequisite for potentially exposed people 'to assess the risks they might run as a result of the choices they had made'.[239] This duty may also arise from the risk posed by certain natural hazards. In *Budayeva v Russia*, the Court characterised providing information as 'one of the essential practical measures needed to ensure effective protection of the citizens

[230] Ibid, para 44; ECtHR, 2nd Sec., *Bône v France,* Decision, 1 March 2005.

[231] ECtHR, 2nd Sec., *Kalender v Turkey,* Judgment, 15 December 2009, para 49.

[232] ECtHR, *Öneryildiz v Turkey,* Judgment, 30 November 2004, Eur Court HR XII 79, pp. 119–121 paras 103–106; ECtHR, 2nd Sec., *Kalender v Turkey,* Judgment, 15 December 2009, para 49.

[233] E contrario, ECtHR, 5th Sec., *Prilutskiy v Ukraine,* Judgment, 26 February 2015, para 37.

[234] See Sect. 4.2.2.2.

[235] ECtHR, *Guerra and Others v Italy,* Judgment, 19 February 1998, Eur Court HR I 7; Starmer (1999), pp. 202–204; Hilson (2009), pp. 355–358; Seminara (2016), pp. 745–746.

[236] ECtHR, *Guerra and Others v Italy,* Judgment, 19 February 1998, Eur Court HR I 7, para 60; Hilson (2009), p. 356.

[237] ECtHR, *Guerra and Others v Italy,* Judgment, 19 February 1998, Eur Court HR I 7.

[238] ECtHR, *Öneryildiz v Turkey,* Judgment, 30 November 2004, Eur Court HR XII 79, p. 115 para 90; ECtHR, *Budayeva and others v Russia,* Judgment, 20 March 2008, Eur Court HR II 267, p. 289 para 132.

[239] ECtHR, *Öneryildiz v Turkey,* Judgment, 30 November 2004, Eur Court HR XII 79, p. 121 para 108.

concerned'.[240] Due to the lack of land planning policies, the Court found the circumstances had required the authorities to inform the inhabitants of the increased risk in advance.[241]

3. Under additional circumstances, positive obligation can amount to a *duty to take preventive operational measures* to protect the interest at risk,[242] which is also known as the 'duty to prevent'.[243] To determine when the positive obligation to take preventive operational measures arises, the Court established a test that became known in the literature as the *Osman Test*.[244] The *Osman* Test has become the Court's 'main tool for dealing with cases involving the duty to prevent'.[245] According to this test, the authorities have violated their positive obligation if the authorities *knew or ought to have known* at the time of the existence of *a real and immediate risk* to a protected interest of an *identified* individual or individuals and if they failed to take *measures within the scope of their powers* which, judged *reasonably*, might have been *expected to avoid* that risk.[246] In this context, 'an immediate risk is one that is present and continuing'.[247] If the abstract legislative and administrative framework will not provide effective protection of a Convention right, measures that are more concrete may be required under these additional circumstances.[248] For instance, since the state had not implemented land planning policies in *Budayeva v Russia*, the Court found that the circumstances had obliged the authorities to arrange emergency evacuations in advance.[249] A prerequisite for this would have been observation posts that would

[240] ECtHR, *Budayeva and others v Russia,* Judgment, 20 March 2008, Eur Court HR II 267, p. 294 para 152.

[241] Ibid.

[242] ECtHR, *Osman v United Kingdom,* Judgment, 28 October 1998, para 115; Grabenwarter and Pabel (2021), § 20 paras 21–22.

[243] Sossai (2018), p. 124; Starmer (1999), pp. 196, 199–202.

[244] The Court famously contoured the so-called 'duty to prevent' in ECtHR, *Osman v United Kingdom,* Judgment, 28 October 1998. In *Osman v United Kingdom,* the applicants' complained that the authorities had failed to appreciate and act on the apparent risk that a seemingly obsessed former teacher represented to the lives and physical integrity of the applicant and his family. The teacher ultimately wounded the applicant and killed his father in a shooting. While the criminal law generally provided for effective deterrence, the question was as to whether the state had been moreover obliged to take preventive *operational measures* to protect the lives of the applicants in light of a series of warning signs.

[245] Ebert and Sijniensky (2015), p. 344.

[246] As established by the Court in ECtHR, *Osman v United Kingdom,* Judgment, 28 October 1998, para 116; see this test also applied in ECtHR, *Akkoç v Turkey,* Judgment, 10 October 2000, Eur Court HR X 389, p. 418 para 78.

[247] High Court of Justice, *W, Re An Application For Judicial Review*, 27 October 2004, NIQB 67, para 17.

[248] ECtHR, *Akkoç v Turkey,* Judgment, 10 October 2000, Eur Court HR X 389, p. 418 para 78; Mowbray (2004), p. 199.

[249] ECtHR, *Budayeva and others v Russia,* Judgment, 20 March 2008, Eur Court HR II 267, p. 294 para 152.

have enabled the specialised surveillance agency to estimate the timing, force and expected duration of the mudslide.[250]

Even if the victim knowingly chooses to break the law despite inherent risks, the state may not remain passive once it becomes aware, provided that the shortcomings pose a *real risk* to the individual's right to life. An example of a situation that requires state action is an individual living in a house that is not in accordance with land planning or construction law and thereby poses a *real risk* to the right to life.[251] If the state's conduct can be construed as encouraging or at least acknowledging the unlawful individual conduct, the responsibility may be attributed to the state and not the victim.[252] This obligation to act applies regardless of whether the threat emanates from an industrial plant[253] or a natural hazard,[254] as the threat reaches the level of a *real risk*.

For instance, the state would also have to carry out evacuations if the persons concerned refuse to evacuate due to the immediacy and seriousness of the risk. Experience shows that time and again some people refuse to leave their homes despite evacuation orders.[255] Some feel the need to protect their homes and possessions against pillages, while others do not take the warning seriously, especially in case of regular evacuation orders.[256] If people reject evacuation efforts, even though a very serious threat to their lives or physical integrity has become imminent, their goal is usually not to expose themselves to the respective harm. On the contrary, the mentioned reasons for refusing evacuation, such as people's 'disaster fatigueless', or their intention to protect their home in the unsubstantiated belief to be able to handle the threat, demonstrate a disjunction between their goals and the means. Such disjunction qualifies as a 'reasoning failure', which has been presented in Chap. 1.[257] As a result, forced evacuations in case of *very serious* and *immediate* threats to lives or physical integrity are justified as a case of reasoning failure, and necessary to protect autonomy. Thus, positive obligations may arise 'even if the person affected robustly disclaims having any subjective fears'.[258] This is the case even if the individual recklessly exposes his or her life to the risk, despite having the necessary information and means to

---

250 Ibid, p. 295 para 154.

251 ECtHR, *Öneryildiz v Turkey,* Judgment, 30 November 2004, Eur Court HR XII 79, p. 113 para 80.

252 Ibid, pp. 119–121 paras 104–106; ECtHR, 2nd Sec., *Özel and Others v Turkey,* Judgment, 17 November 2015, paras 174–176.

253 ECtHR, *Öneryildiz v Turkey,* Judgment, 30 November 2004, Eur Court HR XII 79, p. 113 para 80.

254 ECtHR, 2nd Sec., *Özel and Others v Turkey,* Judgment, 17 November 2015, paras 174–176.

255 Gold et al. (2005).

256 Dow and Cutter (1998).

257 See Sect. 1.7.1.2.

258 House of Lords, *Re Officer L,* 31 July 2007, UKHL 36, para 20, cited in ECtHR, 4th Sec., *Van Colle v United Kingdom,* Judgment, 13 November 2012, para 61.

protect oneself.[259] This finding also reverberates in international soft law instrument, such as the 'Operational Guidelines on Protecting Persons in Natural Disasters' by the Inter-Agency Standing Committee.[260] However, from a proportionality perspective, the interference with individual's autonomy as guaranteed by rights, such as Article 8(1) and Article 2 of Protocol No 4 of the ECHR, must end once the interference no longer pursues this legitimate aim.[261] If the interference extends for longer periods, it may become disproportionate and amount to a violation as a result.[262]

In addition to the factors relating to the threat, there are also three factors related to the victims that affect the standard of due diligence on the part of the state to provide *effective* protection. The first factor refers to the theoretical options to reduce one's own vulnerability that may be practically impaired due to the individual's personal circumstances in terms of available means.[263] In such cases, the state may have to allocate resources to individuals if necessary to prevent *real risks* to their rights.[264] Positive obligations can therefore also be of an economic and social character, even if the ECHR mainly enshrines civil and political rights.[265] For instance, *Fadeyeva v Russia*[266] concerned the impact of air pollution from a steel plant on the applicant, who lived in specially designed buffer zone.[267] Despite the theoretical possibility to move away, the Court acknowledged how it would have been 'very difficult' for the applicant to change her personal situation.[268] *Inter alia*, the Court took note of the applicant's financial constraints that made moving away 'almost unfeasible'.[269] The Court found a failure on the part of the state to offer the applicant an effective solution to resettle.[270] If the individual cannot afford the theoretically available means of protection, the rise of such a *duty to take preventive measures* is also conceivable for the protection of the right to life in the event of *real risks* from natural hazards. However, to respect personal autonomy and the interests of the community as a whole, the prerequisite for such a *duty to take preventive measures* would be that no other risk reduction, such as timely evacuation, is possible other than resettling.

---

[259] ECtHR, *Öneryildiz v Turkey,* Judgment, 30 November 2004, Eur Court HR XII 79, p. 121 para 108.

[260] Inter-Agency Standing Committee (2008), Guideline A.1.8.

[261] See generally on the proportionality of restrictions of an individual's freedom of movement, ECtHR, 5th Sec., *Gochev v Bulgaria,* Judgment, 26 November 2009, paras 49–50.

[262] See generally ibid, para 49.

[263] ECtHR, *Fadeyeva v Russia,* Judgment, 9 June 2005, Eur Court HR IV 255.

[264] ECtHR, *Airey v Ireland,* Judgment, 9 October 1979, Eur Court HR (ser A) 32; Dröge (2003), p. 388.

[265] Dröge (2008), para 7.

[266] ECtHR, *Fadeyeva v Russia,* Judgment, 9 June 2005, Eur Court HR IV 255.

[267] Ibid, p. 263 para 11.

[268] Ibid, p. 289 para 121.

[269] Ibid.

[270] Ibid, pp. 288–290 paras 116–123, 133.

A second factor that can give rise to positive obligations relates to the mental capacity of the victim. The more the individual's autonomy is inherently diminished due to immaturity, mental disability, or mental illness, the less voluntary the decision-making is.[271] Consequently, if potential victims belong to these groups, it may be necessary to implement legal or physical obstacles to prevent them from the consequences of their diminished capacity for autonomous decision-making.[272] For instance, the Court noted that the right to life positively obliges states to build fencing or barbed wire to prevent children from entering an active military firing zone on the basis that children are more vulnerable than adults.[273] Similarly, the state's protective framework would have to ensure that a mentally ill person's life-ending decision corresponds in fact with his or her free will to fulfil the state's obligation under the right to life. For instance, *Haas v Switzerland* concerned a man who had been suffering from a severe bipolar affective disorder for decades and who requested access to assisted suicide without the requirement of obtaining a medical prescription.[274] In contrast to the applicant's request, the Court found that Switzerland's requirement of a medical prescription based on a full psychiatric assessment was a suitable means to fulfil its obligation under the right to life towards the applicant.[275] Considering that the objective circumstances entail the strongest presumption of nonvoluntariness, that is, a *certainly and immediately* fatal threat, in conjunction with facts indicating a diminished capacity of voluntary decision-making, effective protection requires the highest possible diligence in regulating the risk. As such, the case law demonstrates that the required legislative and administrative framework needs to protect respective persons from the foreseeable consequences of their inherently diminished capacity for autonomous decision-making. This requirement also affects the state's obligation in the context of natural hazards. For example, when drawing up evacuation plans, special consideration would have to be given to people with such diminished capacity within the population.

Third, beyond cases of inherently diminished capacity for autonomous decision making, the victim's lack of information or mistaken beliefs also tend 'to diminish or defeat voluntariness'.[276] As such, the state's due diligence obligation may require more efforts, the less familiar the possibly exposed people are with the risk. For instance, the Court emphasised with respect to a construction site that particular safety measures are required if the site is located in a residential area.[277] The safety measures would have to take account of the fact that the general public is less

[271] Dröge (2003), pp. 322–324; see generally Le Grand and New (2015), pp. 106, 116–117.

[272] See, e.g., ECtHR, 2nd Sec., *Oruk c Turquie,* Judgment, 4 February 2014, para 64; ECtHR, *Cevrioğlu v Turkey,* Judgment, 4 October 2016, para 67.

[273] ECtHR, 2nd Sec., *Oruk c Turquie,* Judgment, 4 February 2014, paras 59, 62, 64.

[274] ECtHR, *Haas v Switzerland,* Judgment, 20 January 2011, Eur Court HR I 95, pp. 101–102 paras 6–7.

[275] Ibid, pp. 118–119 para 58.

[276] Feinberg (1989), p. 152; see further Le Grand and New (2015), pp. 112–113.

[277] ECtHR, *Cevrioğlu v Turkey,* Judgment, 4 October 2016, paras 66–67.

familiar with the risks, than professional construction workers.[278] To the extent that a positive obligation has arisen, this also has implications for the state response to natural hazards. The degree of prior experience of the population with the expected natural hazards would influence the content of the positive obligation, particularly in terms of providing information.

On the flip side, an individual's specialised knowledge may reduce the scope of the state's obligation to protect, as the case of *Vladimirov v Bulgaria*[279] demonstrates. In *Vladimirov v Bulgaria*, the applicant bought and built on a plot of land located in an area known to be affected by landslides.[280] As a result of the later continuation of the landslide activity, the structure of the applicant's building was gravely damaged.[281] He unsuccessfully sought compensation from the state at the domestic level for failing to take measures to mitigate landslide activity and its destructive consequences.[282]

The application also failed before the European Court of Human Rights, which found no link between the damage and the state's failure to take measures that the applicant may have legitimately expected.[283] Both the Court and the domestic court found that the landslide could have occurred regardless of whether the authorities did nothing or took effective measures to counteract the landslide.[284] The only way for the state to reduce the damage to the applicant would have been for the state not to issue a building permit or to require the applicant to take out risk mitigation measures such as insurance. However, such measures could not have been legitimately expected from the state according to the Court. Instead, the reduction or avoidance of the damage had been the responsibility of the applicant.[285] The applicant had bought the land and initiated the building process 'in the full knowledge of the landslide activity in the surrounding area and the potential danger that this represented'.[286] Moreover, in view of the commercial context of the construction project, the Court held 'that it is the role of a competent entrepreneur to ensure that he or she is in possession of all relevant information before investing or conducting transactions, as well as to ensure that such an investment is fit for purpose'.[287] The Court further noted that the applicant could have taken out building insurance to reduce damages, but had not.[288] Thus, the combination of factual possibility and the individual's

[278] Ibid, para 67.

[279] ECtHR, *Vladimirov v Bulgaria,* Decision, 25 September 2018.

[280] Ibid, paras 4, 16–17.

[281] Ibid, para 17.

[282] Ibid, paras 18–20.

[283] Ibid, paras 34, 41.

[284] Ibid, para 41.

[285] Ibid, para 37.

[286] Ibid.

[287] Ibid.

[288] Ibid, paras 17, 37.

expertise, which particularly empowered him to make decisions in pursuit of his goals, relieved the state of an obligation to intervene in order to protect A1-P1.

3.2.3.3 The Consequent Impact of Biases and Heuristics on the Scope of Obligation

Building on the last presented factor of the victim's lack of information or mistaken beliefs that also tend 'to diminish or defeat voluntariness', known biases or heuristics may also affect the scope of obligations, primarily related to the right to life. For instance, risk management still often operates on 'poorly evidenced assumptions about how humans respond both to risk and to hazard events once they occur'.[289] Regularly, the asymmetry between the anticipated rational response of people and reality has disastrous consequences on people's chances of survival.[290] As such, scholars see the potential to increase effectiveness if risk management took greater account of behavioural studies.[291] If the state is aware of such culturally induced misperceptions of *real risks*, which may lead to presumably unintended significant consequences for the protected interest, this knowledge may oblige the state to adjust the protective measures accordingly. On the one hand, knowledge of the respective development of a widespread social phenomenon may give rise to the duty to establish a *protective domestic legislative and administrative framework*. On the other hand, knowledge of a specific case may give rise to the *duty to take preventive operational measures*.

However, before natural hazard risk reaches this level of certainty, it is doubtful that biases and heuristics already provide a sufficient basis for extending positive obligations to preventive and mitigative risk reduction in order to protect individuals' rights. Many preventive and mitigating measures interfere with the autonomy of the individual, as Chap. 4 explores in detail.[292] A divergence between the person's intended goal and the employed means to achieve this goal does not suffice to justify paternalistic interferences.[293] Even then, the respective threat to an individual's interests must have reached a minimum level of intensity. The more intense the intervention, the more certain and dangerous the threat to the autonomy of the individual must be to require said intervention. With respect to the less intrusive measures, other normative factors prevent the rise of a state's positive obligation to reduce the influence of biases and heuristics on people's decision-making in the context of natural hazards. Such measures could be, for example, funded structural adjustments, which could provide additional protection against the consequences of distorted risk perception, especially with regard to property. However, such an

---

[289] Crosweller and Wilmshurst (2013), p. 561.

[290] Ibid; Buckle (2012), pp. 493–494.

[291] Crosweller and Wilmshurst (2013), pp. 560–561; Glöckner (2016), p. 21.

[292] See Sects. 4.1.4 and 4.2.

[293] See Sect. 4.2.2.1.

imposition under positive obligations would not be compatible with protecting the rights of the collective as a whole. The investment required of the society as a whole under positive obligations must not only be proportionate to the degree of the individual's control over his or her own sphere. The fair balance must also take account of the risk's foreseeability and susceptibility to mitigation, as the following subsection shows in detail. The inherent difficulties in predicting natural hazards in specific locations usually reduce the demands on the state to invest resources in terms of funded structural adjustments.

3.2.4 *The Legal Relevance of the Ability to Reduce the Impact of a Natural Hazard*

Even if the individual's free choice is diminished, the rise and scope of a positive obligation further depends on what the state can *factually* and *reasonably* do to avert a risk to one's right under the ECHR. Accordingly, even if a *real risk* materialises, a state is not automatically responsible.[294] For instance, as death inevitably follows on from birth, the mere ending of life does not engage a state's responsibility.[295] Instead, state responsibility depends on whether the *foreseeability* of the threat and its *susceptibility to mitigation* would have reasonably allowed for protective measures.

In the following subsections, the impact of these limiting factors on the state's due diligence is examined in the context of natural hazards. As part of the contextual examination, this subsection also addresses the criticism voiced by commentators of the respective case law. Kristian Cedervall Lauta and Jens Elo Rytter have argued for a broader positive obligation than in the developed general principles based on their interpretation of the foreseeability and susceptibility to mitigation of natural hazards.[296] Drawing on the intellectual breakthroughs in the understanding of disasters in recent decades,[297] they deny inherent differences between risks from natural and human made hazards. This subsection refutes their argument by demonstrating the legally relevant differences between natural and human made hazards in terms of foreseeability and susceptibility to mitigation. In doing so, the examination draws upon the scientific understanding of risk from natural hazards developed in Chap. 2.[298] An in-depth discussion of the voiced criticisms serves to achieve the aim of this chapter. By demonstrating that the ECHR is not designed to demand comprehensive disaster risk reduction ('DRR'), the discussion underlines the need for complementing member states' risk management approach from the bottom up. In addition, the

[294] McBride (1999b), HR44; Xenos (2012), pp. 74–75.

[295] McBride (1999b), HR44.

[296] Lauta and Rytter (2016), pp. 130–131.

[297] See Sect. 2.2.3.

[298] See Sect. 2.3.

detailed discussion of the criticism expressed contributes to improving commentators' understanding of this interdisciplinary issue. To that aim, the following subsection begins by introducing foreseeability and the susceptibility to mitigation as limiting factors for the state's due diligence in relation to common natural hazards.

3.2.4.1 The Role of Foreseeability and Susceptibility to Mitigation

The foreseeability of the risk and its susceptibility to mitigation are important factors in determining the proportional scope of a positive obligation. First of all, it is a general principle in international law, in virtually all domestic law systems and all areas of law,[299] that responsibility only arises for causal conduct that is not 'involuntary or at least involves no element of free choice'.[300] Accordingly, the principle of '*ad impossibilia nemo tenetur*'[301] entails that the *impossible* cannot be subject to obligation, nor responsibility.[302] In the broad sense, impossibility refers to an event that is irresistible or unforeseen.[303] However, the state is not automatically responsible even if a risk is known as a general danger and its effect to a specific area could have been avoided with the greatest possible effort. Instead, the state's liability is mainly restricted by the contextual interpretation of the '*reasonably* expected conduct' of the state.[304] As such,

> [i]n determining whether or not a positive obligation exists, regard must be had to the fair balance that has to be struck between the general interest of the community and the interests of the individual, the search for which is inherent throughout the Convention.[305]

To avoid imposing an impossible or disproportionate burden on the state, one precondition for the *rise* of a positive obligation is that the state authorities must have known or ought to have known of the legally relevant risk.[306] Moreover, the scope of obligation depends 'on reasonableness, which brings in consideration of the circumstances of the case, the ease or difficulty of taking precautions and the resources

[299] International Law Commission (1980), p. 75 paras 34–35, for an overview of respective state practice, see pp. 77–98; Hentrei and Soley (2011), para 1; Dellinger (2017), pp. 458–461; Paddeu (2012), pp. 384–385; see Palmisano (2007), para 19.

[300] International Law Commission (2001), Commentary on DA 23 para 1.

[301] 'Nobody is held to the impossible', see Fellmeth and Horwitz (2021), 'Ad impossibilia nemo tenetur', p. 19.

[302] International Law Commission (2001), Commentary on DA 23 para 1; Paddeu (2012), p. 466; Hentrei and Soley (2011), para 12; Dellinger (2017), p. 483; Paddeu (2017), p. 125.

[303] International Law Commission (1980), p. 69 para 13; see Palmisano (2007), para 19; Paddeu (2012); International Law Commission (2001), Commentary on DA 23.

[304] Lavrysen (2018), paras 716–717; Eissen (1993), p. 137.

[305] See, e.g., ECtHR, *Rees v United Kingdom,* Judgment, 17 October 1986, Eur Court HR (ser A) 106, para 37.

[306] Lavrysen (2018), pp. 712–713.

available'.[307] In this regard, the degree of knowledge affects the scope of obligation.[308] As such, the Court has held that 'the more predictable a hazard, the greater the obligation to protect against it'.[309] On the flip side, since the interpretation of 'reasonableness' may not impose an unbearable or excessive burden on the authorities,[310] the interpretation needs to take account of the unpredictability of situations and the operational choices that the state needs to make in terms of priorities and resources.[311]

Based on the effect of the degree of its foreseeability and its susceptibility to mitigation on the scope of obligation,[312] the presented general principles developed by the Court can only be applied to risks that share comparable characteristics in terms of foreseeability and susceptibility to mitigation. This is the reason why the Court has developed a different set of general principles for human made hazards. In addition to natural hazards, the Court has also developed general principles relating to 'dangerous activities' as a possible origin of a disaster.[313] A comparison of the respective general principles reveals that the context affects the rise and scope of preventive state obligations, as well as the intensity of their review.

While this book attributes the differences between the general principles relating to natural and human made hazards to the inherent differences in foreseeability and susceptibility to mitigation, the Court has admittedly not explained the different treatments. In the absence of explanations from the Court, Lauta and Rytter have offered other explanations for these differences and, building on them, have criticised that more stringent requirements only apply to the conduct of states in cases of dangerous industrial activities.[314] According to them, the Court's 'more lenient approach to the prevention of natural disasters [sic] as compared to industrial disasters' needs reconsideration.[315] To them, the only valid reason for a differentiation could be a factual difference in the ability to regulate them. In this regard, they cannot find a factual difference justifying the stricter scrutiny of industrial activities

---

[307] House of Lords, *Re Officer L,* 31 July 2007, UKHL 36, para 21, cited in ECtHR, 4th Sec., *Van Colle v United Kingdom,* Judgment, 13 November 2012, para 61.

[308] Lavrysen (2018), p. 713.

[309] ECtHR, *Finogenov and Others v Russia,* Judgment, 20 December 2011, Eur Court HR VI 365, p. 412 para 243.

[310] See, e.g., ECtHR, *Rees v United Kingdom,* Judgment, 17 October 1986, Eur Court HR (ser A) 106, para 37.

[311] ECtHR, 3rd Sec., *Molie v Romania,* Decision, 1 September 2009, para 41.

[312] Lavrysen (2018), p. 713.

[313] ECtHR, *Budayeva and others v Russia,* Judgment, 20 March 2008, Eur Court HR II 267, p. 290 para 137; ECtHR, 1st Sec., *Kolyadenko and Others v Russia,* Judgment, 28 February 2012, para 161; ECtHR, 2nd Sec., *Özel and Others v Turkey,* Judgment, 17 November 2015, para 171; Bartolini (2018), p. 20; Sommario and Venier (2018), p. 42; Lauta and Rytter (2016), p. 112; International Law Commission (2013), para 51.

[314] Lauta and Rytter (2016), p. 119.

[315] Ibid, p. 130.

over natural hazards.[316] While they concede the inability to regulate natural hazards per se,[317] they argue that 'everything rendering nature a threat to human life can' be regulated.[318] For example, they refer to zoning regulations and certain building codes that could entirely deter flood risks. Pointing to the lack of a factual difference in the ability to protect people's interests from natural or human made hazards, they find the Court's differentiation in relation to the scope of state obligations 'implausible'.[319] Their conclusion is that stricter positive obligation could apply to natural hazards.[320]

To rebut Lauta and Rytter's arguments, the remainder of this subsection demonstrates the differences between natural hazards and industrial activities in terms of foreseeability and susceptibility to mitigation, as well as the implications for the due diligence standard. Considering that disaster always results from an array of causal factors, it is further necessary to discuss the rules for determining whether natural or human made factors constitute the legally relevant 'origin of harm'.

3.2.4.2 The Different Standards of Protection Depending on the Disaster's 'Origin'

To explain the reasons for the less strict due diligence of the state towards natural hazards compared to industrial activities, it is appropriate to start by setting out the object of criticism, that is, the differences in the general principles. In relation to the positive obligation to protect the right to life, the origin of the disaster firstly affects the rise of obligation. As noted above, the Court outlined the applicability of positive obligation relating to natural hazards by qualifying the required threat to the right to life.[321] Positive obligations would arise if the circumstances of the case 'point to the *imminence of a natural hazard* that had been *clearly identifiable*'.[322] This would apply in particular to cases of 'a *recurring calamity* affecting a *distinct area* developed for human habitation or use'.[323] In contrast, according to the Court,

---

[316] Ibid, p. 122.

[317] Ibid.

[318] Ibid.

[319] Ibid, pp. 123, 130.

[320] Ibid, pp. 119–131, see especially pp. 130–131.

[321] ECtHR, 2nd Sec., *Özel and Others v Turkey,* Judgment, 17 November 2015, para 170; Xenos (2007), pp. 236–238.

[322] ECtHR, *Budayeva and others v Russia,* Judgment, 20 March 2008, Eur Court HR II 267, p. 290 para 137; ECtHR, 2nd Sec., *Özel and Others v Turkey,* Judgment, 17 November 2015, para 171 (emphasis added).

[323] ECtHR, *Budayeva and others v Russia,* Judgment, 20 March 2008, Eur Court HR II 267, p. 290 para 137; ECtHR, 2nd Sec., *Özel and Others v Turkey,* Judgment, 17 November 2015, para 171 (emphasis added).

dangerous industrial activities meet this requirement *a fortiori*, as they are dangerous by their very nature to a specific area.[324]

Secondly, the two contexts entail different due diligence standards.[325] As noted above, the Court has only vaguely contoured the due diligence relating to natural hazards. The due diligence would include 'appropriate spatial planning and controlled urban development'.[326] Yet, the Court omitted to qualify the term 'appropriate' and 'controlled'. As such, the obligation remains more open to interpretation, and consequently offers less judicial protection. In contrast, the Court established specified and comprehensive requirements to the regulatory measures to ensure effective protection in the context of dangerous activities. As such, the Court stipulated in *Öneryildiz v Turkey* that the regulatory measures must be designed for the 'special features of the activity in question, particularly with regard to the level of potential risk to human lives'.[327] More specifically, they must govern 'the licencing, setting up, operation, security and supervision of the activity and must make it compulsory for all those concerned to take practical measures to ensure the effective protection of citizens whose lives might be endangered by the inherent risks'.[328] Lastly, it was found that the regulations must contain 'appropriate procedures, taking into account the technical aspects of the activity in question, for identifying shortcomings in the processes concerned and any errors committed by those responsible at different levels'.[329] In comparison with the vague remarks on the due diligence relating to natural hazards, the Court gave specific indications on measures that meet the standard of effective protection against industrial activities. Moreover, as for industrial activities, the Court notably required a secondary procedure to supervise possible shortcoming or human error, which would not be required in the context of protection against natural hazards.

Thirdly, the differentiation between industrial activities and natural hazards affects the standard of proportionality. For industrial activities, the Court reiterated the well-established standard to not impose an 'impossible or disproportionate burden' with view to the authorities' priorities and resources.[330] By contrast, in cases relating to natural hazards, the Court afforded this consideration 'even greater

[324] ECtHR, 1st Sec., *Kolyadenko and Others v Russia,* Judgment, 28 February 2012, para 158; ECtHR, *Öneryildiz v Turkey,* Judgment, 30 November 2004, Eur Court HR XII 79, p. 110 para 71; ECtHR, *Budayeva and others v Russia,* Judgment, 20 March 2008, Eur Court HR II 267, p. 289 para 130.

[325] Bartolini (2018), p. 20; Sommario and Venier (2018), pp. 42–43.

[326] ECtHR, 2nd Sec., *Özel and Others v Turkey,* Judgment, 17 November 2015, para 174; ECtHR, *Budayeva and others v Russia,* Judgment, 20 March 2008, Eur Court HR II 267, p. 289 para 133.

[327] ECtHR, *Öneryildiz v Turkey,* Judgment, 30 November 2004, Eur Court HR XII 79, p. 115 para 90.

[328] Ibid; ECtHR, *Budayeva and others v Russia,* Judgment, 20 March 2008, Eur Court HR II 267, p. 289 para 132.

[329] ECtHR, *Öneryildiz v Turkey,* Judgment, 30 November 2004, Eur Court HR XII 79, p. 115 para 90.

[330] See, e.g., ECtHR, *Osman v United Kingdom,* Judgment, 28 October 1998, para 116.

weight'. The Court stated the reason that these events are as such beyond human control, which distinguishes them from the dangerous activities of a human made nature.[331]

Also in the context of A1-P1, the Court found clear language to describe the different consequences. It held that 'natural disasters [sic], which are as such beyond human control, do not call for the same extent of State involvement as dangerous activities of a man-made nature'.[332] The obligation to protect would consequently be larger for the latter.

3.2.4.3 The Reasoning for the Differing Standards of Protection

In contrast to this book, Lauta and Rytter argue that the Court could, and should, offer a stricter standard of legal protection in cases where natural hazards threaten rights protected under the ECHR. Their argument is partly based on the assertion that there are no factual differences that justify a stricter standard of industrial activities over natural hazards.

It is true that due to intellectual breakthroughs in disaster studies, it is often possible to reduce the impact of natural hazards, even though the natural hazard itself may be unavoidable.[333] However, Lauta and Rytter's argument overlooks the fact that the scope of positive obligation does not depend solely on the *de facto* possibility of protection, but also on the degree of foreseeability and susceptibility to mitigation.[334] As such, the understanding that not all risks are equal is pivotal.[335] As Chap. 2 has demonstrated, risks are neither equally foreseeable nor susceptible to mitigation.[336] In fact, the obstacles to the efficiency of risk reduction measures are the degree of uncertainties relating to the threat, the risk-absorbing system, as well as the side-effects of risk reducing measures. In this respect, it should be noted that some human made hazards, particularly those emanating from installations for instance, are inherently more predictable and more easily susceptible to effective mitigation than natural hazards. This is due to the long-term certainties regarding the range of possible threats and the possibly affected area. Such long-term certainty increases the efficiency and effectiveness of risk reduction. The fact that a hazard is human made provides the opportunity to mitigate the risk agent itself, which is not possible with natural hazards because they are beyond control. Not only can the resilience of the risk absorption system be increased, but the

[331] ECtHR, *Budayeva and others v Russia,* Judgment, 20 March 2008, Eur Court HR II 267, p. 290 para 135.

[332] Ibid, p. 299 paras 173–175; ECtHR, 4th Sec., *Hadzhiyska v Bulgaria,* Decision, 15 May 2012, para 15.

[333] See Sect. 2.2.3.

[334] Balcerzak (2020), p. 170.

[335] Renn et al. (2011), p. 234.

[336] See Sects. 2.3 and 2.4.

hazard-causing activity can also be stopped or changed to reduce the risk.[337] Consequently, the Court has asserted in the context of 'natural disaster' [sic] that the obligation to prevent could only involve measures designed to reduce these events' *impact* to a minimum.[338] *E contrario*, the Court noted that the means to reduce the hazard risk itself do not exist. As such, the hazard itself is 'beyond control'. This shows that natural hazards and human made hazards have inherently different difficulties in determining the probability of a risk for specific locations. Given the knowledge of the infinite number of uncertain risks to each member of society, and the need to distribute limited collective resources fairly, it makes sense to focus collective resources primarily on sufficiently specifiable risks. Moreover, expectations on investments of collective resources reasonably increases as the risk becomes more specific. Consequently, the different general principles established by the Court in the context of disasters do not follow from the culturally traditional distinction between disasters triggered by natural and human made hazards, as Lauta and Rytter suggest. Instead, the inherent differences in the foreseeability of the threat in a specific location and its susceptibility to mitigation are the reason for the differences in the scope of positive obligations.[339]

Beyond the disaster context, this reasoning permeates the entire jurisprudence on positive obligations,[340] as a juxtaposition of involving threats to Article 2 of the ECHR controlled by private parties and the state respectively can show. As such, the basic positive obligation to create a domestic legislative and administrative framework to provide protection under Article 2(1) 1 of the ECHR becomes a 'duty to take operational measures to prevent that risk from materialising' given sufficiently specific knowledge of a relevant threat.[341] The required specificity of the threat to a right can either be supplied by identifying the potential targets[342] or by specifying the risk itself.[343] With respect to the latter, the obligation can also arise when the victims are unidentifiable, but the risk can be identified and localised.[344] In these circumstances, the obligation amounts to a 'general obligation to protect society'.[345] The latter may especially apply to situations involving natural hazards or

[337] See Sect. 2.3.3.

[338] ECtHR, 2nd Sec., *Özel and Others v Turkey,* Judgment, 17 November 2015, para 173.

[339] Balcerzak (2020), p. 170.

[340] Ebert and Sijniensky (2015), pp. 356–357.

[341] ECtHR, *Osman v United Kingdom,* Judgment, 28 October 1998, para 116.

[342] ECtHR, *Mastromatteo v Italy,* Judgment, 24 October 2002, Eur Court HR VIII 151, p. 195 para 69.

[343] McBride (1999b), HR47.

[344] Grabenwarter and Pabel (2021), § 20 para 22, referring to ECtHR, *Maiorano et autres c Italie,* Arrêt, 15 décembre 2009, para 107; Seminara (2016), pp. 737–738, referring to ECtHR, 3rd Sec., *Georgel and Georgeta Stoicescu v Romania,* Judgment, 26 July 2011, para 59.

[345] Grabenwarter and Pabel (2021), § 20 para 22, referring to ECtHR, *Maiorano et autres c Italie,* Arrêt, 15 décembre 2009, para 107; Seminara (2016), pp. 737–738, referring to ECtHR, 3rd Sec., *Georgel and Georgeta Stoicescu v Romania,* Judgment, 26 July 2011, para 59.

environmental pollution.[346] Yet, if the state is in control of the rise of a risk, then the due diligence is stricter.[347] Consequently, when assessing the necessity of the use of force, the Court has considered the circumstances surrounding the administration of force with '*most careful scrutiny*'.[348] With respect to the life of bystanders of policing operations, the Court established the strictest standard for expected conduct. It held that the state has to 'take *all feasible precautions* in the choice of means and methods of a security operation … with a view to *avoiding* and, in any event, to minimising, incidental loss of civilian life'.[349] In its relationship to the targeted individual, the Court has further held that the state has the positive obligation to regulate and organise operations 'in such a way as to minimise to *the greatest extent possible* any risk'[350] to their lives. As such, the established standard of minimising any risk to *the greatest extent possible* under Article 2(2) of the ECHR still establishes a stricter standard than in relation to risks controlled by private third-parties.[351] Consequently, the examination of risks controlled by private parties and the state respectively not only points to differences in their foreseeability and susceptibility to mitigation depending the origin of risk. The juxtaposition of the respective case law also shows how these differences correspond to the scope of due diligence.

Thus, contrary to Lauta and Rytter's assertion, this subsection demonstrated that the ability to protect people's interests varies depending on the origin of the harm. Although the assessment depends on the circumstances of the case, risks from industrial installations are inherently more specific than natural hazards in terms of the range of possible threats and the area possibly affected. The resulting varying difficulty in taking precautions justifies a different scope of due diligence as compared to natural hazards.

3.2.4.4 Case Law Examples in the Context of Natural Hazards

With these findings in mind, it is useful to consider some examples from the case law to demonstrate the interpretation of foreseeability and susceptibility to mitigation in the context of different natural hazards. An example of a case where a positive obligation was excluded for lack of foreseeability and susceptibility to mitigations is *Hadzhiyska v Bulgaria*.[352] *In casu*, the applicant's house was damaged

---

346 McBride (1999b), HR47.

347 ECtHR, 3rd Sec., *Nehyet Günay et autres c Turquie,* Arrêt, 21 octobre 2008, para 79; Ebert and Sijniensky (2015), pp. 356–357.

348 ECtHR, *Ergi v Turkey,* Judgment, 28 July 1998, para 79 (emphasis added), referring to ECtHR, *McCann and Others v United Kingdom,* Judgment, 27 September 1995, Eur Court HR (ser A) 324, paras 148–150.

349 ECtHR, *Ergi v Turkey,* Judgment, 28 July 1998, para 79 (emphasis added).

350 ECtHR, *Makaratzis v Greece,* Judgment, 20 December 2004, Eur Court HR XI 195, pp. 228–229 para 60 (emphasis added).

351 ECtHR, 3rd Sec., *Nehyet Günay et autres c Turquie,* Arrêt, 21 octobre 2008, para 79.

352 ECtHR, 4th Sec., *Hadzhiyska v Bulgaria,* Decision, 15 May 2012.

by a flooding following heavy rain.[353] The applicant alleged that the relevant authorities had violated her right to property by failing to clean the riverbed, which had impeded the flow of water and led to flooding.[354] She further claimed that no dams or other protective structures had been put in place to protect her village from flooding and that no monitoring or warning systems had been implemented.[355] Yet, the Court rejected a violation of the right to property.[356] In the Court's rejection of the application, the Court noted that the applicant had neither been able to establish how the consequences of the rainfall could have been foreseen in the specific area or prevented.[357] In fact, it remained unclear whether the measures requested by the applicant could have prevented or mitigated the damage to her house. Consequently, there was no causal relationship between the damage to the applicant's house and the state's conduct.[358] So, although property was destroyed, the state had not violated its due diligence.

In contrast, *Budayeva v Turkey* is an example of a case in which the risk was sufficiently foreseeable and susceptible to mitigation.[359] In 2000, a series of mudslides swept through the town of Tyrnauz, resulting in several casualties and damaged houses. Records, dating back to 1937, show that the area was regularly hit by mudslides.[360] Due to this fact, the inhabitants and authorities were generally aware of the local hazard and were used to its occurrence during certain seasons.[361] A mud retention dam and a mud retention collector protected the town for 35 years, until the dam was seriously damaged by heavy mudslides in 1999.[362] The dam was not repaired despite several warnings by the state agency responsible for monitoring weather hazards in the relevant area and the Head of the District Administration.[363] Over the course of almost 1 year, these warnings repeatedly emphasised the *imminent risk* of large-scale mudslide and the necessary measures to avoid said risk. These measures included restoration work to the dam as well as observation posts to monitor and issue an emergency warning if necessary.[364] Yet, the authorities did not implement any of these proposed measures.[365]

The Court first noted that the authorities knew of the probability of hazards. Mudslides regularly occurred in this area, and the existence of the defence

[353] Ibid, para 4.

[354] Ibid, para 5.

[355] Ibid.

[356] Ibid, paras 16–17.

[357] Ibid, para 16.

[358] Ibid.

[359] ECtHR, *Budayeva and others v Russia,* Judgment, 20 March 2008, Eur Court HR II 267.

[360] Ibid, pp. 276–277 para 13.

[361] Ibid, p. 277 paras 15, 18.

[362] Ibid, p. 277 para 16.

[363] Ibid, pp. 277–278 paras 19–25.

[364] Ibid.

[365] Ibid, p. 278 para 25.

mechanisms indicates a general awareness of the specific risk.[366] When assessing whether the authorities also had prior knowledge of the potentially devastating consequences, the Court referred to the repeated warnings over the course of almost 1 year. These warnings highlight the increased risks for the people and the indispensable need to set up observation posts for the purpose of providing an emergency warning if necessary.[367] The Court thus concluded that the authorities 'at various levels were aware that any mudslide, regardless of its scale, was capable of causing devastating consequences'.[368] Further, the available information left no doubt about the scope and timing of the necessary work on the defence infrastructure to protect lives.[369] In assessing the level of difficulty of mitigation, the Court noted that the state had ultimately allocated funds for the reconstruction of the defence mechanism after the disaster.[370] Consequently, the burden of repairing the defence system necessary to protect lives would not have been 'impossible or disproportionate'.[371]

The presented cases highlight how Lauta and Rytter's argument that 'everything rendering nature a threat to human life can' be regulated ignores the obstacles that reality poses to this undertaking. Instead, the foreseeability of a risk and the ease or difficulty of reducing it differ from case to case, and not only in the context of natural hazards. To not impose an 'impossible or disproportionate burden' on the state, the scope of due diligence depends on striking a fair balance between individual and community interests, informed by the foreseeability and susceptibility of the threat. As a result of the inherent uncertainties of most natural hazards, the goals of positive obligations relating to natural hazards are to effectively anticipate and facilitate the protection of rights from imminent or current disasters. Due to the nature of natural hazards, some risks only become *certain* once they are imminent. In particular, the time, location and extent of future earthquakes and floods can only be specified with sufficient certainty in the short term.[372] An extension of the scope of positive obligations through scientific progress could, according to their current legal interpretation, only be brought about by better long-term predictions of natural hazards for certain regions, beyond regularly occurring natural hazards. In this respect, however, Chap. 2 has already explained why progress in the accuracy of long-term advance warnings in relation to common meteorological or geophysical natural hazards is hardly expected.[373]

---

[366] Ibid, p. 293 para 147.

[367] Ibid, pp. 293–294 para 148.

[368] Ibid, p. 294 para 149.

[369] Ibid.

[370] Ibid, p. 286 para 118.

[371] Ibid, pp. 294–295 paras 149, 157.

[372] See Sects. 2.3.2.1 and 2.3.2.2.

[373] See Sect. 2.3.2.3.

3.2.5 *The Determination of the 'Origin of the Threat' Under the ECHR*

So far, this section has demonstrated that positive obligations of member states in relation to natural hazards particularly revolve around response-oriented measures, even in the light of evidence on people's risk perceptions. To show this, the section has examined how the obligation of '*effective protection*' is a function of the level of individual autonomy loss on the one hand, balanced fairly with the capacity and needs of the community as a whole on the other hand.[374] As a result of these normative requirements, positive obligations only require necessary measures that can reasonably be expected to protect a right under the ECHR from a *real risk*. It follows that the characteristics and circumstances of the risk decisively affect the scope of due diligence, that is, its foreseeability and the extent to which the victim and the state can reduce it. In case of natural hazards, the inherent uncertainty in determining the timing, location and magnitude of future natural hazards result in a less strict due diligence compared to industrial activities. However, when assessing a case, it usually remains a challenge to identify the legally relevant risk among a multitude of causal factors involved. Especially in the disaster context, this challenge of determining the origin of a threat has received much attention in IDL and disaster studies. As discussed in Chap. 1,[375] even when natural hazards are involved, a disaster only occurs through the contribution of human behaviour.[376]

Against this background, and in conjunction with the Court's omission to clarify the criteria for determining the 'origin of the threat', the commentators Lauta and Rytter have criticised the Court for arbitrarily determining the 'origin of the threat' relevant for the strictness of positive obligations.[377] Lauta and Rytter have doubted the practical feasibility of delineating the 'origin of the threat'.[378] They critically claim in their analysis of the Court's case law that disaster studies have overturned 'a naïve essentialist understanding of what the source of a disaster fundamentally *is*'.[379] They point to the fact that disaster studies identify the origin for the occurrence and extent of harm in combination with *vulnerability*, *exposure* and *lack of capacities* besides the *hazard* itself.[380] They criticise the Court for not taking account of this holistic conceptualisation of harm as a product of several risk factors, when it determines the 'origin of the threat'.[381]

---

374 See, e.g., ECtHR, *Powell and Rayner v United Kingdom,* Judgment, 21 February 1990, Eur Court HR (ser A) 172, para 41.

375 See Sect. 1.5.2.

376 Jaeckel (2001), p. 155; Field et al. (2012), p. 69.

377 Lauta and Rytter (2016), p. 122.

378 Ibid, p. 121.

379 Ibid.

380 Ibid, pp. 119–122; see further Fisher (2010), pp. 551–552; United Nations Inter-Agency Secretariat of the International Strategy for Disaster Reduction (2004), pp. 36–37.

381 Lauta and Rytter (2016), pp. 120–121.

As an example, they refer to the *Kolyadenko v Russia* judgment. *Kolyadenko v Russia* concerned a serious, life-threatening flood in Vladivostok, where the applicants lived close to a river and a drinking water reservoir.[382] After rainfall had been much more intense than forecasted, the evacuation of reservoir water became necessary to prevent a dam from breaking.[383] Over the course of almost 2 years prior to the flood, several authorities warned the District Administration about the throughput capacity of the river channel. The warnings indicated that the river was partly cluttered with debris and household waste and was overgrown with bushes and small trees.[384] According to Lauta and Rytter, the Court 'might just as well have chosen to treat [the harm] as being proximately caused by a natural hazard', instead of categorising it as industrial hazard.[385] This could have resulted in a more lenient due diligence standard. In this regard, they maintain that the 'hybridity between man-made and natural hazards' could impede the determination of the 'origin of harm'.[386]

To dispel this accusation, it is necessary to address the criticism and to approximate the rules for the Court's determination of the 'origin of the threat' among an array of causal factors. The results of this discussion are also useful in demonstrating the barriers to a more comprehensive DRR obligation despite the knowledge of the impact of human induced climate change on the intensity and frequency of extreme weather events. In particular, the interpretation of a stricter due diligence so far fails due to difficulties in attributing particular damages to the impacts of human induced climate change as the 'decisive cause'.

Contrary to the criticisms in the literature, the Court's identification of the origin of harm for the purpose of determining the due diligence is not 'arbitrary'.[387] To understand the Court's determination of the 'origin of harm', it is first important to note that the Court maintains a different notion of causation than is used in disaster studies. The scientific notion of causation identifies the factual relationship between causes and effects. Accordingly, from a scientific point of view, it is in fact almost impossible to clearly distinguish the *factual origin* of a disaster,[388] since disasters are the multi-causal 'result from a complex web of factors'.[389] However, the finding of a *factual causation* is 'over-inclusive' for the attribution of responsibility.[390] The textbook example argues that the fathering of a murderer qualifies as one causal precondition of a future murder, but this should not sufficient to attribute

[382] ECtHR, 1st Sec., *Kolyadenko and Others v Russia,* Judgment, 28 February 2012, para 9.

[383] Ibid, paras 26–31, 51.

[384] Ibid, para 15.

[385] Lauta and Rytter (2016), p. 121.

[386] Ibid, pp. 121–122.

[387] Ibid, p. 122.

[388] Cubie (2017), pp. 245–247; Hübler (2017), p. 85; Macalister-Smith (1985), p. 3.

[389] Bartolini (2018), p. 15; see further Turner (1978), p. 14; see further International Law Commission (2009), para 36.

[390] Lagnado and Gerstenberg (2017), p. 569.

responsibility to the father of the murderer.[391] For this reason, *causation in the normative sense* takes account of fundamental principles of fairness and policy considerations to contour which of the infinite number of contributory causes for harm are normatively relevant.[392] The Court's determination of the 'origin of threat' builds on this *normative conceptualisation of causation*. In a two-tier approach, the Court assesses both the factually causal link between a threat and the (potential) harm, and its 'decisiveness' in causing the harm.

3.2.5.1 The Determination of a Factual Causal Nexus

First, the attribution of harm to state conduct presupposes a factual causal nexus.[393] The determination of a factual causal nexus relies on empirical understanding of the relationships between human conduct and effects.[394] This test for causation is embodied in the '*conditio sine qua non*' test, which is synonymously known as the 'but for' test.[395]

Notably, despite all progress, science is sometimes still incapable of determining with certainty whether causal nexuses exist. An example of such uncertainty constitutes the ongoing Lusi mud eruption in Indonesia, which may have been triggered by an earthquake or by drilling activities.[396] Since 29 May 2006, a mud volcano on Java has not stopped erupting. It has killed 13 people and impacted on the lives of 36,000 people.[397] Scientists still seek to determine whether an earthquake on 26 May 2006 or the drilling of a gas exploration well set off the volcanic eruption.[398] Since the general rule says that 'the party alleging something is obliged to prove it',[399] from a legal point of view the hazard is to be considered natural until the opposite is proven. Thus, if the case were to be tried under the ECHR, the state's responsibility for the deaths and damage would be assessed under a less strict due diligence.

Similarly, scientific uncertainties have so far prevented the attribution of flood damage to human made climate change in terms of factual causation. Despite advancements in 'attribution science', scientists did not succeed in proving that

[391] For more comparative cases, see Woollard (2015), pp. 17–18.

[392] Plakokefalos (2015), p. 478; for an overview of the discussion of the criterion of culpa in international law since the nineteenth century, see International Law Commission (1980), pp. 190–201 paras 492–511; van de Poel and Fahlquist (2012), p. 884; Hart and Honoré (1985), pp. 11–12.

[393] Lagnado and Gerstenberg (2017), p. 568; Hart and Honoré (1985), pp. 10, 23; see further Epstein (1973), p. 161.

[394] Kellner and Durant (2011).

[395] Plakokefalos (2015), pp. 476–477; Hart and Honoré (1985), pp. 111–114; Lagnado and Gerstenberg (2017), pp. 568–569.

[396] Hübler (2017), p. 86.

[397] EM-DAT, CRED/UCLouvain, Brussels, Belgium.

[398] See, e.g., Miller and Mazzini (2018); Davies et al. (2011); EM-DAT categorises the disaster as technological accident, see EM-DAT, CRED/UCLouvain, Brussels, Belgium.

[399] See, e.g., Ambrus (2014), p. 236.

individual flood damages would not have occurred without climate changes.[400] So far, climate scientists can calculate the changes in average precipitation frequency and intensity compared to pre-industrial times and attribute them to climate change.[401] Based on those findings, science can estimate the share of the total damage caused by floods in a region over a certain period of time due to climate change.[402] For individual events, however, science can only statistically estimate the extent to which the event's occurrence or magnitude can be attributed to climate change.[403] Furthermore, it is possible to estimate the probability with which the characteristics of the individual event can be explained by the known impacts of climate change.[404] In terms of establishing the causation of harm, such estimates do not meet the necessary standard of proof to attribute individual flood damage directly to climate change.[405] As a result, the obstacles in attributing damages to specific climate change inducing activities prevent a stricter due diligence to protect. In fact, if individual flood damage could be attributed to climate change, the due diligence would firstly be stricter due to the existing national and international binding obligations to adapt society to climate change. Second, the state's responsibility under the ECHR would also depend on whether it has sufficiently regulated greenhouse gas emissions. The scientific challenges preventing the application of a stricter due diligence underline the need for national bottom-up adjustments in risk management. To reduce disaster losses associated with the projected increases in flood frequency and intensity, national risk management needs to be complemented.

3.2.5.2 The Determination of the 'Decisive Cause'

Beyond the requirement of a factual nexus, a normative judgment determines which contributing factor should be deemed the cause of harm. In this regard, the Court has held that the 'decisive cause' of the harm must be determined.[406] While European philosophy has contributed comparably little to further contour these normative limitations,[407] the conceptualisation of causation for normative purposes is central in legal theory.[408] The delineation of the cause in the normative sense is usually referred

---

[400] Maljean-Dubois (2018), para 2; Clarke et al. (2022), pp. 6–9.

[401] Minnerop and Otto (2020), p. 49.

[402] Clarke et al. (2022), p. 9.

[403] Ibid.

[404] Otto et al. (2017).

[405] Maljean-Dubois (2018), para 2; Clarke et al. (2022), pp. 6–9.

[406] EComHR, *Tugar v Italy,* Decision, 18 October 1995, Eur Comm HR 83A 26, p. 29; ECtHR, *Lopes de Sousa Fernandes v Portugal,* Judgment, 19 December 2017, para 201; Lavrysen (2018), p. 710.

[407] Hart and Honoré (1985), p. 9.

[408] Ibid, Ch 1; Moore (2019), para 1; Pollock (1901), pp. 35–36.

to in terms of proximity or remoteness.[409] Generally, 'there are strong similarities in the legal uses of causation in all presently existing legal systems'.[410] As a consequence, scholars characterise certain standards to identify the legally relevant sequence leading to harm as general principles of law.[411] Consequently, doctrines such as those relating to the 'breaking of the causal chain'[412] are applied in the Court's determination of the 'origin of the threat'.[413] However, it must be pointed out that since the determination of the proximate cause is a normative judgment based on considerations of fairness and policy, the standards differ in detail across different areas of law.[414]

Against this background, some conclusions can be drawn about the determination of the 'origin of threat' for the purpose of determining the scope of the positive obligation. As such, the Court declares that a 'natural disaster' [sic] is 'as such beyond human control'.[415] With the modern understanding of disasters in mind, the Court is to be understood in such a way that the *decisive reason* of the threat must be 'beyond human control'. The case law provides two examples that the Court considered beyond human control. The Court instanced meteorological events in *Budayeva v Russia*,[416] and earthquakes in *Özel v Turkey*, as 'events over which States have no control'.[417] In both examples, the human made vulnerability, that is, the non-compliance with safety and construction standards,[418] was a '*conditio sine qua non*' for the extent of the harm, but not the *decisive* cause and therefore not the 'origin of threat'. Instead, the decisive factor, the hazard, was induced entirely, or at least predominantly, without human activity or choice and as such considered 'natural'. In contrast, in the contested decision in *Kolyadenko v Russia*, the Court acknowledged that the decisive reason for the flood wave itself was not the initial

---

409 Plakokefalos (2015), p. 475; International Law Commission (2001), DA 31 para 10.

410 Moore (2019), para 1; see International Law Commission (2001), DA 31 para 10.

411 See Pusztai (2017).

412 Commonly, all legal systems agree that another actor's action generally qualifies as intervening cause if a third party, or the affected individual, *voluntarily* and *responsibly* acts subsequently to the obliged actor's conduct, and in a way, which is *causally significant* for the manifestation of harm. This *voluntary* conduct does not need to be intentional, however, mere negligence on part of the intervening actor does not 'break the causal chain', see Moore (2019), para 3; Woollard (2015), pp. 17–18.

413 EComHR, *Tugar v Italy,* Decision, 18 October 1995, Eur Comm HR 83A 26, p. 29; see Lavrysen (2018), p. 710; Stahl (2012), pp. 175–176; for a respective example from German constitutional law, see BVerfG, *Nachrüstung,* Judgment, 16 Dezember 1983, BVerfGE 66, 39, at pp. 63–64 para 66; Michael and Morlok (2023), p. 299 para 497.

414 Hart and Honoré (1985), p. 325; for an comparison of the different standards in German civil, criminal and public law, see Rönnau et al. (2004); Moore (2019), para 1.

415 ECtHR, *Budayeva and others v Russia,* Judgment, 20 March 2008, Eur Court HR II 267, p. 299 para 174.

416 Ibid, p. 290 para 135.

417 ECtHR, 2nd Sec., *Özel and Others v Turkey,* Judgment, 17 November 2015, paras 170, 173.

418 Ibid, para 175; ECtHR, *Budayeva and others v Russia,* Judgment, 20 March 2008, Eur Court HR II 267, pp. 293–296 paras 147–160.

meteorological phenomenon.[419] While the exceptionally heavy rain was a '*conditio sine qua non*' for the flood, from a perspective of 'proximity', it was the urgent evacuation of water from the human made facility that caused the flood.[420] Consequently, the Court classified the manifested harm as being decisively caused by the human made activity, despite the involvement of a natural hazard.

It follows from this case review that, contrary to Lauta and Rytter's accusation of arbitrariness, the origin of the threat in cases involving natural hazards is determined according to established and reasoned rules. To determine the decisive cause, evidence of actual causal factors is normatively assessed on the basis of fairness and policy considerations, rather than on the basis of prima facie evidence. In particular, the notion of causation used in disaster studies does not influence the determination of the 'origin of threat' under these rules and thus the scope of due diligence.

3.3 Conclusion

This chapter has demonstrated that international law does not currently protect people from the consequences of neglected long-term DRR in the context of natural hazards. There is a current lack of specialised international obligations to prevent or mitigate the increasing disaster losses related to natural hazards. With respect to the generally applicable obligations under the ECHR, this chapter has also demonstrated that only in the sphere of disaster relief are the member states obliged to do '*everything within the authorities' power*', and to take appropriate measures in response to *imminent* and *clearly identifiable* natural hazards.[421] The reason for this narrow and response-oriented scope of obligation lies in the object and purpose underpinning positive obligations on the one hand, combined with the inherent uncertainties of common natural hazards on the other hand.

In this respect, the analysis has demonstrated that the scope of positive obligations depends on what is contextually necessary to protect the individual's autonomy in relation to a protected interest under the ECHR. This aim sets the minimum standard for *effective* protection, which is, however, subject to limiting principles. The principle of proportionality, the margin of appreciation doctrine, and the principle of subsidiarity influence what the Court may consider necessary to fulfil the principle of effectiveness in a particular case. These principles contribute to the aim of achieving a 'fair balance that has to be struck between the competing interest of the individual and of the community as a whole'.[422] Building on these aims, the interpretation of positive obligations strikes the fair balance by requiring necessary

---

[419] ECtHR, 1st Sec., *Kolyadenko and Others v Russia,* Judgment, 28 February 2012, para 164.

[420] Ibid.

[421] ECtHR, *Budayeva and others v Russia,* Judgment, 20 March 2008, Eur Court HR II 267, p. 290 para 137; ECtHR, 2nd Sec., *Özel and Others v Turkey,* Judgment, 17 November 2015, para 171.

[422] ECtHR, *Powell and Rayner v United Kingdom,* Judgment, 21 February 1990, Eur Court HR (ser A) 172, para 41.

measures that can reasonably be expected to protect a right under the ECHR from a *real risk*. In the context of natural hazards, the temporal and spatial indeterminacy of most natural hazards consequently prevents the rise of obligations for long-term risk reducing measures, even if these would be cost-efficient. Only in exceptional cases, that is, in cases of imminent and clearly identifiable natural hazards, measures to reduce vulnerability may be required to protect the right to life and property. Since this threshold is usually reached when only little time is left before the hazard's manifestation, the positive obligation consists of the preparation of effective disaster relief, such as evacuations in most cases. While evacuations can be realised in the short term, buildings cannot be moved or retrofitted. For this reason, the obligation under general law mainly translates into a response-oriented obligation to protect, which has a practical role primarily in relation to the protection of life.

In sum, this chapter has shown that there is a legal gap regarding the protection of people from the consequences of their distorted risk perception, especially regarding their property. Given the discrepancies in people's perceptions and the facts about risks and mitigation options outlined in Chap. 2, the law currently does not make use of the potential to reduce disaster losses. For this reason, the following chapter offers proposals for appropriate measures that are compatible with the current legal framework. The insights into the biases and heuristics provide a valuable basis for developing lawful measures that counteract these cultural and cognitive mechanisms without interfering with individual rights, such as corrective communication and financial incentives. In addition, the ever-increasing costs to the community due to natural hazards justify more coercive regulation that is more effective in reducing disaster costs. Such measures include spatial planning and regulations to control urban development which have proved to be effective in reducing social disaster risks.

References

Ambrus M (2014) The European Court of Human Rights and standards of proof. In: Gruszczyński L, Wouter W (eds) Deference in international courts and tribunals: standard of review and margin of appreciation. Oxford University Press, Oxford, pp 235–253

Ambrus M (2017) The European Court of Human Rights as governor of risk. In: Ambrus M, Rayfuse RG, Werner W (eds) Risk and the regulation of uncertainty in international law, 1st edn. Oxford University Press, Oxford, pp 99–115

Arai-Takahashi Y (2015) Proportionality. In: Shelton D (ed) The Oxford handbook of international human rights law. Oxford University Press, Oxford, pp 446–468

Aust A (2013) Modern treaty law and practice, 3rd edn. Cambridge University Press, Cambridge

Baade B (2017) Der Europäische Gerichtshof für Menschenrechte als Diskurswächter. In: Beiträge zum ausländischen öffentlichen Recht und Völkerrecht, vol 263. Springer, Heidelberg

Balcerzak M (2020) The 'acquis' of the Council of Europe in the sphere of disaster preparedness and response. CLR 25:155–171. https://doi.org/10.12775/CLR.2019.004

Bartolini G (2015) La definizione di disastro nel progetto di articoli della Commissione del diritto internazionale. Rivista Di Diritto Internazionale 98(1):155–162

Bartolini G (2017) A universal treaty for disasters? Remarks on the International Law Commission's draft articles on the protection of persons in the event of disasters. Int Rev Red Cross 99(3):1103–1137. https://doi.org/10.1017/S1816383119000067

Bartolini G (2018) A taxonomy of disasters in international law. In: Zorzi Giustiniani F, Sommario E, Casolari F, Bartolini G (eds) Routledge handbook of human rights and disasters. Routledge, Abingdon, pp 10–26

Bartolini G, Natoli T, Riccardi A (2015) Report of the expert meeting on the ILC's draft articles on the protection of persons in the event of disasters: international law and disasters working papers series 03. Roma Tre University Department of Law

Bossuyt M (2015) Judicial activism in Strasbourg. In: Wellens K (ed) International law in silver perspective: challenges ahead. Brill, Leiden, pp 31–56

Brölmann C (2005) Law-making treaties: form and function in international law. Nordic J Int Law 74(3):383–403. https://doi.org/10.1163/157181005774939887

Buckle P (2012) Preparedness, warning and evacuation. In: Wisner B, Gaillard JC, Kelman I (eds) The Routledge handbook of hazards and disaster risk reduction. Routledge, London, pp 493–504

Çalı B (2020) Specialized rules of treaty interpretation: human rights. In: Hollis DB (ed) The Oxford guide to treaties, 2nd edn. Oxford University Press, Oxford, pp 504–523

Chatterjee R, Shiwaku K, Das Gupta R, Nakano G, Shaw R (2015) Bangkok to Sendai and beyond: implications for disaster risk reduction in Asia. Int J Disaster Risk Sci 6(2):177–188. https://doi.org/10.1007/s13753-015-0055-4

Childs D (2013) Implementation of the Hyogo Framework for action: summary of reports 2007–2013. https://www.undrr.org/quick/11319. Accessed 19 June 2023

Clarke B, Otto F, Stuart-Smith R, Harrington L (2022) Extreme weather impacts of climate change: an attribution perspective. Environ Res Clim 1(12001):1–25. https://doi.org/10.1088/2752-5295/ac6e7d

Classen CD (2015) AEUV Art. 196. In: von der Groeben H, Schwarze J, Hatje A (eds) Europäisches Unionsrecht: Vertrag über die Europäische Union, Vertrag über die Arbeitsweise der Europäischen Union, Charta der Grundrechte der Europäischen Union, 7th edn. Nomos, Baden-Baden

Costa J-P (2008) The European Court of Human Rights: consistency of its case-law and positive obligations: speech at Leiden University. NQHR 26(3):449–454. https://doi.org/10.1177/016934410802600308

Costa J-P (2013) The relationship between the European Court of Human Rights and the national courts. Eur Hum Rights Law Rev 3:264–274

Cot J-P (2007) Margin of appreciation. In: Wolfrum R, Peters A (eds) Max Planck Encyclopedia of Public International Law. https://opil.ouplaw.com/display/10.1093/law:epil/9780199231690/law-9780199231690-e1438. Accessed 19 June 2023

Craven M (2000) Legal differentiation and the concept of the human rights treaty in international law. Eur J Int Law 11(3):489–519. https://doi.org/10.1093/ejil/11.3.489

Crawford E (2011) Proportionality. In: Wolfrum R, Peters A (eds) Max Planck Encyclopedia of Public International Law. https://opil.ouplaw.com/display/10.1093/law:epil/9780199231690/law-9780199231690-e1459. Accessed 19 June 2023

Creta A (2018) Integrating human rights into disaster management: normative, operational and methodological aspects. In: Zorzi Giustiniani F, Sommario E, Casolari F, Bartolini G (eds) Routledge handbook of human rights and disasters. Routledge, Abingdon, pp 132–148

Crosweller HS, Wilmshurst J (2013) Natural hazards and risk: the human perspective. In: Rougier J, Hill LJ, Sparks RSJ (eds) Risk and uncertainty assessment for natural hazards. Cambridge University Press, Cambridge, pp 548–569

Cubie D (2017) The international legal protection of persons in humanitarian crises: exploring the acquis humanitaire. Hart, Oxford da Costa K (2014) Can the observance of human rights of individuals enhance their resilience to cope with natural disasters? Proc Econ Financ 18:62–70. https://doi.org/10.1016/S2212-5671(14)00914-9

DasGupta R, Shaw R (2017) Disaster risk reduction: a critical approach. In: Kelman I, Mercer J, Gaillard JC (eds) The Routledge handbook of disaster risk reduction including climate change adaptation. Taylor & Francis, Milton, pp 12–23

Davies SE (2012) Natural disasters and the responsibility to protect. German Yearb Int Law 55:149–174

Davies R, Manga M, Tingay M, Swarbrick R (2011) Discussion: fluid transport properties and estimation of overpressure at the Lusi Mud Volcano, East Java Basin (Tanikawa et al., 2010). Eng Geol 121(1–2):97–99. https://doi.org/10.1016/j.enggeo.2011.03.010

Dellinger M (2017) Rethinking force majeure in public international law. Pace Law Rev 37(2):455–506. https://doi.org/10.58948/2331-3528.1944

Dietlein J (2005) Die Lehre von den grundrechtlichen Schutzpflichten. Zugl.: Münster (Westfalen), Univ., Diss., 1991, 2nd edn. Münsterische Beiträge zur Rechtswissenschaft, vol 58. Duncker & Humblot, Berlin

Dörr O (2018) Article 31. General rule of interpretation. In: Dörr O, Schmalenbach K (eds) Vienna Convention on the law of treaties: a commentary, 2nd edn. Springer, Heidelberg, pp 559–616

Dow K, Cutter SL (1998) Crying wolf: repeat responses to hurricane evacuation orders. Coastal Manag 26(4):237–252. https://doi.org/10.1080/08920759809362356

Dröge C (2003) Positive Verpflichtungen der Staaten in der Europäischen Menschenrechtskonvention. Beiträge zum ausländischen öffentlichen Recht und Völkerrecht, Bd. 159. Springer, Heidelberg

Dröge C (2008) Marckx case. In: Wolfrum R, Peters A (eds) Max Planck Encyclopedia of Public International Law. https://opil.ouplaw.com/display/10.1093/law:epil/9780199231690/law-9780199231690-e1796. Accessed 19 June 2023

Ebert FC, Sijniensky RI (2015) Preventing violations of the right to life in the European and the Inter-American human rights systems: from the Osman Test to a coherent doctrine on risk prevention? Hum Rights Law Rev 15(2):343–368. https://doi.org/10.1093/hrlr/ngv001

Eissen M-A (1993) The principle of proportionality in the case-law of the European Court of Human Rights. In: Macdonald RS, Matscher F, Petzold H (eds) The European system for the protection of human rights. Nijhoff, Dordrecht, pp 125–146

EM-DAT, CRED/UCLouvain, Brussels, Belgium. www.emdat.be. Accessed 19 June 2023

Epstein RA (1973) A theory of strict liability. J Leg Stud 2(1):151–204. https://doi.org/10.1086/467495

European Commission (2021) Commission staff working document: overview of natural and man-made disaster risks the European Union may face. SWD(2020) 330 final/2

Farber DA (2014) International law and the disaster cycle. In: Caron DD, Kelly MJ, Telesetsky A (eds) The international law of disaster relief. Cambridge University Press, Cambridge, pp 7–20

Fawcett JES (1987) The application of the European Convention on Human Rights, 2nd edn. Clarendon Press, Oxford

Feichtner I (2007) Subsidiarity. In: Wolfrum R, Peters A (eds) Max Planck Encyclopedia of Public International Law. https://opil.ouplaw.com/display/10.1093/law:epil/9780199231690/law-9780199231690-e1477. Accessed 19 June 2023

Feinberg J (1989) Harm to self. The moral limits of the criminal law, vol 3. Oxford University Press, New York

Fellmeth AX, Horwitz M (2021) Guide to Latin in international law, 2nd edn. Oxford University Press, New York

Field CB, Barros V, Stocker TF, Dahe Q (2012) Managing the risks of extreme events and disasters to advance climate change adaptation: special report of the Intergovernmental Panel on Climate Change. Cambridge University Press, New York

Fisher D (2010) Legal implementation of human rights obligations to prevent displacement due to natural disasters. In: Kälin W, Williams R, Koser K, Solomon A (eds) Incorporating the guiding principles on international displacement into domestic law: issues and challenges. American Society of International Law, Washington, D.C., pp 551–591

Fitzmaurice M (2015) Interpretation of human rights treaties. In: Shelton D (ed) The Oxford handbook of international human rights law. Oxford University Press, Oxford

General Assembly (1987) International decade for natural disaster reduction: GA Res 42/169. UN Doc A/RES/42/169

General Assembly (2014) Report of the International Law Commission: sixty-sixth session. UN Doc A/69/10

General Assembly (2016) Protection of persons in the event of disasters: GA Res 71/141. UN Doc A/RES/71/141

General Assembly (2017) Report of the Open-Ended Intergovernmental Expert Working Group on indicators and terminology relating to disaster risk reduction: GA Res 71/276. UN Doc A/RES/71/276

General Assembly (2021) Resolution adopted by the General Assembly on 9 December 2021: GA Res 76/119. UN Doc A/76/119

Gerards JH (2019) General principles of the European Convention on Human Rights. Cambridge University Press, Cambridge

Glöckner A (2016) Psychology and disaster: why we do not see looming disasters and how our way of thinking causes them. Glob Policy 7:16–24. https://doi.org/10.1111/1758-5899.12289

Gold S, Zucchino D, Braun S (2005) Hundreds refuse to evacuate. Los Angeles Times, 6 September 2005. https://www.latimes.com/archives/la-xpm-2005-sep-06-na-katrina6-story.html. Accessed 19 June 2023

Golsong H (1993) Interpreting the European Convention on Human Rights beyond the confines of the Vienna Convention on the law of treaties? In: Macdonald RS, Matscher F, Petzold H (eds) The European system for the protection of human rights. Nijhoff, Dordrecht, pp 147–162

Grabenwarter C, Pabel K (2021) Europäische Menschenrechtskonvention, 7th edn. Juristische Kurz-Lehrbücher. C.H. BECK, München

Greer S, Wildhaber L (2012) Revisiting the debate about 'constitutionalising' the European Court of Human Rights. Hum Rights Law Rev 12(4):655–687. https://doi.org/10.1093/hrlr/ngs034

Hart H, Honoré T (1985) Causation in the law, 2nd edn. Clarendon Press, Oxford

Hentrei S, Soley X (2011) Force majeure. In: Wolfrum R, Peters A (eds) Max Planck Encyclopedia of Public International Law. https://opil.ouplaw.com/display/10.1093/law:epil/9780199231690/law-9780199231690-e1042. Accessed 19 June 2023

Herdegen M (2020) Interpretation in international law. In: Wolfrum R, Peters A (eds) Max Planck Encyclopedia of Public International Law. https://opil.ouplaw.com/display/10.1093/law:epil/9780199231690/law-9780199231690-e723. Accessed 19 June 2023

Hesselman M (2015) Regional human rights regimes and humanitarian obligations of states in the event of disaster. In: Zwitter A, Lamont CK, Heintze H-J, Herman J (eds) Humanitarian action: global, regional and domestic legal responses. Cambridge University Press, Cambridge, pp 202–227

Heun W (2011) Staatliche Risikosteuerung und Verfassung. RW Rechtswissenschaft 2(4):376–399. https://doi.org/10.5771/1868-8098-2011-4-376

Hilson C (2009) Risk and the European Convention on Human Rights: towards a new approach. Camb Yearb Eur Leg Stud 11:353–375. https://doi.org/10.5235/152888712802730693

Hoffmann L (2009) The universality of human rights. Law Q Rev 125:416–432

Hübler A-KJ (2017) Staatliche Verhaltenspflichten im völkerrechtlichen Katastrophenfall. Schriften zum Völkerrecht, Bd. 227. Duncker & Humblot, Berlin

Inter-Agency Standing Committee (2008) Human rights and natural disasters: operational guidelines and field manual on human rights protection in situations of natural disaster. Brookings-Bern Project on Internal Displacement

International Law Association (2004) Berlin Conference (2004): international human rights law and practice. https://www.ilahq.org/en_GB/documents/conference-report-berlin-2004-9. Accessed 19 June 2023

International Law Commission (1966) Draft articles on the law of treaties with commentaries. Yearbook of the International Law Commission 1966, vol II, A/CN.4/SER.A/1966/Add.1, pp 187–274

International Law Commission (1980) Yearbook of the International Law Commission 1978: documents of the thirtieth session (excluding the report of the Commission to the General Assembly). UN Doc A/CN.4/SER.A 1978/Add.l (Part 1)

International Law Commission (2001) Draft articles on responsibility of states for internationally wrongful acts, with commentaries. Yearbook of the International Law Commission 2001, vol. II (Part Two) and corrigendum. Supplement no. 10 (A/56/10), chp.IV.E.1

International Law Commission (2009) Second report on the protection of persons in the event of disasters. UN Doc A/CN.4/615

International Law Commission (2013) Sixth report on the protection of persons in the event of disasters. UN Doc A/CN.4/662

International Law Commission (2016a) Draft articles on the protection of persons in the event of disasters, with commentaries. Yearbook of the International Law Commission, 2016, vol II, Part Two, pp 26–58

International Law Commission (2016b) Protection of persons in the event of disasters: comments and observations received from governments and international organizations. UN Doc A/ CN.4/696

Jablonski S (2014) Hochwasserschutzrecht: Herausforderungen - Rechtsgrundlagen - Ansatzpunkte und Instrumente. Leipziger Schriften zum Umwelt- und Planungsrecht, vol 26. Nomos, Baden-Baden

Jaeckel L (2001) Schutzpflichten im deutschen und europäischen Recht: Eine Untersuchung der deutschen Grundrechte, der Menschenrechte und Grundfreiheiten der EMRK sowie der Grundrechte und Grundfreiheiten der Europäischen Gemeinschaft. Leipziger Schriften zum Völkerrecht, Europarecht und ausländischen öffentlichen Recht, vol 4. Nomos, Baden-Baden

Jahn J (2014) Normative guidance from Strasbourg through advisory opinions: deprivation or relocation of the convention's core? ZaöRV 74:821–846

Jansen-Wilhelm S (2015) A duty to accept humanitarian assistance under the ICESCR. In: Zwitter A, Lamont CK, Heintze H-J, Herman J (eds) Humanitarian action: global, regional and domestic legal responses. Cambridge University Press, Cambridge, pp 174–201

Kälin W (2012) The human rights dimension of natural or human-made disasters. German Yearb Int Law 55:119–147

Kellett J, Caravani A (2013) Financing disaster risk reduction: a 20 year story of international aid. Global Facility for Disaster Reduction and Recovery at the World Bank and the Overseas Development Institute. https://cdn.odi.org/media/documents/8574.pdf. Accessed 19 June 2023

Kellner M, Durant IC (2011) Causation. In: Fenyves A, Karner E, Koziol H, Steiner E (eds) Tort law in the jurisprudence of the European Court of Human Rights. De Gruyter, Berlin, pp 449–500

Klatt M (2011) Positive obligations under the European Convention on Human Rights. ZaöRV 71(4):691–718

Kothari M, Kälin W (2005) Relief and rehabilitation efforts remain problematic one year after Asian Tsunami, say UN experts. The Brookings Institution. https://www.brookings.edu/on-the-record/relief-and-rehabilitation-efforts-remain-problematic-oneyear-after-asian-tsunami-say-un-experts/. Accessed 19 June 2023

Kotzur M (2012) EU law on disaster preparedness and response. German Yearb Int Law 55:253–278

Kotzur M (2015) TFEU Article 196. In: Geiger R, Khan D-E, Kotzur M (eds) European Union treaties: a commentary. Treaty on European Union, Treaty on the functioning of the European Union. C.H. BECK, München

Krieger H (2014) Positive Verpflichtungen unter der EMRK: Unentbehrliches Element einer gemein-europäischen Grundrechtsdogmatik, leeres Versprechen oder Grenze der Justiziabilität? ZaöRV 74(2):187–213

Lagnado DA, Gerstenberg T (2017) Causation in legal and moral reasoning. In: Waldmann M (ed) The Oxford handbook of causal reasoning. Oxford University Press, New York

Lauta KC (2016) Human rights and *natural* disasters. In: Breau SC, Samuel K (eds) Research handbook on disasters and international law. Edward Elgar, Cheltenham, pp 91–110

Lauta KC, Rytter JE (2016) A landslide on a mudslide? Natural hazards and the right to life under the European Convention on Human Rights. J Hum Rights Environ 7(1):111–131. https://doi.org/10.4337/jhre.2016.01.05

Lavrysen L (2018) Causation and positive obligations under the European Convention on Human Rights: a reply to Vladislava Stoyanova. Hum Rights Law Rev 18(4):705–718. https://doi.org/10.1093/hrlr/ngy027

Le Grand J, New B (2015) Government paternalism: nanny state or helpful friend? Princeton University Press, Princeton

Legg A (2012) The margin of appreciation in international human rights law: deference and proportionality, Oxford monographs in international law. Oxford University Press, Oxford

Macalister-Smith P (1985) International humanitarian assistance: disaster relief actions in international law and organization. Springer, Dordrecht

Macdonald RS (1993) The margin of appreciation. In: Macdonald RS, Matscher F, Petzold H (eds) The European system for the protection of human rights. Nijhoff, Dordrecht, pp 83–124

Mahoney P (1990) Judicial activism and judicial self-restraint in the European Court of Human Rights: two sides of the same coin. Hum Rights Law J 11:57–88

Maljean-Dubois S (2018) Climate change litigation. In: Wolfrum R, Peters A (eds) Max Planck Encyclopedia of Public International Law. https://opil.ouplaw.com/display/10.1093/law-mpeipro/e3461.013.3461/law-mpeipro-e3461. Accessed 19 June 2023

Marochini M (2014) The interpretation of the European Convention on Human Rights. Zbornik Radova Pravnog Fakulteta u Splitu 51(1):63–84

Matscher F (1993) Methods of interpretation of the convention. In: Macdonald RS, Matscher F, Petzold H (eds) The European system for the protection of human rights. Nijhoff, Dordrecht, pp 63–82

McBride J (1999a) Proportionality and the European Convention on Human Rights. In: Ellis E (ed) The principle of proportionality in the laws of Europe. Hart, Oxford, pp 23–36

McBride J (1999b) Protecting life: a positive obligation to help. Eur Law Rev Hum Rights Surv 24:43–54

McGrogan D (2014) On the interpretation of human rights treaties and subsequent practice. NQHR 32(4):347–378. https://doi.org/10.1177/016934411403200403

Merrills JG (1993) The development of international law by the European Court of Human Rights, The Melland Schill monographs in international law, 2nd edn. Manchester University Press, Manchester

Michael L, Morlok M (2023) Grundrechte, 8th edn. NomosLehrbuch. Nomos, Baden-Baden

Miller SA, Mazzini A (2018) More than ten years of Lusi: a review of facts, coincidences, and past and future studies. Mar Pet Geol 90:10–25. https://doi.org/10.1016/j.marpetgeo.2017.06.019

Minnerop P, Otto F (2020) Climate change and causation: joining law and climate science on the basis of formal logic. Buff Environ Law J 27(1):49–86. https://doi.org/10.2139/ssrn.3522519

Moore M (2019) Causation in the law. In: Zalta EN (ed) The Stanford Encyclopedia of Philosophy. https://plato.stanford.edu/entries/causation-law/. Accessed 19 June 2023

Mowbray A (2004) The development of positive obligations under the European Convention on Human Rights by the European Court of Human Rights. Human rights law in perspective, vol 2. Hart, Oxford

Mowbray A (2005) The creativity of the European Court of Human Rights. Hum Rights Law Rev 5(1):57–79. https://doi.org/10.1093/hrlrev/ngi003

Mowbray A (2010) A study of the principle of fair balance in the jurisprudence of the European Court of Human Rights. Hum Rights Law Rev 10(2):289–317. https://doi.org/10.1093/hrlr/ngq006

Mowbray A (2015) Subsidiarity and the European Convention on Human Rights. Hum Rights Law Rev 15(2):313–341. https://doi.org/10.1093/hrlr/ngv002

Nettesheim M (2021) AEUV Art. 196. In: Grabitz E, Hilf M, Nettesheim M (eds) Das Recht der Europäischen Union, 73rd edn. C.H. BECK, München

O'Connell DP (1970) International law, 2nd edn. Stevens & Sons, London
O'Donnell TA (1982) The margin of appreciation doctrine: standards in the jurisprudence of the European Court of Human Rights. Hum Rights Q 4(4):474–507. https://doi.org/10.2307/762206
Opsahl T (1993) The right to life. In: Macdonald RS, Matscher F, Petzold H (eds) The European system for the protection of human rights. Nijhoff, Dordrecht, pp 207–223
Otto FEL, Skeie RB, Fuglestvedt JS, Berntsen T, Allen MR (2017) Assigning historic responsibility for extreme weather events. Nat Clim Chang 7(11):757–759. https://doi.org/10.1038/nclimate3419
Paddeu FI (2012) A genealogy of force majeure in international law. Br Yearb Int Law 82(1):381–494. https://doi.org/10.1093/bybil/brs005
Paddeu F (2017) Justification and excuse in international law: concept and theory of general defences. Cambridge University Press, Cambridge
Palmisano G (2007) Fault. In: Wolfrum R, Peters A (eds) Max Planck Encyclopedia of Public International Law. https://opil.ouplaw.com/display/10.1093/law:epil/9780199231690/law-9780199231690-e1955. Accessed 19 June 2023
Pedersen OW (2013) Environmental risks, rights and Black Swans. Environ Law Rev 15(1):55–62. https://doi.org/10.1350/enlr.2013.15.1.176
Petzold H (1993) The convention and the principle of subsidiarity. In: Macdonald RS, Matscher F, Petzold H (eds) The European system for the protection of human rights. Nijhoff, Dordrecht, pp 41–62
Peukert W (2009) Artikel 1 des 1. ZP (Schutz des Eigentums). In: Frowein JA, Peukert W (eds) Europäische Menschenrechtskonvention: EMRK-Kommentar, 3rd edn. N.P. Engel, Kehl am Rhein, pp 639–670
Philip D (2015) Humanitarian assistance and the right to water: an ASEAN region perspective. In: Zwitter A, Lamont CK, Heintze H-J, Herman J (eds) Humanitarian action: global, regional and domestic legal responses. Cambridge University Press, Cambridge, pp 302–329
Plakokefalos I (2015) Causation in the law of state responsibility and the problem of overdetermination: in search of clarity. Eur J Int Law 26(2):471–492. https://doi.org/10.1093/ejil/chv023
Polakiewicz J (2019) Council of Europe (COE). In: Wolfrum R, Peters A (eds) Max Planck Encyclopedia of Public International Law. https://opil.ouplaw.com/display/10.1093/law:epil/9780199231690/law-9780199231690-e607. Accessed 19 June 2023
Pollock F (1901) The law of torts: a treatise on the principles of obligations arising from civil wrongs in the common law. Stevens & Sons, London
Popovski V (2014) State negligence before and after natural disasters as human rights violations. In: Hobson C, Bacon P, Cameron R (eds) Human security and natural disasters. Routledge, London, pp 94–110
Priest SJ, Suykens C, van Rijswick HFMW, Schellenberger T, Goytia S, Kundzewicz ZW, van Doorn-Hoekveld WJ, Beyers J-C, Homewood S (2016) The European Union approach to flood risk management and improving societal resilience: lessons from the implementation of the floods directive in six European countries. E&S 21(4):50. https://doi.org/10.5751/ES-08913-210450
Pusztai DM (2017) Causation in the law of state responsibility. University of Cambridge, Cambridge
Raju E, da Costa K (2018) Governance in the Sendai: a way ahead? Disaster Prev Manag 27(3):278–291. https://doi.org/10.1108/DPM-08-2017-0190
Renn O, Klinke A, van Asselt M (2011) Coping with complexity, uncertainty and ambiguity in risk governance: a synthesis. Ambio 40(2):231–246. https://doi.org/10.1007/s13280-010-0134-0
Rönnau T, Faust F, Fehling M (2004) Durchblick: Kausalität und objektive Zurechnung. JuS:113–118
Russell D (2010) Supplementing the European Convention on Human Rights: legislating for positive obligations. North Ireland Leg Q 61(3):281–294. https://doi.org/10.53386/nilq.v61i3.455
Sands P, Peel J, Fabra Aguilar A, MacKenzie R (2018) Principles of international environmental law, 4th edn. Cambridge University Press, Cambridge

Saunders I (2014) International disaster relief law and Article 38(1)(c) of the statute of the International Court of Justice: the forgotten source of international law. In: Caron DD, Kelly MJ, Telesetsky A (eds) The international law of disaster relief. Cambridge University Press, Cambridge, pp 29–45

Scheinin M (2017) The art and science of interpretation in human rights law. In: Andreassen BA, Sano H-O, McInerney-Lankford S (eds) Research methods in human rights: a handbook. Edward Elgar, Cheltenham, pp 17–37

Schweizer M (2016) Nudging and the principle of proportionality: obliged to nudge? In: Mathis K, Tor A (eds) Nudging - possibilities, limitations and applications in European law and economics. Springer, Cham, pp 93–119

Seminara L (2016) Risk regulation and the European Convention on Human Rights. Eur J Risk Regul 7(4):733–749. https://doi.org/10.1017/S1867299X00010163

Simma B (1994) From bilateralism to community interest in international law. Hague Recueil des Cours 250(6):221–384. https://doi.org/10.1163/1875-8096_pplrdc_A9789041104199_02

Sinclair I (1984) The Vienna Convention on the law of treaties, Melland Schill monographs in international law, 2nd edn. Manchester University Press, Manchester

Sommario E, Venier S (2018) Human rights law and disaster risk reduction. QIL Zoom-in 49:29–47

Sossai M (2018) States' failure to take preventive action and to reduce exposure to disasters as a human rights issue. In: Zorzi Giustiniani F, Sommario E, Casolari F, Bartolini G (eds) Routledge handbook of human rights and disasters. Routledge, Abingdon, pp 119–131

Sousa L, Dimova S, Fuchs M, Pinto A, Nikolova B, Iannaccone S (2015) State of implementation of the Eurocodes in the European Union: support to the implementation, harmonization and further development of the Eurocodes. JRC Science for Policy Report. EUR 27511 EN

Spano R (2014) Universality or diversity of human rights?: Strasbourg in the age of subsidiarity. Hum Rights Law Rev 14(3):487–502. https://doi.org/10.1093/hrlr/ngu021

Spence R, So E (2021) Why do buildings collapse in earthquakes?: building for safety in seismic areas. Wiley-Blackwell, Hoboken

Spieker H (2015) International norms informing domestic disaster response schemes. In: Zwitter A, Lamont CK, Heintze H-J, Herman J (eds) Humanitarian action: global, regional and domestic legal responses. Cambridge University Press, Cambridge, pp 149–173

Stahl S (2012) Schutzpflichten im Völkerrecht - Ansatz einer Dogmatik: Ein Beitrag zu Grund, Inhalt und Grenzen der völkerrechtlichen Schutzpflichtendogmatik im Bereich konventionell geschützter Menschenrechte. Beiträge zum ausländischen öffentlichen Recht und Völkerrecht, Bd. 232. Springer, Heidelberg

Starmer K (1999) European human rights law: The Human Rights Act 1998 and the European Convention on Human Rights. Legal Action Group, London

Stoyanova V (2018) Causation between state omission and harm within the framework of positive obligations under the European Convention on Human Rights. Hum Rights Law Rev 18:309–346. https://doi.org/10.1093/hrlr/ngy004

Sykes K (2014) Hunger without frontiers: the right to food and state obligations to migrants. In: Caron DD, Kelly MJ, Telesetsky A (eds) The international law of disaster relief. Cambridge University Press, Cambridge, pp 190–207

Thorp T (2013) International climate law and the protection of persons in the event of disasters. N Z J Public Int Law 11(2):427–482

Trouwborst A (2006) Precautionary rights and duties of states. Nova et vetera iuris gentium. Martinus Nijhoff, Boston

Trouwborst A (2009) Prevention, precaution, logic and law: the relationship between the precautionary principle and the preventative principle in international law and associated questions. Erasmus Law Rev 2(2):105–127

Turner BA (1978) Man-made disasters. The Wykeham Science Series, vol 53. Wykeham, London

UN General Assembly (2016) Report of the Open-Ended Intergovernmental Expert Working Group on indicators and terminology relating to disaster risk reduction. UN Doc A/71/644

United Nations Inter-Agency Secretariat of the International Strategy for Disaster Reduction (2004) Living with risk: a global review of disaster reduction initiatives, Volume II - Annexes. United Nations, Geneva

United Nations Office for Disaster Risk Reduction (2015) Sendai Framework for Disaster Risk Reduction 2015–2030. UN Doc A/CONF.224/L.2

van de Poel I, Fahlquist JN (2012) Risk and responsibility. In: Roeser S, Hillerbrand R, Sandin P, Peterson M (eds) Handbook of risk theory: epistemology, decision theory, ethics, and social implications of risk. Springer, Dordrecht, pp 877–907

van Dijk P, van Hoof GJ (1998) Theory and practice of the European Convention on Human Rights, 3rd edn. Kluwer Law International, The Hague

Villiger ME (2009) Commentary on the 1969 Vienna Convention on the law of treaties. Martinus Nijhoff, Leiden

Wilkinson D (1993) The Council of Europe Convention on civil liability for damage resulting from activities dangerous to the environment: a comparative review. Eur Environ Law Rev 2(5):130–134

Woollard F (2015) Doing and allowing harm. Oxford University Press, Oxford

World Conference on Disaster Reduction (2005) Hyogo Framework for Action 2005–2015: building the resilience of nations and communities to disasters. UN Doc A/CONF.206/6

Xenos D (2007) Asserting the right to life (Article 2, ECHR) in the context of industry. German Law J 8(3):231–253. https://doi.org/10.1017/S2071832200005551

Xenos D (2012) The positive obligations of the state under the European Convention of Human Rights. Routledge research in human rights law. Routledge, New York

Zorzi Giustiniani F (2018) Something old, something new: disaster risk reduction in international law. QIL Zoom-in 49:7–27

Chapter 4
The Limitation to Disaster Risk Reduction by Fundamental Rights

Humans are not necessarily 'rational', but such irrationality must not immediately be assumed to be a negative thing; in many cases it is simply a response to a different set of priorities and an alternative way of reaching decisions about how best to manage their safety and that of those around them. (Crosweller and Wilmshurst 2013, p. 563)

The previous chapter has demonstrated that neither specialised international law, nor the generally applicable obligations under the European Convention on Human Rights ('ECHR')[1] respond to the ever-increasing disaster losses in the context of natural hazards. In particular, the advances in the research on disaster risk reduction ('DRR') and on people's distorted perceptions discussed in Chap. 2 have not broadened the scope of positive human rights obligations of member states of the Council of Europe ('member states') to include measures that decrease disaster losses. Chapter 3's findings have complemented the discussion in Chap. 1 that domestic legislation does not currently prevent or mitigate the increase in disaster losses related to natural hazards.[2] Given this state of the current regulatory regimes, this book argues that member states should adopt additional measures to mitigate the consequences of distorted risk perception in order to reduce disaster losses. This argument also builds on the findings on people's misperception of risks established in Chap. 2 and Chap. 1's discussion of the consequences on both the individual and the collective interests. To examine how member states should consequently complement their risk management, this chapter and the following explore what legal and political measures states could implement to mitigate the consequences of distorted risk perception related to natural hazards.

---

[1] On the importance of the ECHR see Sect. 1.6. However, it should be noted that national constitutions sometimes provide stronger individual protection than the ECHR. The ECHR only establishes minimum standards, see generally Petzold (1993), pp. 60–61.

[2] See Sect. 1.1.1.

C. A. Simmig, *Of Risks and Normative Responses*,
https://doi.org/10.1007/978-3-031-41104-5_4

This chapter begins by exploring the lawfulness of measures advocated for by experts in order to mitigate the consequences of distorted risk perception in relation to natural hazards, while also discussing their advantages and disadvantages. With an additional aim to contribute a legal perspective to the interdisciplinary discourse on distorted risk perception, this chapter highlights the shortcomings of demands placed on the state by commentators to protect individuals for their 'own good'. This aim of protection is referred to hereafter as a 'paternalistic aim'. Notably, the finding of distortions in people's risk perception has often invited commentators to argue for state interventions based on paternalistic aims. One paternalistic rationale is the protection of legal interests, particularly life and property, from the consequences of natural hazards. Another paternalistic rationale builds on the claim that people would assess risks differently if they were not influenced by prejudices and heuristics. In this respect, the state should help people realise their 'authentic self'. However, a fruitful discourse on measures to mitigate the consequences of distorted risk perception needs to take account of the value of autonomy as guaranteed by fundamental rights and freedoms. The principle of individual autonomy constrains the implementation of some additional DRR measures, despite the benefits that these measures can provide to individuals. In this regard, it is important to acknowledge that risks in the context of natural hazards are not necessarily involuntarily borne. Studies argue that decisions to continue living in zones prone to natural hazards are more likely to be the result of individual subjective assessments of the risks and benefits despite available alternatives.[3] In light of these subjective interests and values, this chapter shows the limited scope within which paternalistic aims justify measures to mitigate the consequence of distorted risk perception. Conversely, the chapter's legal analysis demonstrates that the aim of safeguarding common capacities and resources from the consequences of individual choices, that is, a non-paternalistic aim, can provide a more expansive justification for DRR measures that interfere with individuals' rights. In doing so, the chapter aims to identify lawful measures to mitigate the consequences of distorted risk perception related to natural hazards.

With this chapter's aims in mind, the analysis begins by examining whether DRR instruments of differing effectiveness interfere with the fundamental rights under the ECHR. Given the scope of this book's research undertaking explained in Chap. 1,[4] this examination is limited to the permissibility of DRR measures on the basis of Europe's shared fundamental rights as enshrined in the ECHR. As such, this chapter does not purport to provide a complete analysis of the lawfulness of DRR measures in terms of each member state's constitutional framework. Secondly, the chapter limits its consideration of DRR to certain hazards. Some DRR instruments can be legally assessed independently of the natural hazard type, such as in the case of disaster risk communication. However, for other instruments, such as the traditional

---

[3] Dibben (2008), p. 292; Kelman and Mather (2008); Dominey-Howes and Minos-Minopoulos (2004), pp. 285–286.

[4] See Sect. 1.6.

instrument of coercive legislation, the assessment of permissibility depends on the specific case. Thus, the diversity of natural hazards, and the resulting wide range of options to regulate the risks they pose, make it impossible to provide a complete overview of all hazards and how their regulation may impinge on individual autonomy.[5] For this reason, the legal analysis of coercive DRR instruments in this chapter is restricted to a closer assessment of the measures in place to reduce risks in the context of hydrometeorological and geophysical hazards. The focus is on these hazards as they are among the most common natural hazards in Europe.[6] They also cause the greatest economic damage.[7] After having established that the most effective DRR measures may interfere with individuals' rights, the chapter then explores how these interferences can be justified. In particular, it examines whether and to what extent the paternalistic and non-paternalistic rationales usually advanced in the context of risk management justify encroachments. As a result, this chapter shows that the ever-increasing cost of the consequences of distorted risk perception to the community provide the stronger basis to lawfully implement even coercive DRR measures that interfere with individuals' rights.

4.1 DRR Instruments and Their Relationship to Fundamental Rights

The analysis begins by examining typical DRR instruments in terms of their (potential) effectiveness and their relationship to individuals' fundamental rights. Not all DRR instruments necessarily interfere with fundamental rights. In fact, some reduce risks by stimulating risk-reducing behavioural changes in individuals without interfering with their rights. For this reason, they are a valuable tool in risk management. It is also worth noting that the consideration of behavioural studies could increase the effectiveness of these DRR instruments, and thus their value in risk management.[8] Yet, although such DRR instruments have undeniable value in risk management, they are comparatively less effective in protecting life and property than coercive instruments. Legal coercion promises the highest effectiveness in achieving the desired behaviour. The flip side of this higher effectiveness is that coercive measures typically interfere with fundamental rights and thus require justification. Certain circumstances may justify such interference, with the extent of justification

[5] To illustrate the range of possible legal encroachments, consider just a few of the common regulations to contain COVID-19. Measures to shut down businesses have encroached upon the professional freedom, the prohibition of religious gatherings has encroached on the freedom of religion, the ban or limitation of demonstrations has encroached on the freedom of assembly, the prohibition to leave certain areas has interfered with the freedom of movement and so forth, see Kunig and Kämmerer (2021), GG Article 2 para 103.

[6] EM-DAT, CRED/UCLouvain, Brussels, Belgium.

[7] Ibid.

[8] Camerer and Kunreuther (1989) and Safarpour et al. (2020).

depending on the underlying rationale, as this chapter later shows. For a detailed analysis, this section begins with the review of preventive measures that stimulate individuals to change their behaviour before this section assesses coercive instruments.

4.1.1 Disaster Risk Communication

Disaster risk communication is a key instrument to change people's behaviour towards risks. It may encourage people to change their behaviour in a risk-reducing manner, which contributes to the protection of threatened lives and property, while not interfering with individuals' rights and freedoms.[9] State practice agrees with the importance of disaster risk communication as an effective and nonintrusive mean, even though studies often find its potential has not been fully realised. For instance, in relation to the example mentioned in Chaps. 1 and 2 of the misconceptions of the people of Santorini about the risks of the volcano,[10] Dominey-Howes and Minos-Minopoulos noted that there is a lack of educational initiatives to overcome such misconceptions.[11]

To be effective, the state should further inform the public on the capacity of publicly installed DRR measures and what risks remain despite these efforts. As an example of the relevance of this observation, one can refer to Japan's risk communication in relation to tsunamis. After the 2011 Tōhoku earthquake and tsunami, which caused the Fukushima Daiichi nuclear disaster, experts criticised Japan's risk communication to the public. The image of Japan as absolutely safe not only suppressed open discussion of risks in Japanese society,[12] it also led people to ignore the emergency warning of the incoming tsunami and to rely on the sea walls that had been constructed as protections against tsunamis.[13] The axiomatic trust in the tsunami protection was a result of the prevailing and unrebutted 'zero risk' culture.[14] Thus, effective disaster risk communication should oppose myths of a 'zero risk society'.[15]

---

[9] Le Grand and New (2015), pp. 15–16, 42.

[10] See Sects. 1.1.1 and 2.1.1.

[11] Dominey-Howes and Minos-Minopoulos (2004), p. 307.

[12] Nöggerath et al. (2011), p. 37.

[13] O'Mathúna et al. (2018), pp. 33–34.

[14] Ibid.

[15] See Sect. 2.1.5.

4.1.2 *Nudging*

Despite the fundamental role of disaster risk communication, other instruments can be more effective in prompting people to adjust their behaviour towards natural hazards. In this regard, 'the currently fashionable idea of "nudging"' promises a more effective instrument to reduce people's risky behaviour,[16] such as living in zones prone to natural hazards. Nudges are policies that steer people in a certain direction, while still allowing them to deviate.[17] The concept of nudging is particularly appealing to disaster risk management for being not only a low-cost steering tool, but for being a less intervening instrument than legal prescriptions or prohibition.[18] In fact, nudges ultimately respect people's choice, while attempting to manipulate them.[19] The following discussion first contextualises how this concept could increase the protection of lives and property against natural hazards, before examining the conditions for its permissibility in the light of the legal protection of autonomy.

4.1.2.1 'Framing' as Example for Nudging

The 'framing of information' is one form of nudging with particular relevance to DRR.[20] Framing seeks to intentionally configure 'the semantics in ways that play on people's propensity to make mistakes'.[21] With respect to DRR, scholars advocate for using the knowledge on cognitive processes to improve individual decision-making.[22] The influence of heuristics, such as the phenomenon known as probability neglect, has already been presented in Chap. 2.[23] It describes the tendency to neglect probability when making a decision under uncertainty. The more strongly people feel about an outcome, the more probabilities can be neglected. In recognition of this phenomenon, information on possible risks should firstly be presented in a vivid way.[24] If people cannot visualise worst-case scenarios, people may even perceive the duty to reduce identified risks as pure 'obstructionism'.[25] For instance, prior to the Fukushima Daiichi nuclear disaster, a Japanese utility representative

[16] Le Grand and New (2015), p. 1, see further Ch 8; see further van Aaken (2017), p. 83.

[17] Sunstein (2015), p. 417; Le Grand and New (2015), p. 154; van Aaken (2017), p. 83.

[18] Meier (2021), p. 104.

[19] Sunstein (2015), p. 439.

[20] See generally Le Grand and New (2015), pp. 136–137.

[21] Weyman and Barnett (2016), p. 164.

[22] Glöckner (2016), p. 17.

[23] See Sect. 2.1.1.

[24] See Le Grand and New (2015), p. 101.

[25] See Baan and Klijn (2004), p. 116.

dismissed worries about a possible failing of the backup electrical generators because it would 'make it impossible to ever build anything'.[26]

People's decision-making is also influenced by semantic risk patterns, that is, socially and culturally internalised conceptions of risk characteristics that do not necessarily 'withstand scientific examination'.[27] In this regard, framing should reflect the conceptualisation of disasters as a combination of human and natural factors to counter culturally developed biases in society.[28] This is because, in general, people find human made risks less acceptable than natural risks.[29] As such, studies found that if people recognise human influence on the rise and impact of a *prima facie* natural hazard, it can adjust semantic risk patterns.[30] For instance, communicating the relationship between flooding and river course regulations can lead people to perceive floods as 'human made'.[31] This results in a higher 'dread level' which changes how the individual evaluates a risk.[32]

Yet, the message needs to avoid sparking feelings of helplessness, which may result in denial of the risk or its acceptance despite available risk reducing options. Thus, the message should not only aim to elicit an emotional response by the recipient. If the message further presents 'information on how to understand and deal with those emotions, it becomes possible to alert vulnerable persons to anticipate their feelings and desires in ways that promote mindful choice'.[33] Raising public awareness for DRR options in a way that promotes mindful choices is particularly important with respect to natural hazards. As Chap. 2 showed, natural hazards have an innate semantic risk pattern of being inevitable, which often impedes agency for preventive actions, unlike industrial risks.[34] Moreover, the framing of available risk reducing options in a way that takes into account loss aversion can encourage people to choose the communicator's preferred option.[35] Studies suggest that the framing of risk in terms of expected losses is twice as powerful than framing it in terms of expected gains.[36] The reason is the loss aversion bias, which describes that people tend to value losses more highly than gains.[37] Making use of such framing techniques is expected to steer more people to opt for DRR with respect to natural hazards.

---

[26] Perrow (2011), p. 48.

[27] Renn (2008), p. 107.

[28] Wachinger et al. (2013), p. 1062.

[29] See Sect. 2.1.

[30] Renn (2008), p. 113; Wachinger et al. (2013), p. 1062; Baan and Klijn (2004), pp. 117–118.

[31] Baan and Klijn (2004), pp. 116–119, also cited in Wachinger et al. (2013), p. 1062.

[32] Baan and Klijn (2004), pp. 116–119, also cited in Wachinger et al. (2013), p. 1062.

[33] Buck and Ferrer (2012), pp. 717–718.

[34] See Sect. 2.1.4.

[35] Weyman and Barnett (2016), p. 164; Safarpour et al. (2020).

[36] Tversky and Kahneman (1992), p. 310.

[37] Ibid, p. 298.

4.1.2.2 Nudging as Infringement of Personal Autonomy

While disaster risk communication aims at making information properly understood, framing seeks to drive people's perception towards a defined result.[38] The mere effort to use language that avoids the creation or perpetuation of distorted risk perception falls in the ambit of disaster risk communication.[39] In contrast, framing intently uses the available knowledge on the cognitive and cultural mechanisms behind decision-making to elicit a specific response.[40] For this reason, commentators have criticised nudging as manipulative and unethical.[41] The criticism is predicated on an understanding of personal autonomy as 'the capacity to be one's own person, to live one's life according to reasons and motives that are taken as one's own and *not the product of manipulative or distorting external forces*'.[42] If nudges are in fact 'manipulative or distorting external forces', they interfere with autonomy and may consequently even be subject to legal scrutiny. In this regard, some commentators have argued that nudges can in principle interfere with fundamental rights that protect personal autonomy or personal development.[43] Under the ECHR, nudges may encroach on Article 8(1) that protects personal autonomy as an aspect of 'private life' under certain circumstances.[44] More likely, it is an interference with national fundamental rights, such as personal freedom as guaranteed under Article 2(1) of the *Grundgesetz für die Bundesrepublik Deutschland* [Basic Law for the Federal Republic of Germany][45] which offers a wider scope of protection in this respect.[46]

Although the legality of nudging has overall received only little attention in the literature until recently,[47] criteria for assessing the permissibility of nudges have started to develop. According to Anne van Aaken, nudges that take advantage of people's cognitive processes 'to push them towards an idea of a "good life"' constitute an impermissible form of manipulation.[48] In contrast, 'choice-supporting nudges', which seek to initiate a learning process to correct biases, would attract

---

[38] Cross (1998), p. 28; Le Grand and New (2015), pp. 136–137.

[39] See Le Grand and New (2015), p. 135.

[40] Weyman and Barnett (2016), p. 164; Edenhofer et al. (2014), p. 162; Kunreuther et al. (2014), p. 160; Glöckner (2016).

[41] Bovens (2009); see Hansen and Jespersen (2013).

[42] Christman (2020) (emphasis added), quoted in Schweizer (2016), p. 98, also quoted in van Aaken (2017), p. 90.

[43] Van Aaken (2017), pp. 101–103.

[44] For a discussion as to how nudges may infringe Article 8 of the ECHR, see ibid.

[45] Grundgesetz für die Bundesrepublik Deutschland [Basic Law for the Federal Republic of Germany], 23 May 1949.

[46] Meier (2021), pp. 105–154.

[47] Van Aaken (2017), p. 84; Schweizer (2016), p. 94.

[48] Van Aaken (2017), pp. 92–96; for a discussion of van Aaken's argument, see Schweizer (2016), pp. 99–101.

less scrutiny.[49] Nevertheless, if nudges aim to realise the individual's assumed preference by invisibly correcting emotions, the nudge would qualify as manipulation.[50] Van Aaken's focus on the 'invisibility' of nudges reverberates in Luc Boven's findings that 'the less transparent the nudge is, the greater is the threat to autonomy'.[51] Other commentators similarly agree with the importance of the level of 'transparency' in the legal assessment of nudges.[52] However, in contrast to van Aaken, Mark Schweizer argues that the nudged person not only needs to be unaware of the nudge's effect, but also needs to be 'unaware of the manipulative cues' to qualify as impermissible manipulation.[53] In this regard, Schweizer gives the examples of subliminal advertising or the secret installation of distorting mirrors to trick a person into losing weight by making the person look bigger.[54] He convincingly substantiates this additional impermissibility requirement with the fact that no choice is ever made in a truly neutral context.[55] Since there was 'no right to a context-free choice',[56] nudges seeking an emotional reaction cannot in itself be reasonably construed as a state's interference with personal autonomy.

Building on this literature review, most nudges, including those proposed above, would not interfere with personal autonomy. Although some of the above-mentioned nudges seek to change the emotional response to natural hazards, they are primarily designed to correct unconscious cognitive processes by emphasising certain information. As such, the nudges do not aim to trigger an automatic, emotional response, which would qualify as manipulation, but instead seek to initiate a learning process. The proposed framing is intended to make the modern conceptualisation of disasters more salient. The aim of the proposed framing is to broaden people's informed understanding and must therefore be construed as enhancing rather than limiting autonomy. Even if the intended effect of the nudge was invisible, the manipulative cue is visible. As a result, the previously presented nudges do not trigger legal scrutiny.

---

[49] Van Aaken (2017), pp. 92–100.

[50] Ibid, p. 96.

[51] Bovens (2009), p. 209; for a different view on nudging's impact on autonomy, see Sunstein (2015), pp. 437–439.

[52] Schweizer (2016), pp. 99–102; Meier (2021), p. 113.

[53] Schweizer (2016), p. 101.

[54] Ibid, pp. 100–101.

[55] Ibid, pp. 101–102; for a similar conceptualisation of autonomy, see Meier (2021), p. 120, citing Hacker (2018), pp. 106–107.

[56] Schweizer (2016), p. 114.

4.1.3 Financial Incentives

Other ways of changing people's behaviour towards risks could be to introduce negative or positive financial incentives, such as taxation on 'risky' behaviours, or subsidising the change of behaviour.[57] Similar to nudges, negative or positive financial incentives are a 'stealth' attempt to change individuals' behaviour towards a specific end and may be paternalistic in certain circumstances.[58] However, economic incentives can hardly be described as 'manipulative'.[59] Impermissible manipulations, as described above, seek an automatic, emotional response through invisible means. With respect to economic incentives, both the manipulative reference and the desired effect are transparent to the addressee and as such, do not aim to garner an automatic emotional response, which would constitute an interference with people's guaranteed autonomy. Thus, in contrast to some nudges, they usually do not elicit legal scrutiny for interfering with personal autonomy.

For this reason, financial incentives are a valuable instrument in disaster risk management as they can have a large effect on people's behaviour while still preserving their choice.[60] For instance, a state can use relocation subsidies as a tool to decrease people's voluntary exposure to disaster risks, such as living in areas prone to natural hazards. Italy began to pursue this strategy at the beginning of this century when it started offering families relocation funds to escape the particularly dangerous zone surrounding Mount Vesuvius.[61] Financial incentives can also be used to encourage potentially vulnerable people to make damage-reducing investments. On the one hand, financial incentives can stimulate self-insurances to reduce the damage in case of a disaster.[62] On the other hand, financial incentives may also motivate individuals to invest in self-protection which reduces the probability of a loss.[63] Once again, Italy's risk management provides a practical example of this strategy. In its 2019 Budget Law, the Italian government introduced the so-called 'Sisma Bonus'.[64] It offers tax deductions of between 50% and 85% of the total cost and up to €96,000 over 5 years to private individuals who seismically upgrade their homes.[65] The percentage depends on how much the building's seismic risk classification has

[57] Notably, Sunstein excludes material incentives from the definition of 'nudges', see Sunstein (2015), p. 417; arguing for the conceptualisation of financial incentives as 'nudges' Meier (2021), pp. 92–93; Le Grand and New (2015), pp. 51, 138.

[58] See Le Grand and New (2015), p. 124.

[59] Sunstein (2015), p. 443.

[60] Ibid.

[61] Edwards (2016), Pasha-Robinson (2016) and Arie (2003).

[62] Mol et al. (2020).

[63] Ibid; Michel-Kerjan and Kunreuther (2011).

[64] Bilancio di previsione dello Stato per l'anno finanziario 2019 e bilancio pluriennale per il triennio 2019–2021, Law 145/2018, 31 December 2018, Gazzetta Uciale della Repubblica Italiana 302.

[65] Formisano et al. (2019), p. 11; Artino et al. (2020), pp. 10274–10275.

been reduced.[66] To give an idea of the overall effect, it is noteworthy that a study has estimated the average costs of seismic upgrading measures to be €12,780, and of seismic retrofitting measures to be €75,298.16.[67] Based on a case study, the study has estimated that on average, individuals would be eligible to tax deductions of €8946, and €60,238.53 respectively.[68] Against this background, and considering that the high costs are one of the main barriers to private individuals,[69] the 'Sisma Bonus' is expected to be an effective instrument to increase seismic upgrading by private parties.

4.1.4 The Regulation of Risk-Taking

The value of the measures discussed so far, which could be employed to encourage changes in people's behaviour, lies in their ability to preserve individual choice. Nevertheless, in terms of their effectiveness in achieving the desired behaviour, they are inferior to the more traditional measures of legal bans or prescriptions.[70] However, legal measures that force individuals to change behaviour interfere with individual autonomy the most.[71] As such, DRR regulations potentially encroach on fundamental rights and therefore require justification.

With respect to hydrometeorological and geophysical hazards, Chap. 2 has already mentioned spatial planning and regulations to control urban development as effective measures to reduce social disaster risks.[72] Such measures may be aimed either at avoiding exposure to the hazard or at increasing the defence of potentially exposed persons. Yet, despite their protective purpose, typical regulations can interfere with fundamental rights such as the right to property, as the following examples of regulations show. While this section presents possible interferences, the conditions for justifying these encroachments are examined in the second section of this chapter in detail.

4.1.4.1 The Ban on Erecting New Buildings in Certain Zones

First, disaster risks can be reduced by regulations prohibiting the construction of new buildings in certain zones that are prone to natural hazards. While fundamental rights do not oppose the implementation of such DRR measures to *terra nullius* or

[66] Formisano et al. (2019), pp. 11–12.

[67] Ibid, p. 11.

[68] Ibid, p. 14.

[69] Artino et al. (2020), p. 10275.

[70] See generally Schweizer (2016), p. 115.

[71] Le Grand and New (2015), p. 138; van Aaken (2017), p. 96.

[72] See generally Greiving et al. (2006).

to public property, the application to private property of natural or legal persons may encroach on the right to property.[73] The right to property is guaranteed by Article 1 of the Protocol No 1 of the ECHR ('A1-P1'), the interpretation of which has been described as 'a useful synthesis of basic principles common to most legal systems'.[74] As a general rule, A1(1)1-P1 protects against any factual or legal situation that restricts the enjoyment of one's property.[75] With respect to the first of the two-tier review process, the European Court of Human Rights ('the Court') generally applies a low-threshold for admitting an interference with A1-P1, which then requires justification.[76] As such, the concept of 'possession' under A1-P1 not only encompasses immovable or movable property, but also protects 'legitimate expectations' to obtain the effective enjoyment of a proprietary asset.[77] In other words, A1-P1 may also protect the future development of owned land. For instance, the Court has considered the granting of an irrevocable outline planning permission an appropriate basis for the applicants' 'legitimate expectation of being able to carry out their proposed development' on their purchased land.[78] In this regard, the Court has construed construction bans or restrictions under planning law as interference with the right to property under A1(2)-P1 and thus require justification.[79] It should be noted, however, that the concept of 'legitimate expectations' requires more 'than a mere hope and [must] be based on a legal provision or a legal act such as a judicial decision'.[80]

4.1.4.2 Forced Resettlement from Certain Zones

To further avoid risk exposure, states could also enforce the resettlement of people who live in areas that are prone to natural hazards. In this respect, Chap. 1 has already pointed out a particular difficulty in European disaster risk management.[81] Many areas were already inhabited when they were classified as risk zones.[82] It stands to reason that resettlement measures may interfere with the right to property. For instance, if a state enforces the purchase of properties prone to natural hazards

73 See Ploeger and Groetelaers (2007).

74 Tarlock and Albrecht (2018), p. 49.

75 Grabenwarter and Pabel (2021), § 25 paras 1, 16; Ploeger and Groetelaers (2007), p. 1430.

76 Ploeger and Groetelaers (2007), p. 1430.

77 Grabenwarter and Pabel (2021), § 25 para 3.

78 ECtHR, *Pine Valley Developments Ltd and Others v Ireland,* Judgment, 29 November 1991, Eur Court HR (ser A) 222, para 51.

79 On construction bans, see ECtHR, *Allan Jacobsson v Sweden (No 1),* Judgment, 25 October 1989, Eur Court HR (ser A) 163, paras 53–54; on restrictions under planning law, see ECtHR, *Pine Valley Developments Ltd and Others v Ireland,* Judgment, 29 November 1991, Eur Court HR (ser A) 222, para 56.

80 ECtHR, *Kopecký v Slovakia,* Judgment, 28 September 2004, Eur Court HR IX 125, p. 143 para 49.

81 See Sect. 1.1.1.

82 Giese (2011), p. 204; Artino et al. (2020), p. 10273.

for the purpose of DRR, the transfer of ownership constitutes an expropriation that falls into the ambit of A1(1)2-P1.[83]

The state may even interfere with the right to property when it demolishes houses that were built without a permit and in violation of town planning law, as these can also be considered a 'possession' under certain circumstances.[84] In this regard, the Court applies the principle of autonomous interpretation, that is, the Court interprets the concept of 'possessions' autonomously and independently from the meaning in national legislation.[85] The parties' classification of a particular interest in their domestic law is not decisive for the Court's assessment.[86] In the Court's view, an *a priori* acceptance of classifications under domestic law would be incompatible with the ECHR's object and purpose to protect human rights detached from the parties' discretion in the particular case.[87] If the parties were able to determine the meaning of a term by means of domestic legislation, the contracting state might intentionally, or innocently, circumvent the Convention's granted protection.[88] As a result, an asymmetry of the definition of 'possession' under national law and the ECHR is possible.[89] Thus, in relation to illegally constructed buildings, they can still be understood as a 'possession' if the state has tolerated the illegal construction for a certain period of time.[90] Such circumstances may give rise to 'a "legitimate expectation" of being able to continue to enjoy that possession' on the part of the individual.[91] Consequently, the demolition of this created 'substantive interest' by domestic authorities still constitutes an interference with an individual's 'possession' under A1(2)-P1 and need justification.[92]

---

[83] Tarlock and Albrecht (2018), pp. 49–50; Cremer (2006), p. 1294 para 88.

[84] See, e.g., ECtHR, *Hamer v Belgium,* Judgment, 27 November 2007, Eur Court HR V 73, p. 94 para 77; ECtHR, *Ivanova and Cherkezov v Bulgaria,* Judgment, 21 April 2016, para 69.

[85] See generally EComHR, *Keller v Germany,* Decision, 4 March 1998; EComHR, *Scientology Kirche Deutschland e.V. v Germany,* Decision, 7 April 1997.

[86] See generally Stahl (2012), p. 65; Letsas (2007), p. 42.

[87] ECtHR, *Engel and Others v Netherlands,* Judgment, 8 June 1976, Eur Court HR (ser A) 22, para 81.

[88] Letsas (2004), p. 281.

[89] See generally Letsas (2007), p. 42.

[90] ECtHR, *Öneryildiz v Turkey,* Judgment, 30 November 2004, Eur Court HR XII 79, p. 128 paras 127–129; ECtHR, *Keriman Tekin et Autres c Turquie (French),* Judgment, 15 November 2016, paras 40–43; Ploeger and Groetelaers (2007), p. 1429.

[91] ECtHR, *Hamer v Belgium,* Judgment, 27 November 2007, Eur Court HR V 73, p. 94 para 76.

[92] Ibid, p. 94 para 77; ECtHR, *Ivanova and Cherkezov v Bulgaria,* Judgment, 21 April 2016, para 69.

4.1.4.3 Regulations to Reinforce Buildings Retrospectively

Finally, regulations could aim to improve the protection of buildings against natural hazards by prescribing and enforcing appropriate building codes. However, ordering the reinforcement of buildings that complied with building code requirements when they were constructed may interfere with the right to property. Even though no landmark cases have been decided by the Court on this issue, most Western constitutions protect the owner's trust in the inapplicability of new laws to pre-existing and lawfully established facts under the right to property.[93] This follows from the application of the general rule against retroactive legislation.[94] As such, even if zoning codes or building codes change due to technical or social developments, the right to property generally prohibits authorities to request adjustments to the so-called 'prior nonconforming use'. Consequently, orders making the continued enjoyment and use of the lawfully constructed property conditional on its retrofitting interfere with the protected 'use of the property' under A1(2)-P1 and would require justification.

4.2 The Justifiability of Interfering DRR Measures

This chapter's analysis of DRR instruments has shown that while measures enforcing DRR can be most effective in protecting life and property from natural hazards, they typically interfere with fundamental rights. However, as this section's analysis shows, such interferences can be justified to safeguard common capacities and resources from the consequences of individual choices. This justification derives from the key philosophy underpinning the legal system 'that every individual should be free to act as he or she perceives to be in self-interest, subject only to limits established to protect the interests of others'.[95]

Conversely, although interventions can also be justified based on paternalistic aims, the conditions for such justifications are so narrow that they exclude coercive risk reducing measures with long-term effect. This narrow scope is due to the value of autonomy that attaches to the manner in which a decision is made and carried out, and not to the outcome of a specific decision. Consequently, personal risk decisions are generally protected based on the value of autonomy and public authorities

---

[93] On the interpretation of Article 17 of the Charter of Fundamental Rights of the European Union, see Calliess (2022), EU-GRCharta Article 17 para 9; on the interpretation of Article 5 of the Austrian Basic Law on the General Rights of Nationals, see Giese (2009); on the interpretation of 'grandfather clauses' under the US constitution, see Washington Supreme Court, *Sumner v First Baptist Church,* Wash. 2d 1, 639 P.2d 1358 97; see further Reynolds Jr (1988).

[94] Reynolds Jr (1988), pp. 99–100.

[95] Green (1981), p. 11.

should therefore not restrict competent adults based on paternalistic aims.[96] By also examining paternalistic aims to justify intervening measures in this section, the analysis addresses commentators' calls for measures to mitigate the consequences of distorted risk perception to protect the individuals for their 'own good'. As Chap. 1 discussed, one's 'own good' is seen in the protection of legal rights, such as the protection of health, life and property from natural hazards, and the realisation of the individual's 'authentic self' from the effects of a distorted perception of risk.[97] In contrast to this school of thought, the most promising basis for long-term coercive regulation is the ever-increasing cost to the community due to natural hazards, which can be reduced cost-effectively through DRR. Although the evidence on biases and heuristics cannot justify the coercive enforcement of such measures, their considerable potential to effectively reduce disaster risks should not be undervalued. As demonstrated in the first section, the insights into the biases and heuristics nevertheless provide a valuable basis for developing lawful measures that counteract these cultural and cognitive mechanisms but do not interfere with individual rights, such as corrective communication and financial incentives.

To demonstrate that non-paternalistic rationales justify the above identified interferences in contrast to the paternalistic rationale, the following subsection first introduces the general justification requirements under the ECHR. Building on the justification requirements, the analysis shows that while paternalistic aims fulfil the first requirement, in most cases they do not fulfil the second requirement, that is, of an appropriate balance of competing interests.

4.2.1 Overview of the Justification Requirements Under the ECHR

While only some provisions of the ECHR, such as Articles 8–11, explicitly provide for limitations of rights, the European Court of Human Rights ('the Court') has read the possibility of limitation into other Articles of the ECHR as well.[98] Although the requirements for justification vary in stringency depending on the right encroached upon, the necessary elements are the same. It follows that the justification presupposes the interference's lawfulness, its pursuit of a legitimate aim, and its proportionality to ensure that individual rights are safeguarded effectively.

[96] Alemanno (2016), p. 199; see further Le Grand and New (2015), pp. 111–135; Flanigan (2017), p. 294.

[97] See Sects. 1.7.1.1 and 1.7.1.2.

[98] Gerards (2013), pp. 466–467.

4.2.1.1 The Principle of Lawfulness and Legitimate Aims

First, an interference by the state can usually only be justified if it is 'lawful'.[99] This means that the interference must be in compliance with a domestic law, on the one hand, and that law must be of a certain quality, on the other hand.[100] In this regard, the sufficient accessibility, preciseness and foreseeability of the law are decisive.[101] The Court understands the term 'law' in its substantial meaning, instead of its formal meaning.[102] Consequently, the classification as a 'law' does not depend, for example, on whether the regulation has been published in accordance with national procedural rules.[103] Accordingly, the notion may even include established practices beside statutory laws.[104]

Secondly, the interference must either pursue at least one of the 'legitimate aims' listed in the impugned right,[105] or must serve the fulfilment of a conflicting positive obligation towards the affected individual. For instance, a positive obligation arising from the right to life can be the basis for justifying an interference with a person's right to physical integrity.[106] These two constellations reflect the presented different rationales for justification, and which also shape the argumentation for more DRR in response to distorted risk perception. Which of the two constellations is present influences the proportionality test that is also required to be satisfied, as the contextual analysis in the second and third subsection shows.

4.2.1.2 The Proportionality Principle

The principle of proportionality requires a proper balance of the competing interests to permit an interference.[107] That is, the 'State's acts must be a rational and reasonable exercise of means towards achieving a permissible goal, without unduly encroaching on protected rights'.[108] The principle of proportionality, which in its modern form can be traced back to the Prussian administrative law of the eighteenth

---

[99] Arai-Takahashi (2015), pp. 450–451; Ploeger and Groetelaers (2007), p. 1430.

[100] See, e.g., in the context of Article 8 of the ECHR ECtHR, *Halford v United Kingdom,* Judgment, 25 June 1997, Eur Court HR III, para 49 and in the context of Article 10 of the ECHR ECtHR, *Magyar Kétfarkú Kutya Párt v Hungary,* Judgment, 20 January 2020, para 93.

[101] ECtHR, *The Sunday Times v United Kingdom (No 1),* Judgment, 26 April 1979, Eur Court HR (ser A) 30, paras 48–49; Ploeger and Groetelaers (2007), p. 1430; Arai-Takahashi (2015), pp. 453–454.

[102] ECtHR, 3rd Sec., *Špaček, sro v the Czech Republic,* Judgment, 9 November 1999, para 57.

[103] Ibid.

[104] Ploeger and Groetelaers (2007), p. 1430.

[105] Arai-Takahashi (2015), pp. 450–451.

[106] See EComHR, *X v Germany,* Decision, 9 May 1984.

[107] Van Dijk and van Hoof (1998), p. 80; Arai-Takahashi (2015), p. 447.

[108] Crawford (2011), para 1.

century,[109] is today recognised in many areas of international law,[110] and in the constitutional jurisprudence of many countries.[111] Particularly among European tribunals, this principle plays a pivotal role. Both European human rights systems, that is, the Charter of Fundamental Rights of the European Union[112] and the ECHR, rely on this principle to assess the permissibility of interferences with fundamental rights. In fact, the proportionality test applies to two axes in the Court's case law.[113]

On the one hand, the Court assesses the proportionality between the means employed and the aim sought.[114] As such, in relation to many rights, the Court has required a *reasonable* or *proportionate* relationship between the measures used and the aim pursued.[115] In this regard, for example, the severity and duration of interference can be relevant for the assessment.[116] Yet, the stringency of the assessment depends on the right concerned.[117] For instance, the Court requires an interference in Articles 8–11 of the ECHR to 'be proportionate to the legitimate aim pursued'.[118] By contrast, the Court has established an even 'stricter and more compelling test of necessity' with respect to the right to life by requiring the used force to 'be *strictly* proportionate to the achievement of the [listed] aims'.[119]

On the other hand, the Court seeks a 'fair balance' between competing interests. To that end, the Court considers numerous factors, depending on the nature of the interference and the interests involved, to determine whether an interference imposes a disproportionate or excessive burden on an individual. As the remainder of this chapter demonstrates, the proportionality of an interference depends inter alia on whether it serves the protection of the interests of the general public or the interests of the individual concerned. The latter aim has a paternalistic character, as the intervention is intended to serve the individual's 'own good'.

---

[109] Schweizer (2016), p. 96; Arai-Takahashi (2015), p. 447; Crawford (2011), para 7.

[110] Crawford (2011), paras 1, 23.

[111] Schweizer (2016), p. 96.

[112] Article 52(1) of the Charter of Fundamental Rights of the European Union, 2012/C 326/2.

[113] Arai-Takahashi (2002), p. 193.

[114] Ibid.

[115] Arai-Takahashi (2015), p. 454.

[116] See, e.g., on the proportionality of restrictions of an individual's freedom of movement ECtHR, 5th Sec., *Gochev v Bulgaria,* Judgment, 26 November 2009, paras 49–50; Arai-Takahashi (2002), p. 193.

[117] Gerards (2013).

[118] ECtHR, *Handyside v United Kingdom,* Judgment, 7 December 1976, Eur Court HR (ser A) 24, p. 23 para 49; ECtHR, *Silver and Others v United Kingdom,* Judgment, 25 March 1983, Eur Court HR (ser A) 61, para 97.

[119] ECtHR, 3rd Sec., *Hugh Jordan v United Kingdom,* Judgment, 4 May 2001, para 104 (emphasis added); ECtHR, *McCann and Others v United Kingdom,* Judgment, 27 September 1995, Eur Court HR (ser A) 324, para 149 (emphasis added).

4.2.2 Justifiability Based on Paternalistic Aims

Before examining potential justifications offered by non-paternalistic aims for the observed interferences with individuals' rights inherent in some DRR measures, this subsection begins by demonstrating the inadequacy of paternalistic aims in this regard. In other words, this subsection argues that spatial planning and regulations that interfere in the voluntary occupation of insufficiently robust houses in zones prone to natural hazards cannot be justified based on the aim of protecting individuals from themselves and to realise their 'authentic self'. Admittedly, many natural hazards pose threats to important individual interests, such as those involving one's property, physical integrity and life. The importance of these interests makes the reduction of the respective risks 'a legitimate matter of concern for the government',[120] which meets the first of the necessary justification conditions of a 'lawful and legitimate aim'. However, as far as the second condition of 'proportional' interventions is concerned, the paternalistic aim does not outweigh the value of autonomy expressed in individual risk-taking. In this respect, it must be acknowledged that individual risk-bearing is not only the result of social marginalisation, but can be found in situations of relative prosperity as well.[121] Chapter 1 has already given examples that, although decisions by individuals to inhabit the active volcano's flanks of Mount Etna in Italy may prima facie seem irrational, studies show that this decision is also based on prioritising rewards and is not just the result of social marginalisation.[122] Thus, such studies suggest that this risk-taking is at least partly the result of competent risk assessment, which should be respected by the authorities, even if others perceive the actions as physically or morally harmful or possibly dangerous to the person concerned.[123]

The examination of paternalistic aims is prompted by voices in the interdisciplinary discourse that attach greater weight to protection against the consequences of distorted risk perceptions in the proportionality test than to the value of autonomy. Distorted risk perception could result in so-called 'reasoning failures', which are a relevant, albeit controversial, permission to intervene in voluntary risk-taking.[124] Such failures describe a 'disjunction between the ends we want and how to get them'.[125] As Chap. 1 discussed, they are understood as a mild form of 'autonomy failure' that would allow the state to ensure that individuals act autonomously

[120] See Le Grand and New (2015), p. 104.

[121] See Sect. 1.1.1 and the introduction to this Chapter.

[122] Dibben (2008), p. 292; Kelman and Mather (2008); Dominey-Howes and Minos-Minopoulos (2004), pp. 285–286.

[123] ECtHR, 5th Sec., *Prilutskiy v Ukraine,* Judgment, 26 February 2015, para 32; see Dröge (2003), p. 329; see Jablonski (2014), p. 83.

[124] Arguing that such failures do not justify interventions: Flanigan (2017), pp. 306–308; arguing that these failures may entail justified interventions by the state, Le Grand and New (2015), Ch 5; see further Feinberg (1989).

[125] Le Grand and New (2015), p. 103.

enough when they engage in self-harming behaviour.[126] In this regard, the influence of cognitive and cultural mechanisms on people's decision-making processes, which can lead to systematic and predictable errors, are discussed as such reasoning failures.[127] Commentators argue that the profound empirical evidence on people's decision-making processes would challenge the traditional argument for deference of individual choice that rests on the reference to rational agency.[128] While this found disjunction would not amount to the individual's incompetence, 'it is nonetheless a failure truly to govern our own lives according to our goals'.[129] This rationale would also apply in the context of natural hazards, where a distorted perception of risk can prevent people from taking DRR measures that they would implement if they properly understood the fact.[130] In response to such lines of argumentation, the analysis in this section shows that respect for the value of autonomy requires a more differentiated approach to determine the extent to which paternalistic regulation justified. To that effect, both philosophical and legal studies agree that paternalistic motives justify state interventions only in a very narrow context.

To conceptualise the differentiated approach to assessing paternalistic interventions, it is useful to also draw on insights from moral and political philosophy. Although the Court has assessed cases involving paternalistic aims in the past, it has not developed a general theory of their permissibility. This is not remarkable since the Court typically rules on a case-by-case basis without explicit elaboration of the theoretical or systematic foundation.[131] However, in contrast to the Court, representatives of moral and political philosophy have developed general theories to assess the permissibility of state interventions to protect individuals from themselves. For this reason, the analysis begins with an overview of the latter in order to provide an analytical framework for examining the Court's approach to justifications based on paternalistic aims. In fact, the juxtaposition shows that the Court's assessment of state interventions that are aimed to protect individuals demonstrates parallels to the differentiated approach that has emerged in moral and political philosophy. By assessing distorted risk perception related to natural hazards under the derived differentiated approach, this subsection reveals shortcomings of paternalistic demands placed on the state. While arguments for more DRR measures often stem from paternalistic motives, they are insufficient to justify long-term DRR given the indeterminacy and sudden manifestation of most natural hazards.

[126] Feinberg (1989), pp. 117–127; Le Grand and New (2015), pp. 119–132; see Sect. 1.7.1.2.

[127] Tversky and Kahneman (1974), p. 1131.

[128] Conly (2013), p. 189.

[129] Le Grand and New (2015), p. 119.

[130] Spence and So (2021), pp. 2–3; Ivčević et al. (2021).

[131] See Sect. 3.2.1.

4.2.2.1 Permitted Paternalism in Moral and Political Philosophy

The seminal contributions, first by Joel Feinberg, and later by Julian Le Grand and Bill New, have conceptualised the permissibility of state interventions in cases of 'reasoning failures'. Whether and how a state may intervene with individuals depends on the 'degrees of reasoning failure and the concomitant reduction in well-being' on the one hand, and on the impact on autonomy on the other hand.[132] As such, the permissibility firstly depends on the objective factors relating to the threat. These objective factors must suggest the 'nonvoluntariness' of an individual's risk-taking.[133] When a 'presumption of nonvoluntariness' is established, the personal importance the individual attaches to the conduct or even the result may suspend the assumption of a reasoning failure.[134] In this respect, subjective factors relating to the potential victim also inform the permissibility of interventions. However, when it comes to natural hazards, particularly floods and earthquakes, there is usually already a lack of objective factors necessary for a 'presumption of nonvoluntariness'.

A so-called 'presumption of nonvoluntariness'[135] permits a third-party to investigate whether the individual's conduct is sufficiently voluntary.[136] Such presumption refers to conduct that is statistically unusual, and therefore suggest that the actor may be ignorant or mistaken about the risk, or suffering from a compulsion or incapacity.[137] Le Grand and New give the example of the desire to swim in waters in which crocodiles are known to live.[138] Feinberg cites Mill's example of seeing 'a person attempting to cross a bridge which had been ascertained to be unsafe'.[139] However, the justified intensity of intervention decreases as the impact of the threat on individual autonomy also decreases. As such, even temporary interfering with the individual's conduct is only justified 'as long as there is a *significant* harm to be prevented'.[140] For instance, the observation of someone mistaking cherry jam for strawberry jam would not justify a forcible intervention, even if it was only temporary.[141] On the flip side, the justified intensity of temporary intervening measures increases as the risk of harm and the degree of irrevocability of harm increases.[142]

---

[132] Le Grand and New (2015), p. 132.

[133] Feinberg (1989), pp. 124–142.

[134] Feinberg (1971), p. 110; Le Grand and New (2015), pp. 120–121; Goodin (1993), pp. 235–236.

[135] Feinberg (1989), pp. 124–147.

[136] Ibid, p. 126.

[137] Ibid, p. 124.

[138] Le Grand and New (2015), p. 120.

[139] Mill (1863), p. 186, cited by Feinberg (1971), p. 112.

[140] Le Grand and New (2015), pp. 111, 120–121 (emphasis added); Feinberg (1989), p. 126; see further Maclean (2009), p. 28; Renn (2008), p. 96.

[141] Feinberg (1989), p. 118.

[142] Le Grand and New (2015), p. 120; Feinberg (1989), pp. 117–127.

Even if the expected harm is serious, in which both the destruction of private homes and especially death is, the justified intensity of intervention further depends on the harm's *imminence*. With respect to Mill's example of an unsafe bridge, if time would not allow to warn the person, the seizing of that person would not unjustifiably infringe his or her liberty, as 'there was a solid presumption, in advance of checking, that this person did not wish to run the risk'.[143] Yet, a warning is the appropriate measure if enough time is left before the person sets a foot on the bridge.[144] Thus, the concept of reasoning failures does not justify the restriction of just any ultimately harmful behaviour.[145] For instance, the failure to engage in exercise, eat healthy food, or attend medical check-ups would not warrant state intervention solely on the grounds of reasoning failures.[146] In this regard, the concept of 'reasoning failures', advocated by the majority of commentators, recognises that happiness is a state of mind which one cannot conceptualise in abstract ends or means. While health and welfare may be ends in themselves to some, to others they may merely constitute the means to self-fulfilment.[147] Consequently, a paternalistic rationale to promote individuals' health and welfare in general would unjustifiably substitute people's ends with a value-judgment about the legitimacy of those ends.[148]

In the context of natural hazards, it is particularly the criterion of *sufficient certainty* that undermines a 'presumption of nonvoluntariness', even if the potential harm is assessed as serious. In practice, as Chap. 2 exposed in detail,[149] science usually remains uncertain, whether, when, or where a natural hazard may manifest.[150] The certainty of forecasts for hydrometeorological hazard significantly decreases beyond a few days.[151] For geophysical hazards, commentators even describe forecasting to be 'in a primitive stage'.[152] In fact, early warning systems currently only provide a warning between seconds and minutes.[153] As such, science will often not be able to forecast with sufficient probability the manifestation of a natural hazards in a *specific* place in the *foreseeable* future.

---

143 Feinberg (1971), p. 112; Mill (1863), p. 186.

144 Mill (1863), p. 186.

145 Flanigan (2017), p. 304.

146 Ibid.

147 Maclean (2009), p. 28.

148 Le Grand and New (2015), p. 102.

149 See Sect. 2.3.2.

150 Renn (2008), p. 178.

151 Edwards and Challenor (2013), pp. 112–113.

152 Lomnitz and Wisner (2012), pp. 315–316, citing National Research Council (U.S.) (2003), p. 149.

153 Lomnitz and Wisner (2012), p. 318.

4.2.2.2 Justifications for Paternalistic Interferences Under the ECHR

In contrast to the presented approach in moral and political philosophy, the jurisprudence of the Court has not addressed the assessment of 'reasoning failures' in a systematic manner. Based on a review of general case law, this section nevertheless shows that the conceptualisation in moral and political philosophy reverberates in the Court's assessment of paternalistic justifications for interferences.

The principle of personal autonomy is an underlying principle of the ECHR[154] as Chap. 3 has already discussed.[155] While this chapter examines what measures the state may lawfully implement, Chap. 3 has inter alia examined the extent to which the consequences of distorted risk perception in the natural hazard context oblige the state to intervene. In doing so, Chap. 3 has already demonstrated how the notion of personal autonomy limits the state's responsibility in terms of its positive obligations to protect Convention rights.[156] The notion of personal autonomy encompasses the freedom to live life according to one's own choices, including engaging in activities that may be perceived as physically or morally harmful or even dangerous for the individual involved.[157] Consequently, even if such activities pose threats to that person's legally protected interests, the state is not obliged to interfere until the threat reaches a certain level of likeliness, seriousness and immediacy.[158] In fact, unless the threat reaches this threshold, such interference may even amount to a violation of the ECHR and would a justification.[159]

A review of the Court's case law in this subsection further shows that to protect the individual's autonomy, the Court has found that paternalistic interventions are less justified when the conduct or situation is less *immediate* in posing a *serious* risk to the individual. In the absence of cases in the disaster context, this analysis derives the criteria for paternalistically justified interventions from general case law. As such, cases relating to, for example, hunger strikes illustrate the high threshold to justify interventions in the individual's autonomy.[160] Such cases are comparable to cases of distorted risk perception related to natural hazards in terms of the individual's attitude towards the threat to the protected interests. People on hunger strikes usually protest a measure or situation,[161] and intend to initiate a change.[162] As such,

[154] ECtHR, 5th Sec., *Prilutskiy v Ukraine,* Judgment, 26 February 2015, para 32; ECtHR, *Pretty v United Kingdom,* Judgment, 29 April 2002, Eur Court HR III 155, p. 193 para 61.

[155] See Sect. 3.2.3.1.

[156] See Sect. 3.2.3.1.

[157] ECtHR, 5th Sec., *Prilutskiy v Ukraine,* Judgment, 26 February 2015, para 32.

[158] See Sect. 3.2.3.2.

[159] ECtHR, 5th Sec., *Prilutskiy v Ukraine,* Judgment, 26 February 2015, para 32; Dröge (2003), p. 330.

[160] Grabenwarter and Pabel (2021), § 20 para 27.

[161] See, e.g., ECtHR, 2nd Sec., *Horoz c Turqui,* Judgment, 31 March 2009, para 9; Dröge (2003), p. 330.

[162] For this reason, Dröge argues that force feeding may serve the non-paternalistic purpose to avert the state's exposure to this kind of extortion, see Dröge (2003), p. 330.

the harmful consequences of the hunger strike to physical integrity, or even to life, are not the *intended end*, but a means to achieve another end. Similarly, living in a risk zone prone to natural hazards is regularly a means to attain the benefits of living with this risk, but the risks are not the *intended end*.

The case law on hunger strikes acknowledges the conflicting obligations on the part of the state.[163] On the one hand, the member state is under a positive obligation to protect the right to life under Article 2(1) of the ECHR. On the other hand, the member state needs to respect the individual's right to physical integrity as safeguarded by Article 8(1) of the ECHR, which force-feeding would interfere with. The case law balances these competing interests by finding that a state may intervene if the person 'would be subject to injuries of a *permanent character*, and the forced feeding is even obligatory if an *obvious danger for the individual's life* exists'.[164] Thus, the *seriousness* and *certainty* of harm, as well as its degree of *irrevocability*, play a role in assessing whether the state has to respect the person's decision to take a risk, *in casu*, to refuse food. Consequently, there is a very limited scope to apply paternalistic rationales to justify state interferences in the rights protected under the ECHR. The respective threat to an individual's interests must have reached a minimum level of intensity. Otherwise, the paternalistic interference would undermine the value of autonomy that the ECHR protects.

It follows with respect to the enforcement of risk reduction in the context of natural hazards that *paternalistic* aims only justify interferences under strict conditions. In accordance with the Court's jurisprudence as well as moral and state philosophy, permissible paternalism requires a certain and high possibility of grave, irrevocable, and unintended harm.

In the context of natural hazards, particularly floods and earthquakes, the strict requirements for paternalistically motivated justifications will often not be met until the natural hazard is already imminent. At this stage, involuntary disaster response measures, such as forced evacuations, may not only be justified, but required to fulfil the state's positive obligation to protect the right to life, as Chap. 3 has shown.[165] Yet, for preventive and mitigative DRR measures, such as the above examined regulations in the context of spatial planning and controlled urban development, a justification based on paternalistic aims is very unlikely. For a start, the strict requirements for permissible paternalistic interventions will usually only be met when it is too late for such preventive measures to take place. An exception might be the case of recurring serious natural hazards in a region.[166] However, even then a paternalistic aim can only justify such interventions that are suitable and, above all,

---

[163] EComHR, *X v Germany,* Decision, 9 May 1984, p. 8; ECtHR, *Nevmerzhitsky v Ukraine,* Judgment, 5 April 2005, Eur Court HR II 307, pp. 329–330 paras 93–99.

[164] EComHR, *X v Germany,* Decision, 9 May 1984, p. 8 (emphasis added); see further ECtHR, *Nevmerzhitsky v Ukraine,* Judgment, 5 April 2005, Eur Court HR II 307, paras 93–94.

[165] See Sects. 3.2.3.2 and 3.2.3.3.

[166] See, e.g., ECtHR, *Budayeva and others v Russia,* Judgment, 20 March 2008, Eur Court HR II 267, pp. 276–277 paras 13–15. The regular occurrence of mudslides gave rise to a positive obligation on the part of the state to ensure the protection of the affected individuals' right to life.

necessary to protect the individual's interests once the natural hazard manifests. If a less intrusive but equally effective measure, such as timely evacuation, is available, it takes precedence. For many natural hazards, for instance hydrometeorological hazards, timely evacuations are usually able to protect individuals' physical integrity and life.

Overall, competing arguments in academic and societal debate that justify intrusive DRR measures solely on the basis of the consequences of distorted risk perception for individuals are generally not cogent. The examination of both the jurisprudence of the Court and the discussion in moral and political philosophy shows that such paternalistic goal can only justify interventions within a very limited framework. The high threshold often precludes the justification of interventions that enforce the avoidance or mitigation of disaster risks. Consequently, their justification cannot be based on the paternalistic rationale of realising the people's 'authentic self'.

4.2.3 Justifiability Based on Non-Paternalistic Aims

In contrast to the examined paternalistic aims, the harm principle can justify more far-reaching interferences. As discussed in Chap. 1,[167] the harm principle restricts the exercise of autonomy when activities affect the legitimate interests of others.[168] Even though voluntary exposure to a natural hazard ostensibly affects only the individual, this risk, like virtually any risk, can also affect a third party or the community as a whole. For instance, seat-belt regulation is often considered a classic paternalistic example. In fact, however, seatbelt regulations are an example of impure paternalism,[169] since it not only protects the individual from 'risk to self'.[170] On a closer look, such legislation further protects communal interests against the negative effects of individual choices. For instance, individual choice may ensue medical costs, which are partially borne by society as a whole, once the risk manifests.[171] This so-called 'public charge argument' adds a socially harmful dimension to effectively every private risk.[172] In addition to costs borne by the community, such as medical costs, private risk-taking can directly affect other private parties as well. In the context of seat belt regulations, it was noted that a person not wearing a seat belt in an accident is less likely able to help other persons involved in the

167 See Sect. 1.7.1.3.

168 Alemanno (2016), pp. 198–199.

169 Dworkin (1972), p. 68.

170 Alemanno (2016), pp. 197, 199–200.

171 Ibid, p. 199; see further Dworkin (1972), p. 65; see Flanigan (2017), pp. 309–313.

172 Kleinig (1984), pp. 92–94; Suber (2012), p. 634.

accident.[173] Admittedly, the risk behind such examples primarily poses a threat to the interests of the risk-taking individual. However, its manifestation can also have secondary negative consequences for communal interests, such as the ability to provide first aid to others. On this basis, the harm principle underpins many governmental regulations of individual behaviour, such as mandatory insurances for cars or social security to protect society from financial burdens.[174] In fact, Suber notes that

> [i]n a welfare state which shifts costs to compensate those who harm themselves, virtually all self-harm will be other-harm too; hence, virtually every corner of life could be regulated by law without violating the harm principle…[175]

As such, the voluntary inhabitation of a zone prone to natural hazards also has a public dimension, even if primarily individual interests are affected. On the one hand, it has already been pointed out in Chap. 1 that disasters usually trigger expensive disaster response and reconstruction measures that consume public resources.[176] On the other hand, the destruction of commercial structures by natural hazards may also have economic ripple effects on the broader community.[177] For instance, if large-scale natural hazards destroy businesses, people lose their jobs, which then decreases the community's tax base. In this regard, Timothy Beatley sees the risk of 'serious harms' to the larger community if the construction and operation of commercial structures in high-risk areas are not regulated.[178]

The consequent applicability of the harm principle to justify interferences in the individual's sphere gives rise to the challenge of protecting the interests of the community without undermining the protection of individual interests. This section began by outlining the general requirements for this balancing exercise and found in this regard that the proportionality test inter alia depends on whether the interference serves public or individual interests. As such, with respect to the former, that is, a non-paternalistic aim, the Court examines whether the interference is proportionate to the legitimate aim pursued and whether the aims invoked are 'relevant and sufficient'.[179] To that end, the Court contrasts the disadvantages for the beneficiary of a convention right with the weight of the legitimate aim pursued.[180] At the same time, the Court's assessment of the 'fair balance' between community and individual interests is characterised by its consideration of the state's margin of

[173] BVerfG, *Verfassungsmäßigkeit der Gurtanlegepflicht für Kraftfahrzeugführer,* Judgment, 24 July 1986, 1 BvR 331/85.

[174] Heun (2011), p. 26.

[175] Suber (2012), p. 634.

[176] See Sect. 1.7.1.3.

[177] Beatley (1989), p. 16.

[178] Ibid.

[179] Grabenwarter and Pabel (2021), § 18 para 16.

[180] Ibid.

appreciation,[181] which should go 'hand in hand with a European supervision'.[182] The remainder of this section takes a closer look at the justification for the interventions in the context of zoning and building regulations identified in the first section of this chapter based on the interests of the community as a whole.

4.2.3.1 General Remarks on the Justifiability of Interferences in the Context of Spatial Planning and Controlled Urban Development

The public interest can justify interventions that do not meet the high requirements for paternalistically motivated interventions. As the necessary legitimate aim for interventions in the context of spatial planning and controlled urban development, the right to property under A1-P1 requires the pursuit of public (or general) interest.[183] These interests include legitimate political purposes, such as economic, social or other policies in the public interests.[184] So far, the Court has only rejected the legislature's judgment of what falls into the ambit of a public interest when it is 'manifestly without reasonable foundation'.[185] Not only is this burden minimal,[186] but the Court has specifically accepted the adoption of land and city development plans, and the securing of land in connection with land development plans, as covered under the notion of public interest in the past.[187] This must apply all the more when the measures serve to control disaster risks, which is a task of high public interest.[188]

While the Court has generally set a low threshold for meeting the criterion of pursuing a matter of public interest,[189] it has examined the proportionality test in

---

[181] Ibid, § 18 para 20.

[182] ECtHR, *Handyside v United Kingdom,* Judgment, 7 December 1976, Eur Court HR (ser A) 24, para 49.

[183] The justification of an interference with A1-P1 requires that the interference is required by the *public interest* in the case of deprivations of property or is in accordance with the *general interest* in the case of restrictions to control the use of property. Despite the terminological difference, the Court has treated the terms as synonymous in the past. See Peukert (2009), Artikel 1 des 1. ZP, p. 657 para 42.

[184] EComHR, *James and Others v United Kingdom,* Judgment, 21 February 1986, Eur Court HR (ser A) 91, para 45.

[185] ECtHR, *Jahn and Others v Germany,* Judgment, 30 June 2005, Eur Court HR VI 55, pp. 80–81 para 91; Grabenwarter and Pabel (2021), § 25 para 19.

[186] Tarlock and Albrecht (2018), p. 50, citing van Dijk and van Hoof (1998).

[187] See, e.g., ECtHR, *Sporrong and Lönnroth v Sweden,* Judgment, 23 September 1982, Eur Court HR (ser A) 52, para 69; ECtHR, 4th Sec., *Skibińscy v Poland,* Judgment, 14 November 2006, para 86.

[188] See, e.g., the assessment of the task of flood protection by the German Federal Administrative Court in BVerwG, Decision, 22 July 2004, 7 CN 1.04, at p. 11.

[189] Tarlock and Albrecht (2018), p. 50.

detail.[190] As such, the goal of disaster risk control, as a high public interest, must be given more weight than is usually the case in spatial planning. This public interest needs to be contrasted against the disadvantages imposed on the individual. In doing so, the Court considers the circumstances of the individual case when weighing up the interests. On the one hand, it makes a difference in the quantification of the individual's interest based on whether the respective property was lawfully or unlawfully acquired or constructed. As described in this chapter, unlawfully acquired or erected 'possessions' can still fall into the ambit of A1-P1 under certain circumstances.[191] However, how legitimate the persons' expectation is to continue the enjoyment of that possession depends on the circumstances of the case.[192] For instance, it may be relevant whether the individual attempted to exploit a weakness in the system,[193] and the degree of fault on the part of the individual. On the other hand, some interferences by the state are more intrusive and therefore place higher demands on their justification. To illustrate this connection, the analysis returns to the justifiability of the interventions identified in the first section of this chapter.

4.2.3.2 The Justification of Forced Resettlement from Certain Zones

The first section of this chapter identified deprivation of property under A1(1)2-P1 with the aim of forcing people to move away from risk zones as an effective but most serious interference with A1-P1. As such, this interference is generally disproportionate.[194] Deprivation refers to the legal or de facto extinction of the individual's rights.[195] As analysed above, measures to resettle people who live in areas that are prone to natural hazards may fall into this ambit. Although, deprivation of property usually upsets the 'fair balance' to the detriment of the individual, it may be tendered legitimate with the payment of compensation.[196] In this regard, *de jure* or *de facto* expropriations normally require the payment of full compensation to achieve a fair balance, even if the expropriation serves the reduction of disaster risks.[197]

---

[190] Gerards (2013), p. 469.

[191] ECtHR, *Öneryildiz v Turkey,* Judgment, 30 November 2004, Eur Court HR XII 79, p. 128 paras 127–129; ECtHR, *Keriman Tekin et Autres c Turquie (French),* Judgment, 15 November 2016, paras 40–43; ECtHR, *Hamer v Belgium,* Judgment, 27 November 2007, Eur Court HR V 73, p. 94 para 77; Ploeger and Groetelaers (2007), p. 1429.

[192] ECtHR, *Hamer v Belgium,* Judgment, 27 November 2007, Eur Court HR V 73, p. 94 para 76.

[193] See, e.g., ECtHR, *National & Provincial Building Society, Leeds Permanent Building Society and Yorkshire Building Society v United Kingdom,* Judgment, 23 October 1997, para 109.

[194] Ploeger and Groetelaers (2007), p. 1431; Peukert (2009), Artikel 1 des 1. ZP, p. 660 para 53.

[195] Grabenwarter and Pabel (2021), § 25 paras 10–13.

[196] Ibid, § 25 paras 22–25.

[197] For a respective case study of different jurisdictions, see Tarlock and Albrecht (2018).

4.2.3.3 The Justification of Bans on Erecting New Buildings in Certain Zones

The first section of this chapter also found that bans on the construction of new buildings in risk zones interfere with A1(2)-P1 by imposing controls over the use of property. In contrast to the justification of expropriations, the prescription or prohibition of a certain use of the respective property do not usually require the payment of compensation.[198] Particular in the context of land planning, the Court has considered the community's general interest to be pre-eminent.[199] This is due to the essentially evolutionary nature of the owners' rights in this context.[200] Consequently, it is compatible with A1-P1 for the state to impose and maintain various building restrictions or bans for different risk zones.[201] Mere ownership of land does not per se confer the right to build on it. While urban and regional planning regulation may reduce the value of the regulated land, the state does not normally have to pay compensation to the owner.[202] However, the greater the impairment, the higher the demands on the state to justify the respective regulation.[203] Exceptionally, the burdens on the individual through construction restrictions may be so severe that appropriate compensation may be necessary to render the building restrictions legitimate.[204]

4.2.3.4 The Justification of Regulations to Reinforce Buildings Retrospectively

Finally, the first section of this chapter also established that obliging individuals to upgrade a house to new construction standards in order to withstand natural hazards constitutes an interference with A1(2)-P1 because this would also impose controls over the use of the property. In regard to retrospective conditions on the use of lawfully erected property, greater weight must be given to the owner's interest than with regard to the prohibition of erecting new buildings. As stated in the first section of this chapter, the owner has a legitimate expectation of the continued use of his property. To justifiably interfere with this trust without a duty to compensate, it is not sufficient for the state to merely aim to reduce merely theoretical dangers to public

---

[198] ECtHR, *Depalle v France,* Judgment, 29 March 2010, Eur Court HR III 233, p. 269 para 91; Grabenwarter and Pabel (2021), § 25 para 14.

[199] ECtHR, *Gorraiz Lizarraga and Others v Spain,* Judgment, 27 April 2004, Eur Court HR III 255, pp. 281–282 para 70.

[200] Ibid.

[201] Tarlock and Albrecht (2018), p. 49.

[202] Ibid, pp. 49, 53–54. This interpretation is also reflected in German case law on the right to build in risk zones, see BVerwG, Decision, 22 July 2004, BVerwGE 121, 283.

[203] Tarlock and Albrecht (2018), p. 50; Köck (2017), pp. 168–171.

[204] See, e contrario, ECtHR, *Depalle v France,* Judgment, 29 March 2010, Eur Court HR III 233, p. 269 para 91; on the corresponding interpretation by German courts, see Tarlock and Albrecht (2018), pp. 53–54.

safety. In fact, the European legal practice reflects this reasoning. For instance, the law of several member states allows authorities to oblige an individual to upgrade lawfully erected buildings to protect important public interests against threats, such as from natural hazards.[205] Germany, for example, combines these important public interests in the concept of 'public safety'. Public safety refers to 'the whole public legal order, individual life, health and freedom as well as the institutions of government and public goods like public utilities'.[206] Austria, on the other hand, defines the scope of application more narrowly and only includes threats to life and health or the threat of serious economic damage to the general public.[207]

To strike the balance between the individual's right to peaceful enjoyment of property and important public interests, orders to retrofit usually also require the existence of a *specific danger*.[208] The 'danger' concept traces—as far as Germany and Austria are concerned—back to the Prussian police law of the nineteenth century and refers to 'a situation or condition, in which in case of an unimpeded course of events a condition or a conduct will with sufficient probability lead to an injury of public safety'.[209] A danger is *specific* if the time, place, and circumstances are clearly determined or determinable. In contrast, a so-called *abstract danger* is insufficient to justify retrospective orders to upgrade a lawfully erected building.[210] An *abstract danger* exists when general experience suggests that certain types of behaviour or conditions lead to an injury.[211] According to the general conceptualisation of a *specific danger*, the injury must also be expected in the foreseeable future,[212] even though it must not amount to a 'danger in delay'.[213] However, such a strict standard of expected temporal proximity is not compatible with the effective protection of important legal interests such as life and health. This strict standard would in fact practically exclude the defence against many risks. As shown, the spatial and temporal occurrence of many natural hazards cannot be precisely predicted. Consequently, orders to upgrade may be compatible with the right to property even if there is no sufficient probability of occurrence in the foreseeable future, so long as the occurrence is not completely improbable.[214] In this case, however, the danger must be substantial. This means that the possibilities for averting the danger or rescue are not sufficient according to the current state of knowledge about typical

[205] For Germany see, e.g., Finkelnburg et al. (2018), pp. 207–214; for Austria, see Giese (2009, 2011).

[206] Heun (2011), pp. 16–17.

[207] Giese (2009), pp. 58–59; Giese (2011), pp. 224–227.

[208] See Finkelnburg et al. (2018), pp. 207–214; Giese (2009), pp. 58–59; Giese (2011), pp. 224–227.

[209] Heun (2011), p. 16; Finkelnburg et al. (2018), p. 164 para 3.

[210] Giese (2009), p. 59; Giese (2011), p. 226.

[211] Finkelnburg et al. (2018), p. 164 para 3.

[212] BVerwG, Judgment, 26 June 1970, IV C 99.67 ; Finkelnburg et al. (2018), p. 164 para 3.

[213] Giese (2009), p. 59; Giese (2011), p. 226.

[214] See in the context of fire safety requirements, Hessischer Verwaltungsgerichtshof, Decision, 19 October 1999, NVwZ-RR 2000, 581, p. 582; Bavarian Administrative Court, Decision, 3 April 2020, 15 ZB 19.1024.

damage processes.[215] This assessment depends on the characteristics of the natural hazard and on the location of the house and its structural conditions in the individual case.

However, even then, the measures need to be proportional to the non-paternalistic aim.[216] This means that the measures need to be necessary to prevent the realisation of the *specific danger*, while they must protect the right to property as much as possible.[217] As a result, without compensation, a state may not order the individual to upgrade a vulnerable building to the optimal level of protection, but only to the minimum level necessary to ensure effective protection.[218] Moreover, as a consequence of the proportionality principle, construction measures take precedence over the revocation of a building or use permit.[219]

4.3 Conclusion

This chapter has legally examined a number of DRR measures recommended by experts and found that none of them violate the individual's interests if certain conditions are met. It has first shown that the state has a number of DRR tools at its disposal that reduce risks by promoting behavioural change among individuals. The analysis showed that disaster risk communication, the 'framing' of information, and the provision of financial incentives can contribute to risk reduction without interfering with the rights of individuals. Instead, they contribute to people's autonomous decision-making. Although these characteristics make them important tools for disaster risk management, these instruments are ultimately less effective than legally coercive tools.

If legally coercive instruments interfere with fundamental rights, they need a justification. In this regard, this chapter has demonstrated that paternalistic aims may justify some DRR measures that interfere with the rights of individuals. However, paternalistic motives only justify interferences if the threat to autonomy has intensified in terms of *seriousness*, *imminence*, and *certainty*. Moreover, the measures must offend the individual's autonomy no more than necessary to ensure its protection. As a result, paternalistic aims are usually not sufficient to justify interventions with fundamental rights that enforce long-term prevention or mitigation of disaster risks, such as through the implementation of building and zoning laws. On the one hand, most natural hazards are uncertain in terms of the time and place of their occurrence. On the other hand, less restrictive measures than building

---

[215] Hessischer Verwaltungsgerichtshof, Decision, 19 October 1999, NVwZ-RR 2000 581, p. 582; Bavarian Administrative Court, Decision, 3 April 2020, 15 ZB 19.1024.

[216] Giese (2009), p. 59; Finkelnburg et al. (2018), pp. 211–212.

[217] Giese (2009), p. 59; Finkelnburg et al. (2018), pp. 211–212.

[218] See, e.g., Hamburgisches Oberverwaltungsgericht, Decision, 4 January 1996, NVwZ-RR 1997, 466, para 14.

[219] Giese (2009), p. 59; Giese (2011), p. 227.

and zoning laws are available to protect autonomy from most natural hazards, such as (forced) evacuations once the hazard becomes imminent. This means that even though paternalistic arguments are often used in the debate for more effective risk management, these can only justify encroachments on fundamental rights within a very narrow scope. Instead, the aim to protect individuals from themselves largely limits the state's options to the choice-preserving but less effective instruments.

In contrast, the aim of protecting communal interests may allow more far-reaching interferences with fundamental rights. For example, expropriation and retrofitting orders for buildings in high-risk zones are very effective long-term DRR measures. At the same time, they impose intensive interventions to the right to property. Nevertheless, community interests can justify them even though additional compensation is sometimes necessary to strike a fair balance between individual and community interests. It can thus be stated that the state could basically also legally undertake drastic but effective DRR measures in the field of spatial planning and controlled urban development to protect the community's interests from costs, such as those related to disaster response and reconstruction. In comparison, an encroachment based on paternalistic aims would not be justifiable even with compensation payments.

In response to this book's second sub-question, this means that the state could legally implement very effective measures to realise the social and economic benefits of DRR. However, the analysis of justification conditions, especially regarding retrospective land planning and building requirements, leads to the conclusion that such effective measures will unlikely solve the major problem of populated risk zones in Europe. To explain this, two circumstances should be highlighted. On the one hand, the measures are very cost-intensive due to the compensation payments that are often necessary to achieve a fair balance. On the other hand, such coercive measures would probably be met with strong political resistance. In a democratic state, risk management must take account of people's preferences when deciding which risks and DRR measures are acceptable, as Chap. 5 explores in more detail. As shown, many continue to live in risk areas despite the possibility of moving away or upgrading their homes. Moreover, many not only tolerate the risks of natural disasters, but also benefit from risk-taking. With respect to the invoked example of people inhabiting areas prone to volcano eruptions, their established livelihood may depend on the benefits of living with this risk.[220] In such cases, in which the restriction of private risks would be inappropriate or 'out of step with public sentiment', the state may have to make use of less intervening risk management measures such as risk communication and financial incentives.[221] The political dimension may also explain why disaster risk management still relies mainly on disaster response measures for effective protection.[222]

---

[220] Dibben (2008), p. 292; Kelman and Mather (2008), pp. 190–191; Dominey-Howes and Minos-Minopoulos (2004), pp. 285–286.

[221] Le Grand and New (2015), p. 139; Camerer and Kunreuther (1989), pp. 582–584.

[222] See Sects. 1.1.1 and 1.1.2.

The previous chapters have addressed the questions of what the state can, must and may do to protect life and property against natural hazards. The following chapter explores how societies could adapt their decision-making procedure in which society determines the trade-off between the minimum necessary and maximum possible protection. To decrease the influence of distorted risk perceptions on democratic decision-making, the next chapter argues for implementing deliberative processes in the collective decision-making process.

References

Alemanno A (2016) Risk and regulation. In: Burgess A, Alemanno A, Zinn JO (eds) Routledge handbook of risk studies. Routledge, Abingdon, pp 191–203

Arai-Takahashi Y (2002) The margin of appreciation doctrine and the principle of proportionality in the jurisprudence of the ECHR. Intersentia, Antwerp

Arai-Takahashi Y (2015) Proportionality. In: Shelton D (ed) The Oxford handbook of international human rights law. Oxford University Press, Oxford, pp 446–468

Arie S (2003) Volcano neighbours refuse to move. The Guardian, 31 August 2003. https://www.theguardian.com/world/2003/aug/31/italy.sophiearie. Accessed 19 June 2023

Artino A, Caponetto R, Evola G, Margani G, Marino EM, Murgano E (2020) Decision support system for the sustainable seismic and energy renovation of buildings: methodological layout. Sustainability 12(10273):1–21. https://doi.org/10.3390/su122410273

Baan PJ, Klijn F (2004) Flood risk perception and implications for flood risk management in the Netherlands. Int J River Basin Manag 2(2):113–122. https://doi.org/10.1080/15715124.2004.9635226

Beatley T (1989) Towards a moral philosophy of natural disaster mitigation. Int J Mass Emerg Disasters 7(1):5–32. https://doi.org/10.1177/028072708900700102

Bovens L (2009) The ethics of nudge. In: Grüne-Yanoff T, Hansson SO (eds) Preference change: approaches from philosophy, economics and psychology. Springer, Dordrecht, pp 207–219

Buck R, Ferrer R (2012) Emotion, warnings, and the ethics of risk communication. In: Roeser S, Hillerbrand R, Sandin P, Peterson M (eds) Handbook of risk theory: epistemology, decision theory, ethics, and social implications of risk. Springer, Dordrecht, pp 693–724

Calliess C (2022) EU-GRCharta Art. 17. In: Calliess C, Ruffert M (eds) EUV/AEUV: Das Verfassungsrecht der Europäischen Union mit Europäischer Grundrechtecharta, 6th edn. C.H. BECK, München

Camerer CF, Kunreuther H (1989) Decision processes for low probability events: policy implications. J Policy Anal Manag 8(4):565. https://doi.org/10.2307/3325045

Christman J (2020) Autonomy in moral and political philosophy. In: Zalta EN (ed) The Stanford Encyclopedia of Philosophy. https://plato.stanford.edu/entries/autonomy-moral/. Accessed 19 June 2023

Conly S (2013) Against autonomy: justifying coercive paternalism. Cambridge University Press, Cambridge

Crawford E (2011) Proportionality. In: Wolfrum R, Peters A (eds) Max Planck Encyclopedia of Public International Law. https://opil.ouplaw.com/display/10.1093/law:epil/9780199231690/law-9780199231690-e1459. Accessed 19 June 2023

Cremer H-J (2006) Kapitel 22: Eigentumsschutz. In: Grote R, Marauhn T (eds) EMRK/GG: Konkordanzkommentar zum europäischen und deutschen Grundrechtsschutz. Mohr Siebeck, Tübingen, pp 1222–1345

Cross FB (1998) Facts and values in risk assessment. Reliab Eng Syst Saf 59(1):27–40. https://doi.org/10.1016/S0951-8320(97)00116-6

Crosweller HS, Wilmshurst J (2013) Natural hazards and risk: the human perspective. In: Rougier J, Hill LJ, Sparks RSJ (eds) Risk and uncertainty assessment for natural hazards. Cambridge University Press, Cambridge, pp 548–569

Dibben CJ (2008) Leaving the city for the suburbs—the dominance of 'ordinary' decision making over volcanic risk perception in the production of volcanic risk on Mt Etna, Sicily. J Volcanol Geotherm Res 172(3–4):288–299. https://doi.org/10.1016/j.jvolgeores.2007.12.014

Dominey-Howes D, Minos-Minopoulos D (2004) Perceptions of hazard and risk on Santorini. J Volcanol Geotherm Res 137(4):285–310. https://doi.org/10.1016/j.jvolgeores.2004.06.002

Dröge C (2003) Positive Verpflichtungen der Staaten in der Europäischen Menschenrechtskonvention. Beiträge zum ausländischen öffentlichen Recht und Völkerrecht, Bd. 159. Springer, Heidelberg

Dworkin G (1972) Paternalism. Monist 56(1):64–84. https://doi.org/10.5840/monist197256119

Edenhofer O, Pichs-Madruga R, Sokona Y, Farahani E, Kadner S, Seyboth K, Adler A, Baum I, Brunner S, Eickemeier P, Kriemann B, Savolainen J, Schlömer S, von Stechow C, Zwickel T, Minx JC (eds) (2014) Climate Change 2014: Mitigation of Climate Change: Contribution of Working Group III to the Fifth Assessment Report of the Intergovernmental Panel on Climate Change. Cambridge University Press, Cambridge

Edwards C (2016) Italy puzzles over how to save 700,000 people from wrath of Vesuvius. The Local, 13 October 2016. https://www.thelocal.it/20161013/evacuation-plan-for-vesuvius-eruption-naples-campania-will-be-ready-by-october. Accessed 19 June 2023

Edwards TL, Challenor PG (2013) Risk and uncertainty in hydrometeorological hazards. In: Rougier J, Hill LJ, Sparks RSJ (eds) Risk and uncertainty assessment for natural hazards. Cambridge University Press, Cambridge, pp 100–150

EM-DAT, CRED/UCLouvain, Brussels, Belgium. www.emdat.be. Accessed 19 June 2023

Feinberg J (1971) Legal paternalism. Can J Philos 1(1):105–124. https://doi.org/10.1080/00455091.1971.10716012

Feinberg J (1989) Harm to self. The moral limits of the criminal law, vol 3. Oxford University Press, New York

Finkelnburg K, Ortloff KM, Otto C-W (2018) Öffentliches Baurecht: Band II: Bauordnungsrecht, Nachbarschutz, Rechtsschutz, 7th edn. Recht - Wirtschaft - Steuern. C.H. BECK, München

Flanigan J (2017) Seat belt mandates and paternalism. J Moral Philos 14(3):291–314. https://doi.org/10.1163/17455243-46810050

Formisano A, Vaiano G, Fabbrocino F (2019) Seismic and energetic interventions on a typical South Italy residential building: cost analysis and tax detraction. Front Built Environ 5. https://doi.org/10.3389/fbuil.2019.00012

Gerards J (2013) How to improve the necessity test of the European Court of Human Rights. Int J Constitutional Law 11(2):466–490. https://doi.org/10.1093/icon/mot004

Giese K (2009) Die nachträgliche Vorschreibung von Auflagen im Baurecht. Baurechtliche Blätter 12(2):47–61. https://doi.org/10.1007/s00738-009-0616-2

Giese K (2011) Baurechtliche Maßnahmen zum Schutz des Baubestandes vor Hochwassergefahren. Baurechtliche Blätter 14(5):203–231. https://doi.org/10.1007/s00738-011-0026-0

Glöckner A (2016) Psychology and disaster: why we do not see looming disasters and how our way of thinking causes them. Glob Policy 7:16–24. https://doi.org/10.1111/1758-5899.12289

Goodin RE (1993) Democracy, preferences and paternalism. Policy Sci 26(3):229–247. https://doi.org/10.1007/BF00999718

Grabenwarter C, Pabel K (2021) Europäische Menschenrechtskonvention, 7th edn. Juristische Kurz-Lehrbücher. C.H. BECK, München

Green HP (1981) The role of law in determining acceptability of risk. Ann N Y Acad Sci 363(1):1–12. https://doi.org/10.1111/j.1749-6632.1981.tb20712.x

Greiving S, Fleischhauer M, Wanczura S (2006) Management of natural hazards in Europe: the role of spatial planning in selected EU Member States. J Environ Plann Manag 49(5):739–757. https://doi.org/10.1080/09640560600850044

Hacker P (2018) Nudging and autonomy: a philosophical and legal appraisal. In: Micklitz H-W, Sibony A-L, Esposito F (eds) Research methods in consumer law: a handbook. Edward Elgar, Cheltenham, pp 77–118

Hansen PG, Jespersen AM (2013) Nudge and the manipulation of choice. Eur J Risk Regul 4(1):3–28. https://doi.org/10.1017/S1867299X00002762

Heun W (2011) Risk management by the government and the constitution. In: Duttge G, Lee SW (eds) The law in the information and risk society. Universitätsverlag Göttingen, Göttingen, pp 15–29

Ivčević A, Mazurek H, Siame L, Bertoldo R, Statzu V, Agharroud K, Estrela Rego I, Mukherjee N, Bellier O (2021) Lessons learned about the importance of raising risk awareness in the Mediterranean region (North Morocco and West Sardinia, Italy). Nat Haz Earth Syst Sci 21(12):3749–3765. https://doi.org/10.5194/nhess-21-3749-2021

Jablonski S (2014) Hochwasserschutzrecht: Herausforderungen - Rechtsgrundlagen - Ansatzpunkte und Instrumente. Leipziger Schriften zum Umwelt- und Planungsrecht, vol 26. Nomos, Baden-Baden

Kelman I, Mather TA (2008) Living with volcanoes: the sustainable livelihoods approach for volcano-related opportunities. J Volcanol Geotherm Res 172(3-4):189–198. https://doi.org/10.1016/j.jvolgeores.2007.12.007

Kleinig J (1984) Paternalism. Clarendon Press, Oxford

Köck W (2017) Rechtliche Anforderungen an das Bauen in Überschwemmungs- und Risikogebieten. In: Faßbender K, Köck W (eds) Aktuelle Fragen und Entwicklungen im Hochwasserschutzrecht: Dokumentation des 21. Leipziger Umweltrechtlichen Symposions des Instituts für Umwelt- und Planungsrecht der Universität Leipzig und des Helmholtz-Zentrums für Umweltforschung - UFZ am 07. und 08. April 2016, 1st edn. Nomos, Baden-Baden, pp 147–172

Kunig P, Kämmerer JA (2021) Art. 2. In: Kämmerer JA, Kotzur M (eds) Grundgesetz-Kommentar Gesamtwerk, 7th edn. C.H. BECK, München, pp 105–202

Kunreuther H, Gupta S, Bosetti V, Cooke R, Dutt V, Ha-Duong M, Held H, Llanes-Regueiro J, Patt A, Shittu E, Weber E (2014) Integrated risk and uncertainty assessment of climate change response policies. In: Edenhofer O, Pichs-Madruga R, Sokona Y, Farahani E, Kadner S, Seyboth K, Adler A, Baum I, Brunner S, Eickemeier P, Kriemann B, Savolainen J, Schlömer S, von Stechow C, Zwickel T, Minx JC (eds) Climate Change 2014: Mitigation of Climate Change: Contribution of Working Group III to the Fifth Assessment Report of the Intergovernmental Panel on Climate Change. Cambridge University Press, Cambridge, pp 151–205

Le Grand J, New B (2015) Government paternalism: nanny state or helpful friend? Princeton University Press, Princeton

Letsas G (2004) The truth in autonomous concepts: how to interpret the ECHR. Eur J Int Law 15(2):279–306. https://doi.org/10.1093/ejil/15.2.279

Letsas G (2007) A theory of interpretation of the European Convention on Human Rights. Oxford University Press, Oxford

Lomnitz C, Wisner B (2012) Earthquake. In: Wisner B, Gaillard JC, Kelman I (eds) The Routledge handbook of hazards and disaster risk reduction. Routledge, London, pp 310–321

Maclean AR (2009) Autonomy, informed consent and medical law: a relational challenge, Cambridge law, medicine, and ethics, vol 8. Cambridge University Press, Cambridge

Meier M (2021) Verhaltenswissenschaftlich inspiriertes Verwaltungshandeln: Herausforderungen und Perspektiven zur Umsetzung staatlichen Nudgings in Deutschland. Verwaltungswissenschaften in juristischer Perspektive, Bd. 5. Nomos, Baden-Baden

Michel-Kerjan E, Kunreuther H (2011) Disaster management. Redesigning flood insurance. Science 333(6041):408–409. https://doi.org/10.1126/science.1202616

Mill JS (1863) On liberty, World's classics, 2nd edn. Ticknor and Fields, Boston

Mol JM, Botzen WJW, Blasch JE (2020) Risk reduction in compulsory disaster insurance: experimental evidence on moral hazard and financial incentives. J Behav Exp Econ 84:1–22. https://doi.org/10.1016/j.socec.2019.101500

National Research Council (U.S.) (2003) Living on an active earth: perspectives on earthquake science. National Academies Press, Washington, D.C. https://doi.org/10.17226/10493
Nöggerath J, Geller RJ, Gusiakov VK (2011) Fukushima: the myth of safety, the reality of geoscience. Bull At Sci 67(5):37–46. https://doi.org/10.1177/0096340211421607
O'Mathúna DP, Dranseika V, Gordijn B (eds) (2018) Disasters: core concepts and ethical theories, Advancing global bioethics, vol 11. Springer, Cham
Pasha-Robinson L (2016) Mount Vesuvius eruption risk: emergency plans to evacuate 700,000 finalised. Independent, 14 October 2016. https://www.independent.co.uk/news/world/europe/mount-vesuvius-emergency-evacuation-eruption-plans-finalised-a7360686.html. Accessed 19 June 2023
Perrow C (2011) Fukushima and the inevitability of accidents. Bull At Sci 67(6):44–52. https://doi.org/10.1177/0096340211426395
Petzold H (1993) The convention and the principle of subsidiarity. In: Macdonald RS, Matscher F, Petzold H (eds) The European system for the protection of human rights. Nijhoff, Dordrecht, pp 41–62
Peukert W (2009) Artikel 1 des 1. ZP (Schutz des Eigentums). In: Frowein JA, Peukert W (eds) Europäische Menschenrechtskonvention: EMRK-Kommentar, 3rd edn. N.P. Engel, Kehl am Rhein, pp 639–670
Ploeger HD, Groetelaers DA (2007) The importance of the fundamental right to property for the practice of planning: an introduction to the case law of the European Court of Human Rights on Article 1, Protocol 1. Eur Plan Stud 15(10):1423–1438. https://doi.org/10.1080/09654310701550876
Renn O (2008) Risk governance: coping with uncertainty in a complex world, Earthscan risk in society series. Routledge, London
Reynolds OM Jr (1988) The reasonableness of amortization periods for nonconforming uses—balancing the private interest and the public welfare. Wash Univ J Urban Contemp Law 34:99–132
Safarpour H, Sarani M, Safi-Keykaleh M (2020) Necessity of focus on the disaster risk perception: lessons from the 2019 floods in Iran. Disaster Med Public Health Prep:1–2. https://doi.org/10.1017/dmp.2019.165
Schweizer M (2016) Nudging and the principle of proportionality: obliged to nudge? In: Mathis K, Tor A (eds) Nudging - possibilities, limitations and applications in European law and economics. Springer, Cham, pp 93–119
Spence R, So E (2021) Why do buildings collapse in earthquakes?: Building for safety in seismic areas. Wiley-Blackwell, Hoboken
Stahl S (2012) Schutzpflichten im Völkerrecht - Ansatz einer Dogmatik: Ein Beitrag zu Grund, Inhalt und Grenzen der völkerrechtlichen Schutzpflichtendogmatik im Bereich konventionell geschützter Menschenrechte. Beiträge zum ausländischen öffentlichen Recht und Völkerrecht, Bd. 232. Springer, Heidelberg
Suber P (2012) Paternalism. In: Gray CB (ed) The philosophy of law: an encyclopedia. Routledge, New York, pp 632–635
Sunstein CR (2015) The ethics of nudging. Yale J Regul 32(2):413–450. https://doi.org/10.2139/ssrn.2526341
Tarlock D, Albrecht J (2018) Potential constitutional constraints on the regulation of flood plain development: three case studies. J Flood Risk Manag 11(1):48–55. https://doi.org/10.1111/jfr3.12274
Tversky A, Kahneman D (1974) Judgment under uncertainty: heuristics and biases. Science 185(4157):1124–1131. https://doi.org/10.1126/science.185.4157.1124
Tversky A, Kahneman D (1992) Advances in prospect theory: cumulative representation of uncertainty. J Risk Uncertain 5(4):297–323. https://doi.org/10.1007/BF00122574
van Aaken A (2017) Judge the nudge: in search of the legal limits of paternalistic nudging in the EU. In: Alemanno A, Sibony A-L (eds) Nudge and the law: a European perspective. Hart, Oxford

van Dijk P, van Hoof GJ (1998) Theory and practice of the European Convention on Human Rights, 3rd edn. Kluwer Law International, The Hague

Wachinger G, Renn O, Begg C, Kuhlicke C (2013) The risk perception paradox-implications for governance and communication of natural hazards. Risk Anal 33(6):1049–1065. https://doi.org/10.1111/j.1539-6924.2012.01942.x

Weyman A, Barnett J (2016) Heuristics and biases in decision making about risk. In: Burgess A, Alemanno A, Zinn JO (eds) Routledge handbook of risk studies. Routledge, Abingdon, pp 157–166

Chapter 5
The 'Better Argument' in Legitimate Risk Governance

The material well-being of a democratic society depends on its ability to rationally manage a nearly limitless variety of often competing risks. The integrity of such a society's commitment to self-governance depends on its ability to fashion procedures that are genuinely deliberative, open, and democratic. (Kahan et al. 2006, p. 1109)

The previous chapter has examined to what extent member states of the Council of Europe ('member states') may implement measures recommended by experts to mitigate the consequences of distorted risk perception without violating individual rights under the European Convention on Human Rights[1] ('ECHR'). In this regard, Chap. 4 concluded that the insights into the biases and heuristics examined in Chap. 2 provide a valuable basis for the development of lawful measures that counteract these cultural and cognitive mechanisms, without impinging upon individual rights. Such measures include corrective communication and financial incentives. Furthermore, spatial planning and regulations to control urban development as effective measures to reduce social disaster risks can be justified, though individual compensation payments may become necessary. With the identified possibilities of lawful DRR measures to mitigate the consequences of distorted risk perception in mind, this chapter draws attention to the lack of public demand and explores potential avenues to overcome this obstacle. As discussed in Chap. 1, there is a reasonable expectation that the same psychological mechanisms that distort individuals' risk perception also impact the collective risk evaluation.[2] Psychological studies suggest that people tend to underestimate or overestimate scientifically determined probabilities of harm. Such findings not only challenge the 'voluntariness' of *individual* decision-making, but *collective* decision-making processes as well. Biases

[1] Convention for the Protection of Human Rights and Fundamental Freedoms, opened for signature 4 November 1950, 213 UNTS 221 (entered into force 3 September 1953).

[2] See Sect. 1.1.2.

C. A. Simmig, *Of Risks and Normative Responses*,
https://doi.org/10.1007/978-3-031-41104-5_5

can either impede or jumpstart public desire for policy change, even if the scientifically determined probability and seriousness of risks has not changed. For this reason, common heuristics and biases in people's risk perception likely feed into the lack of private and public DRR measures relating to natural hazards. Doubts about the 'authenticity' of such collective decisions arise from studies suggesting that people make distinct choices when they rely on epistemologically robust facts and act in awareness of their desires about the future.[3] Against this background, this chapter turns to the third research sub-question of this book by examining how member states should adjust their collective decision-making processes to mitigate the influence of distorted risk perception while respecting citizens as autonomous and equal.

To that end, this chapter argues for the integration of deliberative processes in political policy-making in order to decrease the influence of distorted risk perception in public risk management decisions. Although definitions of the term deliberation differ, it essentially 'is debate and discussion aimed at producing reasonable, well-informed opinions in which participants are willing to revise preferences in light of discussion, new information, and claims made by fellow participants'.[4] Thus, deliberation is primarily a reciprocal exchange of arguments with the aim of reaching agreement on the validity of statements and on the 'better argument' in a transparent process.[5] To reach consensus or compromise, deliberation asks to reflect on the underlying values and worldviews with the aim of reaching a reasoned agreement that all parties can endorse or at least tolerate.[6] As a result, according to the deliberative ideal, the decision-making is based on 'the unforced force of the better argument',[7] instead of 'the status of the participants, sublime strategies of persuasion or sociopolitical pressure'.[8]

To illustrate the merits of this bottom-up approach in the context of disaster risk governance,[9] this chapter first demonstrates the practical merit of the deliberative ideal to respond to this influence while respecting citizens as autonomous and equal and contours the necessary structure of deliberative processes. In doing so, this chapter presents practical suggestions based on political science and behaviour studies for mitigating people's biased risk perceptions relating to natural hazards. The presentation is based on empirical studies that have demonstrated the effectiveness of such deliberative processes. Moreover, this chapter complements the practical merits of the proposals based on the theory of deliberative democracy. To that end, this chapter argues that the theory of deliberative democracy strikes the most reasonable balance between procedural and instrumental requirements on

[3] Ivčević et al. (2021).
[4] Chambers (2003), p. 309.
[5] Renn (2008), pp. 155, 294, 333.
[6] Ibid, pp. 155, 187–188.
[7] Habermas (2015), p. 37.
[8] Renn (2008), pp. 294, 333.
[9] Gunderson (2018), p. 719.

politically legitimate public decisions by facilitating equal participation, while accounting for a reasonable quality of the results for all.[10] As such, this chapter refutes competing approaches that prioritise expertise over laypeople's risk judgments when evaluating the acceptability of risks for society. These competing proposals for dealing with the distorted perception of risk have a long history, have never disappeared, and are put forward regularly. The intuitive appeal of these competing arguments makes proposals that rely on osmotic learning processes seem costly and ineffective. The continuous popularity of these competing proposals makes it necessary to discuss their shortcomings. While the polity could undoubtedly benefit from improved means of determining people's 'authentic' risk acceptance, this improvement can only come from an overall improvement in the political and public process within the democratic system.[11]

5.1 The Benefit of Deliberation for the 'Authenticity' of Risk Evaluations

To substantiate the claim that deliberative processes can mitigate the influence of distorted risk perception relating to natural hazards, all while respecting citizens as autonomous and equal, it is first necessary to explore the deliberate ideal and its application to the aforementioned cognitive and cultural risk perception mechanisms. The conceptualisation of the deliberative ideal offers a differentiated benchmark to assess the reasonableness of risk evaluations by differentiating facts and values and allowing the fact of pluralism so long as the outcome is acceptable to all. This section secondly contours the appropriate structure of deliberative processes to achieve this deliberative ideal, that is, the search for the 'better argument' through debate. Last, it presents empirical evidence for the effectiveness of such structured deliberative processes in practice.

5.1.1 The Respect for the Fact of Pluralism Under the Deliberative Ideal

In its ideal form, the discursive structure of deliberation produces 'good' and epistemically robust outcomes by exchanging *reasoned* arguments.[12] An examination of the conceptualisation of *reasoned* arguments reveals a benchmark for appraising risk assessments in collective decision-making that can improve the quality of collective decisions without undermining the fact of plurality.

[10] Habermas (1996), p. 304.

[11] Green (1981), p. 11.

[12] Knight and Johnson (1994), p. 286.

5.1.1.1 The Reference Point for 'Reasoned' Arguments

The aim of reasoned arguments 'is to frame pressing problems, to identify attractive, feasible solutions to them, and to persuade rather than compel those who may be otherwise inclined to recognize their attractiveness and feasibility'.[13] Political science sometimes characterises reasoned arguments as 'truth-tracking'[14] or 'truth-seeking'.[15] However, the reference to 'truth' in this context requires some cautionary clarifications of its meaning in democratic theory.[16]

A pragmatic account of 'truth' in the context of democratic theory does not raise the claim to have the 'right' answer that is justified in every context, but an answer that stands up to reason and evidence in the relevant context.[17] Thus, a pragmatic account of 'truth' in the context of democratic theory must be understood in terms of 'epistemic robustness'.[18] As such, the conceptualisation of 'truth' suggests a division of *epistemic or technical knowledge* and *political or moral knowledge* in the search for the 'better argument'.[19] Based on these different categories of knowledge is it possible to assess whether arguments are reasoned without interfering with the prerogative of citizens to evaluate facts as autonomous agents.

With respect to epistemic knowledge, the better argument for the pursuit of 'epistemic robustness' is to give science a leading role in establishing the facts in public decision-making processes. According to Rawls, the working out of public reason 'must rely upon current knowledge as recognized by common sense and the existing scientific consensus'.[20] The reasonableness of this benchmark for establishing epistemic facts can be illustrated by juxtaposing the superior certainty and reliability of science in determining facts vis-à-vis people's intuitive risk perceptions. Empirical studies in many fields have shown that the existing algorithmic methods are 'almost invariably equal to or superior' to risk determination methods that rely on human judgment.[21] The reason is that the 'human brain is a relatively inefficient device for noticing, selecting, categorizing, recording, retaining, retrieving, and manipulating information for inferential purposes'.[22] This inefficiency of the human brain is particularly hindering in disaster risk analysis, which requires the consideration of an

[13] Ibid.

[14] Estlund (2008); Christiano (2012), who refers to 'truth sensitivity'; see further Chambers (2021), p. 153, who refers to Habermas conception of democracy.

[15] Chambers (2021), pp. 158–159; Misak (2009), p. 35; Talisse (2009), p. 46.

[16] Holst and Molander (2019), p. 541; Holst (2012), p. 41; Schäfer (2006), p. 188; Estlund and Landemore (2018).

[17] Habermas (2015), p. 37; Misak (2009), pp. 32–34.

[18] Chambers (2021), p. 154.

[19] See generally, Cerovac (2016); Sunstein and Pildes (1997), pp. 135–136.

[20] Rawls (1971), p. 548.

[21] Grove and Meehl (1996), p. 293; van Coile (2016), pp. 32–38; see further Holst and Molander (2019), p. 553.

[22] Grove and Meehl (1996), p. 316; see further Glöckner (2016), pp. 17–18.

array of interconnected and complex factors.[23] Risk analysis may, for example, require that conditional factors be taken into account, such as when calculating the *conditional probability* of a house collapsing given the occurrence of an earthquake. Risk analysis may also require calculating how likely a system failure is due to *independent causes*, for instance, the probability of the failure of a primary system and a back-up system from independent causes. A mathematical calculation of the probability of a disaster can consider such conditional, mutually exclusive, or independent factors.[24] In contrast, 'intuition tends to betray us', the more interconnected and complex a system is.[25] Thus, algorithmic methods promise a greater 'epistemic robustness' than people's intuitive perception of identical facts. For this reason, recourse to scientific risk analysis is the 'better argument' for determining the factual basis. Consequently, John Dewey put 'science at the heart of public deliberation'.[26] Thus, the goal of deliberation should assign science a legitimate role as benchmark for determining factual basis in the public decision-making process.[27]

It must be pointed out, however, that biases not only influence lay people's risk perception, but also that of experts and their research hypothesis.[28] Although some commentators assign experts an 'impartial conscience' and 'neutral competence',[29] experts are not automatically bias-free.[30] In fact, findings in cognitive psychology indicate how implicit biases may similarly shape expert discourse.[31] Afterall, '[c]ognitive biases are no respecters of academic qualifications'.[32] However, if experts pursue well-established scientific methods and reasoning rules, it may reasonably decrease the likelihood of scientifically unsubstantiated or biased judgments.[33] Peer review processes and testing the experts' judgments in different fora,[34] for example, can prevent or at least minimise unreliable judgements.[35]

However, science's superiority in exploring and describing reality to the best of its ability differs from the task of deliberation to interpret the obtained findings.[36] Since a pragmatic account of 'truth' does not claim that there is a 'correct' risk

---

[23] See Renn (2008), pp. 178–179.

[24] Van Coile (2016), pp. 32–35.

[25] Ibid, p. 37.

[26] Moore (2018), p. 641, who refers to Dewey (1927).

[27] Howse (2000), p. 2330.

[28] Renn (2008), p. 307.

[29] See Fischer (1990), p. 24.

[30] See Sunstein (2005b), p. 126; Schudson (2006), p. 500; Thompson (1990), p. 22; Holst and Molander (2019), pp. 553–556; Holst and Molander (2017), p. 241, with many references.

[31] Moore (2018), p. 647, citing Fischer (2000); Holst and Molander (2017), p. 241.

[32] Runciman (2018), p. 183.

[33] Holst and Molander (2019), p. 553; Holst and Molander (2017), p. 242, citing Sunstein (2002b), Ch 3.

[34] Holst and Molander (2017), pp. 242–243.

[35] Ibid, pp. 241–243.

[36] Moore (2018), pp. 641–642, citing Kitcher (2011); Stoll (2003), p. 268; van Coile (2016), p. 37; Gunderson (2018), p. 720.

evaluation,[37] experts' risk evaluation should not be given a privileged position in the negotiation of the *if* and *how* of risk regulation.[38] Instead, experts' rationales should compete with lay people's rationales under deliberative democratic theory. By basing the outcome on the persuasiveness of 'the force of the better argument',[39] respect for the fact of pluralism is secured.

5.1.1.2 Risk Perception Patterns Through the Lens of the Deliberative Ideal

Based on the difference between epistemic facts and moral judgements, a benchmark emerges for assessing whether the influence of intuitive risk perception affects the 'reasonableness' of an argument in the deliberative process. While the deliberative ideal accepts value diversity, the risk evaluation must be epistemically robust. In this regard, science is the benchmark for epistemic knowledge. Thus, if cognitive or culturally shaped perception mechanisms distort the facts on which the individual assessment is based, the assessment is 'unreasoned'. As a result, some of these identified cognitive and cultural mechanisms, mapped in Chap. 2,[40] give cause to suspect a disjunction between people's actual risk perception and how people would evaluate risks if they properly understood the facts.[41] This is because these mechanisms systematically and predictably affect people's ability to process risk information.[42] With the relevance of 'truth' in terms of 'epistemic robustness' in mind, such disjunction would render an argument unreasoned within the deliberative process.

As such, it would be wrong to ignore that psychology has found that the less time has passed since a risk manifested itself, the more dangerous people tend to perceive it to be.[43] As this chapter has shown, after harm has occurred, the 'probability neglect' can give rise to sudden demands from the public for reducing the experienced risk.[44] However, the manifestation of a natural hazard does not change the determined probability of future harm in principle.[45] In this respect, Sunstein and Pildes warn that the occurrence of corresponding public demands are not 'a function of different values, but of what can properly be viewed as cognitive errors based on false beliefs about the actual probabilities of certain events'.[46] This is not to say that a tragic event should not be a reason to reconsider policy. However, the reasonable

---

[37] Sunstein and Pildes (1997), pp. 135–136.

[38] See Renn (2008), p. 96.

[39] Habermas (2015), p. 37.

[40] See Sect. 2.1.

[41] Spence and So (2021), pp. 2–3; Ivčević et al. (2021).

[42] Alemanno (2016), p. 201; Tversky and Kahneman (1974), p. 1131.

[43] Sunstein (2002a), p. 64.

[44] Ibid.

[45] See Sect. 2.3.1.

[46] Sunstein and Pildes (1997), p. 136.

suspicions of people’s temporarily distorted perception of facts reinforce the importance of an ‘appropriately structured deliberative process’ before responding to ‘snapshots of public opinions’ in risk policies.[47]

Similarly, the after-the-fact knowledge of how a calamity could have been prevented can create the impression that respective adjustments will eliminate the risk in the future. Such an assertion neglects the multitude of possible manifestations of natural hazards. The measures that would have been effective in a particular case do not necessarily lead to the same protective effect in similar manifestations of natural hazards. Thus, corresponding public demands are likely to be ‘factually erroneous’ as they are factually inapt to achieve the intended end.[48] In fact, the inference from the realisation of risk to blame points towards an expectation of absolute safety, which is, however, technically unattainable.[49] In contrast to this constructed narrative, the mere fact that a risk has materialised is not synonymous with a policy failure. Rather, in many cases, the previous policy has been the democratically negotiated compromise before the manifestation of risk. This invites structured deliberation to find an agreement on the validity of facts.[50] These facts concern the probability of harm as well as the effectiveness of options to reduce the risk.

However, caution is necessary to not prematurely attribute every deviation between expert and lay evaluation of risks to factually erroneous risk perception. An example illustrating the need for prudent assessment has already been presented in Chap. 2. This showed that the public’s demand for risk regulation may also depend on the risk’s context, such as its origin of harm, even if the expected harm is the same. The survey of prevailing semantic risk patterns has suggested that the reduction of disaster risks in the context of natural hazards may face more obstacles in a democratically constituted state. People dread human made hazards more than natural hazards and are therefore more likely to neglect the latter. Moreover, the so-called ‘crisis effect’ is known to dissipate more quickly after a disaster triggered by natural hazards.[51] The impression of ‘human made disasters’ generates stronger and longer lasting emotions.[52] The deviation between experts’ and laypeople’s risk evaluation may be due to either different perceptions of facts or different values. One explanation for this deviation is seen in the attribution of scientifically unfounded character traits to natural hazards by laypersons, which gives rise to a suspicion of factually erroneous perception. In the private sphere, a different treatment towards undesired damage depending on the origin rather than the objective probability and personal controllability may indeed indicate a misperception of the facts. This erroneous perception can refer to the neglect of probability or the overestimation of personal control in case of the hazard’s manifestation.

---

[47] Ibid, p. 135.

[48] Ibid.

[49] See Sects. 2.1.5 and 2.3.1.4.

[50] Sunstein and Pildes (1997), p. 135.

[51] Baan and Klijn (2004), pp. 114, 118; Stefanovic (2003), p. 242.

[52] Baan and Klijn (2004), p. 118.

For the collective decision-making process, however, this section argues that a value-based explanation for the different treatment of natural and human made hazards is conceivable. Where limited resources force society to prioritise among an infinite number of involuntary risks, the equitable allocation of available resources also depends on the origin of harm from a philosophical point of view. Protective measures against interpersonal harm are more essential for the existence of society than protection against comparable natural processes and for this reason have a higher normative priority in the governance of contingencies.[53] The reason for the different stringency of conflicting moral obligations derives from the difference between the moral principle of justice and beneficence for social organisation. Consequently, the unequal treatment of risks of different contexts in risk regulation is the 'better argument', as the following subsections substantiate in detail.

To that aim, the examination presents the ethical flaws of competing proposals to ignore such differences. The case is repeatedly made in the public and academic debate for linking the allocation of resources to the goal of maximising lives saved with available resources.[54] Risk evaluation should ignore contextual differences relating to the risk's origin and whether it is voluntarily or involuntarily borne to prevent emotion-based and thus irrational decisions that contradict 'sound science'.[55] This regularly proposed reorientation of the risk evaluation process would allegedly facilitate consistent and thus more predictable risk regulations.[56] The detailed examination of these competing proposals in the following subsection demonstrates that they fail to present the 'better argument' for public risk management. While the deliberative ideal respects a plurality of values, there are established ethical values that impose certain limitations.

5.1.1.2.1 Contextualising the Competing Proposal in Academic and Public Debates

According to the competing school of thought, the state should regulate conduct and invest in risk reduction in accordance with the scientifically asserted probability and gravity of harm to human health.[57] The quantitative logic to maximise the number of saved lives, with its perceived 'straightforward intuitive appeal',[58] regularly echoes in the academic and political debate of public risk regulation. To achieve the

[53] Cranor (1993), p. 129; see further Hansson (2012), p. 32; see Kamm (2007), pp. 14, 17, 291–292, 295; Breakey (2015), p. 1203.

[54] Breyer (1993), Laudan (1994), Graham and Wiener (1997), Cross (1998), Sunstein (2002b), Adler and Posner (2006) and Revesz and Livermore (2008).

[55] Sunstein (2002b), pp. 7, 49; see further Cross (1998), p. 35; discussed in Shrader-Frechette (2005).

[56] Laudan (1997), pp. 24–27.

[57] Cross (1998), p. 36; see further Cranor (1993), pp. 117–118, 122–123; Ames et al. (1987), p. 277; see Gonçalves (2013), pp. 123–124; Sunstein (2004a, b).

[58] Cross (1998), p. 38; see for a similar description Cranor (1993), p. 127; Greenacre and Fleshner (2017), p. 35; Beatley (1989), p. 11.

goal of maximising the number of lives saved, two risk evaluation methods have been proposed in the academic community. While both proposals focus on the expected consequences of the risk as ultimate benchmark for its evaluation, their proposed method for the risk comparison differs.

First, some scholars propose to make risk regulation dependent on passing a cost-benefit assessment ('CBA') test.[59] A typical CBA converts the multi-dimensional benefits and disadvantages of running risks into monetary values.[60] Thus, risks to life are converted to costs and compared with the costs of regulating the risk and the loss of other benefits.[61] The yardstick for assessing public investments in risk reduction would have to be whether it minimises costs and maximises net benefits. Shrader-Frechette summarises this approach as requiring 'policymakers to save the cheapest lives first, to save the most lives for the fewest dollars'.[62] Proponents of this approach to maximise the number of saved lives defend CBA as rational over otherwise 'uninformed stabs in the dark'[63] that result in 'inconsistent' risk evaluations.[64] This line of argumentation resorts to an economic logic that refers to the 'efficient use of resources'.[65] The standard economic model argues that the optimal allocation of resources minimises waste, and maximises the beneficial yield to each individual.[66] Following this method, a society would increase the reduction of disaster risks relating to natural hazards. In fact, a broad body of research demonstrates the economic benefits of DRR. These economic benefits are understood as avoided losses, in comparison to the mitigation cost.[67] In these terms, DRR is found economically more effective than the response and recovery approach.[68] Moreover, projections expect the cost-benefit ratio to only improve with ongoing scientific and technological progress.[69]

---

[59] Laudan (1994); Sunstein (2002b), p. 6.

[60] Meghani (2014), p. 983; Christiansen and Hallsson (2017), p. 63.

[61] Laudan (1994), pp. 9–12, 16, 18–22, 167; Sunstein (2002b), pp. 14–15, 30, 49, 79, 122.

[62] Shrader-Frechette (2005), p. 94.

[63] Sunstein (2002b), p. 6.

[64] Laudan (1997), pp. 24–27.

[65] Cranor (1993), p. 126; Lateef (2011), pp. 289–290; see further Rakić (2018), p. 150.

[66] Cranor (1993), pp. 123, 126–129; Mirrlees (1982); Ames et al. (1987), p. 277; see further Gonçalves (2013), pp. 123–124; Kahan et al. (2006), pp. 1074–1076.

[67] See for example, the study by Rose et al. (2007). This study examined a statistical sample of 5500 Federal Emergency Management Agency (FEMA) mitigation grants between 1993 and 2003. It found the overall benefit-cost ratio to be 4:1. Another study found 102 of 117 case studies report 'average cost-benefit ratios above the economic equilibrium', see Hugenbusch and Neumann (2016), p. 29. Reasons for usual uncertainties in calculating the economic benefits of DRR are addressed in Childs (2013), p. 12 and in Shreve and Kelman (2014), p. 214, also cited in Albris et al. (2020), pp. 8–9.

[68] Newman et al. (2017), p. 380.

[69] Childs (2013), p. 8.

Another proposal to maximise the number of saved lives relies on the risk evaluation method known as 'risk-risk comparison'.[70] This method typically evaluates the acceptability of risks by directly comparing the consequences of risks.[71] Such comparison uses scales, such as the 'annual probability of death, the risk per hour of exposure, and the overall loss in life expectancy'.[72] According to proponents of this method, such direct comparison would 'help put risks in psychological perspective', which would improve the understanding and appreciation of risks.[73] Examples of this competing argument in academic and public debate refer to various contexts of risk regulation.[74] As such, scholars have emphasised that society should not pursue large quantities of minor or non-existent hazards over 'the few really serious hazards, such as tobacco or saturated fat'.[75] For instance, industrial toxins, such as carcinogenic wood preservatives or formaldehyde, would receive 'exaggerated' attention, although unhealthy diets and the lack of exercise would kill five times as many people per year.[76] In terms of prioritising risks of human made or natural hazards in risk management, Carl F Cranor also raises the question of whether a state

> should use its authority and resources to intervene to prevent a firm from possibly harming a small number of people as a consequence of its activities (because they are exposed to a substance that causes cancer, for example) or use its authority and the same amount of money to prevent the deaths of a larger number of people from natural causes.[77]

In fact, natural hazards kill more people than human made hazards. For instance, in the past 20 years, disasters triggered by natural hazards have killed almost 17 times more Europeans in member states of the Council of Europe than human made hazards.[78] The rationale to link the scope of protective measures to the number of expected deaths has further reverberated during the early stage of the Coronavirus Disease 2019 ('COVID-19') pandemic in 2020. In March 2020, when only a few had died from COVID-19, public discourse has sometimes challenged the proportionality of protective state measures with quantitative comparisons to other causes of death, such as car accidents, heart disease, cancer, and the common flu.[79] As such, political voices cautioned that '[w]e don't shut down our economy because tens of

---

70 Cross (1998), p. 36.

71 Covello (1991), pp. 80–92; Stoll (2003), p. 337.

72 Covello (1991), p. 79.

73 Ibid.

74 Cross (1998).

75 Ames et al. (1987), p. 277.

76 Sunstein (2002b), p. 8; Laudan (1994), pp. 18–20; Laudan (1997), p. 10, discussed in Shrader-Frechette (2005).

77 Cranor (1993), p. 128.

78 Between 2003 and 2023, 165,353 Europeans have died in disasters triggered by natural hazards in CoE member states, while technological disaster killed 9778 Europeans, see EM-DAT, CRED/UCLouvain, Brussels, Belgium (as per 10 April 2023). However, it should be noted that EM-DAT considers situations or events as disasters, which overwhelms local capacity, necessitating a request to national or international level for external assistance as disaster.

79 The White House (2020a); similarly, The White House (2020c).

thousands of people die on the highways. It's a risk we accept so we can move about'.[80] In other words, since we accept deaths of car accidents, we should not be more restrictive to prevent deaths from COVID-19. Obviously, this argument is already built on what has turned out to be false epistemic assumptions about the lethality of the disease. Contrary to what the argument implies, deaths from COVID-19 have significantly exceeded accidental deaths in many countries. Apart from this flaw, the argument ignores the fact that the scope of measures depends on more than one criterion when it compares death numbers as the reference point for assessing the scope of protective measures. In fact, while the arguments are predicated on a supposedly pure 'epistemically robust' comparison of facts, they inherently incorporate a value judgment. The ethical shortcomings arising from this are pointed out in the following subsection.

5.1.1.2.2 The Hidden (and Flawed) Value Judgment Behind the Competing Proposals

By solely focussing on the expected consequences of risks and risk reduction, the competing proposals implicitly draw upon the theory of utilitarianism. Utilitarianism is a branch of consequentialist ethical theory that centres on the maximisation of happiness and well-being for the majority in case of conflicting moral obligations.[81] To this end, utilitarianism determines the morality of conduct based on the (expected) utility of its consequences.[82] The presented competing proposals interpret the utilitarian goal of maximising utility in terms of the number of saved lives.[83] This means that, according to this rationale, the '*risk* of loss of life from one cause is just as important as a numerically identical risk of loss of life from another cause'.[84] As such, the competing proposals for reorienting risk evaluation offer one simple overriding rule.[85] One can agree that this simplicity and the goal of maximising utility have an 'intuitive appeal'.[86] However, the alleged appeal of utilitarianism, as 'one of the simplest and most powerful methods possible',[87] diminishes when considering other ethical and state philosophical values.

[80] The United States' Senate Homeland Security Committee Chairman Ron Johnson in an interview with Gilbert (2020).

[81] de Lazari-Radek and Singer (2017); Haworth (1984), p. 5; Gomez (2017), p. 175; Rakić (2018), p. 149.

[82] Ross and Athanassoulis (2012), pp. 838–839; Smart (1973); Byskov (2020), pp. 262–263.

[83] Zack (2011), Ch 1; see further Lateef (2011), p. 290.

[84] Cranor (1993), p. 127.

[85] Ross and Athanassoulis (2012), p. 835; Williams (1973), pp. 136–137.

[86] See, e.g., Cross (1998), p. 38; Greenacre and Fleshner (2017), p. 35.

[87] Williams (1973), pp. 136–137.

First, both presented utilitarian risk evaluation methods make no distinction between *voluntarily* and *involuntarily* borne risks.[88] When *risk-risk comparisons* equate, for example, the risks involved in driving a car and living next to a nuclear plant, the comparison ignores the fact that the individual's ability to influence these two risks differs significantly.[89] The consequences of both risks may be unwanted, however, participating in traffic is typically a personally chosen risk, while the construction of a nuclear plant next to one's house is typically an involuntarily imposed risk.[90] The method's ignorance of this difference is even more evident in the above presented example of comparing the risks of industrial toxins with the risks of lack of exercise. As such, risk-risk comparisons unjustifiably neglect the value of autonomous choice. This is also the reason why Dr Anthony Fauci, the head of the National Institute of Allergy and Infectious Diseases in the United States, correctly called a comparison between the risks of a traffic accident and a COVID-19 infection 'a false equivalency'.[91] The two risks do not compare in terms of voluntariness and control of the individual over the risks, and thus differ in normative terms. Particularly at the time the pandemic began, the lack of protective tools, and the unavoidability of coming in contact with potentially infectious people in public, left individuals' very little choice in bearing the risk of an infection.

Similarly, while proposed application of *CBA* does take into account the benefits of running a risk as opposed to the risk-risk comparison method, it also ignores the distinction between voluntarily and involuntarily borne risks. When the proposed CBA compares the sum of costs, which includes the risk of death as converted to monetary values, with the sum of benefits from running a risk, it does not differentiate between those bearing the risks and those benefitting from the risk.[92] While 'high risk of harm and even the risk of death may both be acceptable if one and the same individual stands to gain from the act',[93] a disconnect between risks and benefits may be unacceptable to those affected. When this proposed CBA aggregates the costs and benefits for a collective, it does not take this relevant difference into account.[94]

Even with respect to the *involuntary* born risks, the competing arguments do not provide the 'better argument' due to ethical flaws. As such, the proposed 'rationalisation' of risk management unjustifiably neglects relevant differences between *involuntarily* borne risks for social organisation. For instance, the state may justifiably discriminate in the allocation of resources, such as time, personnel, supplies, and financial resources. Particularly, it is philosophically permissible for a society

[88] See Möller (2012), p. 60; Hansson (2004); Dworkin (2015); Cranor (1993), p. 128; van de Poel and Fahlquist (2012), pp. 890–895; Shrader-Frechette (2005), pp. 103–104; Stoll (2003), p. 337.

[89] Stoll (2003), p. 337.

[90] Shrader-Frechette (2005), p. 99.

[91] The White House (2020b).

[92] Ross and Athanassoulis (2012), p. 839; Shrader-Frechette (2005), p. 99.

[93] Ross and Athanassoulis (2012), p. 839.

[94] Hansson (2012), p. 48; Möller (2012), p. 60.

to invest more resources in the reduction of *involuntarily* borne *human made* risks than in *natural* risks, even if the expected outcome may be the same.

The justification for this differentiation derives from the guiding idea of the ethical theory of non-consequentialism. In case of conflicting moral obligations, contemporary non-consequentialism determines the order of precedence in accordance with the moral obligation's so-called *stringency*.[95] The more stringent an obligation, the 'much stronger considerations are needed to justify' its violation.[96] In this respect, non-consequentialism considers the introduction of a previously not present threat morally more objectionable, than not interfering with an independently present threat.[97] That is because the introduction of a previously not present threat constitutes a violation of the *harm principle*,[98] while not interfering with an independently present threat constitutes a violation of the principle of *beneficence*.[99] According to non-consequentialism, not doing harm is a more stringent moral obligation than not allowing harm to happen. It follows 'that we must go to greater trouble in order to avoid harming [people] ... than we must in order to prevent them from being harmed'.[100]

This guiding idea of the higher stringency of the *harm principle* over the *principle of beneficence* in cases of conflicting obligations also affects the order of precedence among a state's positive moral obligations towards its citizens. With respect to the priorities for the functioning of society, it should be 'one thing to die in a natural disaster [sic], such as an exploding volcano or an earthquake, and quite another to be a victim of a murder or of a reckless or negligent release of a toxic substance'.[101] Accordingly, political philosopher, Adam Smith, notes that the principle of justice, as well as beneficence, are necessary conditions for 'a good society'.[102] However, justice would be 'the main pillar that upholds the whole edifice',[103] while beneficence is an 'ornament which embellishes'.[104] Thus, a society without beneficence can subsist, 'though not in the most comfortable state', while predominant injustice would destroy it.[105] If beneficence is 'less essential to the existence of society than justice',[106] then it follows that protective measures against interpersonal harm take precedence over the protection against comparable natural processes. For instance,

[95] For a comprehensive examination of the different combinations, see Kamm (2007), Ch 9; see further Breakey (2015), pp. 1203–1214.

[96] Woollard and Howard-Snyder (2022), para 1.

[97] Kamm (2007), p. 18.

[98] Cranor (1993), pp. 127–128; Lateef (2011), p. 290; see further Schneewind (2010), p. 251; Kalokairinou (2018), p. 222; Smith (2002), p. 309; Lin and Anderson-Shaw (2009), p. 216.

[99] Cranor (1993), pp. 127–128; Kalokairinou (2018), p. 223.

[100] Scheffler (2004), p. 216.

[101] Cranor (1993), p. 127.

[102] Campbell (1967), p. 574.

[103] Smith (2002), p. 101.

[104] Ibid.

[105] Ibid.

[106] Ibid.

the state would have to give precedence to maintaining police protection against abstract human threats over medical care.[107] As for the context of disaster risks, even if the consequences would be factually the same, a society should give precedence to the reduction of human made risks over risks from natural hazards. For this reason, if risk-risk-comparisons are used for evaluating risks, they should only apply to contextually similar risks. In practice, this is commonly the case. For example, the United Kingdom Health and Safety Executive has advanced procedures for comparing the consequences of chemical risks, that is, contextually similar risks, as a basis for evaluating their acceptability.[108]

The examination in this subsection has revealed that deviations between the risk evaluation of experts and laypersons require a careful identification of the underlying cause, as the deliberative ideal accommodates the diversity of values. The deliberate ideal of reasoned arguments imposes only one restriction on value decisions, namely that 'all possibly affected persons could agree as participants in rational discourses'.[109] In this regard, established ethical values frame the search for the 'better argument'.

5.1.2 The Requirement of an Appropriate Structure of Deliberative Processes

Considering the importance of respecting citizens as equal and autonomous, deliberative processes offer a distinct advantage in the method of mitigating the influence of unreasoned risk perception on collective decision-making. The deliberative process aims to mitigate the influence of unreasoned risk perception on deliberative processes though persuasion by the 'better argument'.[110] To arrive at this desired result, deliberative processes needs to be appropriately structured. This structure of deliberate processes concerns the composition of the participants and their attitudes, the procedural norms, and the moderation of the process.[111] To enable a competent and fair process, all major stake holders (or their representatives) must be involved.[112] In relation to risk evaluations, which often involve complex risks including uncertainties that allow for different legitimate interpretations of their acceptability, input from scientists, policy makers, stakeholders and the affected public is needed.[113] Moreover, the communication rules must limit the ability of individual stake

[107] Kamm (2007), p. 296.

[108] Renn (2008), p. 149; Renn and Klinke (2016), pp. 208–209.

[109] Habermas (1997), p. 107.

[110] Knight and Johnson (1994), p. 286.

[111] Chambers (2021), pp. 152–154; Pateman (2012), p. 8.

[112] Dietz (1994), p. 305.

[113] Renn (2008), p. 294.

holders to dominate the process.[114] Inter alia, this requires ensuring unconstrained communication among participants.[115] The facilitator should be accepted by all participants as neutral in relation to the participants and the risk evaluation under discussion.[116] In terms of content, the participants should define the mandate of the deliberation and contour the permissible outcomes.[117] In the context of risk management, the process ultimately aims to find a compromise or even consensus between those who believe that the risk of natural hazards should be ignored and those who believe that the potential harm justifies additional DRR measures.[118]

To identify and mitigate the influence of unreasoned risk perception on individuals' risk evaluation without undermining the equal respect for the autonomy of each citizens, the deliberative process presupposes that all participants are open to new information and discussion of arguments.[119] As the assessment of psychological evidence on risk perception under the deliberative ideal has shown, it would be a mistake for experts to attribute every deviation to a participant's alleged inability to interpret empirical evidence in risk evaluations. Similarly, it would be a mistake for participants to perceive experts as 'uncompassionate technocrats'.[120] Instead, the collaborative search for the 'better argument' requires that all 'parties are willing to accept the rationale of the other party's position and to understand, and maybe even empathize with, the other party's view'.[121] The broadening of the perspective supports the individual actors in the mental reconstruction of their evaluation.[122]

This goal of mutual empathy requires all participants to present their own views in a way that gives the other participants a reasonable chance to understand the argument's basis.[123] In this respect, a practical concern refers to the asymmetry of knowledge between experts, representatives, and lay people.[124] The success of deliberation inter alia depends on the experts' effort to make the content and basis of their judgment reasonably understood by citizens and experts outside their subject area. Otherwise the decision cannot derive from the competition for 'the better argument'. Building on the insights into the cultural background of today's risk perception patterns presented in Chap. 2, the following discussion contours some pitfalls in the communication of risks and DRR in more detail.

---

114 Dietz (1994), p. 305; see further Renn (2008), pp. 294, 319; Gunderson (2018), p. 721.

115 Dietz (1994), p. 305; Gunderson (2018), pp. 719–721.

116 Renn (2008), p. 319.

117 Ibid, p. 318.

118 See generally, ibid, pp. 187–188.

119 Chambers (2003), p. 309; Renn (2008), pp. 319–320.

120 Renn (2008), p. 320.

121 Ibid.

122 Ibid, p. 305.

123 Gutmann and Thompson (2004), pp. 5, 136, 146; see generally Moore (2018), p. 643.

124 Bohman (1999), p. 596.

5.1.2.1 Demands on Risk Communication

When communicating disaster risks, participants could mitigate the effects of cognitive and cultural mechanisms by using language that increases the chances of being properly understood by the recipients.[125] To this end, experts should avoid terminology that has been found to feed into distorted perceptions of risk. This open-ended task depends on continuous social science research on the effect of language on risk perception and the respective adaptation on the part of the participants of deliberation. Since a detailed summary of the research findings on this relationship is beyond the scope of this book, it restricts itself to some salient examples of unhelpful narratives.

First, the terminology of 'natural disasters' perpetuates a still 'deeply engrained' and 'difficult to shake' bias that 'natural disasters' are inevitable.[126] The term 'natural disaster' is therefore not appropriate for this task and should be avoided.[127] The term's abandonment is considered necessary to avoid the common misconception 'that if disasters are natural there is little that can be done, except by preparing to respond to them'.[128] Instead, the used terminology should recognise the 'unnaturalness' of disasters to convey the potential for risk reduction and the public and private accountability in disasters.[129] In line with the modern disaster conceptualisation presented in Chap. 1,[130] the terminology of 'disasters triggered by natural hazards', 'disasters due to vulnerability to natural hazards' or 'socio-natural disaster' are more apt to effectively communicate risks, since they do not insinuate the impossibility of effective prevention.[131]

Another salient example for inadequate terminology for disaster risk communication refers to technical terms to describe hazard frequencies in terms of return periods. For instance, the term of a '100-year event' has been identified as inadequate for public disaster risk communication.[132] In common usage, these terms have been found to have ambiguous interpretations that may even give rise to people's false perception of a deterministic behaviour of natural hazards.[133] Thus, disaster risk communication should 'translate' such scientific findings for the public to increase its effectiveness.[134] In this respect, studies have emphasised that people

---

[125] Freer et al. (2013), p. 222; see further Faulkner et al. (2007).

[126] Sun (2016), p. 32; see Raju and da Costa (2018), pp. 282–283; see further Chmutina and von Meding (2019).

[127] Briceño (2015), p. 1; Wachinger et al. (2013), p. 1062; Raju and da Costa (2018), p. 285; Chmutina and von Meding (2019).

[128] Briceño (2015), p. 1; see further Chmutina and von Meding (2019), pp. 289–290.

[129] Raju and da Costa (2018), pp. 282–283; Briceño (2015), p. 5.

[130] See Sect. 1.5.2.

[131] Briceño (2015), p. 1; Chmutina and von Meding (2019), p. 290.

[132] Freer et al. (2013), p. 198; Rougier (2013), pp. 33, 36.

[133] Freer et al. (2013), pp. 198, 222; Rougier (2013), p. 33.

[134] Freer et al. (2013), p. 222; see further Faulkner et al. (2007).

understand probabilities better in percentages than in frequencies.[135] For example, instead of calling a flood risk a '500-year event', it could be expressed as a level of protection of 99.8% per year.[136] The expression '500 year event' can be understood as an expectation of '500 years' of safety. In contrast, the expression of probabilities in percentage counteracts the human tendency to understand disasters triggered by natural hazards as something temporally deterministic by making it clear that the level of protection each year is less than 100%.[137]

5.1.2.2 Communicating and 'Translating' (Un)Certainty and Confidence

Second, to facilitate a value-based debate on the basis of good information about the facts, all participants must be able to assess the informational value of scientific knowledge. In view of the findings in Chap. 2, this requires to establish that there are gradations in the reliability of scientific findings. Chapter 2 drew attention to the widespread, sometimes almost religious belief in the ability of science to provide definitive facts.[138] Even if science cannot completely predict the future, it offers additional information that likely improves the basis to make decisions for the future. Yet, as Chap. 2 has explored,[139] it follows from probability theory that the informative value of risk analyses depends on the available epistemic knowledge about involved factors, and the amount of historical data.[140] To indicate the remaining uncertainty related to the correctness of a determination, model or estimated probability, scientists assign so-called confidence intervals or levels.[141] The higher the confidence level value, the more reliable the presented scientific result.

Participants in the deliberate process must be able to interpret the outcome and reliability of research. However, time and again, scientists notice a lack of knowledge to interpret the informative value of risk determination among decision-makers.[142] Due to policymakers' 'scientific illiteracy',[143] even the assignment of 'probabilities to describe risk will have limited value and can even mislead the decision maker'[144] unless the presentation is accompanied by adequate explanations. Against this background, scientists, such as Ruben van Coile, find 'a basic understanding of probability is increasingly turning into a necessity for decision

---

135 Baan and Klijn (2004), p. 118.

136 Ibid.

137 Ibid.

138 See Sect. 2.1.5.

139 See Sects. 2.3.1 and 2.3.2.

140 German Advisory Council on Global Change (1998), p. 53.

141 Van Coile (2016), p. 32; Rougier (2013), pp. 29–32; German Advisory Council on Global Change (1998), pp. 52–53; Mastrandrea et al. (2010); Intergovernmental Panel on Climate Change (2005).

142 See van Coile (2016), p. 38.

143 Albris et al. (2020), p. 6.

144 Renn et al. (2011), p. 234.

makers'.[145] However, so is the requirement for experts to express findings in a way that is reasonably understandable to the recipient. Notably, outside the circle of scientists, studies have shown that understanding the calculation and interpretation of confidence intervals is difficult even for university students.[146] As a result, today's debate culture lacks effective communication of the informative value of scientific progress. For instance, the COVID-19 pandemic revealed shortcomings in the communication of research results in public debate on scientific uncertainties.[147] The public witnessed the self-correcting process of science when key findings on the virus, effective protection, and treatment changed over time. However, the lack of effective management of expectations caused frustration and damaged the public's trust in science. In fact, a study from France found, for example, that trust in science has dropped by 10%.[148] Yet studies have also shown that this shortcoming can be countered, as the 'frustration was not due to the changes themselves but to poor communication for why these changes were necessary'.[149] In this regard, studies analysing media coverage and opinions on the presentation of scientific uncertainty found that

> [w]hile specialist journalists understood that scientific knowledge evolves and the process is fraught with uncertainty, non-specialist reporters and commentators expressed frustration over changing public health guidelines, leading to the politicization of the pandemic response and condemnation of elected officials' decisions.[150]

These results show that even low confidence levels do not necessarily diminish the value of research findings in the deliberative process, but when they are poorly communicated, this affects the formation of public opinion. The substantive quality of a deliberative process, as well as the procedural success that requires trust, depends on the effective communication of the value of information, which includes the communication of the level of confidence. Managing participants' expectations of scientific research in public discourse through effective communication of the level of confidence can help to maintain trust in science as the most reasonable benchmark for facts.[151]

To facilitate substantive discussion, experts should use layperson-friendly language and presentation techniques. The presentation methods of the Intergovernmental Panel on Climate Change are good examples of transparent communication and presentation of confidence levels in a way that is understandable to scientific laypersons. To translate these scientific expressions of the confidence level

---

[145] Van Coile (2016), p. 38.

[146] Henriques (2016); Rashidah Paujah Ismail et al. (2018), p. 61.

[147] Capurro et al. (2021) and Caulfield et al. (2021).

[148] Caulfield et al. (2021), p. 406, citing Matthews (2020).

[149] Capurro et al. (2021), p. 2181 (11).

[150] Ibid, p. 2181 (1).

[151] Ibid; Caulfield et al. (2021).

to laypersons, a quantitative metric or qualitative metric can be used.[152] In a quantified metric, the confidence level indicates the level of faith that a repetition of the examination would result in the same result.[153] This may be expressed probabilistically,[154] or by using qualifiers that express quantitatively calibrated confidence levels.[155] An example of the latter formed the basis of the Fourth Assessment Report of the Intergovernmental Panel on Climate Change ('IPCC') as set out in Table 5.1.[156]

On the other hand, the confidence level can also be translated qualitatively. In this respect, the Fifth Assessment Report of the IPCC provides an example worth highlighting (Fig. 5.1). The Fifth Assessment Report of the IPCC relied on a qualitative definition that 'intended to synthesize author teams' judgments about the validity of findings as determined through their evaluation of evidence and agreement'.[157]

This metric takes into account the confidence of the scientific community at large in the accuracy of research findings. When experts explain the information value of scientific results to participants in the deliberative process, the degree of agreement among competent observers is essential information.[158]

5.1.3 *The Empirical Effectiveness of Deliberative Fora*

Empirical studies and experiences show that, in practice, deliberative processes can achieve their theoretical promise of mitigating unreasoned risk perception on people's decision-making in practice. Considering that critics regularly dismiss the

Table 5.1 Quantitatively calibrated levels of confidence in the Fourth Assessment Report of the IPCC. (Intergovernmental Panel on Climate Change 2005)

Terminology	Degree of confidence in being correct
Very High confidence	At least 9 out of 10 chance of being correct
High confidence	About 8 out of 10 chance
Medium confidence	About 5 out of 10 chance
Low confidence	About 2 out of 10 chance
Very low confidence	Less than 1 out of 10 chance

[152] Mastrandrea et al. (2010), p. 1; Intergovernmental Panel on Climate Change (2005), p. 3, which stipulated a quantitative metric for expressing the confidence level.

[153] Intergovernmental Panel on Climate Change (2005), para 13.

[154] Mastrandrea et al. (2010), p. 1.

[155] Ibid, Annex A, referring to Intergovernmental Panel on Climate Change (2005), para 13; see further on the development Mastrandrea et al. (2011).

[156] Intergovernmental Panel on Climate Change (2005), para 13.

[157] Mastrandrea et al. (2010), Annex A.

[158] Moore (2018), p. 644.

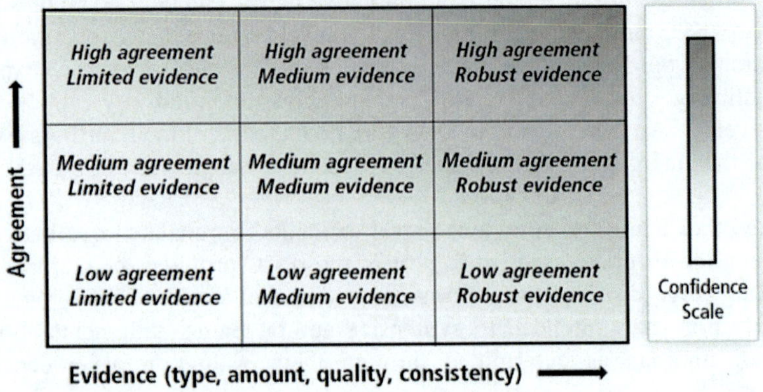

Fig. 5.1 A depiction of evidence and agreement statements and their relationship to confidence. Confidence increases towards the top-right corner as suggested by the increasing strength of shading. Generally, evidence is most robust when there are multiple, consistent independent lines of high-quality evidence. (Reproduced Figure 1 from Mastrandrea et al. 2010)

deliberative process as 'utopianism',[159] it is useful to point to this empirical evidence. The main objection by critics refers to the presence of 'erroneous laypeople's knowledge and intuitive biases' which, they argue, would weaken the quality of the outcome in practice because only rigorous scientific scrutiny could overcome this influence.[160]

In contrast to this objection, empirical studies and experience demonstrate that the deliberative model of participation 'is specifically suited for dealing with risk issues and it can be well combined with analytic processes of knowledge generation and processing'.[161] Numerous empirical studies have shown that citizens are effective, efficient and rational problem solvers who seek fact-based solutions to policy problems.[162] High motivation on the part of the participants can even overcome weaknesses in the structure of the deliberative process.[163] Ample case studies even conclude that the influence of unreasoned cognitive biases on the outcome can be mitigated in the deliberate process.[164]

Beyond the theoretical settings, deliberative processes in the form of 'citizen panels' have been implemented in various countries, for instance in the context of urban planning.[165] Citizens panels are allowed to co-determine the outcome of a

[159] Cf. Renn (2008), pp. 306–309; cf. Gunderson (2018), pp. 717–718.

[160] For an overview of respective critics, see Renn (2008), p. 306.

[161] Ibid, p. 304.

[162] Chambers (2021), p. 152, citing Dryzek et al. (2019); Gastil et al. (2008); for further case study references, see Renn (2008), pp. 309, 350.

[163] See references cited in Renn (2008), p. 313.

[164] For plenty references, see ibid, pp. 309, 350.

[165] For an overview and evaluation of experiences with these applications, see ibid, pp. 347–350.

public decision.[166] Independent scholars have evaluated these applications as being able of '[e]liciting the preferences and educated responses of citizens in a rather short time'.[167] Even those who rate the process as time-consuming emphasise the effectiveness of the outcome.[168] In the context of environmental governance, public participation in decision-making has resulted in 'better formulated and more legitimate' decisions.[169] For this reason, risk management agencies around the world use 'scientific advisory councils, stakeholder roundtables, citizens' advisory groups and other forms of public outreach' to improve their legitimacy base for decisions and practices.[170]

5.2 The Strength of Deliberative Democracy Under Normative Political Theory

This chapter has so far shown the implication of distorted risk perception on collective decision outcomes and how appropriately structured deliberation mitigates their effects while respecting citizens as autonomous in evaluating risks. Ample empirical evidence suggests that deliberative processes can mitigate the unreasoned effects of common heuristics and biases in risk perception in the public decision-making process. With the practical merit of deliberation in mind, this section further substantiates the case for deliberative democracy based on normative political theory. Decision-making processes based on the deliberative ideal are not only capable of mitigating the influence of distortions in risk perception on the collective decision-making outcome, but can also strengthen their political legitimacy.[171] As introduced in Chap. 1,[172] the normative political concept of political legitimacy refers to the basis upon which a government obtains the right to coercively enforce laws.[173] Political theory usually assesses political legitimacy in terms of two sources of legitimacy. These sources are procedural or *input*-oriented legitimacy, which requires the authority's actions to be responsive to the '*authentic preferences* of citizens',[174] and instrumental or *outcome*-oriented legitimacy, which relates to the production of 'good outcomes'.[175]

---

166 See generally Gunderson (2018), p. 729.

167 Renn (2008), p. 350 with many references.

168 Gunderson (2018), p. 717.

169 Ibid, pp. 715–716, citing Dietz and Stern (2008), p. 226.

170 Renn (2008), p. 291.

171 Gunderson (2018), pp. 715–716, citing Dietz and Stern (2008), p. 226.

172 See Sect. 1.1.3.

173 Paletta (2011), pp. 870–871.

174 Scharpf (1997), p. 19; Christiano and Bajaj (2022), para 2.2.1.

175 Brettschneider (2005), p. 424; Holst (2012), p. 50.

The following section examines the source of political legitimacy within the theory of deliberative democracy theory. It examines in detail how the deliberative democracy model facilitates the requirement of participating equally in the determination of public decisions, while also promoting the 'common good',[176] and how this distinguishes it from other democratic theories. Finally, this section examines the theory's compatibility with the practical challenges posed having the goal of a functioning society in mind.

5.2.1 *The Source of Political Legitimacy in Deliberative Democracy*

While different variants of the theory of deliberative democracy exist,[177] it essentially derives legitimacy for decision-making from the 'weighing of reasons or an exchange of arguments for or against a given view'.[178] To ensure the fairness of the procedure, citizens must have *free* and *equal* access to the deliberative procedure.[179] Citizens are considered *free* if they are endowed with rights, liberties, and powers of citizenship irrespective of their view of life.[180] *Equal access* to the deliberative procedure includes all relevant public fora, as well as the citizen's right to participate and to inform themselves.[181]

Deliberate theories in the tradition of Habermas[182] and Gutmann and Thompson[183] combine these procedural features with criteria relating to the quality of outcomes.[184] As such, outcomes are not already legitimate as soon as a popular will has crystallised.[185] Instead, the legitimacy of political outcomes derives 'from the discursive structure of an opinion- and will-formation that can fulfill its socially integrative function only because citizens expect its results to have a reasonable *quality*'.[186] On the one hand, this conceptualisation of political legitimacy contributes to improving the epistemic quality of final decisions.[187] On the other hand, the outcome must be

---

176 Chambers (2017), p. 270; Fung (2007), p. 449.

177 Baade (2017), p. 311; Chambers (2003), p. 309.

178 Estlund and Landemore (2018), p. 120.

179 Knight and Johnson (1994), pp. 285–286; Christiano (2009), pp. 2–4; Gunderson (2018), pp. 719–720.

180 Christiano (2009), p. 3; Knight and Johnson (1994), p. 285.

181 Christiano (2009), p. 3; Knight and Johnson (1994), pp. 285–286.

182 Habermas (1996).

183 Gutmann and Thompson (2004).

184 Peter (2017), para 4.3.

185 Knight and Johnson (1994), pp. 281–287.

186 Habermas (1996), p. 304.

187 See Habermas (2015), pp. 36–39.

such that all affected people can agree, or can at least be expected to agree, due to the force of the better argument.[188]

In this vein, deliberate democracy builds on the legacy of consent as the source of legitimacy.[189] The goal of deliberation is not necessarily a complete consensus among participants concerning the issue.[190] On the contrary, deliberate democracy acknowledges that the 'fact of pluralism' excludes the settlement on a 'comprehensive doctrine'.[191] A comprehensive agreement on an issue would presuppose 'the oppressive use of state power'.[192] While it would consequently be unreasonable to expect a complete consensus on an issue, a reasonable person would seek a consensus on the scope of considerations that are relevant to justify a decision.[193] Based on this interpretation of consensus, political legitimacy then depends on the ability to give reasons and evidence that all reasonable citizens have reason to approve of.[194] Thus, deliberate democracy derives legitimacy from 'consent', while giving it 'a more complex and richer interpretation'.[195]

5.2.2 *The Strength of the 'Responsiveness'-Concept of Deliberative Democracy*

A particular strength of the theory of deliberative democracy is that its discursive structure not only serves a procedural function by responding to people's preferences, but also produces 'acceptable' and epistemically robust reasons.[196] This strength becomes clear in direct comparison with other theories of democratic legitimacy, such as aggregative democracy.[197] Political theory generally describes democracy as a collective decision-making system that equally considers every member's interests.[198] To that end, 'it is fairly uncontroversial' that democratic

---

188 Ibid, p. 37; see generally Holst (2012), p. 51; Misak (2009), p. 33; Baade (2017), p. 313; cf. Schumpeter (2010), p. 226.

189 Peter (2017), para 3.3.

190 Chambers (2003), p. 309; Christiano (2009), pp. 7–8; Misak (2009), p. 33; Estlund and Landemore (2018), pp. 123–125.

191 Rawls (1987).

192 Ibid, p. 4 Fn 7.

193 Ibid, p. 13 Fn 21; Christiano (2009), pp. 8–9.

194 Baade (2017), p. 311; Misak (2009), p. 33; Chambers (2017), p. 268; Knight and Johnson (1994), p. 284; Peter (2017), para 4.3.

195 Chambers (2003), p. 308.

196 Chambers (2017), pp. 268–270.

197 See Muirhead (2015) and Bernholz (1966); see further Knight and Johnson (1994); see generally Estlund and Landemore (2018), p. 125.

198 See Baade (2017), pp. 308, 314–315; Waldron (2012), pp. 187, 191–197; Christiano and Bajaj (2022), para 1.

systems seek to respond to people's preferences.[199] However, democracy models differ in their approach to accomplish 'systematic responsiveness' to people's preferences.[200] In fact, political theories have offered different conceptualisations of the procedural requirement to equally consider every member's interests.[201] For instance, both deliberative democracy and aggregative democracy require that public decisions take into account the preferences of citizens. Of these two theories, however, only deliberative democracy produces 'good outcomes' for all, as an examination of its conceptualisation shows.

The theory of aggregative democracy interprets democratic legitimacy in terms of procedures that determine and enforce the majority's expressed opinion.[202] Thus, when the theory of aggregative democracy is applied to risk management decisions, legislation would reflect the preferences of the majority.[203] Since an exchange of reasons is not necessary, this majority could be determined by 'a simple referendum'.[204] The minority is 'expected to accept those laws and policies because the process of generating them was democratic'.[205] A creditable strength of this conceptualisation of democracy is that it places a high emphasis on the values of liberty and political equality.[206] Aggregative democracy presumes that all individuals have rational preferences, and for this reason policies should derive from their aggregated views.[207] In this vein, it builds on the model of the *homo oeconomicus* used in economic theory, that is, an agent who seeks to maximise the satisfaction of his or her interests.[208]

However, the theory of aggregative democracy reveals a thin conceptualisation of the 'common good'.[209] It is built primarily on the procedural justification and not on the substantive quality of the outcomes for all concerned.[210] As such, aggregative democracy represents a formalistic understanding of democracy that often excludes the substantive limitations of the majority's expressed preferences.[211] It has been claimed that such an approach 'undercuts the possibility that ideas in their own might matter, that there might be better or worse ideas, and that this

[199] Christiansen and Hallsson (2017), p. 60.

[200] Goodin (1993).

[201] See Baade (2017), pp. 308, 314–315; Waldron (2012), pp. 187, 191–197; Christiano and Bajaj (2022), para 1.

[202] Baade (2017), pp. 308–310.

[203] Meghani (2009), p. 133.

[204] Ibid.

[205] Ibid, p. 131.

[206] Fung (2007), p. 449.

[207] Ibid, pp. 448–449; Meghani (2009), p. 131.

[208] Baade (2017), p. 309.

[209] Fung (2007), pp. 448–449; Meghani (2009), p. 131.

[210] Fung (2007), p. 449.

[211] Baade (2017), p. 309.

better-or-worseness might have a consequence for politics'.[212] Another shortcoming of this theory is that governance exclusively based on majority decisions could unacceptably narrow the meaning of political equality.[213] It is true that elections and majority rule often 'serve as the expression of a deeper idea, that of popular control'.[214] However, the aggregative theory's exclusive reliance on utilitarian justification patterns may unacceptably ignore the legitimate interests of the minority.[215] To that effect, pure majority rule runs the risk of creating a 'majority tyranny'.[216] Consequently, scholars hold that this conceptualisation of democracy, as the invariable enforcement of the majorities' aggregated preferences, could not be understood as democratic quality.[217] The European Court of Human Rights Court also supports this conclusion. As it has repeatedly held, the ideal of democracy cannot be reduced to decisions that enforce the majority's preferences at all costs:

> Although individual interests must on occasion be subordinated to those of a group, democracy does not simply mean that the views of a majority must always prevail: a balance must be achieved which ensures the fair and proper treatment of minorities and avoids any abuse of a dominant position.[218]

On the basis of these theoretical considerations, politically legitimate risk management should not be reduced to simply being responsive to the majority's expressed preferences. These considerations support the theory of deliberative democracy that systematically responds to the various perspectives in society while also setting the condition that collective decisions are acceptable to those concerned.

5.2.3 The Compatibility of a Pragmatic Approach with Deliberative Theory

So far, this section has presented how the theory of deliberative democracy derives political legitimacy from a balance between the consideration of citizens' preferences and the 'common good' in public decision-making processes. In practice, however, the goal of a functioning society is incompatible with the performance of ideal deliberation among all citizens. In practice, every state, even a democratic state, requires a degree of labour division and consequently decides most policy

---

212 Muirhead (2015).

213 Waldron (2012), p. 198, with further references; Kitcher (2011), pp. 63–65.

214 Kitcher (2011), p. 65.

215 Baade (2017), pp. 315–316.

216 Christiano and Bajaj (2022), para 2.2.3.

217 Baade (2017), pp. 312–313.

218 ECtHR, *Young, James and Webster v United Kingdom,* Judgment, 13 August 1981, Eur Court HR (ser A) 44, para 63; the Court confirmed this interpretation in ECtHR, *Chassagnou and Others v France,* Judgment, 29 April 1999, Eur Court HR III 21, p. 65 para 112 and in ECtHR, *Sørensen and Rasmussen v Denmark,* Judgment, 11 January 2006, Eur Court HR I 1, pp. 29–30 para 58.

issues through elected representatives or through regulatory agencies.[219] In fact, the representation of citizens through elected agents is to some extent inevitable when political communities reach a certain degree of complexity.[220] This is not only due to the excessive amount of time that comprehensive participation would demand from all citizens.[221] Participation of all members of society is also technically unrealistic as such procedures entail significant costs and delays in the decision-making process.[222] A division of labour, on the other hand, makes it possible to make a collective decision that strikes a balance between quality, time and effort. In this regard, further elaboration is needed on how 'this noble goal'[223] can be put into practice without affecting the basis of the political legitimacy, such as equal standing.

5.2.3.1 Compatibility of Representative Democracy and Deliberative Democracy

The implementation of representative structures in deliberate democracy does not necessarily affect political legitimacy. In fact, political legitimacy does neither theoretically, nor practically, depend on the performance of ideal deliberation among all citizens.[224] Besides the presented conceptualisation of deliberative democracy in its pure form, a plethora of intermediate positions exists in theory and in practice. While the concept of input-legitimacy derives from the idea of liberty and equality,[225] this does not necessarily require direct democracy. Instead, deliberative democracy built on representative structures may also satisfy this requirement if democratic oversight and accountability is possible.[226] On the one hand, representative arrangements often even serve the practical implementation of deliberate ideals as they are able to 'frame and channel deliberation and decision making among the people'.[227] On the other hand, if representative democracy incorporates fora that enable a structured deliberation with respect to legislation, it has 'a justification that is not necessarily at odds with the political equality'.[228] As such, representative democracy and deliberate democracy are compatible.[229]

---

219 Schäfer (2006), p. 187; Baade (2017), pp. 316–317; Christiano and Bajaj (2022), paras 4, 4.3; Waldron (2012), pp. 200–201.

220 Schäfer (2006), p. 187; Baade (2017), pp. 316–317; Christiano and Bajaj (2022), paras 4, 4.3; Waldron (2012), pp. 200–201.

221 Strøm (2000), pp. 266–267.

222 Ibid; Gunderson (2018), p. 728; Baade (2017), pp. 313, 317.

223 Renn (2008), p. 332.

224 Baade (2017), pp. 312–313; see Moravcsik (2004), p. 337.

225 Christiano and Bajaj (2022), paras 2.2.1, 2.2.3; Fung (2007).

226 Waldron (2012), p. 200.

227 Ibid.

228 Ibid.

229 Chambers (2003), p. 308.

5.2.3.2 Demands on Democratic Accountability of Experts

While representative democracy can be politically legitimised, and even 'superior to direct democracy',[230] the requirement of treating 'participants as autonomous agents to whom power and coercion must be justified'[231] demands adequate institutionalisation of democratic oversight.[232] A particular challenge in the context of disaster risk management is the democratic control of experts. As disaster risk management is a controversial and complex ethical, political, and scientific issue,[233] experts' role in the decision-making process is *in principle* not only acceptable, but reasonable collective decision-making partly depends on experts' input.[234] However, with respect to the reality of collective decision-making within the member states, some commentators criticise an excessive and democratically insufficiently controlled reliance on expert evaluations in some policy areas. Modern democracies would increasingly delegate risk regulation to depoliticised expert bodies, such as audit and regulatory agencies or advisory committees.[235] Such a delegation of decisions to experts 'can amount to a de facto alienation of control'.[236] The reliance on experts in modern democracies has led some scholars to compare the current role of science to a fifth branch of government.[237] With a more critical tone, Steve Rayner characterises the current period as the 'age of assessment'[238] that would uplift the role of science from informing policy towards driving policy.[239] The rise of the concept of scientifically determined risk management would even yield 'a decline of democracy',[240] and was describes as 'post-politics'.[241] The COVID-19 pandemic has given fresh impetus to critical questions concerning the weight of expert knowledge and opinion in state decision-making as well as their accountability.[242] The pandemic has put the spotlight on epidemiologists, public health experts, and virologists, in navigating the disaster response.[243] Their advice became an authority for the justification of unprecedented protective measures. The displayed reliance on

[230] Waldron (2012), p. 200.

[231] Chambers (2017), p. 270.

[232] Ibid, pp. 268, 270; Holst (2012), p. 53.

[233] Lauta (2018), p. 50.

[234] Moore (2018), pp. 641–642; Jasanoff (2003), pp. 158, 161.

[235] Holst (2014), p. 2; Holst and Molander (2017), p. 235; Holst and Molander (2019), p. 542.

[236] Moore (2014), p. 54.

[237] Jasanoff (1994); see further Vibert (2007).

[238] Rayner (2003).

[239] Rayner (2007), p. 166.

[240] See Lauta and Faure (2016), p. 183; Rayner (2007), pp. 168, 171.

[241] Swyngedouw (2010), pp. 225–227.

[242] Lavazza and Farina (2020) and Boschele (2020).

[243] Staudenmaier (2020); Lavazza and Farina (2020), pp. 1–2.

the experts' input quickly gave rise to public debate 'whether virologists "have too much influence" over the measures'.[244]

Given the role of the people in supporting expert-generated policies, the dystopian fear of post-democracy in European decision-making is exaggerated.[245] Nevertheless, the brief overview of critical voices highlights the need to address means to ensure democratic oversight regarding experts' contributions to collective decision-making. While the argument put forward in this chapter for implementing deliberative processes does not involve delegating decisions to experts, the control of experts' contributions to deliberation is nevertheless challenging. Afterall, the division of labour is rooted in the fact that experts can contribute something that others cannot.[246] Similar to representative structures, deliberate democracy has 'no problem *in principle* with dependence on science within democratic politics',[247] 'as long as citizens are also able to exercise some form of democratic oversight'.[248] In this regard, the well-founded and serious warnings concerning the loss of democratic oversight over unelected experts in decision-making processes requires an explanation of how trust in the experts can be justified.[249]

To that end, scholars in political science ask for the existence of 'some independent basis for believing the experts to be trustworthy'.[250] This can be, for example, a record of reliable judgment in the past, or the presence of a system that involves critical scrutiny by other experts.[251] Notably, the process through which competent observers determine the degree of agreement, and its public transparency and accessibility play an important role.[252] These competent observers may include peers, as well as experts from other relevant disciplines.[253] This exposure facilitates to review the pursuit of established scientific methodology,[254] as well as to uncover hidden value judgments.[255] The value of such review depends on a minimum transparency on the utilised methodology, sources, and data, as well as the impartiality of the reviewing process.

Again, the COVID-19 pandemic illustrates shortcomings in the operationalisation of the current system of peer review processes. Time and again, research results were widely disseminated before they were tested for methodological substance within the scientific community. For instance, Annals of Internal Medicine, a

[244] Staudenmaier (2020).

[245] Baade (2017), p. 319; with respect to the European Union, see Moravcsik (2002, 2004).

[246] Bohman (1999), p. 596; see Bouchard (2016), p. 588.

[247] Moore (2018), p. 642.

[248] Chambers (2017), p. 268.

[249] Baade (2017), p. 319; Bouchard (2016).

[250] Gutmann and Thompson (2004), pp. 5, 146; see further Holst and Molander (2017), p. 242.

[251] Gutmann and Thompson (2004), pp. 5, 146; Bouchard (2016), pp. 593–594.

[252] Moore (2018), p. 644.

[253] Holst and Molander (2017), p. 242.

[254] Ibid, pp. 242–243.

[255] See Murphy and Gardoni (2012), p. 990; Hansson (2012), pp. 32–33.

worldwide renowned medical journal, retracted a widely noticed article on the alleged inefficiency of 'both surgical and cotton masks … in preventing the dissemination of SARS–CoV-2'.[256] Despite the later retraction, hundreds of news outlets, twitter user, and the World Health Organization itself,[257] had featured the article.[258] While mistakes are never completely avoidable, two factors in particular facilitated the release of methodologically unsubstantiated scientific findings. First, medical journals drastically accelerated their publication process.[259] Accordingly, numerous publications in even prestigious medical journals had to be retracted after scientists expressed serious concerns about the methodology and reliability of data.[260] A second factor relates to the increased use of preprint servers to circulate work before completing the peer reviewing process.[261] The motivation of publishing information as quickly as possible is understandable considering the pressing issues posed by the COVID-19 pandemic. Yet, the concomitant spread of insufficiently verified epistemic information likely damaged the public trust in the scientific review system as an independent basis for believing experts. Later retractions of methodologically unsubstantiated articles did not put the genie back into the bottle. To that effect, the former Editor-in-Chief of *The New England Journal of Medicine,* Dr Jerome Kassirer, warned that '[t]he problem with trust is that it's too easy to lose and too hard to get back'.[262] As such, the protection of public trust requires more protection in the operationalisation of peer review processes when met with time pressure.

5.3 The Compatibility with the Member States' Democratic Systems

The developed proposals to mitigate distorted perceptions of risk with the help of deliberative processes resonate with the democratic orientation of the member states. The core of deliberative democracy is inherent in the member states' democracies. While the member states predominantly rely on representative decision-making,[263] they share the common understanding that politically legitimate decision-making by representatives does not allow an elitist disregard for people's

[256] Bae et al. (2020), W23.

[257] World Health Organization, Regional Office for the Western Pacific (2020).

[258] Altmetric (2020).

[259] One study found that medical journals halved the reviewing period based on an assessment of 669 articles, Horbach (2020). Another, and more extensive, statistical study determined the median time between submission to journals' acceptance of COVID-19 articles to be just 6 days in comparison to a typical median of around 100 days, Palayew et al. (2020).

[260] Mehra et al. (2020a, b).

[261] Mayo-Yánez (2020), Else (2020), Bajak Aleszu and Howe (2020) and Caulfield et al. (2021).

[262] Rabin (2020).

[263] Baade (2017), pp. 319–320.

preferences. In practice, the rationale of deliberative democracy constitutes a cornerstone of public decision-making processes in the member states. The member states agree that democratic decision-making processes require the examination of the best available evidence, and the weighing of different perspectives and arguments.[264] In other words, democratic processes in Europe have in common the search for policies that stand up to evidence and reason, and that balance common and individual interests.[265] As such, the member states' democratic models feature the criterion of 'reasoned arguments', which is at the heart of the theory of deliberative democracy. The commitment of the member states to deliberative democracy can also be seen in the fact that some have strengthened and continue to promote the institutionalisation of deliberative fora for specific issues in their democratic systems.[266] To that effect, the member states respond to many voices in the literature that criticise deficits in the equal footing of ordinary citizens in decision-making processes, particularly in the area of risk management decisions.[267] Thus, while the participation of ordinary citizens is largely missing from the decision-making process, the approach put forward in this chapter is compatible with the member states' commitment to democracy.

5.4 The Flaws of Competing Proposals to Respond to Distorted Risk Perception

So far, this chapter has presented deliberative processes as a practically and theoretically substantiated means to mitigate the influence of distorted risk perception on public decision-making processes that is compatible with the member states' commitment to democracy. To further substantiate the merits of this proposal, this section points to the practical and theoretical flaws of two alternative proposals to mitigate the influence of distorted risk perception on public decision-making processes. Seemingly irrational results of democratic decision-making processes have always stoked arguments against the reasonableness of allowing lay people equal standing in collective decision-making processes. The so-called positivist school of thought encompasses arguments for the superior role of scientific concepts and experts over people's expressed preferences in policy decisions.[268] At their core, the positivist arguments all rely on the promotion of *rational* decision-making in public issues,[269] though their conceptualisations of 'rationality' differs. Although most

[264] See ibid, p. 313.

[265] Misak (2009), p. 33; Baade (2017), p. 313.

[266] Reuchamps and Suiter (2016).

[267] Rayner (2003, 2007); Swyngedouw (2010); Vibert (2007); Cerovac (2016), p. 79.

[268] Renn (2008), pp. 96–97, citing Cross (1998) and Coglianese (1999); see further Christoforou (2003), p. 208; cf. Murphy and Gardoni (2012), pp. 989–990.

[269] Roeser et al. (2012), pp. 8–9.

contemporary political philosophy considers democracy, in the sense of equal opportunity for self-government for all, a necessary requirement of political legitimacy,[270] not all political theories consider these democratic values the 'better argument'.[271]

The most far-reaching position argues to empower experts to decide over the acceptability of risks based on their superior knowledge of complex issues.[272] This instrumentalist school of thought assumes the existence of contextually '*objectively rational*' outcomes, and therefore conditions the political legitimacy of the decision-making procedure on its capacity to arrive at these outcomes.[273] Accordingly, if non-democratic processes contribute to better approximate these correct outcomes, political legitimacy would not depend on the inclusion of democratic values in the decision-making process.[274] The second competing proposal is also based on an outcome-based justification for empowering experts in the decision-making. Yet, this school of thought empowers experts with the mandate of extrapolating people's 'authentic' *subjective values*.

An obvious criticism is that these competing approaches are not compatible with the member states' commitment to democracy as a government system. However, even if there were a political willingness to change this commitment, the proposals do not stand up to normative jurisprudential scrutiny. This final section identifies critical theoretical and practical weaknesses of the two competing proposals for mitigating the influence of distorted risk perception on public risk management by empowering experts. The following discussion of these competing proposals for responding to distorted risk perceptions first turns to the school of thought that prioritises expertise for the purpose of promoting supposedly *objectively rational* goals over lay people's preferences. Subsequently, this section discusses the weaknesses of the positivist arguments that prioritise expertise for the purpose of maximising people's 'authentic' *subjective values*.

5.4.1 The Competing Arguments for Objectively Rational Risk Management

One conceptualisation of rationality, articulated in the theory of objective rationality, reflects 'on one's goals, to attempt to determine what preferences one ought to hold'.[275] This theory represents the classical approach in 'decision theory' that inter alia aims to conceptualise what constitutes rational decision making between

[270] Peter (2017), para 4.

[271] Holst (2012), pp. 50–51.

[272] Brennan (2016); Holst (2012), p. 41.

[273] See Peter (2017), para 4.1.

[274] See ibid.

[275] Stewart (1995), p. 57; see further Jensen (2012), p. 407.

different options.[276] Classical 'decision theories' sought to define objectives 'which a rational individual ought to maximize'.[277] Thus, instead of coordinating different means and goals, the theory of objective reason seeks to streamline behaviour and ends.[278] Before discussing the weaknesses of this positivist approach, the analysis provides an overview of the ways in which the idea of objective rationality reverberates in proposals for appropriate risk management and in political theories.

5.4.1.1 Examples in the Literature on Risk Management

For centuries, the objective theory of reason has prevailed among Western thinkers.[279] Even in the more recent past, the notion of objective rationality continues to shape the debate on legitimate risk management. As such, commentators regularly call for more consistency among the regulation of diverse risks, even if this consistency is not supported by people's expressed preferences concerning a risk.[280]

Some commentators argue that society has reached a point where the objectively rational values have already transpired through past risk regulations. The public would want 'better health and more safety overall'.[281] However, in detail, risk regulation would not coherently reflect those values due to people's inconsistent risk perception.[282] Against this background, former Supreme Court Justice Stephen Breyer offered the 'provocative and influential proposal'[283] to create 'a small, centralized administrative group, charged with a rationalizing mission'.[284] This group of experts would improve risk-regulation systems by harmonising risk-related programs with respect to priorities and resource allocation.[285] Since the priorities have already been determined, 'all that is left is the weighing, balancing, and specification of these values: something best left to experts'.[286] While such approaches purport to respond to people's 'already determined' preferences, they implicitly rely on the idea of objective rationality. This becomes transparent in the proposals' goal to streamline the consistency of risk evaluation by reducing the scope of relevant values. While health, safety and rational resource management are legitimate factors, they do not capture the complexity of influential factors in people's risk

276 Beisbart (2012); on the development of the 'rationality' concept in legal studies, see Stoll (2003), pp. 328–330; Roeser et al. (2012), pp. 8–9; Jensen (2012).

277 Jensen (2012), p. 407.

278 Horkheimer (2013), p. 2; see generally Sunstein and Pildes (1997), p. 137.

279 Horkheimer (2013), p. 2.

280 Cross (1998), p. 35; see Sunstein and Pildes (1997), p. 131; see for a critique of such approaches Thompson (1990).

281 Breyer (1993), p. 55.

282 See Sects. 1.1.2 and 2.1.

283 Sunstein and Pildes (1997), p. 145.

284 Breyer (1993), p. 60.

285 Ibid.

286 Evans (2006), p. 222.

evaluation.[287] Thus, this competing approach effectively presumes to determine which factors deserve objective legitimacy and which do not.

In contrast to such disguised arguments for objectively rational risk management, other commentators explicitly reject the legitimacy of subjective values in risk regulation.[288] They argue that the benefits of implementing objective reasoning would even justify abandoning democratic values.[289] This is particularly argued in the context of uncertain, but serious threats, which traditionally play into democracy's weakness. For instance, the record of democracy's capacity to deal with SARS–CoV-2 would force an admission of democracy's inadequacy to respond to uncertain threats.[290] Despite experts' repeated and serious warnings, governments were not sufficiently prepared for the pandemic.[291] Consequently, expertise would deserve prioritisation over lay people's preferences because of experts' specialised methods, training, and experience, their 'ethical or professional commitment to truth-seeking', and their 'willingness to be judged' by other experts.[292] This outcome-driven argument is also particularly expounded in the context of climate change. As such, experts challenge whether democracies are geared to cope with this global threat. It would not be 'entirely clear that democracy is up to the challenge of climate change'.[293] For this reason, some commentators argue that non-democratic decision-making is necessary to take the unpopular, yet necessary measures to respond to this global threat.[294] For instance, Shearman and Smith argue that the necessary measures 'should not be put for democratic approval, or humanity will elect to live as it wishes'.[295]

5.4.1.2 Overview of Knowledge-Based Normative Political Theories

The examples given of calls to prioritise expertise in the evaluation of the acceptability of risks expose two main arguments for the primacy of outcome justification over procedural justification. First, that the quality of results would justify the prioritisation of expertise over people's preferences. Second, that lay people's incompetence to coherently evaluate risks would justify limiting their participation in the decision-making process. These two arguments also reverberate in normative political theory. As such, one group of political theories argues for political systems that

[287] See, e.g., Slovic (1987) and Fischhoff et al. (1978).

[288] For further references, see Shrader-Frechette (1991), pp. 89–99.

[289] Brennan (2016).

[290] See generally Ganesh (2020) and Jones (2020).

[291] See, e.g., Duncan (2020) and Sanger et al. (2020).

[292] Schudson (2006), p. 500; see Fischer (1990), p. 24; see Haring (2010), p. 248; see further Holst and Molander (2019), p. 548.

[293] Jamieson (2014), p. 100.

[294] Cf. Fiorino (2018).

[295] Shearman and Smith (2007), p. 4.

empower a knowledgeable elite to competently decide on substantive issues irrespective of people's subjective preferences. Again, some of these theories waive democratic requirements, while other theories purport to build on democratic values.

5.4.1.2.1 Non-Democratic Governance Systems

Non-democratic proposals for the organisation of state governance argue that political legitimacy derives from outcome-oriented arguments, instead of the non-instrumental values, such as liberty, public justification, and equality.[296] Although the details of proposals differ, their instrumental arguments all draw upon the notion that 'knowledge' should have a superior weight in policy decisions over lay people's preferences.

This notion even predates modern democracies.[297] Plato's recommendation for state governance by philosopher kings already relied on the prioritisation of knowledge in collective decision-making processes.[298] To Plato, this would facilitate the pursuit of objective reason, which would interconnect with success and happiness.[299] Similarly, Aristotle proposed a rule of the wise.[300] The idea of a prioritised role of 'knowledge' in public decision-making was still hardly contentious in the nineteenth century.[301] For example, John Stuart Mill famously argued for giving the educated an additional vote.[302] Accordingly, in the nineteenth and early twentieth century political theories emerged that feature knowledge-based rule.[303] For instance, technocracy describes 'a system of governance in which technically trained experts rule by virtue of their specialized knowledge and position in dominant political and economic institutions'.[304] Another non-democratic political theory constitutes the model of epistocracy that refers to the rule by the people who know best.[305]

Generally, the pure archetype of technocracy and epistocracy as alternatives to democracy had disappeared from academic discourse by the end of the 1980s.[306] However, recent popular decisions, such as the Brexit decision and the election of Donald Trump in 2016, have catalysed the discussion of alternatives to

---

[296] See generally Christiano and Bajaj (2022), paras 2–2.2.3.

[297] Holst (2012), pp. 42–43.

[298] Evans (2006), p. 217; Holst and Molander (2019), p. 541; Holst (2012), p. 43.

[299] Horkheimer (2013), p. 2.

[300] Holst (2012), p. 43; Runciman (2018), p. 122.

[301] For examples of governments with epistocratic characteristics in European history, see Holst (2012), p. 43; Runciman (2018), p. 183.

[302] Mill (1861), p. 168; Holst (2012), p. 43; Runciman (2018), p. 122.

[303] Haring (2010), pp. 160–161.

[304] Fischer (1990), p. 17.

[305] Runciman (2018), p. 180; Holst (2012), p. 41.

[306] Haring (2010), pp. 260–261.

democracy.[307] In particular, Jason Brennan and his 'provocative'[308] arguments for the legitimacy of epistocracies, based on the incompetence of voters to comprehend complexity, have recently attracted much attention.[309] In fact Italy introduced a technocrat-led government in February 2021, after the elected coalition had fallen apart over political differences.

5.4.1.2.2 Elitist Theory of Representative Democracy

A related, yet purportedly democratic theory, constitutes the 'pragmatic elitist theory of representative democracy'[310] that reduces democratic legitimacy to the procedure of electing competent representatives.[311] According to this theory, political legitimacy does not require elected representatives to respond to people's preferences when deciding on substantive issues.[312] On the contrary, it would be the task of successfully elected leaders to 'make policy and law with little regard for the fickle and diffuse demands made by ordinary citizens'.[313]

Proponents, such as Joseph Schumpeter, give two main justifications for placing severe limitations of citizen's participation in governance.[314] First, they claim that the 'classic' interpretation of 'common good' in terms of outcomes that all individuals could subscribe to whether under real or ideal circumstances is 'nonsensical'.[315] The broad range of preferences and values among people would defeat the goal of serving 'an all-embracing general will' of the people.[316] To that effect, the test for 'good outcomes' should rather focus on whether the results 'prove in the long run satisfactory to the people at large'.[317] Based on this rationale, this test may allow the implementation of policies that 'affected parties, in the first instance, either would have failed to agree upon, or would have rejected on the grounds that they entailed unacceptable levels of sacrifice'.[318]

Secondly, proponents of the elitist theory justify placing severe limitations on citizens' participation in governance on the assumption of 'voter incompetence and

---

[307] Estlund and Landemore (2018), p. 126; Runciman (2018), p. 180; see generally Mulligan (2015).

[308] Runciman (2018), p. 123.

[309] Brennan (2014, 2016).

[310] Nunan (2014), p. 89.

[311] Schumpeter (2010), pp. 241, 245; see Baade (2017), p. 310.

[312] Schumpeter (2010), p. 214; see Baade (2017), pp. 310–311; Fung (2007), p. 448, who refers to this theory as 'minimal democracy'.

[313] Christiano and Bajaj (2022), para 4.2.1.

[314] See Held (2006), pp. 146–151.

[315] Schumpeter (2010), pp. 225–227; see Fung (2007), p. 448; Held (2006), pp. 146–148.

[316] Held (2006), p. 147.

[317] Schumpeter (2010), p. 230.

[318] Held (2006), p. 148.

myopia'.[319] A high-level participation of citizens in the legislative procedure would be prone 'to produce bad legislation designed by demagogues to appeal to poorly informed and overly emotional citizens'.[320] To that end, ordinary citizens should 'do no more than vote and then sleep between elections'.[321]

5.4.1.3 Discussion of Positivist Argument for Knowledge-Based Governance

Despite its current resurrection, the idea of incapacitating citizens from participating in political decision-making processes in order to reserve them for elected or unelected elites remains a 'reckless idea'.[322] This is not to deny the substance, nor the relevance of some of the reasons for positivist arguments. However, the positivist responses to those diagnosed problems suffer from philosophical and practical flaws that cast doubt on its preferability over deliberative decision-making processes to mitigate the influence of distorted risk perception.

5.4.1.3.1 Philosophical Objections to the Concept of Objective Rationality

While positivists make correct observations, their conclusions to give up on normative ideals such as equal participation and political equality are 'fundamentally mistaken'.[323] As such, Schumpeter is correct that the pursuit of the 'common good' will not meet everyone's wants. It cannot be expected that people 'reach *political* agreement on a general and comprehensive doctrine'.[324] However, even if these ideals could not fully be realised in the real world,[325] this claim does not justify to replace them with philosophical objectional approaches. To that effect, Andrew Moravcsik has rightly claimed that '[a]ny criticism of real-world democratic legitimacy, or proposal for its enhancement, must be philosophically coherent'.[326] This requirement for philosophical coherence is not met by the positivist approach building on objective rationality. Even if a comprehensive agreement was unattainable, the approach to streamline behaviour and ends, instead of coordinating differences,[327] unacceptably ignores the 'fact of pluralism'.[328] Both knowledge-based governance

---

319 Nunan (2014), p. 96.

320 Christiano and Bajaj (2022), para 4.2.1.

321 Cf. Dryzek (2001), p. 663.

322 Runciman (2018), p. 184; see further Haring (2010), p. 249.

323 Held (2006), pp. 152–153.

324 Rawls (1987), p. 13 Fn 21.

325 See on this point Held (2006), p. 153.

326 Moravcsik (2004), p. 338.

327 See Horkheimer (2013), p. 2.

328 Rawls (1987).

systems presented are based on the idea that an empowered elite could deliver the *objectively better* policies for all if the elite could ignore lay people's preferences. The positivist arguments on risk governance have revealed that several interpretations of '*objectively better*' approaches exist. Yet, all these interpretations either overlook the influence of values or unjustifiably discredit some values as illegitimate.

In this regard, as this chapter has already discussed,[329] when some commentators argue that the outcome of decision-making would qualitatively improve if it were objectified, for instance, with the help of probabilistic concepts,[330] they overlook the influence of values. The inevitability of risk trade-offs in the face of an infinite number of risks to human beings, combined with the finite nature of resources for risk reduction, forces society to select which risks to reduce and which to ignore in public risk management based on facts and values. In the past, philosophical contributions to risk analysis have refuted this idealist belief in the capacity of expertise to deliver a 'purely objective and value free' evaluation of risks that merely relies on a comprehensive review of empirical facts[331] by exposing 'the value-dependence of allegedly value-free risk assessments'.[332] In fact, the question of what risks or goals are acceptable to a society cannot be answered by the best available epistemic knowledge about a risk alone.[333] Consequently, although elements of risk evaluation 'may be defined in scientific, objective terms, … the content of these terms cannot be reduced to meaningful numbers that have more than ephemeral value in the decision-making process'.[334] Instead, the evaluation of risk requires the weighing of values which differ among people.[335] For instance,

> [o]ne person might judge the paving of a wetland for the development of a shopping center as a benefit if they dislike wetlands for aesthetic reasons, whereas someone else might judge this as a cost because they value natural areas and the species that live in wetlands.[336]

Thus, claims that experts could objectively evaluate risks, for instance, with the help of probabilistic concepts,[337] are built on 'a regressive pursuit of false Gods'.[338] In fact, such an approach is not objective, but implicitly includes value judgements through the selection of values deemed relevant.[339] Consequently, it is important to differentiate between science's task of describing reality to the best of its ability, and

[329] See Sect. 5.1.1.2.

[330] Cross (1998); see Sunstein and Pildes (1997), p. 131.

[331] Haring (2010), p. 249, with further references; Thompson (1990), p. 22.

[332] Hansson (2012), p. 29, with many references; see further Thompson (1990).

[333] Stoll (2003), p. 331; Möller (2012), p. 71.

[334] Green (1981), p. 11.

[335] See Sects. 1.1.3, 1.5.4 and 5.1.1.2.2.

[336] Hartzell-Nichols (2012), p. 948.

[337] See, e.g., Cross (1998).

[338] Thompson (1990), p. 22; see further Hansson (2012), pp. 29, 32–33.

[339] See generally Hansson (2012), pp. 32–33.

'the interpretation the user gives to the obtained results'.[340] Even if the distinction is blurred,[341] the exposure to different expert fora allows to identify and test often implicit value assumptions.[342]

The legitimacy of subjective priorities in responding to epistemic knowledge forecloses the idea that a group of elected or unelected decision-makers could define an 'objective truth' for all irrespective of people's preferences.[343] In fact, modern philosophy denies the existence of true or false moral facts.[344] Even the pursuit of economic efficiency cannot claim objective rationality. Economics usually aims at minimising waste and maximising the beneficial yield to each person.[345] To that effect, the standard economic approach is predicated on the axiom 'that it is better if we all become richer'.[346] Philosopher, such as Sven Ove Hansson, warn that '[e]conomists sometimes lose sight of the fact that this is a value judgment'.[347] Even if this value judgment may be uncontroversial to some, others may assign a higher value to other ends, such as the idea of sustainability.[348] It is for this reason that philosophical contributions to risk research refute the characterisation of risk evaluations as neutral.[349] Thus, the reasoning to streamline behaviour and outcomes in the form of objective rationality embodies a generally unjustified paternalistic approach. To that end, the legitimate plurality of positions is the reason why the various interest groups 'need to convene for making the often painful but necessary trade-offs between conflicting objectives and values'.[350]

5.4.1.3.2 Scepticism Concerning Practical Implementation

Beyond these philosophical objections to the idea of objective rationality, commentators doubt whether the exclusion of citizens from the decision-making process, or even from the election of decision-makers, would yield a stable institutional system that could reliably achieve set goals. First, with respect to the presented non-democratic governance systems, scholars caution against trivialising the practical challenge to regularly recruit a group of experts who are free from personal intentions, and instead motivated to implement the 'best' solution for all.[351] More

340 Van Coile (2016), p. 37; Stoll (2003), p. 268.

341 Hansson (2012), p. 32.

342 See Murphy and Gardoni (2012), p. 990; Hansson (2012), pp. 32–33.

343 See Rawls (1997), p. 771; Cerovac (2016), p. 79.

344 Habermas (2015), p. 36; Cerovac (2016), pp. 77–78.

345 Mirrlees (1982); Cranor (1993), pp. 123, 126.

346 Hansson (2012), p. 32.

347 Ibid.

348 See ibid.

349 Ibid, p. 29.

350 Renn (2008), p. 155.

351 Haring (2010), p. 248; see further Saretzki (1994), p. 361; Held (2006), p. 154.

specifically, critical voices wonder how the recruiting process could practically ensure that only a motivated, qualified, and ideological homogenous group of experts is given power.[352] Considering the lack of accountability mechanisms, mistakes in the recruitment process implicate the danger of 'creating a monster that can't be deflected from its course'.[353]

The elitist theory of representative democracy seeks to solve this problem by establishing an 'institutional arrangement for arriving at political decisions in which individuals acquire the power to decide by means of a competitive struggle for the people's vote'.[354] Thus, the elitist theory trusts that citizens are capable of selecting competent leadership among competitors. Against this background, the question arises as to how citizens can be capable to competently assess leadership candidates, while they are simultaneously denied the capacity to develop a reasonable judgment on substantive issues.[355] To that effect, the argument to empower citizens to elect leadership undermines the reasoning to restrict the idea of political equality. For this reason, most scholars deny the political legitimacy of the elitist theory's proposed design and reasoning.[356]

5.4.2 The Competing Argument for Subjectively Rational Risk Management

Similar to the rejected arguments built on the concept of 'objective rationality', the positivist empowerment of experts to mitigate the influence of bias on collective decisions in the name of 'subjective rationality' has significant weaknesses as well. This second positivist school of thought agrees with the importance of systematically responding to people's subjective values in legitimate decision-making. However, based on the empirical findings on people's 'subjective irrationality', this positivist school of thought argues to strengthen experts' role in the public decision-making process with the goal of exerting people's *authentic* values. At the heart of this school of thought stands the theory of subjective reasoning that is 'concerned with means and ends, with the adequacy of procedures for purposes more or less taken for granted'.[357] In other words, the theory of subjective reasoning does not challenge the reasonableness of the individuals' goals as the theory of objective rationality does.[358] Instead, subjective reasoning describes the effectiveness to which a person's behaviour increases the probability of achieving his or her preferred

[352] Haring (2010), p. 248; see further Saretzki (1994), p. 361.
[353] Runciman (2018), p. 185.
[354] Schumpeter (2010), p. 241.
[355] Held (2006), pp. 153–154.
[356] Walker (1966).
[357] Horkheimer (2013), p. 1.
[358] Stewart (1995), p. 58; see generally Sunstein and Pildes (1997), p. 137.

goals.[359] The embodiment of irrationality would be '[t]o deliberately choose a feasible outcome that is not most preferred, or to deliberately act without regard to maximizing one's objective'.[360] The theory of subjective rationality is the basis of contemporary normative decision theory that often describes this notion as 'means-ends rationality'.[361] In fact, most decision theorists hold today

> that rational agents are allowed to let whatever beliefs and desires they so wish guide their decisions, as long as those beliefs and desires are compatible with the principle of maximizing expected utility.[362]

In light of the scientific findings on public risk perception, positivists doubt the 'subjective rationality' of public risk regulations. Yet, instead of initiating an osmotic learning process, the second positivist school of thought advocates giving experts the task of determining people's authentic values in risk policies.

5.4.2.1 The 'Democratic-Enhancement' Argument

The position of empowering experts to have the last word is built on democratically inspired reasoning. If it was a liberal-democratic state's ideal to respond to the preferences of the people,[363] then '[d]emocratic governments should respond to people's values, not to their blunders'.[364] However, according to this school of thought, this goal could not be achieved by the traditional democratic means, such as polls and public debate, as these would be designed to reflect people's biased risk perception.[365] Based on the mistrust that a structured debate can reduce the influence of distorted risk perception through persuasion, specialists should be empowered to engage 'in a kind of "peer review" of legislative proposals', to prevent the implementation of such unauthentic risk perceptions in the legislative process.[366] On the one hand, if people have scientifically unsubstantiated fear of risks, experts would be 'in a better position to judge whether risks are real' due to their scientific training.[367] On the other hand, if people neglect a risk, experts should extrapolate people's 'authentic opinion' in risk policy-making. The extrapolation should rely on social science's measurements of people's risk perception and preferences to 'reveal

[359] Stewart (1995), pp. 58–59.

[360] Ibid, p. 59.

[361] Roeser et al. (2012), p. 9; see generally Kahan et al. (2006), pp. 1074–1076, who refers to the 'irrational-weigher model'.

[362] Roeser et al. (2012), p. 9.

[363] Christiansen and Hallsson (2017), pp. 59–60; Baade (2017), pp. 308–313.

[364] Sunstein (2005b), p. 126; cf. Christiansen and Hallsson (2017).

[365] Sunstein (2005b); cf. Christiansen and Hallsson (2017), in particular p. 60.

[366] Sunstein (2002a), p. 102.

[367] Ibid; Sunstein (2005b), p. 126; cf. on the merit of Sunstein's argument Christiansen and Hallsson (2017); cf. further Kahan et al. (2006) and Shrader-Frechette (2005).

patterns of "acceptable" risk trade-offs'.[368] Such patterns would indicate the universal parameters in the evaluation of risks that are shared by all citizens. By applying these universal parameters, positivists argue that this model would even be 'implicitly more legitimate than representatives of interest groups because interest groups are by definition not representing all of the citizens, but only an interested faction'.[369] Consequently, the prioritisation of experts' extrapolation of people's 'authentic opinion' in risk policy-making is presented as the most suitable means of realising people's 'real' values.[370] The contradictory risk perception of the public would have to be corrected towards the extrapolated result with the help of risk communication and risk education.[371]

At a first glance, the goal of realising people's 'authentic' values may seem appealing. However, the main weakness of this positivist approach lies in the ability of science to deliver on the promise of identifying the 'authentic' values. As a result, there is a danger of undermining the conceptual basis of political legitimacy. Both points invite more explanation.

5.4.2.2 Practical Restraints of Extrapolation Proposal

First, the argument of basing risk management on extrapolations of people's 'authentic' risk concerns overstretches the reliability of extrapolations. As such, social scientists caution against claims that science could extrapolate people's counterfactual preferences if they believed the facts.[372]

5.4.2.2.1 Doubts About the Reliable Determination of People's 'Authentic' Values

The argument of this positivist school of thought presupposes the ability to reliably capture and map people's 'authentic' values in risk evaluation. However, it is doubtful whether social science has developed a respective method to accomplish this. For instance, the commonly proposed economic risk assessment approaches, such as cost-benefit assessment ('CBA'), reproduce the same presented biases and heuristics.[373] The method of CBA, which converts the multi-dimensional benefits and

[368] Slovic (2000), p. 22.

[369] Evans (2006), p. 221; see further Cross (1998), p. 37.

[370] Sunstein (2005b); see Viscusi (1992), p. 25; cf. Sunstein and Pildes (1997); Breyer (1993), pp. 55–63.

[371] See Renn (2008), p. 96, citing Cross (1998) and Coglianese (1999).

[372] For critical voices, see Christiansen and Hallsson (2017), p. 63; Fischhoff et al. (1978), p. 130; Slovic (1987).

[373] Christiansen and Hallsson (2017), p. 63; Sunstein and Pildes (1997), pp. 128–130; Hartzell-Nichols (2012), p. 948; Shrader-Frechette (2005); Clarke (2010); MacLean (2012), pp. 798–799.

disadvantages of risks into monetary values,[374] can be used to determine how much people are willing to pay to avoid a presented risk, and how much money they would demand to accept that risk.[375] The monetary value assignment often relies on epistemically measured market activity,[376] such as the labour market or consumer products to determine the actually accepted compensation for assuming risks.[377] For instance, if a worker is averagely paid $600 in additional wages for assuming risks of 1/10,000, the value of a statistical life would amount to $6 million.[378] If market data is unavailable, the determination of monetary value often relies on surveys.[379] For instance, surveys may ask participants, how much they are willing to pay to avoid the loss of a coral reef.[380]

Yet, the quantification of people's risk acceptance based on their actual or hypothetical purchases or labour conditions does not necessarily reflect their 'authentic' beliefs and desires.[381] For instance, people's economic decisions may be subject to practical constraints that affect their choices.[382] As such, Zahra Meghani concludes 'that one votes with one's dollars usually only holds for those who have the financial wherewithal to express their beliefs about the values that should govern risk assessment through their purchases'.[383] Furthermore, people may hold different values as private consumers or as a public citizen.[384] As such, MacLean holds that

> [a] reasonable person might shop for the least expensive car while simultaneously supporting legislation to make cars safer and more fuel efficient, even if these regulations drive up the price of automobiles. Laws and social policies can express values in ways that are not available to citizens acting privately in the market.[385]

The frequent divergence of considerations and motivations in the private sphere and in the democratic process is well documented by social science studies.[386] To that effect, the challenge of reliably isolating people's *authentic* values in the evaluation of risks should not be underestimated.

---

374 Meghani (2014), p. 983; Christiansen and Hallsson (2017), p. 63.

375 Christiansen and Hallsson (2017), p. 63; Sunstein and Pildes (1997), pp. 139–141; Viscusi (1992), Ch 2; Viscusi (2015), pp. 1123–1126; Hansson (2007), pp. 163–164.

376 Murphy and Gardoni (2012), p. 985.

377 Viscusi (1992), pp. 7–8; Sunstein (2005a), p. 353.

378 Sunstein (2005a), pp. 352–353; Murphy and Gardoni (2012), p. 985; Sunstein (2005b), p. 132.

379 Sunstein (2005a), p. 353; Murphy and Gardoni (2012), p. 985; MacLean (2012), p. 799.

380 Sunstein (2005a), p. 353; Murphy and Gardoni (2012), p. 985.

381 Meghani (2009), pp. 137–138.

382 Sunstein and Pildes (1997), pp. 140–141; Shrader-Frechette (1991), pp. 72–73.

383 Meghani (2009), pp. 137–138.

384 Sunstein and Pildes (1997), p. 141.

385 MacLean (2012), p. 799.

386 Sunstein and Pildes (1997), p. 141.

5.4.2.2.2 Doubts About the Reliable Extrapolation to Other Contexts

Moreover, it is uncertain that experts can reliably extrapolate how the identified 'authentic values' apply to other risk contexts without inadvertently ignoring the complexity of people's risk perception.[387] To that end, Paul Slovic, as one of the leading theorists in the field of risk perception research, has cautioned that

> [p]erhaps the most important message from this research is that there is wisdom as well as error in public attitudes and perceptions. Lay people sometimes lack certain information about hazards. However, their basic conceptualization of risk is much richer than that of the experts and reflects legitimate concerns that are typically omitted from expert risk assessments. As a result, risk communication and risk management efforts are destined to fail unless they are structured as a two-way process. Each side, expert and public, has something valid to contribute. Each side must respect the insights and intelligence of the other.[388]

Only an experimental cross-check could rebut these theoretical doubts on science's ability to extrapolate people's counterfactual preferences. Without such cross-check, science would request unconditional trust, which in turn undermines the input legitimacy, namely the equal standing in the deliberative process and democratic accountability. Moreover, if it was possible to make all citizens sincerely understand and believe respective facts to cross-check the reliability of projected counterfactual preferences, the question emerges regarding why extrapolation would be preferable over an appropriately structured deliberative process.

5.4.2.3 The Threat of Eroding the Foundation of Democratic Theory

Secondly, this positivist approach of ignoring 'unauthentic' risk perception poses a threat to the conceptual foundation of democratic theory. In contrast to deliberate democracy, the positivist argument is to use risk communication and risk education to re-educate people towards an attitude regarding risk that science has identified as 'authentic'. However, the public decision on the substantive issue would not depend on whether the information manages to successfully adjust people's perceptions.

In this respect, the positivist approach undermines the role of personal autonomy in political legitimacy. If people's value judgments do not change, despite appropriate information on true facts, the concept of autonomy and democracy requires to respect such decisions. To disavow people's preferences because they depart from the expected outcome based on a conception of bias and heuristics comes close to denying the very existence of individual agency.[389] Even if the narrower concept of free will may be controversial in social psychology and in the philosophical branch of determinism, the notion of freedom in normative political theory necessarily

---

[387] Ibid, p. 140.

[388] Slovic (1987), p. 285.

[389] See generally Held (2006), p. 153.

takes the existence of the broader concept of autonomy as a given.[390] This idea presupposes that individuals are principally able to process new information, to reason, and to make respective choices. However, the concept of autonomy does not presuppose a particular outcome of the individual's reasoning process.

The argument to enhance democratic legitimacy by ignoring people's 'unauthentic' preferences after an appropriate deliberative process would also amount to 'an artificial and cryptically elitist conception of democratic deliberation' through the back-door.[391] The latter conception could only be convincing if one distrusts lay people to be open to new information, and ultimately 'believed that rational decision making is best performed by experts'.[392] Such a conclusion would concomitantly negate the normative basis of democracy and would thus render consent in voting or deliberation redundant.[393]

5.5 Conclusion

Given the scientific evidence on the likelihood and seriousness of common natural hazards, experts judge the status quo of private and collective DRR measures in Europe to be inadequate.[394] Scientific findings further suggest that people would often judge the acceptability of risks, such as in relation to natural hazards, differently if they could unbiasedly apply scientific facts in their judgments.[395] In other words, psychology's findings on common disjunctions between means and ends point out that uninformed or intuitive decisions by lay people may not coherently reflect their political views or interests.[396] In the context of natural hazards, the observed perception of deterministic behaviour of natural hazards and the 'probability neglect' in particular distort the authenticity of collective decisions relating to DRR. As such, distortions in risk perception can hinder the public's desire for policy change. Against this background, this chapter explored how the design of the political decision-making process can promote the realisation of the 'authentic' will in policies, while respecting citizens as autonomous and equal.

Based on the ideal of deliberative democracy, this chapter has argued that the better argument seems to be not to respond to the 'initial, often uninformed,

390 See Baade (2017), pp. 320–321.

391 Howse (2000), p. 2337.

392 Fischhoff et al. (1978), p. 149.

393 Urbinati (2014), p. 10, quoting Holmes (1995), p. 196; Rayner (2003), p. 164; Rayner (2007), p. 168.

394 In relation to Germany, see, e.g., Gesamtverband der Deutschen Versicherungswirtschaft e. V. (2021).

395 See Viscusi (1992), p. 25; see Murphy and Gardoni (2012), p. 985; Christiansen and Hallsson (2017), pp. 62–64; Ivčević et al. (2021).

396 See generally Fung (2007), p. 449.

preferences of citizens … [as the] basis for evaluating risks a community faces'.[397] Indeed, empirically proven, deliberative processes can produce 'good', that is, acceptable to all citizens concerned, and epistemically robust outcomes in reality. The goal of 'epistemically robust outcomes' in deliberative processes gives experts a legitimate role in establishing the *epistemic or technical knowledge* necessary for determining what risks society find acceptable. Yet, with respect to the negotiation of the *if* and *how* of risk regulation, deliberative theory requires equal access for all citizens to the deliberative procedure to derive input-oriented legitimacy.[398] Thus, the conceptualisation of deliberate democracy requires that experts and lay people have equal standing as participants in deliberation and are thus equally entitled to contribute to the exchange of reasons and arguments.[399] This conceptualisation is also reflected in the prevailing school of thought on risk management that puts scientific concepts on equal footing as those of other stakeholders and the general public.[400]

It has been demonstrated in empirical studies and experience that both laypeople and experts can reflect on their biases through deliberation. Yet, the realisation of this success depends on appropriate structure and implementation of deliberative processes. This concerns the maintenance of a fair exchange of reasoned arguments, the openness of participants to new information and discussion of arguments,[401] and the effort of each participant to give the other participants a reasonable chance to understand his or her point of view. In this context, the asymmetry of scientific knowledge poses particular challenges for experts. On the one hand, with the cultural backgrounds of distorted risk perceptions in mind, experts should avoid narrative patterns that lead to distorted risk perceptions. On the other hand, they should explain the value and reasonable expectations of scientific knowledge.

From a perceptive of normative political theory, the juxtaposition of common democratic theory has substantiated deliberative democracy as the more reasonable theory to balance procedural and outcome-oriented aspects of political legitimacy. In contrast to the 'extreme individualism' of aggregative democracy,[402] the theory of deliberative democracy manages to facilitate equal participation, while also accounting for a reasonable quality of the results for all.[403] In order to ensure this necessary equal standing of experts and laypersons in practice, the chapter has also contoured institutional structures for the substantiation and democratic control of trust in experts' contributions relating to epistemic knowledge.

---

[397] Murphy and Gardoni (2012), p. 990; see further Sunstein and Pildes (1997), pp. 135–136.

[398] See Sect. 5.2.1.

[399] See Walker (1966).

[400] Renn (2008), p. 96, citing Liberatore and Funtowicz (2003) and Jasanoff (2004); see further Stoll (2003), pp. 328–332.

[401] Chambers (2003), p. 309.

[402] Christiano (2020), para 5.

[403] Habermas (1996), p. 304.

Admittedly, given that deliberative processes may prolong decision-making and even increase risk levels if structured inappropriately, it cannot be considered a panacea for every political issue.[404] Yet, despite these downsides, the merits of deliberative processes stand out compared to alternative proposals to mitigate the influence of distorted risk perception on collective decision-making.[405] In this respect, this chapter has further defended the proposal based on deliberative processes against competing positivist proposals that assign a leading role to experts in public decision-making processes with the claim to realise the objectively or subjectively best solution for the 'incompetent' citizen.

First, positivist arguments that rely on the idea of objective rationality to trump people's expressed preferences need to be rejected. Promises to promote 'the needs and functions of the system as a whole' more effectively cannot justify the restriction of liberty and political equality, which entail a right of self-government.[406] Such purely, or at least primarily, outcome-oriented justifications based on a notion of objective rationality reveal normative and practical flaws. On the one hand, these flaws render undemocratically constituted epistocracies 'totally unacceptable and illegitimate from a normative point of view'.[407] Consequently, this analysis has underpinned the position that democratic legitimacy is a necessary requirement of political legitimacy. On the other hand, the discussion of 'objective rationality' has also opposed elitist conceptualisations of democracy that lack respect for people's opinions. The prioritisation of experts' assessment over lay people's preferences would render consent in form of voting or deliberation redundant.[408]

Second, the positivist argument that experts should be empowered to substitute public risk decisions they deem 'unauthentic' fails to stand up to practical and normative concerns. On the one hand, empirical support for experts' ability to reliably extrapolate the 'authentic opinions' of citizens is lacking. On the other hand, the conclusion of this argument undermines the source of democratic legitimacy. To that effect, Robert Howse aptly summarises that democracy

> requires respect for popular choices, even if different from those that would be made in an ideal deliberative environment by scientists and technocrats, *if* the choices have been made in awareness of the facts, and the manner that they will impact on those legitimately concerned has been explicitly considered.[409]

Since democratic theories derive their political legitimacy from the possibility of equal participation of citizens in the decision-making process,[410] experts cannot be granted the last word in the decision-making process, even if the outcome seems

[404] Gunderson (2018), p. 721.

[405] Renn (2008), p. 313.

[406] Christiano and Bajaj (2022), paras 2.2.1, 2.2.3; Walker (1966), pp. 286–289.

[407] Holst (2012), p. 52; see further Fischer (1990), pp. 21–26.

[408] Urbinati (2014), p. 10, quoting Holmes (1995), p. 196; Rayner (2003), p. 164; Rayner (2007), p. 168.

[409] Howse (2000), p. 2330.

[410] See Walker (1966).

irrational to experts' counterfactual expectations.[411] Thus, the conceptualisation of input-legitimacy is incompatible with proposals that seek to override the requirement for democratic approval with the claim to realise the 'subjectively rational' policy. Such paternalistic rationale cannot justify the incapacitation of citizens in the decision-making process.[412]

For these reasons, this chapter has argued that instead of incapacitating people, the consequence should be to enable people to not become victims of their cognitive and cultural mechanisms. As such, the respective findings of subjective irrationality give reason to make the decision-making process as deliberative as possible.

References

Adler MD, Posner EA (2006) New foundations of cost-benefit analysis. Harvard University Press, Cambridge

Albris K, Lauta KC, Raju E (2020) Disaster knowledge gaps: exploring the interface between science and policy for disaster risk reduction in Europe. Int J Disaster Risk Sci 11(1):1–12. https://doi.org/10.1007/s13753-020-00250-5

Alemanno A (2016) Risk and regulation. In: Burgess A, Alemanno A, Zinn JO (eds) Routledge handbook of risk studies. Routledge, Abingdon, pp 191–203

Altmetric (2020) Effectiveness of surgical and cotton masks in blocking SARS–CoV-2: a controlled comparison in 4 patients: overview of attention for article published in Annals of Internal Medicine, July 2020. Web Page. https://annals.altmetric.com/details/79213450. Accessed 19 June 2023

Ames BN, Magaw R, Gold LS (1987) Ranking possible carcinogenic hazards. Science 236(4799):271–280. https://doi.org/10.1126/science.3563506

Baade B (2017) Der Europäische Gerichtshof für Menschenrechte als Diskurswächter. In: Beiträge zum ausländischen öffentlichen Recht und Völkerrecht, vol 263. Springer, Heidelberg

Baan PJ, Klijn F (2004) Flood risk perception and implications for flood risk management in the Netherlands. Int J River Basin Manag 2(2):113–122. https://doi.org/10.1080/15715124.2004.9635226

Bae S, Kim M-C, Kim JY, Cha H-H, Lim JS, Jung J, Kim M-J, Oh DK, Lee M-K, Choi S-H, Sung M, Hong S-B, Chung J-W, Kim S-H (2020) Effectiveness of surgical and cotton masks in blocking SARS-CoV-2: a controlled comparison in 4 patients. Ann Intern Med 173(1):W22–W23. https://doi.org/10.7326/M20-1342

Bajak Aleszu, Howe J (2020) A study said covid wasn't that deadly. The right seized it: how coronavirus research is being weaponized. The New York Times, 14 May 2020. https://www.nytimes.com/2020/05/14/opinion/coronavirus-research-misinformation.html. Accessed 19 June 2023

Beatley T (1989) Towards a moral philosophy of natural disaster mitigation. Int J Mass Emerg Disasters 7(1):5–32. https://doi.org/10.1177/028072708900700102

Beisbart C (2012) A rational approach to risk? Bayesian decision theory. In: Roeser S, Hillerbrand R, Sandin P, Peterson M (eds) Handbook of risk theory: epistemology, decision theory, ethics, and social implications of risk. Springer, Dordrecht, pp 376–404

[411] Howse (2000), p. 2335; see generally Crosweller and Wilmshurst (2013).

[412] See Walker (1966); Sunstein and Pildes (1997), pp. 145–146, who discuss Breyer's proposal of an 'expert cadre'.

Bernholz P (1966) Economic policies in a democracy. Kyklos 19(1):48–80. https://doi.org/10.1111/j.1467-6435.1966.tb02492.x
Bohman J (1999) Democracy as inquiry, inquiry as democratic: pragmatism, social science, and the cognitive division of labor. Am J Polit Sci 43(1):590. https://doi.org/10.2307/2991808
Boschele M (2020) COVID-19 science policy, experts, and publics: why epistemic democracy matters in ecological crises. OMICS 24(8):479–482. https://doi.org/10.1089/omi.2020.0083
Bouchard F (2016) The roles of institutional trust and distrust in grounding rational deference to scientific expertise. Perspect Sci 24(5):582–608. https://doi.org/10.1162/POSC_a_00224
Breakey H (2015) Positive duties and human rights: challenges, opportunities and conceptual necessities. Polit Stud 63(5):1198–1215. https://doi.org/10.1111/1467-9248.12150
Brennan J (2014) Epistocracy within public reason. In: Cudd AE, Scholz SJ (eds) Philosophical perspectives on democracy in the 21st century. Springer, Cham, pp 191–204
Brennan J (2016) Against democracy. Princeton University Press, Princeton
Brettschneider C (2005) Balancing procedures and outcomes within democratic theory: core values and judicial review. Polit Stud 53(2):423–441. https://doi.org/10.1111/j.1467-9248.2005.00536.x
Breyer S (1993) Breaking the vicious circle: toward effective risk regulation. The Oliver Wendell Holmes Lectures, vol 1992. Harvard University Press, Cambridge
Briceño S (2015) Looking back and beyond Sendai: 25 years of international policy experience on disaster risk reduction. Int J Disaster Risk Sci 6(1):1–7. https://doi.org/10.1007/s13753-015-0040-y
Byskov MF (2020) Utilitarianism and risk. J Risk Res 23(2):259–270. https://doi.org/10.1080/13669877.2018.1501600
Campbell WF (1967) Adam Smith's theory of justice, prudence, and beneficence. Am Econ Rev 57(2):571–577
Capurro G, Jardine CG, Tustin J, Driedger M (2021) Communicating scientific uncertainty in a rapidly evolving situation: a framing analysis of Canadian coverage in early days of COVID-19. BMC Public Health 21(1):2181. https://doi.org/10.1186/s12889-021-12246-x
Caulfield T, Bubela T, Kimmelman J, Ravitsky V (2021) Let's do better: public representations of COVID-19 science. FACETS 6(1):403–423. https://doi.org/10.1139/facets-2021-0018
Cerovac I (2016) The role of experts in a democratic society. JECS 7(2):75–88. https://doi.org/10.15503/jecs20162.75.88
Chambers S (2003) Deliberative democratic theory. Annu Rev Polit Sci 6(1):307–326. https://doi.org/10.1146/annurev.polisci.6.121901.085538
Chambers S (2017) Balancing epistemic quality and equal participation in a system approach to deliberative democracy. Soc Epistemol 31(3):266–276. https://doi.org/10.1080/02691728.2017.1317867
Chambers S (2021) Truth, deliberative democracy, and the virtues of accuracy: is fake news destroying the public sphere? Polit Stud 69(1):147–163. https://doi.org/10.1177/0032321719890811
Childs D (2013) Implementation of the Hyogo Framework for Action: Summary of Reports 2007–2013. https://www.undrr.org/quick/11319. Accessed 19 June 2023
Chmutina K, von Meding J (2019) A dilemma of language: "natural disasters" in academic literature. Int J Disaster Risk Sci 10(3):283–292. https://doi.org/10.1007/s13753-019-00232-2
Christiano T (2009) Must democracy be reasonable? Can J Philos 39(1):1–34. https://doi.org/10.1353/cjp.0.0037
Christiano T (2012) Rational deliberation among experts and citizens. In: Parkinson J, Mansbridge J (eds) Deliberative systems: deliberative democracy at the large scale. Cambridge University Press, Cambridge, pp 27–51
Christiano T (2020) Authority. In: Zalta EN (ed) The Stanford Encyclopedia of Philosophy. https://plato.stanford.edu/entries/authority/. Accessed 19 June 2023
Christiano T, Bajaj S (2022) Democracy. In: Zalta EN (ed) The Stanford Encyclopedia of Philosophy. https://plato.stanford.edu/entries/democracy/. Accessed 19 June 2023
Christiansen A, Hallsson BG (2017) Democratic decision making and the psychology of risk. Les ateliers de l'éthique/The Ethics Forum 12(1):51–83. https://doi.org/10.7202/1042278ar

Christoforou T (2003) The precautionary principle and democratizing expertise: a European legal perspective. Sci Public Policy 30(3):205–212. https://doi.org/10.3152/147154303781780443
Clarke S (2010) Cognitive bias and the precautionary principle: what's wrong with the core argument in Sunstein's laws of fear and a way to fix it. J Risk Res 13(2):163–174. https://doi.org/10.1080/13669870903126200
Coglianese C (1999) The limits of consensus: the environmental protection system in transition: toward a more desirable future. Environ Sci Policy Sustain Dev 41(3):28–33. https://doi.org/10.1080/00139159909604620
Covello VT (1991) Risk comparisons and risk communication: issues and problems in comparing health and environmental risks. In: Kasperson RE, Stallen PJM (eds) Communicating risks to the public: international perspectives. Springer, Dordrecht, pp 79–124
Cranor CF (1993) Regulating toxic substances: a philosophy of science and the law, Environmental ethics and science policy series. Oxford University Press, New York
Cross FB (1998) Facts and values in risk assessment. Reliab Eng Syst Saf 59(1):27–40. https://doi.org/10.1016/S0951-8320(97)00116-6
Crosweller HS, Wilmshurst J (2013) Natural hazards and risk: the human perspective. In: Rougier J, Hill LJ, Sparks RSJ (eds) Risk and uncertainty assessment for natural hazards. Cambridge University Press, Cambridge, pp 548–569
de Lazari-Radek K, Singer P (2017) Utilitarianism: a very short introduction. Oxford University Press, Oxford
Dewey J (1927) The public and its problems. Holt, New York
Dietz T (1994) 'What should we do?': human ecology and collective decision making. Hum Ecol Rev 1(2):301–309. https://doi.org/10.1525/sod.2015.1.1.123
Dietz T, Stern PC (2008) Public participation in environmental assessment and decision making. National Academies Press, Washington, D.C.
Dryzek JS (2001) Legitimacy and economy in deliberative democracy. Polit Theory 29(5):651–669. https://doi.org/10.1177/0090591701029005003
Dryzek JS, Bächtiger A, Chambers S, Cohen J, Druckman JN, Felicetti A, Fishkin JS, Farrell DM, Fung A, Gutmann A, Landemore H, Mansbridge J, Marien S, Neblo MA, Niemeyer S, Setälä M, Slothuus R, Suiter J, Thompson D, Warren ME (2019) The crisis of democracy and the science of deliberation. Science 363(6432):1144–1146. https://doi.org/10.1126/science.aaw2694
Duncan DE (2020) "Prepare, Prepare, Prepare": why didn't the world listen to the coronavirus Cassandras? Vanity Fair, 27 March 2020. https://www.vanityfair.com/news/2020/03/why-didnt-the-world-listen-to-the-coronavirus-cassandras. Accessed 19 June 2023
Dworkin G (2015) The nature of autonomy. Nordic J Stud Educ Policy 1(28479):1–8. https://doi.org/10.3402/nstep.v1.28479
Else H (2020) Covid in papers: a torrent of science. Nature 588(7839):553. https://doi.org/10.1038/d41586-020-03564-y
EM-DAT, CRED/UCLouvain, Brussels, Belgium. www.emdat.be. Accessed 19 June 2023
Estlund DM (2008) Democratic authority: a philosophical framework. Princeton University Press, Princeton
Estlund D, Landemore H (2018) The epistemic value of democratic deliberation. In: Bächtiger A, Dryzek JS, Mansbridge JJ, Warren M (eds) The Oxford handbook of deliberative democracy. Oxford University Press, New York, pp 112–131
Evans JH (2006) Between technocracy and democratic legitimation: a proposed compromise position for common morality public bioethics. J Med Philos 31(3):213–234. https://doi.org/10.1080/03605310600732834
Faulkner H, Parker D, Green C, Beven K (2007) Developing a translational discourse to communicate uncertainty in flood risk between science and the practitioner. Ambio 36(7):692–703. https://doi.org/10.1579/0044-7447(2007)36[692:DATDTC]2.0.CO;2
Fiorino DJ (2018) Can democracy handle climate change? Democratic futures. Polity, Cambridge
Fischer F (1990) Technocracy and the politics of expertise. SAGE, Newbury Park

Fischer F (2000) Citizens, experts, and the environment: the politics of local knowledge. Duke University Press, Durham

Fischhoff B, Slovic P, Lichtenstein S, Read S, Combs B (1978) How safe is safe enough? A psychometric study of attitudes towards technological risks and benefits. Policy Sci 9(2):127–152. https://doi.org/10.1007/BF00143739

Freer J, Beven KJ, Neal J, Schumann G, Hall J, Bates P (2013) Flood risk and uncertainty. In: Rougier J, Hill LJ, Sparks RSJ (eds) Risk and uncertainty assessment for natural hazards. Cambridge University Press, Cambridge, pp 190–233

Fung A (2007) Democratic theory and political science: a pragmatic method of constructive engagement. Am Polit Sci Rev 101(3):443–458. https://doi.org/10.1017/S000305540707030X

Ganesh J (2020) Coronavirus and the comeback of the administrative state. Financial Times, 11 March 2020. https://www.ft.com/content/22f51a26-6385-11ea-b3f3-fe4680ea68b5. Accessed 19 June 2023

Gastil J, Black L, Moscovitz K (2008) Ideology, attitude change, and deliberation in small face-to-face groups. Polit Commun 25(1):23–46. https://doi.org/10.1080/10584600701807836

German Advisory Council on Global Change (1998) World in transition: strategies for managing global environmental risks. World in Transition, Berlin

Gesamtverband der Deutschen Versicherungswirtschaft e. V. (2021) Positionspapier des Gesamtverbandes der Deutschen Versicherungswirtschaft für ein zeitgemäßes und nachhaltiges Bauordnungs- und Bauplanungsrecht, das den Herausforderungen durch Klimawandel und Extremwetterereignissen zuverlässig begegnen kann. https://www.gdv.de/resource/blob/66384/3b4b78bbd97fe50268d7bdb1d42a9d58/positionspapier-bauen-data.pdf. Accessed 19 June 2023

Gilbert C (2020) Coronavirus: Sen. Ron Johnson says keep outbreak in perspective. Milwaukee Journal Sentinel, 18 March 2020. https://eu.jsonline.com/story/news/politics/analysis/2020/03/18/coronavirus-sen-ron-johnson-says-keep-outbreak-perspective/5074145002/. Accessed 19 June 2023

Glöckner A (2016) Psychology and disaster: why we do not see looming disasters and how our way of thinking causes them. Glob Policy 7:16–24. https://doi.org/10.1111/1758-5899.12289

Gomez C (2017) Ethics and disaster risk reduction including climate change adaptation. In: Kelman I, Mercer J, Gaillard JC (eds) The Routledge handbook of disaster risk reduction including climate change adaptation. Taylor & Francis, Milton, pp 174–186

Gonçalves VB (2013) The precautionary principle and environmental risk management: contributions and limitations of economic models. Ambient Soc 16(4):121–138. https://doi.org/10.1590/S1414-753X2013000400008

Goodin RE (1993) Democracy, preferences and paternalism. Policy Sci 26(3):229–247. https://doi.org/10.1007/BF00999718

Graham JD, Wiener JB (1997) Risk vs. risk: tradeoffs in protecting health and the environment. Harvard University Press, Cambridge

Green HP (1981) The role of law in determining acceptability of risk. Ann N Y Acad Sci 363(1):1–12. https://doi.org/10.1111/j.1749-6632.1981.tb20712.x

Greenacre M, Fleshner K (2017) Distributive justice in disaster triage. UWOMJ 86(1):35–37. https://doi.org/10.5206/uwomj.v86i1.2162

Grove WM, Meehl PE (1996) Comparative efficiency of informal (subjective, impressionistic) and formal (mechanical, algorithmic) prediction procedures: the clinical-statistical controversy. Psychol Public Policy Law 2(2):293–323. https://doi.org/10.1037/1076-8971.2.2.293

Gunderson R (2018) Global environmental governance should be participatory: five problems of scale. Int Sociol 33(6):715–737. https://doi.org/10.1177/0268580918792786

Gutmann A, Thompson DF (2004) Why deliberative democracy? Princeton University Press, Princeton

Habermas J (1996) Between facts and norms: contributions to a discourse theory of law and democracy. Studies in contemporary German social thought. MIT Press, Cambridge

Habermas J (1997) Between facts and norms: contributions to a discourse theory of law and democracy. Polity Press, Cambridge

Habermas J (2015) Inclusion of the other: studies in political theory. Polity Press, Cambridge

Hansson SO (2004) Weighing risks and benefits. Topoi 23(2):145–152. https://doi.org/10.1007/s11245-004-5371-z

Hansson SO (2007) Philosophical problems in cost–benefit analysis. Econ Philos 23(2):163–183. https://doi.org/10.1017/S0266267107001356

Hansson SO (2012) A panorama of the philosophy of risk. In: Roeser S, Hillerbrand R, Sandin P, Peterson M (eds) Handbook of risk theory: epistemology, decision theory, ethics, and social implications of risk. Springer, Dordrecht, pp 27–54

Haring S (2010) Herrschaft der Experten oder Herrschaft des Sachzwangs? – Technokratie als politikwissenschaftliches "Problem-Ensemble". Zeitschrift für Politik 57(3):243–264. https://doi.org/10.5771/0044-3360-2010-3-243

Hartzell-Nichols L (2012) Intergenerational risks. In: Roeser S, Hillerbrand R, Sandin P, Peterson M (eds) Handbook of risk theory: epistemology, decision theory, ethics, and social implications of risk. Springer, Dordrecht, pp 931–960

Haworth L (1984) Autonomy and utility. Ethics 95(1):5–19. https://doi.org/10.1086/292594

Held D (2006) Models of democracy, 3rd edn. Polity, Cambridge

Henriques A (2016) Students' difficulties in understanding of confidence intervals. In: Ben-Zvi D, Makar K (eds) The teaching and learning of statistics: international perspectives. Springer, Cham, pp 129–138

Holmes S (1995) Passions and constraint: on the theory of liberal democracy. University of Chicago Press, Chicago

Holst C (2012) What is epistocracy? In: Øyen SA, Lund-Olsen T, Vaage NS (eds) Sacred science? On science and its interrelations with religious worldviews. Wageningen Academic Publishers, Wageningen, pp 41–54

Holst C (2014) Why not epistocracy? Political legitimacy and 'the fact of expertise'. In: Holst C (ed) Expertise and democracy. ARENA Centre for European Studies, Oslo, pp 1–11

Holst C, Molander A (2017) Public deliberation and the fact of expertise: making experts accountable. Soc Epistemol 31(3):235–250. https://doi.org/10.1080/02691728.2017.1317865

Holst C, Molander A (2019) Epistemic democracy and the role of experts. Contemp Polit Theory 18(4):541–561. https://doi.org/10.1057/s41296-018-00299-4

Horbach SP (2020) Pandemic publishing: medical journals strongly speed up their publication process for COVID-19. Quant Sci Stud 1(3):1056–1067. https://doi.org/10.1162/qss_a_00076

Horkheimer M (2013) Eclipse of reason. Bloomsbury Revelations, Bloomsbury, London

Howse R (2000) Democracy, science, and free trade: risk regulation on trial at the World Trade Organization. Mich Law Rev 98(7):2329–2357

Hugenbusch D, Neumann T (2016) Cost-benefit analysis of disaster risk reduction: a synthesis for informed decision making. Aktion Deutschland Hilft e.V. https://www.aktion-deutschland-hilft.de/fileadmin/fmdam/pdf/publikationen/ADH_Studie_EN_rev3.pdf. Accessed 19 June 2023

Intergovernmental Panel on Climate Change (2005) Guidance notes for lead authors of the IPCC Fourth Assessment Report on addressing uncertainties. https://www.ipcc.ch/site/assets/uploads/2018/02/ar4-uncertaintyguidancenote-1.pdf. Accessed 19 June 2023

Ivčević A, Mazurek H, Siame L, Bertoldo R, Statzu V, Agharroud K, Estrela Rego I, Mukherjee N, Bellier O (2021) Lessons learned about the importance of raising risk awareness in the Mediterranean region (North Morocco and West Sardinia, Italy). Nat Haz Earth Syst Sci 21(12):3749–3765. https://doi.org/10.5194/nhess-21-3749-2021

Jamieson D (2014) Reason in a dark time: why the struggle against climate change failed - and what it means for our future. Oxford University Press, Oxford

Jasanoff S (1994) The fifth branch: science advisers as policymakers. Harvard University Press, Cambridge

Jasanoff S (2003) (No?) accounting for expertise. Sci Public Policy 30(3):157–162. https://doi.org/10.3152/147154303781780542

Jasanoff S (2004) Ordering knowledge, ordering society. In: Jasanoff S (ed) States of knowledge: the co-production of science and social order. Routledge, London, pp 13–45

Jensen KK (2012) A philosophical assessment of decision theory. In: Roeser S, Hillerbrand R, Sandin P, Peterson M (eds) Handbook of risk theory: epistemology, decision theory, ethics, and social implications of risk. Springer, Dordrecht, pp 405–439

Jones G (2020) 10% less democracy: why you should trust elites a little more and the masses a little less. Stanford University Press, Redwood City

Kahan DM, Slovic P, Braman D, Gastil J (2006) Fear of democracy: a cultural evaluation of Sunstein on risk. Harv Law Rev 119(4):1071–1109

Kalokairinou E (2018) Kantian virtue ethics approaches. In: O'Mathúna DP, Dranseika V, Gordijn B (eds) Disasters: core concepts and ethical theories. Springer, Cham, pp 217–228

Kamm FM (2007) Intricate ethics. Oxford University Press

Kitcher P (2011) Science in a democratic society. Prometheus Books, Amherst

Knight J, Johnson J (1994) Aggregation and deliberation: on the possibility of democratic legitimacy. Polit Theory 22(2):277–296. https://doi.org/10.1177/0090591794022002004

Lateef F (2011) Ethical issues in disasters. Prehosp Disaster Med 26(4):289–292. https://doi.org/10.1017/S1049023X1100642X

Laudan L (1994) The book of risks: fascinating facts about the chances we take every day. Wiley, New York

Laudan L (1997) Danger ahead: the risks you really face on life's highway. Wiley, New York

Lauta KC (2018) Disasters and responsibility. normative issues for law following disasters. In: O'Mathúna DP, Dranseika V, Gordijn B (eds) Disasters: core concepts and ethical theories. Springer, Cham, pp 43–53

Lauta KC, Faure MG (2016) Disaster risk management. In: Burgess A, Alemanno A, Zinn JO (eds) Routledge handbook of risk studies. Routledge, Abingdon, pp 179–188

Lavazza A, Farina M (2020) The role of experts in the Covid-19 pandemic and the limits of their epistemic authority in democracy. Front Public Health 8:1–11. https://doi.org/10.3389/fpubh.2020.00356

Liberatore A, Funtowicz S (2003) 'Democratising' expertise, 'expertising' democracy: what does this mean, and why bother? Sci Public Policy 30(3):146–150. https://doi.org/10.3152/147154303781780551

Lin JY, Anderson-Shaw L (2009) Rationing of resources: ethical issues in disasters and epidemic situations. Prehosp Disaster Med 24(3):215–221. https://doi.org/10.1017/s1049023x0000683x

MacLean D (2012) Ethics and risk. In: Roeser S, Hillerbrand R, Sandin P, Peterson M (eds) Handbook of risk theory: epistemology, decision theory, ethics, and social implications of risk. Springer, Dordrecht, pp 791–804

Mastrandrea MD, Field CB, Stocker TF, Edenhofer O, Ebi KL, Frame DJ, Held H, Kriegler E, Mach KJ, Matschoss PR, Plattner G-K, Yohe GW, Zwiers FW (2010) Guidance note for lead authors of the IPCC Fifth Assessment Report on consistent treatment of uncertainties. http://www.ipcc.ch/site/assets/uploads/2018/05/uncertainty-guidance-note.pdf. Accessed 19 June 2023

Mastrandrea MD, Mach KJ, Plattner G-K, Edenhofer O, Stocker TF, Field CB, Ebi KL, Matschoss PR (2011) The IPCC AR5 guidance note on consistent treatment of uncertainties: a common approach across the working groups. Clim Chang 108(4):675–691. https://doi.org/10.1007/s10584-011-0178-6

Matthews D (2020) French trust in science drops as coronavirus backlash begins. Times Higher Education, 8 June 2020. https://www.timeshighereducation.com/news/french-trust-science-drops-coronavirus-backlash-begins. Accessed 19 June 2023

Mayo-Yánez M (2020) Research during SARS-CoV-2 pandemic: to "preprint" or not to "preprint", that is the question. Med Clin (Engl Ed) 155(2):86–87. https://doi.org/10.1016/j.medcli.2020.05.002

Meghani Z (2009) The US' Food and Drug Administration, normativity of risk assessment, GMOs, and American democracy. J Agric Environ Ethics 22(2):125–139. https://doi.org/10.1007/s10806-008-9133-6

Meghani Z (2014) Risk assessment of genetically modified food and neoliberalism: an argument for democratizing the regulatory review protocol of the food and drug administration. J Agric Environ Ethics 27(6):967–989. https://doi.org/10.1007/s10806-014-9511-1

Mehra MR, Desai SS, Kuy S, Henry TD, Patel AN (2020a) Retraction: cardiovascular disease, drug therapy, and mortality in Covid-19. N Engl J Med. DOI: 10.1056/NEJMoa2007621. N Engl J Med 382(26):2582. https://doi.org/10.1056/NEJMc2021225

Mehra MR, Ruschitzka F, Patel AN (2020b) Retraction—hydroxychloroquine or chloroquine with or without a macrolide for treatment of COVID-19: a multinational registry analysis. Lancet 395(10240):1820. https://doi.org/10.1016/S0140-6736(20)31324-6

Mill JS (1861) Considerations on representative government. Parker, Son, and Bourn, London

Mirrlees JA (1982) The economic uses of utilitarianism. In: Sen A, Williams B (eds) Utilitarianism and beyond. Cambridge University Press, Cambridge, pp 63–84

Misak C (2009) Truth and democracy: pragmatism and the deliberative virtues. In: Geenens R, Tinnevelt R (eds) Does truth matter?: Democracy and public space. Springer, Dordrecht, pp 29–39

Möller N (2012) The concepts of risk and safety. In: Roeser S, Hillerbrand R, Sandin P, Peterson M (eds) Handbook of risk theory: epistemology, decision theory, ethics, and social implications of risk. Springer, Dordrecht, pp 55–85

Moore A (2014) Democratic theory and expertise: between competence and consent. In: Holst C (ed) Expertise and democracy. ARENA Centre for European Studies, Oslo, pp 49–83

Moore A (2018) Deliberative democracy and science. In: Bächtiger A, Dryzek JS, Mansbridge JJ, Warren M (eds) The Oxford handbook of deliberative democracy. Oxford University Press, New York, pp 639–654

Moravcsik A (2002) In defence of the 'democratic deficit': reassessing legitimacy in the European Union. J Common Mark Stud 40(4):603–624. https://doi.org/10.1111/1468-5965.00390

Moravcsik A (2004) Is there a 'democratic deficit' in world politics? A framework for analysis. Gov Oppos 39(2):336–363. https://doi.org/10.1111/j.1477-7053.2004.00126.x

Muirhead R (2015) Anthony Downs, an economic theory of democracy. In: Levy JT (ed) Oxford handbook of classics in contemporary political theory. Oxford University Press, Oxford

Mulligan T (2015) On the compatibility of epistocracy and public reason. Soc Theory Pract 41(3):458–476. https://doi.org/10.5840/soctheorpract201541324

Murphy C, Gardoni P (2012) The capability approach in risk analysis. In: Roeser S, Hillerbrand R, Sandin P, Peterson M (eds) Handbook of risk theory: epistemology, decision theory, ethics, and social implications of risk. Springer, Dordrecht, pp 980–997

Newman JP, Maier HR, Riddell GA, Zecchin AC, Daniell JE, Schaefer AM, van Delden H, Khazai B, O'Flaherty MJ, Newland CP (2017) Review of literature on decision support systems for natural hazard risk reduction: current status and future research directions. Environ Model Softw 96:378–409. https://doi.org/10.1016/j.envsoft.2017.06.042

Nunan R (2014) Proportional representation, the single transferable vote, and electoral pragmatism. In: Cudd AE, Scholz SJ (eds) Philosophical perspectives on democracy in the 21st century. Springer, Cham, pp 87–101

Palayew A, Norgaard O, Safreed-Harmon K, Andersen TH, Rasmussen LN, Lazarus JV (2020) Pandemic publishing poses a new COVID-19 challenge. Nat Hum Behav 4(7):666–669. https://doi.org/10.1038/s41562-020-0911-0

Paletta D (2011) Political legitimacy. In: Chatterjee DK (ed) Encyclopedia of global justice. Springer, Dordrecht, pp 870–872

Pateman C (2012) Participatory democracy revisited. Perspect Polit 10(1):7–19. https://doi.org/10.1017/S1537592711004877

Peter F (2017) Political legitimacy. In: Zalta EN (ed) The Stanford Encyclopedia of Philosophy. https://plato.stanford.edu/entries/legitimacy/. Accessed 19 June 2023

Rabin RC (2020) The pandemic claims new victims: prestigious medical journals. The New York Times, 14 June 2020, updated on 16 June 2020. https://www.nytimes.com/2020/06/14/health/virus-journals.html. Accessed 19 June 2023

Raju E, da Costa K (2018) Governance in the Sendai: a way ahead? Disaster Prev Manag 27(3):278–291. https://doi.org/10.1108/DPM-08-2017-0190

Rakić V (2018) Disaster consequentialism. In: O'Mathúna DP, Dranseika V, Gordijn B (eds) Disasters: core concepts and ethical theories. Springer, Cham, pp 145–156

Rashidah Paujah Ismail N, Abdol Razak F, Baharun N (2018) Investigating students' difficulties in understanding confidence intervals in linear regression models. IJET 7(4.33):60–64. https://doi.org/10.14419/ijet.v7i4.33.23485

Rawls J (1971) A theory of justice. Belknap Press of Harvard University Press, Cambridge

Rawls J (1987) The idea of an overlapping consensus. Oxf J Leg Stud 7(1):1–25. https://doi.org/10.1093/ojls/7.1.1

Rawls J (1997) The idea of public reason revisited. Univ Chic Law Rev 64(3):765. https://doi.org/10.2307/1600311

Rayner S (2003) Democracy in the age of assessment: reflections on the roles of expertise and democracy in public-sector decision making. Sci Public Policy 30(3):163–170. https://doi.org/10.3152/147154303781780533

Rayner S (2007) The rise of risk and the decline of politics. Environ Haz 7(2):165–172. https://doi.org/10.1016/j.envhaz.2007.05.003

Renn O (2008) Risk governance: coping with uncertainty in a complex world, Earthscan risk in society series. Routledge, London

Renn O, Klinke A (2016) Risk governance: concept and application to technological risk. In: Burgess A, Alemanno A, Zinn JO (eds) Routledge handbook of risk studies. Routledge, Abingdon, pp 204–215

Renn O, Klinke A, van Asselt M (2011) Coping with complexity, uncertainty and ambiguity in risk governance: a synthesis. Ambio 40(2):231–246. https://doi.org/10.1007/s13280-010-0134-0

Reuchamps M, Suiter J (2016) A constitutional turn for deliberative democracy in Europe? In: Reuchamps M, Suiter J (eds) Constitutional deliberative democracy in Europe. ECPR Press, Colchester, pp 1–13

Revesz RL, Livermore MA (2008) Retaking rationality: how cost-benefit analysis can better protect the environment and our health. Oxford University Press, Oxford

Roeser S, Hillerbrand R, Sandin P, Peterson M (2012) Introduction to risk theory. In: Roeser S, Hillerbrand R, Sandin P, Peterson M (eds) Handbook of risk theory: epistemology, decision theory, ethics, and social implications of risk. Springer, Dordrecht

Rose A, Porter K, Dash N, Bouabid J, Huyck C, Whitehead J, Shaw D, Eguchi R, Taylor C, McLane T, Tobin LT, Ganderton PT, Godschalk D, Kiremidjian AS, Tierney K, West CT (2007) Benefit-cost analysis of FEMA hazard mitigation grants. Nat Haz Rev 8(4):97–111. https://doi.org/10.1061/(ASCE)1527-6988(2007)8:4(97)

Ross A, Athanassoulis N (2012) Risk and virtue ethics. In: Roeser S, Hillerbrand R, Sandin P, Peterson M (eds) Handbook of risk theory: epistemology, decision theory, ethics, and social implications of risk. Springer, Dordrecht, pp 833–856

Rougier J (2013) Quantifying hazard losses. In: Rougier J, Hill LJ, Sparks RSJ (eds) Risk and uncertainty assessment for natural hazards. Cambridge University Press, Cambridge, pp 19–39

Runciman D (2018) How democracy ends. Profile Books, London

Sanger DE, Lipton E, Sullivan E, Crowley M (2020) Before virus outbreak, a cascade of warnings went unheeded. New York Times, 19 March 2020, updated 22 March 2020. https://www.nytimes.com/2020/03/19/us/politics/trump-coronavirus-outbreak.html. Accessed 19 June 2023

Saretzki T (1994) Technokratie, Technokratiekritik und das Verschwinden der Gesellschaft: Zur Diskussion um das andere politische Projekt der Moderne. In: Lenk K, Greven MT, Kühler P, Schmitz M (eds) Politikwissenschaft als Kritische Theorie: Festschrift für Kurt Lenk. Nomos, Baden-Baden, pp 353–386

Schäfer A (2006) Die demokratische Grenze output-orientierter Legitimation. Integration 29(3):187–200

Scharpf FW (1997) Economic integration, democracy and the welfare state. J Eur Public Policy 4(1):18–36. https://doi.org/10.1080/135017697344217

Scheffler S (2004) Doing and allowing. Ethics 114(2):215–239. https://doi.org/10.1086/379355

Schneewind JB (2010) Autonomy, obligation, and virtue: an overview of Kant's Moral philosophy. In: Schneewind JB (ed) Essays on the history of moral philosophy. Oxford University Press, Oxford, pp 248–276

Schudson M (2006) The trouble with experts – and why democracies need them. Theor Soc 35(5–6):491–506. https://doi.org/10.1007/s11186-006-9012-y

Schumpeter JA (2010) Capitalism, socialism and democracy. Routledge, London

Shearman DJ, Smith JW (2007) The climate change challenge and the failure of democracy. Politics and the environment. Praeger, Santa Barbara

Shrader-Frechette KS (1991) Risk and rationality: philosophical foundations for populist reforms. University of California Press, Berkeley

Shrader-Frechette K (2005) Flawed attacks on contemporary human rights: Laudan, Sunstein, and the cost-benefit state. Hum Rights Rev 7(1):92–110. https://doi.org/10.1007/s12142-005-1004-1

Shreve CM, Kelman I (2014) Does mitigation save? Reviewing cost-benefit analyses of disaster risk reduction. Int J Disaster Risk Reduct 10:213–235. https://doi.org/10.1016/j.ijdrr.2014.08.004

Slovic P (1987) Perception of risk. Science 236(4799):280–285. https://doi.org/10.1126/science.3563507

Slovic P (2000) The perception of risk. Earthscan risk in society. Taylor & Francis, London

Smart JJ (1973) An outline of a system of utilitarian ethics. In: Smart JJ, Williams B (eds) Utilitarianism: for and against. Cambridge University Press, Cambridge, pp 3–74

Smith A (2002) The theory of moral sentiments. Cambridge texts in the history of philosophy. Cambridge University Press, Cambridge

Spence R, So E (2021) Why do buildings collapse in earthquakes?: Building for safety in seismic areas. Wiley-Blackwell, Hoboken

Staudenmaier R (2020) World's top coronavirus experts face fame, scorn amid pandemic. Deutsche Welle, 30 April 2020. https://p.dw.com/p/3bcKi. Accessed 19 June 2023

Stefanovic IL (2003) The contribution of philosophy to hazards assessment and decision making. Nat Haz 28(2–3):229–247. https://doi.org/10.1023/A:1022965604958

Stewart H (1995) A critique of instrumental reason in economics. Econ Philos 11(1):57–83. https://doi.org/10.1017/S0266267100003229

Stoll P-T (2003) Sicherheit als Aufgabe von Staat und Gesellschaft: Verfassungsordnung, Umwelt- und Technikrecht im Umgang mit Unsicherheit und Risiko. Jus Publicum, vol 101. Mohr Siebeck, Tübingen

Strøm K (2000) Delegation and accountability in parliamentary democracies. Eur J Polit Res 37(3):261–290. https://doi.org/10.1023/A:1007064803327

Sun LG (2016) Climate change and the narrative of disaster. In: Peel J, Fisher D (eds) The role of international environmental law in disaster risk reduction. Brill, Leiden, pp 27–48

Sunstein CR (2002a) Probability neglect: emotions, worst cases, and law. Yale Law J 112(1):61–107. https://doi.org/10.2307/1562234

Sunstein CR (2002b) Risk and reason: safety, law, and the environment. Cambridge University Press, Cambridge

Sunstein CR (2004a) Lives, life-years, and willingness to pay. Colum Law Rev 104(1):205–252

Sunstein CR (2004b) Valuing life: a plea for disaggregation. Duke Law J 54(2):385–446

Sunstein CR (2005a) Cost-benefit analysis and the environment. Ethics 115(2):351–385. https://doi.org/10.1086/426308

Sunstein CR (2005b) Laws of fear: beyond the precautionary principle. The Seeley Lectures, vol 6. Cambridge University Press, Cambridge

Sunstein CR, Pildes R (1997) Experts, economists, and democrats. In: Sunstein CR (ed) Free markets and social justice. Oxford University Press, New York, pp 128–150

Swyngedouw E (2010) Apocalypse forever? Theory Cult Soc 27(2–3):213–232. https://doi.org/10.1177/0263276409358728

Talisse RB (2009) Folk epistemology and the justification of democracy. In: Geenens R, Tinnevelt R (eds) Does truth matter?: Democracy and public space. Springer, Dordrecht, pp 41–54

The White House (2020a) Remarks by President Trump, Vice President Pence, and members of the coronavirus task force in press conference. https://trumpwhitehouse.archives.gov/briefings-statements/remarks-president-trump-vice-president-pence-members-coronavirus-task-force-press-conference/. Accessed 19 June 2023

The White House (2020b) Remarks by President Trump, Vice President Pence, and members of the coronavirus task force in press conference. https://trumpwhitehouse.archives.gov/briefings-statements/remarks-president-trump-vice-president-pence-members-c-oronavirus-task-force-press-briefing/. Accessed 19 June 2023

The White House (2020c) Remarks by President Trump, Vice President Pence, and members of the coronavirus task force in press conference. https://trumpwhitehouse.archives.gov/briefings-statements/remarks-president-trump-vice-president-pence-members-coronavirus-task-force-press-briefing-9/. Accessed 19 June 2023

Thompson PB (1990) Risk objectivism and risk subjectivism: when are risks real? Risk Issues Health Saf 1(1):3–22

Tversky A, Kahneman D (1974) Judgment under uncertainty: heuristics and biases. Science 185(4157):1124–1131. https://doi.org/10.1126/science.185.4157.1124

Urbinati N (2014) Democracy disfigured: opinion, truth, and the people. Harvard University Press, Cambridge

van Coile R (2016) Probability. In: Burgess A, Alemanno A, Zinn JO (eds) Routledge handbook of risk studies. Routledge, Abingdon, pp 27–38

van de Poel I, Fahlquist JN (2012) Risk and responsibility. In: Roeser S, Hillerbrand R, Sandin P, Peterson M (eds) Handbook of risk theory: epistemology, decision theory, ethics, and social implications of risk. Springer, Dordrecht, pp 877–907

Vibert F (2007) The rise of the unelected: democracy and the new separation of powers. Cambridge University Press, Cambridge

Viscusi WK (1992) Fatal tradeoffs: public and private responsibilities for risk. Oxford University Press, New York

Viscusi WK (2015) Pricing lives for corporate risk decisions. Vanderbilt Law Rev 68(4):1117–1162. https://doi.org/10.1017/bca.2015.40

Wachinger G, Renn O, Begg C, Kuhlicke C (2013) The risk perception paradox-implications for governance and communication of natural hazards. Risk Anal 33(6):1049–1065. https://doi.org/10.1111/j.1539-6924.2012.01942.x

Waldron J (2012) Democracy. In: Estlund DM (ed) The Oxford handbook of political philosophy. Oxford University Press, New York, pp 187–203

Walker JL (1966) A critique of the elitist theory of democracy. Am Polit Sci Rev 60(2):285–295. https://doi.org/10.2307/1953356

Williams B (1973) A critique of utilitarianism. In: Smart JJ, Williams B (eds) Utilitarianism: for and against. Cambridge University Press, Cambridge, pp 75–150

Woollard F, Howard-Snyder F (2022) Doing vs. allowing harm. In: Zalta EN (ed) The Stanford Encyclopedia of Philosophy. https://plato.stanford.edu/entries/doing-allowing/. Accessed 19 June 2023

World Health Organization, Regional Office for the Western Pacific (2020) Calibrating long-term non-pharmaceutical interventions for COVID-19: principles and facilitation tools, Manila. https://apps.who.int/iris/handle/10665/332099. Accessed 19 June 2023

Zack N (2011) Ethics for disaster. Rowman & Littlefield, Lanham

Chapter 6
Conclusion

> *The way we talk about disasters—how we describe them and the metaphors we use—matters. The frames we choose help determine the solutions we imagine, the resources we dedicate, the institutions we mobilize, the policy approaches we select, and the legal rules we craft. (Sun 2016, p. 290)*

Many people in the member states of the Council of Europe ('member states') continue to expose themselves to risks from natural hazards, for example by living in risk areas, despite existing knowledge about risks and means to reduce them. In this regard, the discussion of the factual ability to determine risks and reduce the impact of natural hazards in Chap. 2 leads to the general conclusion that governments, but also individuals, have a choice between accepting the determined probability and impact of a natural hazard and taking risk-reducing measures. Risk assessments and technical developments offer both the individual and the collective the option of making a conscious decision on whether and how to build in an area at risk. The legal examination of several disaster risk reduction ('DRR') measures in Chap. 4 suggests that member states could lawfully implement measures to effectively reduce disaster risks. However, although DRR saves lives, as well as private assets and taxpayers' money—compared to mere disaster response—society's risk management remains response-oriented.[1] In this regard, Chaps. 1 and 3 discussed that the efforts of many member states fall short of expert-recommended measures and the member states' own political acknowledgements of the benefits of DRR at the global stage. Based on the discussed findings on people's risk perception in the context of natural hazards, it is also doubtful that individuals and collectives will engage more in DRR on their own volition. As the discussion in Chap. 2 concluded, people tend to underestimate the risks from natural hazards due to cognitive and culturally shaped mechanisms in foresight. This affects not only the individual risk

[1] See Sects. 1.7.1 and 1.7.2.

C. A. Simmig, *Of Risks and Normative Responses*,
https://doi.org/10.1007/978-3-031-41104-5_6

evaluation, but also the outcome of collective decision-making processes in democratic states, as Chap. 1 illustrated.

With the benefits of DRR in mind, this book aimed to explore how member states should complement their risk management to facilitate the reduction of disaster losses related to common natural hazards. Based on the analysis of different normative responses in terms of the interests involved in society's response to risks, member states should strengthen DRR from the bottom-up by mobilising individual and collective support in the long-term with the help of discursive methods. First, member states should promote a bias-sensitive and lay-friendly risk communication to mitigate widespread distortions in the perception of risks related to natural hazards. Second, the member states should include deliberative fora in collective decision-making processes to mitigate the impact of distorted risk perception on collective decision-making. Based on the research of distortions in risk perceptions prevailing among people, it can be reasonably expected that more people would agree with experts' evaluation of the benefits of DRR if they properly understood relevant facts relating to themselves and the collective. Nevertheless, effective communication alone is not always enough to initiate behavioural change since people have different preferences and goals in life. If democratic demand generally increases, the member states should therefore further implement DRR measures that economically incentivise DRR or even enforce DRR. The protection of the collective against the preventable costs for the collective provides a legitimate aim for the enforcement of DRR against individuals. Thus, this book concluded a practical potential to increase DRR by mitigating the influence of biases and heuristics in people's evaluation of disaster risks in the context of natural hazards. On the flip side, the results of the analysis of the values involved in public risk management challenge paternalistic approaches to justify risk reducing interferences given the current lack of individual and democratic support. The key research findings of this book are summarised in this chapter.

6.1 Summary of the Analysed Political Reasons for the Neglect of DRR

The analysis of the international discourse presented in Chaps. 1 and 3 has shown that the assessment of experts on the benefits of DRR are widely recognised on the global stage. In numerous non-binding international instruments, states acknowledge the importance of DRR for the future.[2] However, the implementation of DRR at the national and municipal level falls short of these declared political goals. The book concludes that in order to enhance DRR measures, it is imperative to mobilise political will in the member states.

[2] See Sect. 3.1.

6.1.1 *The Benefits of DRR for Member States as Identified by Experts*

If economic and social hardships from future natural hazards are to be reduced, increased efforts to reduce disaster risks are necessary. Adapting land use and the construction methods to the identified risks is recommended as effective measures for reducing disaster risks. Experts' recommendation to place greater emphasis on reducing risk factors requires adjustments to both existing structures and the construction of future buildings. With respect to future buildings, it should be noted that continued urbanisation in areas prone to natural hazards will exacerbate the impact of natural hazards on life and property. Appropriate land use and construction methods are in turn associated with significant benefits. With respect to the large proportion of buildings in Europe that already exist in zones prone to floods and earthquakes, individuals and collectives can reduce risks of disaster losses, for example, by making structural adjustments or taking out insurance. Investing in DRR generally saves lives and leads to significant savings in the form of avoided damage.

6.1.2 *Legitimacy of Recommended DRR Measures*

The legal examination in Chap. 4 found a number of recommended DRR measures that the collective could implement to promote and enforce DRR. Beyond neutral disaster risk communication, the state could also integrate nudges and incentives to support individual decision-making processes to facilitate people's implementation of private DRR measures. Nudges refer to measures that deliberately use behavioural science to steer people's decisions. The insights into the functioning of risk perception patterns offer the possibility to specifically counteract people's distorted risk perceptions by framing information.[3] For instance, in recognition of the probability neglect, information on possible risks should be presented in a vivid way, because if people cannot visualise worst-case scenarios, they tend to deny the probability of harm.[4] In addition, the framing of risk-reducing options in a way that takes loss aversion bias into account can encourage people to choose the option preferred by the communicator. The effectiveness of these measures is simultaneously the biggest point of concern. If the manipulative cue is invisible to the nudged individual, nudges interfere with the value of autonomy. However, the examples discussed in Chap. 4 were identified as below the threshold of intervening in one's autonomy because they correct unconscious cognitive processes by emphasising certain information. On the other hand, incentives can support individuals' decision for DRR, for instance by offering tax deductions for retrofitting buildings or relocation funds

[3] For the difference between disaster risk communication and nudging in terms of information framing, see Sect. 4.1.2.2.

[4] See Sect. 4.1.2.1.

to escape the particularly dangerous zones. Such incentives are a valuable tool for disaster risk management as they can sway the risk evaluation of people who are not convinced by effective communication alone.

Overall, Chap. 4 concluded that prescribing certain building standards or prohibiting people from living or building in certain vulnerable zones promises the most effective realisation of the protection goal. Yet, in the context of uncertain natural hazards, these measures often interfere with individuals' right to property and require justification. In this respect, the protection of the community from preventable consequences of natural hazards provides a 'legitimate aim' for interference with individual rights by enforcing DRR.[5] Even very effective (retrospective) land-use planning and enforcement of building regulations in high-risk areas can be justified on the grounds of community interests. However, such measures may require the payment of compensation to the individual in order to strike a fair balance between the individual right to property and the interests of the community.

6.1.3 *Linking the Lack of Political Will to the Collective Neglect of Probability*

The legal possibility of implementing risk reduction measures, the claimed long-term cost-efficiency of DRR and the scope of projected disaster losses lead to only one conclusion. 'We now know what has to be done, what is needed is the political will to do it',[6] as a statement of the former Secretary General of the United Nations, Kofi Annan, regarding disaster triggered by natural hazards, aptly summarises. Notably, the political will is not only lacking among the elected representation, but also among citizens. Based on the analysis in Chaps. 1 and 2, the book concludes that one factor for the lack of private and public initiative lies in the culturally-shaped cognitive patterns of risk perception that lead people to neglect risks in the context of natural hazards.

People's response to risks depends on their emotions, which in turn are subject to cognitive mechanisms and internalised cultural worldviews that often stand in contrast to scientific facts. As such, people's risk evaluation depends inter alia on the time since the risk's last manifestation. Psychology explains this correlation by claiming that the more vivid the memories are, the more strongly people perceive a situation as unsafe. Thus, recent manifestations of disasters give rise to the 'crisis effect', which describes the phenomenon that the occurrence of natural hazards can (temporarily) increase people's demand for protection. People's perception of the probability of harm and their control to prevent harm is also influenced by other people's conduct and perception of risk, which in turn is shaped by people's historical-cultural relationship with natural hazards. Notably, not long ago, disasters

[5] See Sect. 4.2.3.

[6] Annan (1999).

triggered by natural hazards were considered inevitable natural events, which placed them *a priori* outside the human sphere of influence. The review of recent examples has shown that this narrative still exists,[7] which feeds into people's collective neglect of DRR. Conversely, the rise of the risk reduction concept has also given rise to a widespread mistaken belief that risks could be reduced to zero. The assumption that the state provides absolute safety also reduces the likelihood that individuals take private measures to reduce the risk to their lives, physical integrity, and property. Altogether, the research has illustrated a widespread lack of contextual understanding of probability, uncertainty, and the complexity of risk management. At present, public risk management reflects these distorted risk perceptions because the democratic decision-making process lacks elements to mitigate distorted risk perception.[8]

However, psychological research supports the reasonable expectation that more people would voluntarily opt for more risk reduction if they understood the circumstances correctly. People's response to risks in the context of natural hazards give reason to suspect that individuals suffer from a 'reasoning failure', that is, a disjunction between the goals they seek and their behaviour.

6.2 Weaknesses of Paternalistic Arguments to Justify DRR Enforcement

The fact that experts tend to perceive such disastrous consequences as 'irrational' may explain the significant body of research exploring approaches to overcome the political obstacle of distorted risk perceptions, which this book has discussed. The conceptual and normative examination of these approaches contributes to the relevant literature by arguing that several debated proposals for responding to people's 'reasoning failures' insufficiently consider the value of autonomy and democratic values. The contextual analysis of these values in this book challenges approaches that justify intervening DRR measures with the intention to serve the individual's and collective's 'own good'. As such, some commentators argue that the value of autonomy carries less weight in the balancing of interests than the costs of neglected DRR. Other paternalistic arguments rely on the superior authority of science and expertise which should be empowered to make 'neutral' or 'better' risk evaluations for all. While such discussed approaches all pursue laudable goals, namely the protection of individuals and society from avoidable harm (for their 'own good'), such top-down proposals rely on legally and philosophically incoherent arguments. Despite the different lines of argumentation, the approaches share the weakness of unacceptably neglecting the value of autonomy in individual and collective decision-making.

---

[7] See Sect. 2.2.1.

[8] See Sect. 1.1.2.

6.2.1 *The Autonomy Concept Excludes 'Objectively Rational Risk Evaluations'*

First, the discussion of the requirements of lawful, ethical, and politically legitimate risk management in this book opposes arguments that rely on the authority of science and expertise to justify enforced DRR without democratic support. Such approaches neglect the subjectivity of risk evaluations. Autonomy as a pluralistic conceptualisation of happiness entails that what some perceive as a threat, may be an opportunity to others. Determining how the individual should behave for their 'own good' is not, and should not, be the task of the state, which is instead obliged to respect the fundamental rights of the individual. These even include the individual's freedom to autonomously decide to expose oneself to potential harm.[9] The restriction of individual freedom is possible only to protect the interests of the community from inacceptable consequences of the individual's decision or to protect the individual from so-called autonomy or reasoning failures.

The inextricably intertwined challenges contradict the utopian idea of a general objective rationale for evaluating risk. If the legitimacy of subjective evaluations is accepted, it follows that the evaluation of risks must be made on a case-by-case basis to take context-dependent preferences and perspectives into account. As Howard Raiffa aptly articulates, '[t]here is no absolute standard for safety – nor should there be… "How Safe is Safe Enough?" is a short-hand, catchy sounding phrase that is merely a pitifully weak and misleading simplification of a very complex problem'.[10] In fact, the collective evaluation of risks must account for multifaceted, and partly incommensurable, values and needs, which excludes the existence of objectively rational risk evaluations. The state's response to risks needs to strike a balance between the risk of adverse consequences and the 'costs' of reducing them. These 'costs' include resources necessary for the implementation, the loss of benefits that result from ignoring a risk, and negative side-effects of a risk reducing measure. As an example of such negative side effects, the review of DRR in the context of natural hazards in Chap. 2 has demonstrated how some river training structures may effectively increase the protection against a threat but may create new risks as a corollary.[11] This balancing exercise is further complicated by the fact that knowledge about risks is often fraught with uncertainties. Last, the limit of financial and institutional resources forces societies to set priorities in the management of an infinite number of risks.

Once the subjectivity of risk evaluations is accepted, it must be tolerated that the results of collective risk evaluations will not be valid for eternity but will change over time. This means that '[t]he laws that exist at any given moment … reflect societal values that have reached expression through a complex

[9] See Sect. 3.2.3.1.

[10] Raiffa (1980), p. 339.

[11] See Sect. 2.3.3.2.

socioeconomic-political process. They are not immutable, but are always subject to change'.[12] As such, the societal evaluation of risks will forever be subject of discussion as preferences change over time.

6.2.2 *Explanation for Limited Scope of Positive Obligations*

The conceptual and normative analysis of the individual and collective interests in the management of natural hazards has further challenged paternalistically-motivated interpretations of human rights to derive an extended positive obligation to take DRR measures from the European Convention on Human Rights[13] ('ECHR'). The literature review on the scope of positive obligations has revealed attempts of commentators to derive a more extensive obligation to increase the protection of life and property by taking preventive and mitigative DRR.[14] However, the discussion in Chap. 3 opposes those debated approaches to increase DRR for neglecting the necessary balance of individual and community interests under the ECHR.

Based on the discussion of the object and purpose of the ECHR, the book has conceptualised the interests involved in the interpretation of positive obligations. To respect the value of autonomy, a threat must reach a level of certainty and immediacy before the state may interfere, as Chap. 4 discussed in detail. Thus, instead of applying the 'precautionary principle', the interpretation of the ECHR is based on the 'preventive principle'. On the other hand, the application of the 'preventive principle' seeks to protect society from unreasonable burden. This consideration recognises that even if the state has a factual choice to avoid a risk to an individual with maximal efforts, the state must respond to an infinite number of risks to individuals with limited resources, which forces societies to set priorities while ensuring the equitable distribution of resources.

The consideration of these interests in the context of natural hazards has confirmed the European Court of Human Rights' ('Court') interpretation that a positive obligation to take preventive or mitigative DRR measures only arises in the case of clearly identifiable and imminent natural hazards. This high threshold for positive obligations is a result of the protection of the individual from paternalistic intervention, and the protection of the community from excessive burdens. The knowledge about distorted risk perceptions does not change this fact. In practice, this threshold means that positive obligations rarely extend to long-term disaster risk- preventing or mitigating measures. This follows from the remaining epistemic and statistical uncertainties in relation to natural hazards which impede the long-term prediction of most natural hazards in specific locations as explored in Chap. 2. Thus, positive

[12] Green (1981), p. 11.

[13] Convention for the Protection of Human Rights and Fundamental Freedoms, opened for signature 4 November 1950, 213 UNTS 221 (entered into force 3 September 1953).

[14] See Sect. 3.2.4–3.2.5.

obligations regularly arise in the short term, which allows the state, for example, to save lives through evacuation, but not to adapt already existing buildings.

The discussion has further concluded that this de facto response-oriented interpretation of positive obligations under the ECHR is also unlikely to extend to long-term DRR measures in the foreseeable future. Despite the significant technical and scientific progress in determining the risk and predicting the occurrence of natural hazards, Chap. 2 concluded that uncertainties are likely to persist, especially with regard to the timing and location of their occurrence. This is due to the limited historical data available and the known complexity of modelling natural hazards, which experts consider too complex for long-term predictions. In sum, without legislative initiative in the member states, an expansion of the response-oriented disaster management approach towards increased DRR is unlikely.

6.3 Strengthening DRR from the Bottom Up: Summary of Suggestions and Merits

While this book concludes that paternalistic approaches come with unacceptable disadvantages, the book recommends stakeholders to mitigate distorted risk perception in order to mobilise political will for DRR. In this respect, the book has advanced insights by behavioural and communication scientists that have the potential to help people to properly understand the facts and be aware of their goals and desires for the future. In terms of recommendations, this book relies on the merit that they do not violate fundamental rights and democratic values according to the analysis in Chaps. 4 and 5. At the same time, this bottom-up strengthening of DRR promises to increase the voluntary reduction of disaster risks at the private level and to strengthen democratic support for legal prohibitions and obligations at the collective level.

6.3.1 Adjusting the Institutional Design of Collective Decision-Making Processes

A key recommendation of this book is that member states should integrate deliberative processes in their collective decision-making process to mitigate the impact of distorted risk perceptions. Deliberative processes in public decision-making are geared to facilitate 'authentic decision-making' through a structured exchange of knowledge between all relevant stakeholders, including both experts and laypeople. Based on the model of deliberative democracy, deliberative processes are designed as a moderated search for the 'better argument' by thoughtfully weighing reasons that are epistemically robust and acceptable to all citizens concerned. The discussion in Chap. 5 has demonstrated empirical evidence that a properly structured exchange of reasonable arguments can enable people to challenge their intuitive perceptions of risk by persuading rather than coercing them. The merit of discursive methods of deliberation lies not only in the mitigation of the influence of distorted perceptions of facts on collective decisions, but the inclusion of deliberative processes can also enhance the political legitimacy of the outcome. Deliberative processes respect the procedural value of ensuring equal participation of experts and other stakeholders, while also enhancing the quality of the outcome, which is another source of political legitimacy.

Concurrent with introducing deliberative processes in the collective decision-making process, the analysis recommends that member states introduce adequate institutionalisation of democratic oversight of expert contributions. The discussion of the role of experts concluded that reasonable collective decision-making partly depends on experts' input. This gives rise to practical concerns of how stakeholders can exercise democratic oversight if there is an asymmetry of knowledge between experts, representatives, and laypeople. This asymmetry bears the risk of undermining the division of labour, in which science has the role of presenting information, while the public and individuals then use the information to make informed decisions. For this reason, member states should ensure the existence of an independent basis for trusting experts' contributions. This independent basis can include a transparent and accessible record of an expert's reliable judgment in the past, or a system that provides critical review by other competent experts. The existence of such independent basis for trusting experts' contributions can compensate the obstacle posed by knowledge asymmetry in the exercise of democratic control.

6.3.2 Promoting Bias-Sensitive and Laypeople-Friendly Risk Communication

A further recommendation is directed at the authorities in member states as well as other stakeholders in the communication of facts related to DRR and natural hazards, such as politicians, experts, and the media. First, the analysis in this book indicates that the terminology and metaphors chosen for communicating disaster risks can contribute to reconstruct obsolete perceptions about risks related to natural hazards. As such, disaster risk communication should, for instance, avoid terms that behavioural studies identified to feed into obsolete risk perceptions, such as 'natural disaster'. Notably, even experts in the field of disaster risk management still use this obsolete term.[15] Instead, when communicating disaster risks, stakeholders should use language that has been found to increase the chances of being properly understood by the recipients, as discussed in Chaps. 4 and 5.[16] This also refers to the communication of the probability of natural hazards, the relevance of disaster risks

[15] Chmutina and von Meding (2019).

[16] See Sects. 4.1.1, 4.1.2 and 5.1.2.

factors and the benefits of reducing them, and the level of confidence behind this knowledge.

As a starting point for inducing bias-sensitive and laypeople-friendly risk communication, raising awareness of the impact of certain narratives and alternatives is pivotal. In this regard, a model could be the movement towards gender-neutral language in recent years along with its implementation in media, authorities, and educational institutions. This example shows that institutions and people are capable of developing an awareness of the impact of language and to apply alternative terms offered.

6.3.3 *Reflecting on Strengths and Weaknesses of the Bottom-Up Approach*

A comparison of the advantages and disadvantages of the bottom-up approach confirms the recommendation of this book. This approach supports authentic decisions in an autonomy-promoting way, while it also proved to be effective in swaying people's risk evaluations over time. Thus, the approach contributes to more voluntary implementation and the mobilisation of political support for the lawful enforcement of DRR. Another advantage is that the institutionally required structural adjustments can have positive effects in policy areas that are not related to natural hazards. The influence of reasoning failures is suspected in many areas, such as the failure to reduce greenhouse gas emissions with regard to climate change or vaccine hesitancy.[17] In this respect, implementing this recommendation would provide benefits that can also be generalised.

Nevertheless, the recommended bottom-up approach is not a panacea. The widespread reconstruction of societal thought patterns takes years, which means that some DRR measures may continue to be met with public resistance for some time. The widespread success of the bottom-up approach also depends on the success of mobilising relevant stakeholders to adapt bias-sensitive language, including politicians, experts, and the media. It follows from these down-sides that the success of the bottom-up approach is conditional and cannot be precisely determined in terms of time. However, a key conclusion of the discussion of the values relating to managing risk from natural hazards is that these disadvantages should be accepted in order to reduce disaster losses in the long term through a legal and politically acceptable process.

[17] See Zolkefli (2017), Flanigan (2014) and Wang and Kim (2018).

6.4 Future Research

The limitations of this book invite the identification of potential future studies to further the effectiveness and practical implementation for the recommended bottom-up approach. First, the focus of this book was on the laws and values binding the member states of the Council of Europe, but did not intend to provide a complete analysis of each member state's constitutional framework. Based on the conclusion on the merits of implementing deliberative processes for mitigating the influence of distorted risk perception on collective decision-making, future studies could address the legal implementation in individual member states.

Second, the effectiveness of this approach depends on continuous research. It has emerged from the discussion of the cultural influence on risk perceptions that these are not static. As such, ongoing research on diverging perceptions of risks, as well as the effective design of risk communication towards individuals and in collective decision-making processes is vital for the long-term success of the recommended discursive approach.

6.5 Final Observations

With the goal of reducing disaster losses in mind, the book has identified distorted risk perceptions as a relevant political obstacle to increasing DRR and has provided a socio-legal examination of approaches to overcome the lack of political will to implement lawful DRR measures. Based on the analysis of interests involved in the reduction of disaster risks related to natural hazards, this book recommends a bottom-up approach to strengthen DRR by supporting people in making mindful risk evaluations. Addressing the political obstacle of distorted risk perceptions to DRR at the individual and collective level is critical in light of the ever-increasing disaster losses due to natural hazards, especially with regard to the adverse consequences of climate change. Notably, disaster losses in Europe are likely to increase even more in the future without additional DRR measures given the expected increase in the frequency and intensity of natural hazards in all regions of the world due to environmental degradation and climate change.[18] Admittedly, due to the discussed 'crisis effect',[19] it is likely that the issue of DRR will naturally receive more attention at the individual and collective level when the frequency of natural hazards increases. However, if the state waits until the 'crisis effect' sets in, it may be too late to reap the long-term benefits that appropriate land use and risk-reducing construction

---

[18] Farber (2014), p. 12; Cohen and Bradley (2010), p. 95; International Federation of Red Cross and Red Crescent Societies (2012), p. 21; Cubie and Hesselman (2015), p. 40, who refer to Human Rights Council (2009), paras 8, 23; Crosweller and Wilmshurst (2013), pp. 561–562; Edwards (2013).

[19] See Sect. 1.1.2.

methods currently provide. This is because reconstruction is regularly costlier than adaptation. Also, the foresighted consideration of risks in land-use and risk-reducing building standards during the construction of new buildings is regularly less expensive than retrospective adaptions. Thus, if the benefits of DRR should be maximised, now is the time to take DRR seriously. To help people make decisions consistent with their individual and collective goals for the future and their future desires, it is vital to make people aware that their inaction amounts to a choice. Either they act now or they pay a high price, because prevention is cheaper and safer than the cure.

References

Annan K (1999) An increasing vulnerability to natural disasters. International Herald Tribune, 10 September 1999. https://www.nytimes.com/1999/09/10/opinion/IHT-an-increasing-vulnerability-to-natural-disasters.html. Accessed 19 June 2023

Chmutina K, von Meding J (2019) A dilemma of language: "natural disasters" in academic literature. Int J Disaster Risk Sci 10(3):283–292. https://doi.org/10.1007/s13753-019-00232-2

Cohen R, Bradley M (2010) Disasters and displacement: gaps in protection. J Int Hum Leg Stud 1(1):95–142. https://doi.org/10.1163/187815210X12766020139884

Crosweller HS, Wilmshurst J (2013) Natural hazards and risk: the human perspective. In: Rougier J, Hill LJ, Sparks RSJ (eds) Risk and uncertainty assessment for natural hazards. Cambridge University Press, Cambridge, pp 548–569

Cubie D, Hesselman M (2015) Accountability for the human rights implications of natural disasters: a proposal for systemic international oversight. NQHR 33(1):9–41

Edwards TL (2013) Hydrometeorological hazards under future climate change. In: Rougier J, Hill LJ, Sparks RSJ (eds) Risk and uncertainty assessment for natural hazards. Cambridge University Press, Cambridge, pp 151–189

Farber DA (2014) International law and the disaster cycle. In: Caron DD, Kelly MJ, Telesetsky A (eds) The international law of disaster relief. Cambridge University Press, Cambridge, pp 7–20

Flanigan J (2014) A defense of compulsory vaccination. HEC Forum 26(1):5–25. https://doi.org/10.1007/s10730-013-9221-5

Green HP (1981) The role of law in determining acceptability of risk. Ann N Y Acad Sci 363(1):1–12. https://doi.org/10.1111/j.1749-6632.1981.tb20712.x

Human Rights Council (2009) Report of the Office of the United Nations High Commissioner for Human Rights on the relationship between climate change and human rights. UN Doc A/HRC/10/61

International Federation of Red Cross and Red Crescent Societies (2012) World Disasters Report: focus on forced migration and displacement. https://www.ifrc.org/sites/default/files/2012_WDR_Full_Report.pdf. Accessed 19 June 2023

Raiffa H (1980) Concluding remarks. In: Schwing RC, Albers WA (eds) Societal risk assessment: how safe is safe enough? Springer, Boston, pp 339–341

Sun LG (2016) Climate change and the narrative of disaster. In: Peel J, Fisher D (eds) The role of international environmental law in disaster risk reduction. Brill, Leiden, pp 27–48

Wang J, Kim S (2018) Analysis of the impact of values and perception on climate change skepticism and its implication for public policy. Climate 6(4):99. https://doi.org/10.3390/cli6040099

Zolkefli Y (2017) Evaluating the concept of choice in healthcare. Malays J Med Sci 24(6):92–96. https://doi.org/10.21315/mjms2017.24.6.11